PSYCHOLOGICAL TESTS AND TESTING RESEARCH TRENDS

PSYCHOLOGICAL TESTS AND TESTING RESEARCH TRENDS

PAUL M. GOLDFARB
EDITOR

Nova Science Publishers, Inc.
New York

LIBRARY OF CONGRESS CATALOGING-IN-PUBLICATION DATA
Psychological tests and testing research trends / Paul M. Goldfarb, editor.
     p. cm.
Includes index.
ISBN-13: 978-1-60021-569-8 (hardcover)
ISBN-10: 1-60021-569-6 (hardcover)
1. Psychological tests. I. Goldfarb, Paul M.
BF176.P825   2006
150.28'7--dc22   2006102904

Published by Nova Science Publishers, Inc. ✦ New York

CONTENTS

PREFACE

Psychological testing or Psychological assessment is a field characterized by the use of samples of behavior in order to infer generalizations about a given individual. By samples of behavior, one means observations over time of an individual performing tasks that have usually been prescribed beforehand. These responses are often compiled into statistical tables that allow the evaluator to compare the behavior of the individual being tested to the responses of a norm group. The broad catagories of psychological evaluation tests include: Norm-referenced, IQ/achievement tests, Neuropsychological tests, Personality tests, Objective tests (Rating scale), Direct observation tests, Psychological evaluations using data mining. This book presents new and important research from around the world.

Chapter 1 - *Background:* Over the past 30 years the field of health-related quality of life research has shown continual expansion, with several instruments having been developed for its assessment. Yet, there is still not a clear universally agreed upon definition of the construct. There is general agreement that quality of life is related to perceived physical, mental, and social well-being; but a strong theoretical model that is at once simple, intuitive, and useful for assessment has not been forthcoming. The authors proposed two competing theoretical models, which they have called the *component* and *abstraction* models of quality of life; and they have tested these through the construct validation of a health status instrument that is both brief and simple, the COOP / WONCA.

Method: A multiethnic sample of 365 cancer survivors in Hawaii responded to a slightly modified version of the nine-item COOP / WONCA and the EORTC QLQ-C30 questionnaire. Construct validation of the COOP / WONCA was performed via factor analysis and cross-structure comparison with the QLQ-C30. As a test of the two proposed theoretical models, the results of these construct validation procedures were compared with the hypotheses generated from each theory.

Results: Factor analyses of the COOP / WONCA suggested that a single factor provided the most parsimonious solution, which supported the abstraction model of quality of life. Comparisons with the QLQ-C30 suggested both convergent and discriminant validity. One item, labeled physical fitness, did not perform as well as the others.

Conclusions: The evidence here suggests that the COOP / WONCA provides a valid assessment of health-related quality of life in cancer survivors. A definition of quality of life consistent with an abstraction model (a one-dimensional construct) was supported, suggesting a greater simplicity than is often believed. Although further research is clearly needed, these results suggest that researchers and clinicians needing to assess quality of life simply, and with minimal burden to the respondents, will be well-served by the COOP / WONCA.

Chapter 2 - Cognitive vulnerability is considered as a factor predisposing an individual to depressive episodes. Measures of vulnerability have consistently emphasized perfectionism and dependence as the main factor on which vulnerability is based. Within this cognitive framework Sinclair and Wallston (1999) have proposed the Psychological Vulnerability Scale (PVS). This six-item self-report assesses a pattern of maladaptive beliefs, such as need for others´ approval, very stringent standards and negative attributions.

In this chapter the authors examined the psychometric properties of the PVS in a non-clinical population. The authors determined the construct validity of the PVS through correlations with perceived competence, hostility and affective states. They also investigated the predictive validity of the PVS regarding its contribution to alexithymia, health criteria and well-being.

The sample was composed of 436 participants (23% males and 77% females) with a mean age of 36. The PVS together with measures of perceived competence, hostility, affective states, alexithymia, health criteria and well-being were completed.

The scale showed adequate internal consistency ($\alpha = .76$) and high temporal stability (3 months test-retest reliability = .70). Factor analysis revealed an unifactorial solution, accounting for 47% of the total variance. Item loadings were .58 and above. Construct validity was supported by the positive correlations with measures of hostility and negative affect, and by the negative correlations of the PVS with perceived competence and positive affect. Appropriate predictive validity of the scale was also found. It positively predicted alexithymia, and negatively predicted health behaviors and well-being. However, the contribution of the PVS to the symptoms was lower.

The results provided considerable evidence of the validation of the PVS in a non-clinical population. They also suggest that psychological vulnerability constitutes a maladaptive cognitive style with negative consequences in the physical and psychological domain.

Chapter 3 - *Introduction:* Considering that most of the card- sorting tasks are "one shot", developing tests which demand similar cognitive operations but different stimuli and instructions may be useful for longitudinal studies and for understanding specific components of problem solving ability and brain function. The nine-card sorting test (9CST) involves a purposive and interviewee-centered activity, which deals with three nonverbal sorting principles and their combination by pairs.

Objectives: 1) To study the validity of the 9CST by: a) its correlation with the WCST (construct validity) and b) its capacity to differentiate between frontal vs. non- frontal patients as well as frontal patients vs. healthy subjects (concurrent validity). 2) To study the test-retest and inter-scorer reliability on 40 healthy subjects.

Methods: Validity data were obtained from a sample of 106 volunteers: 32 patients with anterior (frontal) encephalic lesions (A), 30 patients with posterior (temporal, parietal or occipital) encephalic lesions (P) and 44 healthy (H) subjects. The three groups were matched by sex, age, educational background and manual preference and the two groups of patients, also by type of lesion, time since onset of condition and presence of other neurological risks. A neuropsychological battery complemented card-sorting evaluation.

Results: Significant differences were observed between the A and P patients in both card-sorting tests (and in an abbreviated version of the Raven test) but not in the rest of the neuropsychological tests administered considered as a whole. Three 9CST indexes correlated significantly with the WCST indexes of categories, errors and perseverative errors. Neither the WCST nor the 9CST differentiated the P patients from healthy subjects but the difference between A patients and healthy subjects became more evident with the 9CST. A very simple test of face recognition also differentiated betweend the A and P patients but in the opposite direction than the card sorting tests. Reliability coefficients were ≥0.79 for all the 9CST indexes. Practice effects were not observed in the 9CST number of categories completed.

Conclusion: This test of free distribution demonstrated a suitable validity and reliability. It can be a valid screening test to detect frontal impaired patients from healthy people. It also can be useful to detect frontal impaired patients when they are compared with patients impaired in posterior encephalic areas who have similar cognitive resources in alternative tasks such as attention, discrimination, memory, copy and verbal ability. An association between card sorting tests and intelligence, and a bias in sample selection favoring the more skillful non-frontal patients are discussed.

Frontal – Execution- Factor analysis- Internal consistency- Focal brain lesions- Mild cognitive impairment- Discriminant analysis- Face memory.

Chapter 4 - In the first part of this chapter, differences and similarities between static and dynamic measures of intelligence are presented and analysed. Static measures of intelligence are generally obtained by testing either a ratio of mental age to chronological age or a score of deviation from age norm. Dynamic measures of intelligence are generally obtained by administrating novel problem solving tasks to the subjects, supplying them with gradual and balanced assistance that progressively disclose the solution of the problem, and determining the amount of aid the learner needs to be able to solve the problem. The amount of aid is inversely proportional to the modifiability index. The modifiability index is the general propensity to change, and can better measure intelligence.

In the second part of this chapter it is hypothesized that some subjects can obtain a normal score with static test measures and a giftedness score with dynamic test measures. Two experiments were conducted to examine the relationship between dynamic measures and static measures of intelligence in low socio-economic background subjects and in ADHD subjects. In the first experiment 24 subjects with either high (12) or low (12) level of socio-economic background were trained to master problem solving tests with dynamic and static measures of intelligence. In the second experiment 57 subjects, 10 with ADHD-IA, 10 with ADHD-HI, 10 with ADHD-C and 27 controls were trained to master problem solving tests with dynamic and static measures of intelligence. The results showed that subjects with ADHD-C and Controls scored similarly on dynamic and static measure, but subjects with ADHD-HI and subjects with a low level of socio-economic background had lower scores with static test measures and higher scores with dynamic test measures. Results are discussed in terms of their implications for intelligence tests.

Chapter 5 - Self-injurious behaviour (SIB) refers to the direct and deliberate damage of one's own body surface without suicidal intent. This is a considerable health problem occurring at a high frequency in psychiatric inpatients units. In order to design specific therapeutic interventions, the primary diagnostic task is to identify the current external and internal stimulus conditions that contribute directly to the instigation of SIB. But for that purpose we do not have good assessment instruments and therefore the authors developed a new self-reporting questionnaire: the Self-Injury Questionnaire - Treatment Related (SIQ-TR; see Appendix A) which not only assesses the taxonomic specifications of SIB (e.g., type, frequency, duration), but also the affective antecedents and consequences as well as the functions of each type of SIB separately. A validation study in 273 female eating disorder patients showed that it was possible to construct four reliable and valid Emotions Scales (Positive/Negative Affectivity Before/After SIB) and three Functionality Scales (Positive Social Reinforcement, Automatic Positive/Negative Reinforcement). Convergent and divergent validity of the SIB characteristics, the Emotion Scales and the Functionality Scales were calculated by correlating the SIQ-TR with the Self-Harm Inventory, the Self Expression and Control Questionnaire and the Symptom Checklist. Finally, the authors discuss how the SIQ-TR can be used to plan the therapeutic management of SIB.

Chapter 6 - *Objective:* This chapter examines the measurement of eating disorders in the general population using the Survey for eating disorders (SEDs, Götestam and Agras, 1995, Ghaderi, 2002). The chapter is based on a prevalence study of eating disorders in the general female population in Norway.

Method: A total number of 3500 women, representatively recruited from the Norwegian female population, were sent a self-report questionnaire in 2004, including the SEDs, including both DSM-III-R and DSM-IV criteria for eating disorders. Among those, 1521 subjects (45.8%) returned completed forms.

Results: The point prevalence of eating disorders was found to be 2.6%, using DSM-IV. Using DSM-III-R, the point prevalence was 3.6%.

Discussion: The two different versions of the DSM-system gave different results. Methodological issues are discussed focusing on similarities and differences between DSM-III-R and DSM-IV. In addition, a discussion in light of DSM-V for eating disorders is provided.

Chapter 7 - Comparative neuropsychology refers to a line of research where tests originally developed to investigate cognitive processes in animals are modified for use with humans. The authors have used a comparative neuropsychological approach to develop a new test battery specifically for use with clinical populations. The new battery evaluates object discrimination, egocentric spatial abilities, visual and spatial working memory, and cognitive flexibility. The authors have investigated the usefulness of this battery in two clinical groups: in a geriatric population and in patients with Fragile-X syndrome (FXS), a genetic condition associated with mental retardation. Our results in geriatric participants indicate age differences on tasks that evaluate egocentric spatial abilities, cognitive flexibility, and object recognition. The results with FXS patients indicate strengths in egocentric spatial abilities and visual working memories alongside weaknesses in object discrimination, cognitive flexibility, and spatial working memory. These studies illustrate the utility of comparative neuropsychology to the study of cognition in normal and clinical populations. Future directions for novel test development and translation to the clinic are discussed within the comparative framework.

Chapter 8 - This chapter describes the development, test construction, and validation of psychological tests. The authors describe item generation and selection, testing for content validity, developing a standardization sample, testing for reliability (internal consistency, test-retest), assessing for internal test bias, determining the factor structure of a test, and finally testing both the convergent validity and discriminant validity of tests. The authors demonstrate these principles by contrasting the application of these processes with a recently published scale and with a newly developed measure for the assessment of personality disorders.

Chapter 10 - The study examined: a) the factor structure of the Short-Form Sport Orientation Questionnaire (SF-SOQ) (Skordilis and Stavrou, 2005) in two separate groups of athletes, with and without disabilities, through confirmatory factor analysis (CFA) and b) the equivalence of the SF-SOQ factor structure, across the two groups, through multisample analyses. The SF-SOQ incorporates 15 items, under the following three factors: "Competitiveness" (7 items), "Win Orientation" (5 items) and "Goal Orientation" (3 items).The participants were five hundred and thirty (530) athletes, classified in two groups of 273 athletes with disabilities and 257 athletes without disabilities. Three alternative nested models were examined for the first purpose [a: a three first-order correlated factor model (FM_{3C}), b: a three first-order uncorrelated factor model (FM_{3U}), and c: a single first-order factor model (FM_1)]. The results were in accordance to the sport achievement orientation theory (Gill and Deeter, 1988), since: a) the three first-order correlated factor SF-SOQ model-FM_{3C} provided an acceptable fit to the data, whereas the models of: b) three uncorrelated-FM_{3U} and c) single first-order-FM_1 factors, provided poor fit. Accordingly, the multisample analyses revealed that the three sport orientation factors were not equivalent across the two groups. The SF-SOQ items varied, in their relationship to the underlying measurement construct, meaning that these items were perceived and interpreted differently between athletes with and without disabilities. Overall, the SF-SOQ may be used with confidence to examine separate groups of athletes, either with or without disabilities. However, meaningful differences between athletes who differ according to disability status may not be undertaken in the future.

Chapter 11 - The present chapter aims to review the assessment of prospective memory (PM) in healthy subjects and clinical populations. In particular, the purposes of this chapter are three-fold: (1) To evaluate the pros and cons of different types of PM tasks: event-based, time-based and activity-based, (2) To discuss the issue of ecological validity in clinical practice, (3) To evaluate the effect sizes of PM deficits in patients with neurological disorders. Moreover, the authors also illustrate the potential aging effect on PM using both experimental-based and ecologically valid paradigms. The present findings provide a comprehensive view about aging effect by comparing three age groups: young, young old and older old. Three different types of laboratory-based PM showed different aging patterns, event-based PM tasks show a general decline pattern while aging effect of time-based PM only obvious when comparing the young and the young old. Activity-based PM did not show any aging effect, which implies different aging process of three types of PM. However, both executive function and retrospective memory failed to show the relationship with PM with one exception—one high cognitive demanding ecological valid time-based PM (open-and-close door in hotel test), was found consistent significant correlations with executive function, suggesting that executive function is not needed in PM unless PM performance is difficult or competing with other tasks for cognitive resources.

Chapter 12 - The measurement of functional limitations and disability in individuals with multiple sclerosis (MS) has been plagued by definitional ambiguity and measurement limitations. The abbreviated Late Life-Function and Disability Inventory (LL-FDI) was recently developed based on accepted definitions of functional limitations and disability, and has been supported as having strong measurement properties in samples of older adults. This study examined the structural and external aspects of score validity for the LL-FDI in individuals with MS. Individuals with MS completed the LL-FDI and three measures of physical activity. Structural aspects of score validity for the LL-FDI were established using confirmatory factor analysis (CFA). The CFA supported the existence of two factors of personal and social aspects of disability for the disability frequency and limitations subscales of the LL-FDI, and three factors of upper extremity function, basic lower extremity function, and advanced lower extremity function for the functional limitations subscale of the LL-FDI. External aspects of score validity for the LL-FDI were established based on expected differences in mean scores between individuals with relapsing-remitting MS and primary and secondary progressive MS and examination of the pattern of correlations between mean scores with the measures of physical activity. Our results support the structural and external aspects of score validity for the LL-FDI in individuals with MS, and the authors recommend that future researchers use this scale when measuring functional limitations and disability in this population.

Chapter 13 - The concept of "outcomes" has become widely accepted in clinical medicine as a means to evaluate the results of a medical intervention. In the past there was a reluctance to place a high value on patients' perceptions, but it is now generally agreed that patient-based outcomes are a valuable method of determining function and quality of life. In order for any outcome-based instrument to be useful, it must be user-friendly for both the clinician and patient, but it must be also statistically reliable and valid. These goals can be achieved through careful preparation by experts, sufficient feedback from patient groups, and by comparing objective clinical data with the results of the outcome instrument itself.

In this chapter, the authors would like to focus on the following 4 methodological issues and other related topics;

1. Selection of appropriate content for question items

For most outcome instruments, an ordinal scale is used with 3 to 5 choices ranging from a negative extreme to a positive extreme. However, grading schemes sometime use unclear phrasing which results in a misunderstanding by the patient. It is important, therefore, to ensure that the choice of content is comprehensive, yet unambiguous.

2. Relationships among items

Multivariate analyses are often used to statistically evaluate the strength of a relationship between a dependent variable and multiple independent variables. However, the assumption that the relationships are linear may not always be true in the case of outcome measures. It is necessary to use information criteria or data-specific multiple comparisons to check relationships among instrument items.

3. Construct validity

Categorical principal component analysis (CPCA) is a powerful statistical tool to reveal the patterns of shared variation or interrelationships within a score matrix. Through CPCA, items are clustered into related groups and dimensionally rotated. The number of dimensions – in effect, grouping clusters – is determined through scree plot or testing.

4. Evaluation of non-parametric tests

Non-parametric tests are commonly used in psychometric assessment, which involve the analysis of the difference between the median and its 95% confidence interval within a set of data. No standard method for estimation of the result of non-parametric calculations has been determined for evaluating outcomes instruments, but some promising methodologies deserve special attention.

Chapter 14 - The detection of intentional neglect requires time and equipment. In order to simplify its detection, the authors developed new software running on Microsoft Windows®, inverting right-left horizontal movements of the mouse cursor while leaving its vertical movements unchanged. The authors observed on eight successive subjects, that the software increased the expression of attentional neglect and detected intentional neglect. To conclude, they developed a simple, fast and objectively analyzable bedside test to detect and evaluate intentional neglect.

Chapter 15 - Rasch measurement is widely used for measurement of latent variables in psychological testing, education, health status measurement, and other fields. The Rasch model expresses ideal measurement requirements and much research has dealt with testing whether these assumptions are met in real data. Latent variables are often of interest in terms of their relation to other variables, some examples being self rated health as predictor of mortality or psychosocial work environment factors as predictors of job turnover. This chapter deals with prediction of a binary outcome variable using latent variables measured using the Rasch model. Three approaches are compared:\ (i) prediction using the sufficient score, (ii) prediction using the estimated values for each person, and (iii) prediction based on a joint model. Extensions of the Rasch model including uniform differential item functioning and uniform local dependence between items are also discussed. The approaches are illustrated and motivated using an example from occupational epidemiology.

Chapter 16 - This study was an initial psychometric test of the Chinese versions of the Index of Nausea, Vomiting, and Retching (INVR) and the Prenatal Self-Evaluation Questionnaire (PSEQ) in pregnant Taiwanese women. Although there already is evidence that the English-language versions of the scales are reliable and valid, it is important to verify the proper psychometric characteristics of the Chinese versions. Forward and backward translation, and a multiphase instrumentation study describing internal consistency, test-retest reliability, and content validity of the translated versions were conducted. A convenience sample was recruited from prenatal clinics in the south of Taiwan. Three measurement instruments were used in this study: the demographic inventory (DI), the INVR, and the PSEQ. Thirty pregnant women participated in the study. Both the internal consistency and stability coefficients of the INVR and PSEQ were satisfactory. The indices of content validity (CVI) for the Chinese versions of these two instruments were both 1.0, indicating that they are acceptable for use among Taiwanese pregnant women. This was the first instrumentation study of the INVR and PSEQ applied to Taiwanese pregnant women. Researchers could use this study as a model for future translation and application of psychometric instrumentation.

In: Psychological Tests and Testing Research Trends
Editor: Paul M. Goldfarb, pp. 1-3

ISBN: 978-1-60021-569-8
© 2007 Nova Science Publishers, Inc.

Expert Commentary A

NEW DIRECTIONS IN INTELLIGENCE TESTS: THE DYNAMIC MEASURES

Rosa Angela Fabio

Department of Psychology, Faculty of Formation Science,
Catholic University of Milan, Italy

Traditional intelligence test procedures focus only on the child's current level of performance rather than on the child's ability to respond to ongoing experiences (Gutierrez-Clelen and Pena, 2001; Fabio, 2005; Roediger and Karpicke, 2006). In examining different definitions of intelligence, it appears that intelligence is related to the individual's learning ability, to the change processes, and to the modifiability or plasticity of cognitive processes; it is therefore based on a dynamic and not a static concept.

As Elliot (2003) emphasizes, static measures contain some limitations: their tendency to lack an empirically supported theoretical framework (Flanagan and McGrew, 2000), the limited relationship between scores and instructional practices (Reschly and Robinson-Zañartu, 2000), their emphasis upon products rather than psychological processes (Sternberg, 2006; Sternberg and Grigorenko, 2002), their tendency to linguistic and cultural bias (Lopez, 1997) and their inability to guide clinicians in deriving specific interventions for educational difficulties (Fuchs et al., 1987; McGrew, 1994).

In any case, the main problem related to traditional intelligence tests is the rationale: since the concept of intelligence is referred to as a dynamic cognitive process and since the word "adapting" refers to a dynamic quality, it is important to measure it dynamically. For this reason dynamic measures of intelligence can better address dynamic and adaptive behaviour (Fabio, 2005; Sternberg, 2006).

Dynamic assessment (DA) is an umbrella term used to describe a heterogeneous range of approaches that are linked by a common element: instruction and feedback; normally DA is built into the testing process and is differentiated on the basis of an individual's performance. Thus the amount of assistance provided is directly contingent upon the testee's performance and modifiability (Elliot; 2003; Lidz and Elliott, 2000).

A new direction in dynamic assessment is to use flexible access to information and transfer as an index of plasticity and modifiability. As a consequence, indexes of dynamic assessment can measure cognitive processes in the learning phase (when the subject faces new problem solving) and in the transfer phase (when the subject generalises what he has learnt in the learning phase to new, more complex problem solving). This type of measure consists of submitting the learners to more difficult problem solving (over their basic ability), in supplying them with gradual and balanced assistance progressively disclosing the solution of the problem submitted and determining the level of aid adopted by the learner in solving the problem. The level of aid is inversely proportional to the modifiability index. The modifiability index is dynamic and is better related to the definitions of intelligence.

A first misdirection in the use of dynamic assessment is the target group. In a recent review Elliot (2003) listed in an appendix the major approaches of different authors that in different countries use dynamic assessment. Only four of them out of 17 use dynamic assessment to measure normally developing people. They mainly use dynamic assessment for low achieving children, children with learning difficulties and children that come from different countries. In relation to the rationale of dynamic assessment above mentioned, the target group can be also the normal subjects.

A second misdirection is related the type of assistance provided. Since the amount of assistance provided is inversely related to the testee's modifiability, it is important to measure it precisely. So, the critical factor is a precise, balanced standardization of the step-by-step aids supplied to the testee for problem solving.

It is hoped that all the researchers that work with dynamic measures work togheter to create and standardize a general normative system to measure intelligence. The area which need to be explored is also the relationship between evoked potential and behavioural propensity to change. Since evoked response is an electrical brain potential recorded following presentation of a stimulus, it may be that the electrical brain potential is linked to the general propensity to change, even if the latter is a more complex process.

A second area which needs to be explored is if it is possible to improve individual dynamic measures and the amount of improvement.

REFERENCES

Elliot, J. (2003). Dynamic Assessment in Educational Settings: realising potential. *Educational Review, 55*, 221-231.

Fabio, R. A., (2005). Dynamic assessment of intelligence is a better reply to adaptive behaviour and cognitive plasticity. *Journal of General Psychology, 132,* 41-64.

Flanagan, D. P., McGrew, K. S., and Ortiz, S. O. (2000). *The Wechsler Intelligence Scales and Gf-Gc theory: A contemporary approach to interpretation.* Boston: Allyn and Bacon.

Gutierrez-Clellen, V.F. and Pena, E. (2001). Dynamic assessment of diverse children: a tutorial. *Language, Speech, and hearing Services in Schools*, 32, 212-224.

Lidz, C. Y., Elliot, J. (2000). Introduction to dynamic assesment. En: *Advances in Cognition and Educational Practice, vol. 6: Dynamic Assesment: Prevailing Models and Application.* Editado por Carol Lidz y Julian Elliott. Elseiver Science.

Reschly, D.J. and Robinson-Zañartu, C. (2000). Aptitude tests in educational classification and placement. In G. Goldstein and M. Hersen. *Handbook of psychological assessment* (3rd edition) (pp. 183-201). Boston: Allyn and Bacon.

Roediger, H.L., and Karpicke, J.D. (2006). The power of testing memory: basic research and implicatons for educational practice. *Perspectives on Psychological Science,* 1, 181-210.

Sternberg, R. J. (2006). *International Handbook of Intelligence.* Connecticut: Yale University.

Sternberg, R. J., and Grigorenko, E. L. (2002). *Dynamic testing.* New York: Cambridge University Press.

In: Psychological Tests and Testing Research Trends
Editor: Paul M. Goldfarb, pp. 5-6

ISBN: 978-1-60021-569-8

Expert Commentary B

REGARDING PSYCHOLOGICAL TESTING

Louis A. Gottschalk

Department of Psychiatry and Human Behavior, University of California, Irvine Medical
Center, Orange, CA, USA

Psychological testing is making notable progress due to increasing contributions from computerized information high technology.

One area deserving mention is the technology involved in computerised *speech recognition*. In the past, computerized speech recognition, though remarkable, has been useful when applied to the speech of one individual to which the recognition technology can be fruitfully applied after the recognition system has been accustomed to the pronunciation and voice enunciation of each individual separately. There is now available technological software that claims it can successfully and reliably recognize across English speaking persons with initial exposure to their voices, e.g., Dragon naturally speaking 9. Since some psychological testing involves speech recognition and communication, this innovation is noteworthy.

The computerization of the *content analysis of speech and verbal texts* which is now capable of measuring the magnitude of many diverse neuropsychobiological dimensions (anxiety—and six subscales, hostility outward, hostility inward, depression—and seven subscales, social alienation-personal disorganization—i.c., schizophrenia, cognitive impairment, human relations, hope, achievement strivings, quality of life) and immediately comparing the empirical findings for emotional states or traits with norms for these dimensions (Gottschalk and Bechtel, 1982, 1989, 1995, 1998-2003) has had many published applications. Some of these applications have included the field of neuropsychopharmacology and the assessment of the efficacy of psychoactive drugs (Gottschalk, 1999), the rapid detection of cognitive impairment (Gottschalk, Bechtel, Maguire, et al. 2000), the influence of anticancer chemotherapeutic agents (Gottschalk, Holcombe, Jackson, et al.), the development of computerized psychodynamic psychotherapy (Gottschalk, 2000, 2006) , the prediction of treatment outcome (Gottschalk, 1985; Gottschalk, Bechtel, Buchman et al, 2004), the mental status of patients with multiple sclerosis (Van den Noort, Gottschalk, Bechtel, 2006).

In combination with the advances in accurate speech recognition and the computerized measurement of verbal behavior and its quantitative semantic assessment, critical advances have been made in the broad field of psychological testing.

REFERENCES

Gottschalk, L.A. and Bechtel, R.J.. The measurement of anxiety through the computer analysis of verbal samples. *Comprehensive Psychiatry.* 23: 364-369, 1982.

Gottschalk, L.A. Hope and other deterrents to illness. *American Journal of Psychotherapy.* 39:515-524,1985.

Gottschalk, L.A. and Bechtel, R.J.. Artificial intelligence and the computerization of the content analysis of natural language. *Artificial Intelligence in Mediocine.* 1: 131-137, 1989.

Gottschalk, L.A. and Bechtel, R.J.. Computerized measurement of natural language for use in biomedical research. *Computer Methods and Programs in Biomedicine.* 47: 123-130, 1995.

Gottschalk, L.A.. The application of a computerized measurement of the content analysis of natural language to the effects of psychoactive drugs. *Methods and Findings in Experimental and Clinical Pharmacology.* 21: 133-138, 1999,

Gottschalk, L.A., Bechtel, R.J., Maguire, G.A., Harrington, D.E., Levinson, D. M., Franklin, D.L., Caracoma, D. Computerized measurement of cognitive impairment and associated neuropsychiatric dimensions., *Comprehensive Psychiatry.* 41: 326-333, 2000.

Gottschalk, L.A., Holcombe, R., Jackson, D., Bechtel, R.J. Effects os anticancer chemotherapeutic drugs upon cognitive functioi and other neuropsychiatric dimensions in breast cancer patients. *Methods and Findings in Experimental and Clinical Pharmacology.*, 24: 117-122, 2002.

Gottschalk, L.A. and Bechtel, R.J.. *PCAD 2000—Psychiatric Content Analysis and Diagnosis.* Corona del Mar, CA: GB Software (4607 Perham Road; Corona del Mar, CA 92625), 1998-2003.

Gottschalk, L.A., Bechtel, R.J., Buchman, T.G., Ray, S.E. Measurement of hope and associated neuropsychiatric dimensions by the computerized content analysis of speech and verbal texts. In Jacklin Elliott (Ed.) *Research on the Measurement of Hope.* New York: Nova Science Publishers, Inc., 2004.

Van den Noort, S., Gottschalk, L.A., Bechtel, R.J. Computerized content analysis of speech for the assessment of mental function in multiple sclerosis patients. (In press) New York: Nova Science Publishers, Inc. , 2006.

In: Psychological Tests and Testing Research Trends
Editor: Paul M. Goldfarb, p. 7

ISBN: 978-1-60021-569-8
© 2007 Nova Science Publishers, Inc.

Expert Commentary C

THE PSYCHOLOGICAL VULNERABILITY SCALE

B. Rueda
Faculty of Psychology, Madrid, Spain

The construct of vulnerability has been characterized by an extensive theoretical and empirical research that support the relevance of this concept in the scientific field.

Based on clinical perspective, vulnerability has been conceptualized as a profound disturbance in the self-concept or in interpersonal relationships. This psychological disruption can trigger maladaptive attitudes, such as excessive perfectionism and dependency of others' approval. Theorists from this arena have emphasized the importance of measuring vulnerability in the understanding, treatment and prevention of the affective disorders.

Vulnerability has also been widely investigated by health psychologists. Within this domain the scope of vulnerability has been extended, to the extent that it has been regarded as a mechanism that connects personality to a number of potential health outcomes, for example risky perception, maintenance of a healthy lifestyle or illness management.

In an attempt to integrate both clinical and health orientations, Sinclair and Wallston (1999) have proposed the construct of Psychological Vulnerability, that encompasses the dysfunctional beliefs of perfectionism, dependency and depressogenic attributions. The Psychological Vulnerability scale (PVS) has been developed to measure this characteristic, and has been mainly used in patients with chronic disease and in need of therapeutic intervention.

This instrument contains two important features that merits especial attention. First, the scale has been underwent to validational research using not only patients' samples, but also non-clinical populations (see Rueda *et al.*, in this volume). Both methodological strategies have supported the psychometric adequacy and construct validity of the PVS, together with the generalizability of the results. And second, the issue that this instrument contains six items indicates good ease of use, and limited amount of burden when it is administered.

Consequently, although more cumulative evidence is required concerning the testing and use of the scale, preliminary empirical investigation makes the PVS a recommended measure to be applicable for clinical and research purposes.

In: Psychological Tests and Testing Research Trends
Editor: Paul M. Goldfarb, pp. 9-15

ISBN: 978-1-60021-569-8
© 2007 Nova Science Publishers, Inc.

Expert Commentary D

DEMENTIA AND MENTAL DISORDERS: METHODOLOGICAL CONSIDERATIONS

Nora Silvana Vigliecca

Consejo Nacional de Investigaciones Científicas y Técnicas de la Argentina
(CONICET) Centro de Investigaciones de la Facultad de Filosofía y Humanidades
(CIFFyH) y Servicio de Neurocirugía del Hospital Córdoba, Córdoba. Argentina

Motivation: Having my own family suffer the consequences of a psychological misdiagnosis corroborated by "clinical consensus of experts", I feel profoundly concerned about the use that psychiatrists, psychologists and other clinical neuroscience professionals can make of a number of symptoms and mental disorders which have been just theoretically (and also consensually) formulated into a book. I have devoted my professional life to getting better psychological diagnoses and, ironically, now I am suffering myself the impotence of not being able to change a psychiatric diagnosis that can destroy the life of a relative of mine. Therefore, I can understand not only the patient's pain and helplessness particularly when the diagnosis is made based mainly on the "information provided by others", but also, and taking into account my professional training, some methodological mistakes, which are most of the times linked to (and hidden behind) an apparently correct and consolidated professional habit.

The purpose of this comment is to introduce some questions and some practical or theoretical appreciations, which can help analyze if the current paradigm of psychiatric diagnosis by consensus is not incurring in a vicious circle by avoiding some methodological assumptions, which are essential for a correct clinical approach from both the ethical and technical points of view.

There is a big difference between the concepts (and the fascination that they arise) and the way of looking for them in a person, that is, between what is observed and what is interpreted. A clinical interpretation, for example Dementia, can be made from one, two or hundreds of observational indexes. At the present time, both the amount of evidence and particularly the way of showing it apparently are not requirements for getting a demonstration of the relationship between concepts and persons. When professionals are overconfident and convinced that the patient seems to have a typical abstract pattern of impairment, they will simply register the case as having the mental disorder (thus affecting the patient´s future life) and, eventually, this case, as any other case, can become part of scientific research (and can affect in this way the future of scientific knowledge). Besides, as any psychological or physical register (including worldwide drug treatments) can be associated with clinical opinion, the production of research articles with redundant information in their diagnosis component becomes facilitated.

The diffusion of criteria, which the terms "multiple deficits" (or equivalent ones) involve, has become common practice, without a true understanding of the methodological difficulty that these criteria bring about. When in a definition (as in the one of Dementia) a number of not mutually exclusive concepts is mixed up, that is, when multifactorial and multivariate models should lead the professional activity to organize the situation in a more realistic way, paradoxically, professionals resort to univariate and simplistic proposals of analysis to solve the problem by assuming that real persons are abstract archetypes of each syndrome. Likewise, it is also assumed that the clinical "inductive inference" which emerges from that syndrome is the most valuable "measure" to be compared with any other measure, which in many cases is directly or indirectly included in the syndrome due to the multiplicity of variables and indexes the syndrome has taken into account.

The use of multiple interpretation criteria (such as probable, possible or definite; severe or mild; or type A, B or C dementia) for multiple and macro psychological concepts (such as language, memory, execution, praxia, etc. which at once are affected by multiple factors and expressed in multiple ways) without an appropriate operational definition which organizes all the possible *combinations* among them leaves to the discretion of each observer or group of observers (i.e., the clinical consensus) the final interpretation of each case or of each accidental sample of study. The human brain is a very complex entity, and it will become much more complex and unreachable if we make it even more difficult to understand through criteria that cannot be verified. The problem is not the clinical criterion itself but the lack of operational definitions. Concepts are always necessary but their empirical evidences, too. Otherwise, diagnoses can be unfair as they are based on prejudices more than on real judgments.

There should be at least an attempt to consider the multiple and real patient's data statistically to reach a clinical conclusion but, nowadays, everybody seems to be very satisfied with a simplistic approach that literally hides all this information behind the clinical criterion.

What exactly does, for instance in dementia, "deficits in two areas of cognition" mean (American Psychiatric Association, 2000 (DSM IV); Roman et al, 1993)? Does it mean: deficits in two tests, in two subtests, in two items, in X % of the tests, in two statistically extracted psychological factors, in two batteries developed to assess huge psychological functions? From the same point of view, which tests and how many of these tests indicate, for example, the presence of "amnesia", "aphasia", "execution deficits" or "apraxia". The use of absolute numbers (and the sum of them) to describe concepts that are relative in their essence (and, for this reason, *limited to their own contexts and conditions*) can complicate the panorama instead of clarifying it. If a politician or a professor becomes aphasic (showing, of course, problems in verbal memory, comprehension, reasoning, praxia, and so on) and for this reason has to change jobs and becomes annoyed or sad, is he suffering from dementia or just from aphasia? (Probably he is suffering just from aphasia, even when he has more than "two" cognitive functions affected).

Scientists do not usually define what they consider two cognitive deficits *in their particular instruments and subjects*. They do not make explicit the way in which multiple evaluations are organized in a model of interpretation, in spite of having some statistical tools to do it. The psychological operational definition is simply avoided. Moreover, as anatomical operational definitions for expressions such us multiple, extensive, relevant, abnormal, etc., are also avoided, the panorama becomes even more complicated.

Confronted with this situation, clinicians generally rely *at last on just one* source of information, namely intuition, experience, or a colleague's opinion and make an educated guess on a diagnosis. That is the moment when their personal clinical criteria are inexorably mixed up with the universal conceptual criterion, and they do not seem to need anything else (but the repetition of the "the theoretical symptoms") to classify a person. That is the moment when reality is mixed up with an absolute concept, i.e., with no observational indexes at all or with *all the observational indexes fused in an undecipherable, idiosyncratic and unrepeatable impression.* When the operational definition is avoided, the theory (the conceptual definition) becomes irrefutable (a dogma). Consequently, scientific knowledge gets stuck.

The current procedure to come to a dementia diagnosis is, in the best of the cases, to collect some evidence from the action of different professionals and, with all this information, risk an intuitive opinion. But scientific reasoning cannot be built by beginning with a hypothesis (this person has dementia) and by coming to a conclusion (this person has dementia) without showing the *specific rule* by means of which to infer the second statement. Strictly speaking, we should say that, in those particular kinds of studies, patients are classified according to the researcher's personal appreciation. Independent of the sensitivity, specificity and reliability that this appreciation (generally expressed as two categories) may demonstrate, it is still only ONE data of the N evidences collected. In other words, if researchers use one observational index with two final categories of analysis to classify the subjects (for example, normal vs. pathological), they will have two possibilities of responses for each subject. If they add another index with, for example, three categories, they will have six possibilities. But if they use N indexes with N categories, they will have N x N possibilities. The problem is that clinicians are using the N x N possibilities as if they were just two. And clinical research is permanently linking the N x N possibilities (the clinical criterion) with a big subgroup of them (generally another clinical criterion derived from -and included in- the first one (McKhann, Drachmann, Folstein, Katzman, Price, Stadlan, 1984; Roman et al, 1993), thus producing redundant information. Clinical research is permanently trying to confirm the validity of the clinical criterion, which, in fact, has been assumed as valid from the very beginning.

Since the clinical criterion (as a pure interpretation) is present in all the validation procedures or in all the steps of the scientific research (to diagnose a person and a group of persons, to build and to validate a test, to validate a histopathological pattern, etc.) it becomes at once the dependent and the independent variable. So, in the end, we do not know if we are measuring an abstraction or a reality (although the entire psychiatric world may believe in and agree with it, that is not an empirical confirmation of its existence). *As we are using the conceptual definition along with the operational one in a confusing way, the pattern of the patient's cognitive and anatomical data is generally built a priori.* Besides, how can professionals become "experts" (acquire "experience or practice") in just a so-called illness, i.e., in just a conventional entity? Are professionals more expert if they have "read" more about that entity in books?

The solution to clarify this confusing practice would be to always link two or more "autonomous realities" (for example, cognitive *scores* vs. anatomical *measures*) by avoiding, as far as possible, absolute criteria or *a priori* interpretations in the validation process. To stop contaminating the results of the instruments (the real patient's data) from previous conceptual definitions about a certain mental disorder, the researcher opinion should be considered at most as one dichotomous item among others or, better, as an interpretation (i.e., as an inductive inference) in the discussion section of a paper. The theorization phase should be independent of the demonstration one, which at all times should go from empirical indexes towards empirical indexes.

If, in fact, there is a neuropsychological pattern for the different types of dementia, for example, and this pattern has been actually related to the corresponding anatomical pattern, all these patterns (statistically expressed) should be shown in published articles. By using this approach, researchers will discover that not only the individual patients but also the different groups of patients (assessed with different instruments and in different situations) have a distinctive or variable pattern of response, *a real one,* thus favoring the discrimination of authentic scientific concepts. Complex phenomena cannot be reduced to 2 x 2 contingency tables on the basis of conventional categories of interpretation.

In some studies, the unique source of information to report a cognitive impairment is a very widespread test, which has been originally based on just one or two validity studies carried out with small and accidental samples, which, by the way, have been generally divided into two groups of analysis (for example, dementia vs. non dementia) by using the clinical criterion once more. *The cognitive measures incorporate the clinical criterion to confirm validity and the clinical criterion incorporates the cognitive measures to confirm diagnosis.* Nevertheless, as both of them would need an independent validation, the final result is a never-ending circle of affirmations confirming each other through a collection of apparently well-known concepts, which are in fact just the illusion caused by methodological circularity. Although nobody can deny that consensus is the first step within scientific development, we have been dealing with the first step for two decades.

Ideally, in order to consider a psychological technique as scientific we should demonstrate that it is superior (non equal) to not applying anything at all, that is to say, that it is superior (non equal) to the evaluation by common sense or by personal appreciation. When subjective classification criteria are used as reference standards, we are demonstrating that the psychological technique is at most equal to those criteria and, in terms of costs and benefits we might wonder if it is not more useful to continue using the subjective criteria. Many valid tests are based on opinions. But opinions are test items not persons.

When a patient is severely affected, it is not necessary to be a doctor to make a correct "diagnosis". Maybe this is the secret for the consensus criteria reliability. Doctors, relatives, nurses, friends, and so on can read a clinical theoretical criterion in a book and reach a "diagnosis" by comparing intuitively that concept with the concept they have about the patient. Even patients can make this process by themselves. But that has nothing to do with Science. If we do not define our clinical procedures better and quickly, this vulgar (and rather primitive) knowledge will be progressively more difficult to differentiate from the "scientific" criteria we are proposing for the evaluation of mental disorders.

Enumerating the "names" of all the criteria and techniques used in research is not equivalent to an operational definition. The logical reasoning and the methodological premise underlying to a correct empirical approach would be: "if that conceptual definition is true, then we should be able to see in the patient..." Within this context, we can say for example: "In this study we have operationally defined Dementia (or Aphasia or Apraxia, etc.) as Y and/ or Z and/ or N (real) measures" (the consistency among these measures should also have to be shown), but we cannot quote other authors to define our own research conditions. *There cannot be a universal operational definition.*

Papers about dementia or mental disorders usually affirm that subjects have been classified according to "X" clinical (conceptual) criteria, which in fact is a fallacy, because those persons are not concepts. A person is not comparable to a set of words unfolded in a theoretical definition. This person has to do or to show something; some concrete fact has to be registered with precise computations (for example, in a multifactor and multivariate structure) in order for other observers to be able to use it with the same or other subjects. And the precise computations should not be found in a criterion cited in the references; they should be shown in published articles, in the form of a common formula that embraces *all the persons included in the sample and all the data collected (if collected at all) for all those persons.* In scientific research, the "expert opinion" should be that formula. That is the only way to make it possible for us to come to an agreement by using terms that can be understood not only by the current observers of the patient but also by any observer any time. Science is the translation of intuition to these terms but, unfortunately, we are using the translation exactly the opposite way.

Dementia itself and cognitive deterioration, of any etiology and magnitude, are not homogenous phenomena. Neither is the brain, the biosocial environmental factors or the interaction between them. Differentiating the normal from the pathologic implies a great responsibility. But, although this task may be difficult, it cannot be avoided by appealing to dogmas. In the disciplines which lack of a biological marker, there is generally a great confusion of concepts (as "dementia") with observational indexes (as "a low score") hidden behind an apparent plain situation universally accepted. And, although it may sound contradictory, it is this oversimplification of the problem which brings about that feeling of certainty, which is enough to hinder scientific progress.

A *valid evaluation* or procedure is not a definite one. In a validity study, not only the gold standard but also the technique to be proved is relative to the other. The interaction or correlation between two views supposedly pertaining to the same phenomenon does not consider the quality of better/ worse or of cause/ effect. This is also an interpretation, which comes from the state of knowledge. Nevertheless, in the case of Dementia or mental disorders, it is very difficult to affirm that one of the terms is better than the other because both of them are permanently changing in relation to the other, and both of them are equally incipient or exploratory in the current state of knowledge. For example, what gold standard has been established to validate a histopathological dementia study? If a study case has a histopathological evidence of dementia but not the corresponding psychological diagnosis, or vice versa, does it not mean that "both" criteria are fallible or relative? How can they produce (together or alone) then a "definite" diagnosis (McKhann, Drachmann, Folstein, Katzman, Price, Stadlan, 1984; Roman et al, 1993)? Or, from a different point of view, if they are (or at least just one of them is) such perfect criteria, why is it necessary to enumerate the two of them or even several indexes of "definite" in a conceptual definition? If technology keeps developing, will the number of dementia indexes described in clinical criteria keep growing too? A permanent renewal of concepts is not necessarily a multiplication of them.

Technology is developing faster than the capacity human beings have to understand it. But even when we are overwhelmed by a large amount of information, which we are still unable to process, we cannot mix up the method to build a theory and the theory itself with the techniques or the instruments we are circumstantially using to collect data. In some instances, scientists forget that what they usually consider a universal or a "true" concept has generally been originated by the reading of a particular observer with a particular instrument at a given moment and subject.

A scientific theory is a limited perspective to interpret what the evidences might mean in a certain scientific period and context but it is not the method to arrange the way in which these evidences should be collected nor should it be, as it is considered at present, some kind of hegemonic practice to which every scientist has to adhere to in order not to be discriminated. In order to be scientific, a theory should be refutable. However, nowadays there seems to be very few articles, which contradict the current and universal perspective. And what would happen if the current theory (or convention) turns out to be false and we were forcing real people to fit into just a chimerical typology of pathological processes? Should we consider a certain behavior right or wrong on the basis of what most physicians agree or on the basis of what most people actually do? If the current theory has been based on the norms and deviations from the norms about certain variables assessed with certain instruments, then this is a good reason to continue the following "empirical" studies starting from the results of those (or similar) instruments not just from the "names" of those variables.

Behavior techniques are as perfectible as anatomical ones, and behavior affects the brain as much as the brain affects behavior. So far, it has not been demonstrated that one of the directions is stronger than the other. But, if we continue *prioritizing the opinion consensus more than the data consistency,* psychology will never progress.

In order not to lose sight of the problem, it is very useful to get back to the roots: The Scientific Method. Considering this perspective*, there is not a definite diagnosis.* Scientific evaluations are always probable (it is not necessary to explain this quality by means of a conceptual definition) and the probability level cannot be determined *a priori* with a careful description of abstract concepts. So as to be perfectible, scientific concepts are *always relative* to other criterion, objective and repeatable (not merely interpretative) which will precisely help to determine, preferably, the *a posteriori* level of probability.

We cannot compensate for the rudimentary knowledge we have about the relationship between brain and cognition by appealing to beliefs and the support of our colleagues to convince others of the real existence of our data. "Consensus" has been the method par excellence to come to an agreement in any human group (including, dishonest ones) particularly by appealing to the authority criteria as the gold standard. Besides, if two persons (for example two professionals or a professional and a patient's relative or a patient's teacher) share the same belief system (namely the extremely well-known clinical criterion) it is possible for them to interpret reality (the patient) in a similar way. So, something much more solid and humble than "democracy" should be used in Science to differentiate a professional diagnosis from a common one and guarantee the enhancement of knowledge as well as avoid an eventual abuse on a patient.

The clinical "consensus of experts" is not a scientific notion by itself. Nevertheless, it is currently used as the main way to establish which patterns of behavior should be considered as pathological, not only for an individual patient but also for all the patients in the world. Clinical experience and intuition cannot be under discussion because *they will always be present* in an evaluation. But they are unmanageable. So, there are other factors, the repeatable, the perfectible and, in short, the scientific ones to which our efforts should be addressed. Systematic reviews are necessary to identify papers based on opinions vs. papers based on the real patients' data.

Although technical and ethical issues should go together, this does not seem to be the case for the psychiatric ones. The demands of human rights organizations regarding the eventual harm that the current paradigm is causing to patients are apparently ignored in scientific journals. This may be because these organizations are using just persuasive methods to express their complaints. Nevertheless, when researchers who stick to the current paradigm express their opinions about the patient's condition they are using similar methods to justify their decisions, i.e., they are referring to very widespread dissertations rather than to their own results to confirm a diagnosis.

Behavior is the common denominator for many biological and social disciplines. But, if in the current state of knowledge, we cannot define a clear structure to organize complex psychological data, hardly will we be able to understand the imminent behavioral science, i.e., a science that will be nourished by the information provided by all those disciplines, including the genomic one. The analysis of mental disorders, by its nature and intricacy, can be a very good "exercise" in this attempt.

REFERENCES

American Psychiatric Association. . (2000): *Diagnostic and statistical manual of mental disorders*, 4th ed. Washington, D.C.

McKhann, G., Drachmann, D., Folstein, M., Katzman, R., Price, D., and Stadlan, E. M. (1984): Clinical diagnosis of Alzheimer's disease: Report of the NINCDS-ADRDA work group under the auspices of Department of Health and Human Services Task Force on Alzheimer's Disease. *Neurology; 34*: 939-944.

Roman, G. C., Tatemichi, T. K., Erkinjuntti, T., Cummings, J. L., Masdeu, J. C., Garcia, J. H., Amaducci, L., Orgogozo, J. M., Brun, A., Hofman, A., Moody, D. M., O'Brien, M. D., Yamaguchi, T., Grafman, J., Drayer, B. P., Bennett, D. A., Fisher, M., Ogata, J., Kokmen, E., Bermejo, F., Wolf, P. A., Gorelick, P. B., Bick, K. L., Pajeau, A. K., Bell, M. A., DeCarli, C., Culebras, A., Korczyn, A. D., Bogousslavsky, J., Hartmann, A., and Scheinberg, P (1993). Vascular dementia: Diagnostic criteria for research studies: Report of the NINDS-AIREN International Workshop. *Neurology; 43*: 250- 260.

In: Psychological Tests and Testing Research Trends
Editor: Paul M. Goldfarb, pp. 17-38

ISBN: 978-1-60021-569-8
© 2007 Nova Science Publishers, Inc.

Chapter 1

VALIDATING THE COOP/WONCA AS A QUALITY OF LIFE MEASURE IN CANCER SURVIVORS

Ian S. Pagano and *Carolyn C. Gotay*
Cancer Research Center of Hawaii, Biomed C105;
1960 East-West Road; Honolulu, HI 96822 USA

ABSTRACT

Background: Over the past 30 years the field of health-related quality of life research has shown continual expansion, with several instruments having been developed for its assessment. Yet, there is still not a clear universally agreed upon definition of the construct. There is general agreement that quality of life is related to perceived physical, mental, and social well-being; but a strong theoretical model that is at once simple, intuitive, and useful for assessment has not been forthcoming. We therefore proposed two competing theoretical models, which we have called the *component* and *abstraction* models of quality of life; and we have tested these through the construct validation of a health status instrument that is both brief and simple, the COOP / WONCA.

Method: A multiethnic sample of 365 cancer survivors in Hawaii responded to a slightly modified version of the nine-item COOP / WONCA and the EORTC QLQ-C30 questionnaire. Construct validation of the COOP / WONCA was performed via factor analysis and cross-structure comparison with the QLQ-C30. As a test of the two proposed theoretical models, the results of these construct validation procedures were compared with the hypotheses generated from each theory.

Results: Factor analyses of the COOP / WONCA suggested that a single factor provided the most parsimonious solution, which supported the abstraction model of quality of life. Comparisons with the QLQ-C30 suggested both convergent and discriminant validity. One item, labeled physical fitness, did not perform as well as the others.

Conclusions: The evidence here suggests that the COOP / WONCA provides a valid assessment of health-related quality of life in cancer survivors. A definition of quality of life consistent with an abstraction model (a one-dimensional construct) was supported,

---

*Address for correspondence: Ian Pagano, PhD; Cancer Research Center of Hawaii; Biomed C-105; 1960 East-West Road; Honolulu, HI 96822; Phone: (808) 441-3489; Fax: (808) 586-3077; E-mail: ian@crch.hawaii.edu

suggesting a greater simplicity than is often believed. Although further research is clearly needed, these results suggest that researchers and clinicians needing to assess quality of life simply, and with minimal burden to the respondents, will be well-served by the COOP / WONCA.

Keywords: quality of life, cancer, factor analysis, validation, COOP / WONCA, QLQ-C30

INTRODUCTION

In recent decades there has been increased interest in assessing the quality of life of cancer survivors [1], and several instruments have been developed for this purpose [2-5]. However, one problem with assessing quality of life is that there is not a clear universally agreed upon definition [6], and different instruments often have different theoretical underpinnings [7;8]. This creates a certain amount of confusion, which makes it difficult to compare research across studies.

One simple and generally accepted definition of quality of life (also called health-related quality of life or sometimes simply health)[1] is the one written in the preamble to the constitution of the World Health Organization, "Health[2] is a state of complete physical, mental and social well-being and not merely the absence of disease or infirmity" [9]. This definition has not been amended since 1948, suggesting a long-term consensus as to its merits. However, we feel that ambiguity does exist.

From this definition, it is implied that quality of life (or health) is related to three components (physical, mental, and social well-being), all of which are necessary to some degree in order for a person to have a high level of quality of life.[3] However, ambiguity arises because the definition does not imply a cause and effect relationship between quality of life and the three components. To quote the cliché, "Which came first, the chicken or the egg?"

So, one might ask, why is quality of life related to physical, mental, and social well-being? When two variables are correlated, there are three possible explanations: the first variable causes the second, the second variable causes the first, or a third variable causes the first two.[4] These three possibilities are almost axiomatic with respect to the concept of correlation.

While the possibility of a third variable having a causal influence on both QoL[5] and the three components seems plausible (e.g., a disabling disease would almost certainly have that effect), this model would negate the WHO definition of quality of life. To see this, assume that the third variable could be controlled (as in a standard multiple regression analysis). By doing so, the relation between QoL and three components would no longer exist, rejecting the

---

[1] In this paper, we use the term *quality of life* to refer only to health-related quality of life from the individual perspective (sometimes called internal quality of life), and not what is sometimes called external or environmental quality of life (e.g., disease presence, standard of living).

[2] In this definition we interpret the word *health* to mean quality of life.

[3] The WHO definition also suggests that the absence of disease or infirmity is related to quality of life, and we include this in our discussion below regarding Aristotle's eudaimonia theory.

[4] For the sake of simplicity, in this context we are calling the group of component variables (physical, mental, and social well-being) a single variable.

[5] We will often abbreviate quality of life as *QoL*.

WHO definition of QoL. So, this scenario is not implied by the WHO definition, but which of the other two possibilities is most appropriate? Do physical, mental, and social well-being cause QoL, or is it the other way around? Let us look at each possibility in turn.

If the three components have a causal path to QoL, a possible analogy is that a person's quality of life is to her physical, mental, and social well-being, as the volume of a box is to its length, width, and height (in the Aristotelian format, QoL : physical-mental-social : : Volume : length-width-height). By measuring the three components, one can then calculate the outcome. If so, quality of life and volume are both three-dimensional constructs, which can only be understood through an understanding of each of the components (dimensions). We shall refer to this as the *component* model of quality of life (see figure 1).

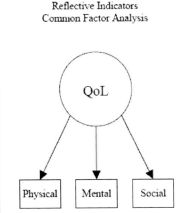

Figure 1. The component and abstraction models of quality of life are shown. Each circle represents a single latent construct and each rectangle represents multiple observed indicators. In the component model, three orthogonal components (P, M, and S) are defined by their observed formative indicators (physical, mental, and social well-being). These three components (dimensions) then define the quality of life (QoL) construct. In the abstraction model, QoL is defined as an abstraction of reflective indicators. Principal component analysis is appropriate when the hypothesized causal pathway is formative (as in the component model), whereas common factor analysis is appropriate when the hypothesized causal pathway is reflective (as in the abstraction model).

However, unlike the dimensions of a box, the components of quality of life are not orthogonal (they are correlated) [10]. For example, we would expect people with low levels of mental well-being to have a tendency to also have low levels of physical and social well-being. Because of this correlation among the components, it is not clear that all three are actually needed in order to characterize quality of life.

To illustrate this, assume that instead of the three-dimensional box used in the analogy above, the object is in fact a two-dimensional sheet of paper. If we were given three measurements for the sheet of paper (e.g., the length of the vertical, the length of the horizontal, and the length of the diagonal), some of this information would be redundant (i.e., correlated). This is of course because only two dimensions exist for calculating the size (area) of a sheet of paper.[6] Because of the correlated nature of the three WHO components of quality

---

[6] Assume that a sheet of paper has negligible thickness.

of life, some of the information contained in them is also redundant, and perhaps not all three are needed to measure quality of life.

The correlation between the three components brings us to the third possible causal explanation for the relation between QoL and the three components. This is the possibility that QoL causes physical, mental, and social well-being. If this theoretical model is the most appropriate, then the three components are necessarily correlated because they all are influenced by QoL.

A possible analogy is with the construct of depression. Quality of life is to physical, mental, and social well-being, as depression is to appetite, sadness, and concentration (in the Aristotelian format, QoL : physical-mental-social : : Depression : appetite-sadness-concentration).[7] Here, depression is hypothesized to be a latent mental construct, which has a causal effect on various observables. Depression is a one-dimensional abstraction, which is understood via several instantiations (appetite, sadness, and concentration).[8] Applying this model to quality of life, QoL could possibly be defined as a one-dimensional abstraction of the instantiations perceived physical, mental, and social well-being. We shall refer to this as the *abstraction* model of quality of life (see figure 1).

Perhaps the earliest conception of an abstraction model of quality of life is *eudaimonia*, which was elaborated by Aristotle in *Nicomachean Ethics* in 350 BCE [11]. Eudaimonia is translated literally as "having a good guardian spirit," which implies happiness, well-being, or flourishing. Aristotle recognized eudaimonia as a state to be achieved through a lifetime of virtuous action combined with a certain amount of good fortune (e.g., necessary goods[9] and freedom from disease), and he viewed it as the ultimate goal in life.

Examining eudaimonia through a present-day scientific lens, we propose that it could be modeled as a one-dimensional latent mental construct in the same way as the abstraction model of quality of life. This latent construct would of course influence other observable variables (as in the depression analogy above), which could be used to measure the unobservable construct. And returning to the WHO definition of quality of life, these observables would likely include perceived[10] physical, mental, and social well-being.

With these foundations, we propose a more complete theoretical model of QoL that combines Aristotle's concept of eudaimonia with the abstraction model of quality of life. We call it the *eudaimonia model of quality of life* (see figure 2). In this model, virtuous action, goods, and objective physical health[11] influence quality of life (eudaimonia), which in turn influences perceived physical, mental, and social well-being.

Ultimately our objective is to test the plausibility of the eudaimonia model via structural equation modeling [12;13], but unfortunately, due to our current resources, this is not presently possible. Therefore, our objective here is less ambitious. We wish to test the

---

[7] The depression construct is deliberately oversimplified here for the purpose of the analogy.

[8] From Wikipedia (http://en.wikipedia.org/wiki/Abstraction), *abstraction* is the process of reducing the information content of a concept, typically in order to retain only information which is relevant for a particular purpose. Instantiations are instances of the abstract concept.

[9] Goods are akin to standard of living.

[10] We wish to emphasize that these observables are strictly the subjective perceptions of the individual, and are not based on any "objective" criteria.

[11] We wish to contrast *objective physical health*, as used here, with the WHO definition of *health*. Objective physical health implies only an objective state of the physical body (akin to a measure of disease existence), and does not imply an internal subjective state of mind.

plausibility of the abstraction versus the component models of quality of life. Should the abstraction model show greater viability, then this would provide incremental validity for the eudaimonia model proposed above, which could be further tested at a later date. Should the component model show greater viability, then this would contradict the proposed eudaimonia model, suggesting that it be at least revised, and perhaps abandoned.

Eudaimonia Model of Quality of Life

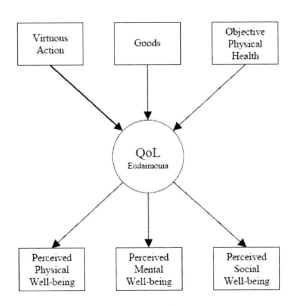

Figure 2. The eudaimonia model of quality of life is shown. It is based on Aristotle's concept of eudaimonia and the abstraction model of quality of life (which is based on the WHO definition of health). Virtuous action is the primary causal pathway to quality of life. However, goods and objective (i.e., not perceived) physical health also have a causal influence. Perceptions of physical, mental, and social well-being are caused by one's level of quality of life.

The question we seek to answer[12] in this chapter is, "How many dimensions are needed to characterize quality of life most efficiently?" We propose that one dimension would suggest the abstraction model, and two or more would suggest the component model. While this might seem a simple enough question, we feel that additional clarification is needed.

First, note the word *efficiently*. As with any unobservable latent construct, it is conceivable that both single- and multi-dimensional definitions could be empirically supported. However, consistent with the principle of Occam's razor,[13] we believe that in order to adopt a theoretical model with a greater number of dimensions, it must be shown that this model is clearly superior to models with smaller numbers. We believe that if a model with a smaller number of dimensions can convey nearly the same information as a model with a

---

[12] We of course cannot provide anything remotely akin to a definitive answer in this small study, and our only hope is to show a modicum of evidence that suggests one answer over another.

[13] From Wikipedia (http://en.wikipedia.org/wiki/Occam%27s_razor), *Occam's razor* is the principle that when multiple competing theories have equal predictive powers, select the one that introduces the fewest assumptions and postulates the fewest hypothetical entities.

greater number, then the smaller model is more efficient (or more parsimonious). In a sense, the "burden of proof" is on the higher-dimensional models.

Second, we feel we need to clarify how we define different dimensions. This basic philosophical question as to the dimensions of quality of life is of course not a new one [10]. However, as discussed above, there is confusion regarding the dimensions of quality of life because what are often considered different dimensions, are in fact correlated with each other. And these correlations imply that the dimensions are not truly distinct (e.g., three correlated dimensions used to measure the area of a sheet of paper are not distinct).

To illustrate by way of analogy again, let us look at the metaphysical concepts of monism, dualism, and pluralism. According to monism, all substances[14] are of one essential essence.[15] This is in contrast to dualism and pluralism, which hold, respectively, that ultimately there are either two or many kinds of substance. In order for the concepts of dualism or pluralism to be shown superior to monism, it would be necessary to demonstrate that two or more ultimate substances are unique. For example, an often studied philosophical question is, "Are the mind and body distinct?" According to dualism as proposed by René Descartes [14], the mind and body are two distinct substances, and the mind could therefore exist without the body. Contrast this with a form of monism called physicalism, which holds that everything is physical, so there can be no mind without body. Following these tenets, it is not possible for both Descartes' dualism and physicalism to both be correct. We would argue that to suggest that they are is to avoid, rather than address the question.

Similarly, with respect to quality of life, we do not believe that a multi-dimensional definition with correlated dimensions has great utility. This would be akin to adopting Descartes' dualist perspective, but also stating that the mind and body are not really separate. We believe that such a definition is ambiguous, leads to confusion, and is not consistent with Occam's razor. Therefore, it is our objective to assess the number of "ultimate substances" (i.e., distinct orthogonal dimensions) necessary to define quality of life in cancer survivors, and to provide a clearer understanding of the QoL domain.

We attempt to do this through the construct validation of a simple quality of life instrument administered to cancer survivors. The instrument we use is the COOP / WONCA [15-19], and we discuss it in the *Measures* section below. What follows is a brief discussion of our approach to construct validation and why we feel it will help answer the question of the number of distinct QoL dimensions.

We base our approach on the recommendations of Pedhazur and Schmelkin [13], who discussed construct validation under three headings: logical analysis, internal-structure analysis, and cross-structure analysis. The first heading, logical analysis, involves careful examination of the definition of the construct to be assessed. We believe that we have done this above with respect to the WHO definition of QoL (health), and we have explained why we feel it contains a certain amount of ambiguity. In an attempt to resolve the ambiguity, we have proposed two competing definitions, which we have called the component and abstraction models of quality of life.

Logical analysis also involves an examination of item content. The items used to assess the construct should cover the domain in question. With respect to the definition of quality of

---

[14] *All substances* refers essentially to everything in existence.

[15] From Wikipedia (http://en.wikipedia.org/wiki/Essence), *essence* is the attribute that makes an object or substance what it fundamentally is.

life we use here, the items should cover physical, mental, and social well-being. We believe that the COOP[16] (discussed below) covers this domain well.

The second heading, internal-structure analysis, involves assessing the validity of a set of indicators (items) reflecting the same construct (or multiple constructs). With this analysis, correlations among items are examined to determine if they can be attributed to hypothesized underlying constructs. With respect to quality of life, we wish to test two competing models: one with a single underlying construct (the abstraction model), and one with two or more underlying constructs (the component model). Arguably the most useful analytic approach for assessing the internal-structure of a set of indicators is factor analysis, and this is the method we use (see *Data Analyses*).

However, while an assessment of internal-structure will demonstrate if a set of items corresponds to a hypothesized construct, it cannot specify what that construct is. Through the process of logical analysis (described above), we can speculate as to the definition of the construct, but this is not the same as having empirical evidence. The given internal structure could be consistent with several different construct definitions, the validity of which cannot be determined through internal-structure analysis. For that we need the third approach to construct validation, cross-structure analysis.

Cross-structure analysis involves testing the relations between the construct, as defined by logical and internal-structure analysis, and other variables. Based on the logical analysis definition, we would expect the construct to be correlated with certain variables, but not correlated with others. For example, if the construct in question were depression and a newly developed instrument were shown to have the hypothesized internal-structure, we would expect this measure to correlate with other established measures of depression (convergent validity). Further, we would expect it to have lower correlations with measures not believed to be measuring to depression (discriminant validity).

In this chapter, we will examine the cross-structure validity of the COOP by comparing it with an instrument that has been established as a multi-dimensional measure of quality of life in cancer survivors, the EORTC QLQ-C30 [20-25] (see *Measures*). This instrument is used to assess various correlated QoL components, which we will compare with the COOP components found via our internal-structure analysis. Specifically, we will examine the convergent and discriminant validity of the COOP through comparisons with the QLQ-C30[17] in a multitrait-multimethod matrix (see *Data Analyses*). For more information on the construct validation approaches of logical analysis, internal-structure analysis, and cross-structure analysis, please refer to Chapter 4 in Pedhazur and Schmelkin [13].

Hence, through the procedures described above, we will test the two competing hypotheses regarding the number of unique (uncorrelated) dimensions needed to define quality of life. The key step will be the factor analysis, which will be used to assess the number of underlying constructs needed to most efficiently describe the domain of quality of life.

---

[16] We will often refer to the COOP / WONCA instrument as simply COOP.

[17] We will often refer to the EORTC QLQ-C30 as QLQ-C30.

METHOD

Participants

The study sample consisted of 365 cancer survivors, 57% of 646 eligible survivors who were invited to participate. The most frequent reasons for nonparticipation were not feeling well enough to take part and being "not interested." Of the participants, 56% were women, 69% were married, 40% had a high school education or less. The mean age was 62 years. Ethnic breakdowns were 36% Japanese, 34% Caucasian, 17% Filipino, 11% Hawaiian, and 2% unknown.

Participants were identified through the Hawai'i Tumor Registry (HTR), a member of the National Cancer Institute-supported Surveillance, Epidemiology, and End Results (SEER) Registry, which maintains records for all cancers diagnosed in the state. Eligibility criteria were histologic confirmation of any kind of cancer diagnosed between four and six months previously, ability to understand English, permission of primary physician, Oahu residency, and 18 years of age or older. Participation was not limited by stage or site of disease, but not all cancer sites were represented (e.g., no survivors had colorectal, head and neck, lung, or ovarian cancer). The most frequent site was breast (34%), followed by prostate (27%). Most survivors had received surgical treatment (83%), but less received radiation (37%), chemotherapy (11%), and hormonal treatment (24%). Most survivors (87%) had localized stage disease.

Procedures

Permission to approach survivors was obtained from their attending physicians before they were contacted. Survivors received a letter introducing the study's intent, followed by a telephone call to set appointments. Data were collected by interviews and self-report, most often at the survivor's home. Interviews were conducted by one of four female research associates, all of whom had completed graduate work in social sciences, as well as extensive training in interviewing cancer survivors.

Measures

We selected two instruments for this chapter. The first is the primary instrument and it is the one we wished to validate as a measure of quality of life in cancer survivors. This instrument is the COOP / WONCA [15-19]. The COOP was not specifically created for the purpose of assessing quality of life in cancer survivors, so it might not seem the best choice for such a task. However, we believed that the COOP was an ideal instrument for several reasons. First, while it was not written specifically for cancer survivors,[18] there are items clearly targeted at the three QoL components (physical, mental, and social well-being) specified in the WHO definition of health. Second, there are two items that appear to directly

---

[18] Note that while it was not written specifically for cancer survivors, it was also not written to preclude them.

assess a one-dimensional QoL construct, and these would be helpful in defining such a construct (if it exists) by acting as marker[19] items. Third, the COOP is brief, and we believe that minimizing the response burden of cancer survivors should be a primary concern. Finally, the COOP offers a novel pictorial approach in the presentation of its items, which might be helpful for survivors who have difficulty understanding verbal questionnaires.

The original COOP charts[20] began development in 1981 as measure of health status, as part of the Dartmouth Primary Care Cooperative Information Project[21] [26;27], and were then revised in 1988 by the WONCA (World Organization of Colleges, Academics and Academic Associations of General Practitioners / Family Physicians) Classification Committee [15]. The COOP is a self-report form that consists of nine charts containing both verbal descriptions and graphic illustrations for assessing functioning during the past two weeks. Each chart includes a title (related to a specific aspect of health), a question about level of functioning (consistent with the title), and both verbal and graphic depictions of five levels of functioning. The charts aid in selecting the appropriate response, which is a Likert-type scale ranging from one to five. Lower numbers represent more favorable levels of health.

For this chapter we made some minor modifications to the COOP. First, we restated the questions to refer to functioning in the past week, instead of the past two weeks. This was done for consistency with the QLQ-C30 (discussed below), which refers to functioning in the past week. Second, we modified some of the graphic illustrations. This was done because of feedback we received, regarding ambiguity, during a pilot study with cancer survivors. The slightly modified COOP instrument we used for this chapter is shown in figure 3.

Reliability and validity studies with the COOP have found it to perform well [15-19;28-38]. In particular, studies have found evidence in support of the instrument's test-retest reliability [16;33;39], internal consistency [33], convergent validity [28;29;33], and discriminant validity [17;29]. Also, studies with cancer survivors have been conducted with the COOP [40-42], but these did not assess the instrument's validity.

With regard to the factor structure of the COOP, at least two published studies have reported on this [29;43]. In one [29], an orthogonal exploratory factor analysis (EFA) was performed with data from migraine sufferers in the Netherlands, in which the items from the COOP, the MOS 36-Item Short Form (SF-36) [44-46], and the EuroQoL [47-50] were combined into a single analysis. The results showed a two factor structure (accounting for 52% of the variance), which appeared to reflect dimensions the authors labeled mental health and physical health. The second study [43] also involved an orthogonal EFA, but the data were obtained from "healthy" individuals in Switzerland. A two factor solution suggesting physical and mental health was also found in this chapter.

---

[19] In a factor analysis, *marker* items are items that load very high on a single factor and very low on all other factors.

[20] The items on the COOP are commonly called charts.

[21] http://www.dartmouth.edu/~coopproj/

COOP / WONCA Charts

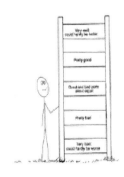

1. Physical Fitness
During the past week...
What was the hardest physical activity you
would be able to do for at least 2 minutes?

Very Heavy — Run, fast pace		1
Heavy — Run, slow pace		2
Moderate — Walk, fast pace		3
Light — Walk, medium pace		4
Very Light — Walk, slow pace		5

2. Feelings
During the past week...
How happy have you been?

Extremely		1
Quite a Bit		2
Moderately		3
Slightly		4
Not at All		5

3. Daily Activities
During the past week...
How much difficulty have you had doing
your usual activities or tasks?

No Difficulty at All		1
A Little Bit of Difficulty		2
Some Difficulty		3
Much Difficulty		4
Could Not Do		5

4. Social Activities
During the past week...
Has your physical or emotional health
limited your usual activities with family,
friends, or others?

Not at All		1
Slightly		2
Moderately		3
Quite a Bit		4
Extremely		5

5. Change in Health
How would you rate your overall health
now, compared to last month?

Much Better		1
A Little Better		2
About the Same		3
A Little Worse		4
Much Worse		5

6. Overall Health (marker)
During the past week...
How would you rate your health in
general?

Excellent		1
Very Good		2
Good		3
Fair		4
Poor		5

7. Social Support
During the past week...
Did you have enough help or support when
you needed it?

Yes, as Much as I Wanted		1
Quite a Bit		2
Some		3
Just a Bit		4
No, None at All		5

8. Quality of Life (marker)
How have things been going for you during
the past week?

	1
	2
	3
	4
	5

9. Pain
During the past week...
How much bodily pain have you had?

No Pain		1
Very Mild Pain		2
Mild Pain		3
Moderate Pain		4
Severe Pain		5

Figure 3. The nine COOP / WONCA charts used for this chapter are shown. These are slightly modified versions of the official charts, which are copyrighted by the Trustees of Dartmouth / COOP Project 1995. Our hypothesized QoL marker items (6 and 8) are indicated parenthetically.

Of note, however, is that in both studies several of the COOP items did not load cleanly on a single factor, and these included the two "QoL marker" items.[22] This suggests that the two factors (mental health and physical health) are both reflecting the same quality of life construct. What distinguishes them is simply the mental versus physical characteristics of the items, independent of QoL. It is our view that this factor solution has minimal utility in assessing quality of life, as it emphasizes a distinction between item characteristics unrelated the construct of interest.

We believe the problem with the factor analyses in both studies is that a varimax rotation procedure was used for determining the factor loadings. Varimax rotation is ideally suited for situations in which multiple distinct factors are hypothesized to exist. However, when a single general factor is hypothesized, such as our hypothesized single QoL construct, varimax rotation is not appropriate [51]. In this situation, an unrotated factor solution should be reported.

With an unrotated factor solution, if a single general construct exists, it will be defined by the first factor. The first factor will account for the highest proportion of the variance, and subsequent factors will account for significantly less variance. Had the authors of the two studies reported unrotated factor solutions, the items might have all loaded highest on the first general factor; and a second weaker factor might have reflected the mental versus physical aspects of the items.[23] Hence, only the first factor would be needed to define quality of life, and the second weaker factor would provide unneeded information as to the items' emphases with respect to physical or mental characteristics.

For the purpose of assessing the cross-structure validity of the COOP, we included a second well-established instrument in this chapter, the EORTC QLQ-C30 (European Organization for Research and Treatment of Cancer Quality of Life Questionnaire for Cancer survivors with 30 items) [20-25]. The QLQ-C30 was developed specifically for cancer survivors, and for this reason we believed it to be well-suited for the purpose of validating the cross-structure of the COOP. The QLQ-C30 defines quality of life as a multi-dimensional construct with several correlated components. These include five functional subscales (physical, role, cognitive, emotional, and social), three symptom subscales (pain, fatigue, and nausea), one global health status subscale, five symptom items (dyspnea, insomnia, appetite loss, constipation, and diarrhea), and one financial difficulties item. Responses are either dichotomous (yes or no) for the physical and role subscales, or Likert-type for the others (see Appendix).

Data Analyses

As discussed above, our primary objective in this chapter was to test two competing theoretical models of quality of life (the component and abstraction models shown in figure 1). To do this we have proposed a construct validation methodology using the COOP / WONCA questionnaire, in which we shall assess internal-structure and cross-

---

[22] We are referring to the two items discussed above (items 6 and 8), which appear to directly assess a one-dimensional QoL construct. See Figure 3.

[23] For more information on the interpretation of unrotated versus varimax rotated factors, refer to Chapter 22 in Pedhazur and Schmelkin [13].

structure. Internal-structure will be assessed via factor analysis, and cross-structure will be assessed via comparisons with the QLQ-C30 in a multitrait-multimethod matrix.

First, for the internal-structure assessment, the most important aspect of the factor analysis is the determination of the most efficient (i.e., most parsimonious) number of factors needed to explain the item variance within the COOP instrument. If one factor is most efficient, then this will support the abstraction model of quality of life. However, if two or more orthogonal factors are needed, then the component model will be supported.

In making this determination there are two major factor analytic techniques available: principal components analysis (PCA) and common factor analysis (CFA)[24] [13;52]. The primary distinction between these two techniques is the amount of item variance available for the factor extraction. PCA attempts to extract all available item variance, but CFA only attempts to extract the variance that is shared among the items (i.e., variance unique to a given item is excluded).

The appropriate technique to use depends on the theoretical model one is using. For the component model of quality of life, PCA is the best approach; but for the abstraction model, CFA is best.[25] This is because in the component model, the items are formative (the causal pathway is from the items to the construct), but in the abstraction model the items are reflective (the causal pathway is from the construct to the items). If the items are reflective it does not make sense to examine variance unique to a given item, because this unique variance cannot be attributed to the factor. In this chapter, because we wished to test both the component and the abstraction models of quality of life, we performed both PCA and CFA analyses.

When performing PCA, two common criteria are often used for determining the "best" number of factors: eigenvalues[26] greater than one and scree test [51;52]. The eigenvalues greater than one criterion states that factors with eigenvalues greater than one should be retained, and the others (with eigenvalues less than one) should be dropped. The scree test involves plotting the eigenvalues[27] versus the factor numbers, and locating the point where the plot forms an "elbow" (the point were the linear trend changes slope). The number of factors to the left of the "elbow" is the "best" number of factors.

We performed a PCA analysis on the COOP data and examined both the eigenvalue greater than one and the scree test criteria to assess the most efficient number of factors. Based on the previous research that examined factor analyses of COOP data [29;43], we predicted that a two factor solution would be found. However, we did not hypothesize physical health and mental health factors. As discussed above (see *Measures*), we did not believe that varimax rotation was appropriate, and we therefore examined the unrotated factor solution.

We hypothesized that the first factor would represent the quality of life construct and that it would account for substantially more (at least twice as much) variance than the second factor. For the second factor, we hypothesized that it would represent the physical versus mental characteristics of the items, which were independent of quality of life. Further, we

---

[24] Common factor analysis should not be confused with confirmatory factor analysis. We do not use confirmatory factor analysis in this chapter.

[25] See Figure 1 for depictions of each theoretical model.

[26] The eigenvalue is the amount of variance accounted for by a given factor.

[27] The number of eigenvalues is equal to the number of items.

hypothesized that the items with the highest loadings on the first factor would be items 6 (overall health) and 8 (quality of life), which we predicted to be QoL marker items. See table 1 for our hypothesized PCA solution.

For CFA, a common criterion for determining the most parsimonious number of factors is the proportion criterion, which specifies the proportion of common variance that is to be explained by the retained factors. We used 67% (two-thirds of the shared variance) as the proportion criterion for this chapter. Assuming the abstraction model of quality of life, we hypothesized that only one factor would be retained when using CFA.

Next, for the cross-structure validation of the COOP, we computed the correlations between each of the COOP items and the QLQ-C30 subscales[28] and presented them in a multitrait-multimethod matrix.[29] This matrix included the COOP factors determined by the internal-structure analyses described above.

We hypothesized that the COOP items would have highest correlations with the most similar subscales on the QLQ-C30, demonstrating convergent validity; and we hypothesized that the correlations between less similar subscales would be lower, demonstrating discriminant validity. With respect to the COOP factors, we hypothesized that a single QoL composite factor, including all nine of the COOP items, would correlate highly with all of the QLQ-C30 functioning scales, but the highest correlation would be with global functioning. This would demonstrate convergent validity. Correlations with the symptom scales were hypothesized to be less, demonstrating discriminant validity.

All analyses were performed using the SAS 9.1 statistical software.[30]

RESULTS

Prior to running analyses, all items on both the COOP and the QLQ-C30 were re-scaled to range from 0 to 100, with 0 indicating the lowest level of functioning and 100 the highest. Missing values were handled with listwise deletion for the factor analyses (10 observations were deleted) and pairwise deletion for calculating correlations. Out of 14,235 possible responses (365 survivors multiplied by the 39 items on the COOP and QLQ-C30 instruments), there were only 24 missing values (less than 0.2% of the total).

As discussed above (see *Data Analyses*), we performed both PCA and CFA factor analyses (unrotated) to determine the most parsimonious number of factors needed to define quality of life with the COOP / WONCA instrument. See table 1 for both the PCA and CFA results.

For the PCA, we used two criteria determining the number of factors,[31] eigenvalue greater than one and scree test. See figure 4 for all nine eigenvalues plotted versus the factor numbers. Two of the eigenvalues were greater than one, suggesting two factors by the first criterion. However, the scree test suggests only a single factor, because the "elbow" is at the

---

[28] The QLQ-C30 subscales we used were the ones defined by the creators of the instrument.

[29] Note that in this context *trait* refers to the various correlated QoL subscales defined in the QLQ-C30, and *method* refers to the two instruments (the COOP versus the QLQ-C30).

[30] http://support.sas.com/documentation/onlinedoc/sas9doc.html

[31] Even though this is a principal component analysis, we use the word *factor* when referring to the components, as this is standard practice in the literature.

second factor number. The proportion of total variance accounted for was 39% for the first factor, and 13% for the second. As we had hypothesized, the first factor accounted for more than twice as much variance as the second (in fact, three times as much).

Principal Component Analysis Scree Plot

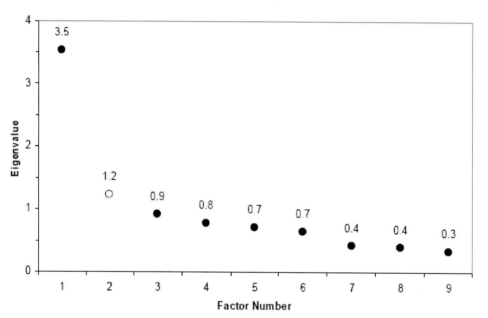

Figure 4. A scree plot of the eigenvalues versus the factor numbers from a principal component analysis (PCA) is shown. The "elbow" is indicated as a hollow circle located at the second factor. This suggests that a single factor solution is the most parsimonious.

In table 1 we report the results from a two-factor solution. We report two factors because this is what we had hypothesized (see *Data Analyses*) and because the eigenvalue greater than one criterion suggested a two-factor solution. We the exception of the physical fitness item (item 1), all of the items loaded well (greater than 0.5) on the first factor, which we have called *QoL*. The two hypothesized marker items, overall health and quality of life (items 6 and 8), had the highest loadings (both were 0.81).

Loadings on the second factor, which have called *Mind-Body*, were mostly as predicted but with a few exceptions. The physical fitness item (item 1) loaded higher than we predicted (+0.66 versus the hypothesized value of +0.40), and the quality of life item (item 8) loaded lower than we predicted (−0.25 versus the hypothesized value of 0.00). These results suggest that the physical fitness item is not an ideal measure of QoL, as it might be too strongly related to "objective physicality" and not the subjective perception of physical well-being. Also, the quality of life item appears to have a slight leaning toward to the mental side of the mind-body continuum, but still reflects a strong QoL loading.

For the CFA, the proportion of shared variance accounted for by the first factor was 71%, which exceeded the proportion criterion we had set to 67%. We therefore report a single-factor solution in table 1. Again, with the exception of the physical fitness item, results were consistent with our hypotheses. Items 2–9 loaded well on the QoL factor, with items 6 (overall health) and 8 (quality of life) serving as marker items. Hence, the factor analytic results presented here (both the PCA and the CFA) support for the abstraction model of quality of life (see figure 1).

Table 1. Factor Analytic Results for the COOP / WONCA

		HYPOTHESIZED		PCA			CFA	
Item	Label	QoL	MB	QoL	MB	h^2	QoL	h^2
1	Physical Fitness	0.6	+ 0.4	0.38	**+ 0.66**	0.58	0.29	0.09
2	Feelings	0.6	− 0.4	**0.66**	− 0.41	0.60	**0.63**	0.40
3	Daily Activities	0.6	+ 0.4	**0.61**	+ 0.52	0.65	**0.50**	0.25
4	Social Activities	0.6	0.0	**0.66**	0.08	0.44	**0.57**	0.32
5	Change in Health	0.4	0.0	**0.52**	− 0.16	0.29	**0.46**	0.21
6	Overall Health	0.8	0.0	**0.81**	0.00	0.65	**0.78**	0.61
7	Social Support	0.6	− 0.4	**0.51**	− 0.42	0.44	**0.44**	0.20
8	Quality of Life	0.8	0.0	**0.81**	− 0.25	0.72	**0.80**	0.64
9	Pain	0.6	+ 0.4	**0.56**	+ 0.26	0.38	**0.47**	0.23
	Proportion	0.4	0.2	0.39	0.13		0.71	

Notes. Under the *Hypothesized* heading, the predicted results for the principal component analysis are shown. There are two orthogonal unrotated components, *QoL* and *MB*, representing quality of life and mind-body (a mental-physical continuum). For the mind-body component, positive values indicate physical characteristics, and negative values indicate mental characteristics. The observed principal component analysis results are shown under the *PCA* heading. The observed common factor analysis results are shown under the *CFA* heading with a single quality of life factor. Within each analysis, the best loadings are shown in **bold**. *Proportion* is the proportion of either the total (PCA) or shared (CFA) variance accounted for by the given component or factor, and h^2 is the communality for each item.

Based on the factor analytic results we created a QoL composite score, which was calculated as the mean of items 2–9. We did not include item 1 (physical fitness) because of the low loading it had on the QoL factor. Coefficient alpha for the QoL composite was 0.81. We then computed the multitrait-multimethod matrix (as described in *Data Analyses*) between the COOP and the QLQ-C30 as an assessment of the cross-structure validity of the COOP. See table 2.

The correlations were mostly consistent with our hypotheses, and showed evidence for convergent and discriminant validity. The QoL composite and the two marker items (6 and 8) all had moderate to high correlations (0.70, 0.68, and 0.57, respectively) with the QLQ-C30 global functioning subscale, suggesting convergent validity. Correlations with all other QLQ-C30 subscales were lower, suggesting discriminant validity. The COOP physical fitness item (item 1) correlated only moderately (0.40) with the QLQ-C30 physical functioning subscale, and this is perhaps further evidence that the item is not well-suited to assess quality of life.

The change in health (item 5) and social support (item 7) items did not have strong correlations with any QLQ-C30 subscales. The highest correlations were with global functioning: 0.27 and 0.33, respectively. From the factor analytic results, these items had the lowest loadings on QoL (excluding physical fitness). This suggests that these items might not be necessary for the COOP, and could possibly be removed.

Table 2. Correlations Between the COOP / WONCA and EORTC QLQ-C30

	COOP / WONCA	1	2	3	4	5	6	7	8	9	QoL
						COOP / WONCA					
1	Physical Fitness										
2	Feeling	0.07									
3	Daily Activities	0.34	0.19								
4	Social Activities	0.17	0.38	0.49							
5	Change in Health	0.12	0.26	0.17	0.17						
6	Overall Health	0.30	0.50	0.42	0.45	0.41					
7	Social Support	0.03	0.31	0.16	0.31	0.22	0.30				
8	Quality of Life	0.13	0.57	0.35	0.43	0.38	0.59	0.41			
9	Pain	0.18	0.20	0.39	0.26	0.25	0.41	0.21	0.38		
QoL	Composite	0.26	0.64	0.62	0.69	0.56	0.79	0.54	0.77	0.61	*0.81*
EORTC QLQ-C30											
	Physical	**0.40**	0.18	0.59	0.42	0.15	0.41	0.14	0.29	0.33	0.49
	Role	0.25	0.18	**0.49**	0.38	0.09	0.28	0.15	0.26	0.26	0.41
	Cognitive	0.07	0.21	0.32	0.34	0.17	0.29	0.15	0.25	0.20	0.37
	Emotional	0.02	**0.45**	0.36	0.49	0.17	0.43	0.28	0.50	0.31	0.57
	Social	0.14	0.29	0.48	**0.62**	0.08	0.35	**0.29**	0.41	0.28	0.54
	Pain	0.20	0.23	0.48	0.37	0.19	0.39	0.27	0.39	**0.72**	0.59
	Fatigue	0.26	0.40	0.59	0.51	0.24	0.52	0.25	0.46	0.35	0.64
	Nausea	0.10	0.26	0.30	0.37	0.15	0.22	0.20	0.30	0.25	0.40
	Global	0.27	0.48	0.49	0.49	**0.27**	**0.68**	0.33	**0.57**	0.35	**0.70**
	Dyspnea	0.21	0.25	0.33	0.29	0.13	0.35	0.15	0.30	0.31	0.40
	Insomnia	0.14	0.28	0.29	0.34	0.19	0.31	0.16	0.26	0.26	0.40
	Appetite Loss	0.19	0.40	0.39	0.50	0.21	0.46	0.32	0.43	0.27	0.58
	Constipation	0.11	0.19	0.19	0.22	0.17	0.28	0.23	0.24	0.20	0.33
	Diarrhea	0.12	0.25	0.25	0.29	0.16	0.18	0.17	0.27	0.16	0.33
	Financial	0.03	0.20	0.29	0.34	0.07	0.20	0.24	0.23	0.26	0.35

Notes. The COOP items were re-scaled to range from 0 to 100 (the same as the QLQ-C30 subscales), with 0 indicating the lowest level of functioning and 100 the highest. The COOP *QoL Composite* is calculated as the mean of items 2–9; coefficient alpha is shown *italicized* in the main diagonal. Correlations between similar "traits" assessed with different "methods" are shown in **bold**. Values greater than 0.10 are statistically significant ($p < 0.05$). See figure 3 for depictions of the nine COOP / WONCA items.

CONCLUSION

Our primary objective in this chapter was to test two competing theoretical models of quality of life in cancer survivors. As shown in figure 1, we have called these the component and abstraction models of quality of life. The fundamental difference between them is the direction of the causal pathway. In the component model, quality of life is defined by the three formative components physical, mental, and social well-being. Whereas, in the abstraction model, physical, mental, and social well-being are reflective of the underlying quality of life construct.

To test these competing models we proposed a construct validation approach with the COOP / WONCA questionnaire. Using the methods of factor analysis and cross-structure comparison with the QLQ-C30, our goal was to determine the most parsimonious factor solution and to test the cross-structure validity of this solution. A one-factor solution would suggest that the abstraction model of quality of life is the most parsimonious; whereas, a solution with two or more (orthogonal) factors would suggest the component model.

The results from this sample of 365 cancer survivors in Hawaii suggest that the abstraction model is more parsimonious than the component model. Both PCA and CFA factor analytic methods demonstrated that a single QoL factor accounted for a substantial amount of variance in the nine COOP items. Although far from conclusive, this suggests that a composite score of the COOP items (excluding physical fitness) can be used as a measure of quality of life, without the need to distinguish between various subscales.

Even though previous research has found a two-factor solution with the COOP [29;43], we do not believe that these results are contradictory. As we discussed (see *Measures*), in those studies a varimax rotation procedure was used, which we believe was not appropriate for assessing a single QoL factor. Had those studies reported an unrotated factor solution, it is possible that a one factor solution would have been found.

For our PCA analyses we do report two factors, but the first factor explains three times more variance than the second (39% versus 13%). Also, the first factor is clearly defined by the two marker items (overall health and quality of life). The second weaker factor was simply an indicator of the tendency of some items to imbue characteristics of "body" versus "mind."

In our CFA analysis, a one-factor solution was also supported. This is consistent with a previous study we conducted with this same sample [53]. In that study, we examined the possibility of modeling QoL as a one-dimensional construct with the QLQ-C30, using item response theory (IRT) methods. The results there also suggested the plausibility of a "unidimensional" QoL construct.

In this chapter, there was one result which ran counter to our expectations, and this was the loading of the physical fitness item. The physical fitness item did not load highly on the QoL factor, but did load highly on the mind-body factor. This suggests that the item was not clearly reflective of the QoL factor, and was instead reflecting a strong "physicality" characteristic, independent of perceived well-being.

Upon closer examination of this item (see figure 3, item 1), we speculate that it emphasizes an almost "objective physicality." That is, the item does not appear to reflect an internal perceived sense of physical well-being; but rather, an external objective measure of athleticism. For example, it is possible to imagine a senior individual who is unable to run at a fast (or even slow) pace, yet this person feels excellent with respect to her physical well-being. As the definition of quality of life we examined here is specific to internal perceived well-being, we do not believe that the physical fitness item on the COOP should be included. We recommend a modified item emphasizing satisfaction with ones level of physical functioning.

In conjunction with the eudaimonia model we presented (see figure 2), we further speculate that the physical fitness item might better fall into the *objective physical health* variable. From Aristotle's view of eudaimonia, physical health (i.e., objective physical health and not perceived well-being) has a causal influence on QoL, and perhaps the COOP physical fitness item could be modeled better here. That is, physical fitness has a causal influence on QoL, rather than being reflective of it. We propose an examination of this hypothesis in future research.

The cross-structure comparison between the COOP and the well-established QLQ-C30 showed evidence in support of the COOP validly measuring quality of life in cancer survivors. In particular, the COOP QoL composite score (calculated as the mean of items 2–9) had a high correlation (0.70) with the QLQ-C30 global functioning subscale. Correlations with the other subscales were all less than 0.70, but ranged from 0.33 to 0.64. Further, the reliability (coefficient alpha) of the COOP QoL composite score was high (0.81).

Hence, the evidence presented here suggests that the COOP is perhaps an ideal instrument for measuring quality of life in cancer survivors. It appears to validity measure a simple one-dimensional quality of life construct, which we believe reduces the potential for unnecessary complexity and confusion that exists with multi-dimensional ones. And this combined with its brevity and pictorial aids, should make it a strong candidate for researchers and clinicians who need to measure QoL.

Finally, while we believe that this chapter offers support for both the abstraction model of quality of life, and the COOP as a valid measure of QoL in cancer survivors, we must emphasize that this chapter suffers from the common limitation of nonrandom (convenience) sampling. All participants were residents of Hawaii who agreed to participate, and it cannot be concluded that the results found here will generalize beyond this sample. That is, while this chapter might contain a certain degree of internal validity, it has no external validity. Therefore, much more research is needed in order to establish whether or not these results are stable across different settings.

ACKNOWLEDGEMENTS

This chapter was supported by a grant from the National Cancer Institute (CA61711). We are grateful for assistance in data collection by Jeffrey Stern, Mary Lynn Fiore, Akiko Lau, Malia Wilson, Daniella Dumitriu, Florence Yee, and Cris Yamabe. The participation of Kaiser-Permanente Hawaii, Kuakini Medical Center, St. Francis Medical Center, Straub Clinic and Hospital, and Queens Medical Center is also greatly appreciated.

REFERENCES

[1]   Kaplan RM. A Broad Look at Outcomes Research. In: Lenderking WR, Revicki DA. *Advancing Health Outcomes Research Methods and Clinical Applications.* McLean, VA: Degnon, 2005.

[2]   McDowell I, Niezgoda HE. Measuring Health. *A Guide to Rating Scales and Questionnaires.* Oxford: Oxford University Press, 1987.

[3]   Bowling A. Measuring Health. *A Review of Quality of Life Measurement Scales.* Milton Keynes: Open University Press, 1991.

[4] Bowling A. Measuring Disease. *A Review of Disease-specific Quality of Life Measurement Scales.* Buckingham: Open University Press, 1995.

[5] McSweeny AJ, Creer TL. Health-related quality-of-life assessment in medical care. *Dis. Mon.* 1995;41:1-71.

[6] Rogerson RJ. Environmental and health-related quality of life: conceptual and methodological similarities. *Soc. Sci. Med.* 1995;41:1373-82.

[7] Fayers P.M., Machin D. Quality of life: Assessment, Analysis and Interpretation. New York: John Wiley and Sons, 2000.

[8] Bruley DK. Beyond reliability and validity: analysis of selected quality-of-life instruments for use in palliative care. *J. Palliat. Med.* 1999;2:299-309.

[9] World Health Organization. Preamble to the Constitution of the World Health Organization as adopted by the International Health Conference, New York, 19-22 June, 1946; signed on 22 July 1946 by the representatives of 61 States (Official Records of the World Health Organization, no. 2, p. 100) and entered into force on 7 April 1948. 1948.

[10] Gotay CC, Blaine D, Haynes SN, Holup J, Pagano IS. Assessment of quality of life in a multicultural cancer patient population. *Psychological Assessment.* 2002;14:439-50.

[11] Aristotle, Irwin T. Nicomachean Ethics, 2nd ed. Indianapolis, IN: Hackett, 1999.

[12] Mueller RO. Basic Principles of Structural Equation Modeling: *An Introduction to LISREL and EQS.* New York: Spring-Verlag, 1996.

[13] Pedhazur EJ, Schmelkin LPS. Measurement, Design, and Analysis: *An Integrate Approach.* Hillsdale, NJ: Lawrence Erlbaum Associates, 1991.

[14] Descartes R, Cress DA. Meditations on First Philosophy: In *Which the Existence of God and the Distinction of the Soul from the Body Are Demonstrated.* Indianapolis, IN: Hackett Publishing Company, 1993.

[15] Bentsen BG, Natvig B, Winnem M. Assessment of one's own functional status. COOP-WONCA questionnaire charts in clinical practice and research. *Tidsskr Nor Laegeforen* 1997;117:1790-3.

[16] Bentsen BG, Natvig B, Winnem M. Questions you didn't ask? COOP/WONCA Charts in clinical work and research. World Organization of Colleges, Academies and Academic Associations of General Practitioners/Family Physicists. *Fam. Pract.* 1999;16:190-5.

[17] Nelson EC, Wasson J, Kirk J, Keller A, Clark D, Dietrich A et al. Assessment of function in routine clinical practice: description of the COOP Chart method and preliminary findings. *J. Chronic Dis.* 1987;40:55S-69S.

[18] Scholten JHG, Van Weel C. Functional Status Assessment in Family Practice: *The Dartmouth COOP Functional health Assessment Charts/WONCA.* Lelystad: MEDITekst, 1992.

[19] Van Weel C. Functional status in primary care: COOP/WONCA charts. *Disabil. Rehabil.* 1993;15:96-101.

[20] Anderson RT, Aaronson NK, Wilkin D. Critical review of the international assessments of health-related quality of life. *Qual. Life Res.* 1993;2:369-95.

[21] Anderson RT, Aaronson NK, Bullinger M, McBee WL. A review of the progress towards developing health-related quality-of-life instruments for international clinical studies and outcomes research. *Pharmacoeconomics.* 1996;10:336-55.

[22] Aaronson NK, Ahmedzai S, Bullinger M, Crabeels CD, Estape J, Filiberti A et al. The EORTC core quality of life questionnaire: Interim results of an international field study. In: Osoba D. *Effect of cancer on quality of life.* Boca Raton: CRC Press, 1991:185-203.

[23] Aaronson NK, Ahmedzai S, Bergman B, Bullinger M, Cull A, Duez NJ et al. The European Organization for Research and Treatment of Cancer QLQ-C30: a quality-of-life instrument for use in international clinical trials in oncology. *J. Natl. Cancer Inst.* 1993;85:365-76.

[24] Aaronson NK, Cull A, Kaasa S, Sprangers MAG. The European Organization for Research and Treatment of Cancer (EORTC) modular approach to quality of life assessment in oncology. *International Journal of Mental Health* 1994;23:75-96.

[25] Aaronson NK, Cull A, Kaasa S, Sprangers MAG. The European Organization for Research and Treatment of Cancer (EORTC) modular approach to quality of life assessment in oncology: An update. In: Spilker B. *Quality of Life and Pharmacoeconomics in Clinical Trials,* 2nd ed. New York: Raven Press, 1995.

[26] Nelson EC, Kirk JW, Bise BW, Chapman RJ, Hale FA, Stamps PL et al. The cooperative information project: Part 2: some initial clinical, quality assurance, and practice management studies. *J. Fam. Pract.* 1981;13:867-76.

[27] Nelson EC, Kirk JW, Bise BW, Chapman RJ, Hale FA, Stamps PL et al. The Cooperative Information Project: Part 1: A sentinel practice network for service and research in primary care. *J. Fam. Pract.* 1981;13:641-9.

[28] Eaton T, Young P, Fergusson W, Garrett JE, Kolbe J. The Dartmouth COOP Charts: a simple, reliable, valid and responsive quality of life tool for chronic obstructive pulmonary disease. *Qual. Life Res.* 2005;14:575-85.

[29] Essink-Bot ML, Krabbe PF, Bonsel GJ, Aaronson NK. An empirical comparison of four generic health status measures. The Nottingham Health Profile, the Medical Outcomes Study 36-item Short-Form Health Survey, the COOP/WONCA charts, and the EuroQol instrument. *Med. Care* 1997;35:522-37.

[30] Kinnersley P, Peters T, Stott N. Measuring functional health status in primary care using the COOP-WONCA charts: acceptability, range of scores, construct validity, reliability and sensitivity to change. *Br. J. Gen. Pract.* 1994;44:545-9.

[31] Landgraf JM, Nelson EC, Hays RD. Assessing Function: Does It Really Make a Difference? A Preliminary Evaluation of the Acceptability and Utility of the COOP Function Charts. In: Lipkin M. *Functional Status Measurement in Primary Care: Frontiers of Primary Care.* New York: Springer-Verlag, 1990:150-65.

[32] Larson CO, Hays RD, Nelson EC. Do the pictures influence scores on the Dartmouth COOP Charts? *Qual. Life Res.* 1992;1:247-9.

[33] Linaker OM, Moe A. The COOP/WONCA charts in an acute psychiatric ward. Validity and reliability of patients' self-report of functioning. *Nord. J. Psychiatry.* 2005;59:121-6.

[34] Lindegaard PM, Bentzen N, Christiansen T. Reliability of the COOP/WONCA charts. Test-retest completed by patients presenting psychosocial health problems to their general practitioner. *Scand J. Prim. Health Care.* 1999;17:145-8.

[35] McHorney CA, Ware JE, Jr., Rogers W, Raczek AE, Lu JF. The validity and relative precision of MOS short- and long-form health status scales and Dartmouth COOP charts. Results from the Medical Outcomes Study. *Med. Care.* 1992;30:MS253-MS265.

[36] Meyboom-De Jong B, Smith RJA. Studies with the Dartmouth COOPCharts in General Practice: Comparison with the Nottingham Health Profile and the General Health Questionnaire. In: Lipkin M. *Functional Status Measurement in Primary Care: Frontiers of Primary Care*. New York: pringer-Verlag, 1990:132-49.

[37] Nelson EC, Landgraf JM, Hays RD. The COOP Function Charts: A System to measure Patient Function in Physicians' Offices. In: Lipkin M. *Functional Status Measurement in Primary Care: Frontiers of Primary Care*. New York: Springer-Verlag, 1990:97-131.

[38] Nelson EC, Landgraf JM, Hays RD. The COOP Function Charts: Single Item Health Measures for Use in Clinical Practice. In: Stewart A, Ware J. *Measuring Functional Status And Well Being: The Medical Outcomes Study Approach*. Durham, NC: Duke University Press, 1990.

[39] Nelson EC, Landgraf JM, Hays RD, Wasson JH, Kirk JW. The functional status of patients. How can it be measured in physicians' offices? *Med. Care*. 1990;28:1111-26.

[40] Schuit KW, Sleijfer DT, Meijler WJ, Otter R, Schakenraad J, van den Bergh FC et al. Symptoms and functional status of patients with disseminated cancer visiting outpatient departments. *J. Pain Symptom Manage*. 1998;16:290-7.

[41] Sneeuw KC, Aaronson NK, Sprangers MA, Detmar SB, Wever LD, Schornagel JH. Evaluating the quality of life of cancer patients: assessments by patients, significant others, physicians and nurses. *Br. J. Cancer*. 1999;81:87-94.

[42] Van Bokhorst-de Van der Schuer MA, Langendoen SI, Vondeling H, Kuik DJ, Quak JJ, van Leeuwen PA. Perioperative enteral nutrition and quality of life of severely malnourished head and neck cancer patients: a randomized clinical trial. *Clin. Nutr.* 2000;19:437-44.

[43] Perneger TV, Chamot E, Etter JF, Richard JL, Gallant S, Ricciardi P et al. Assessment of the COOP charts with and without pictures in a Swiss population. *Qual. Life Res.* 2000;9:405-14.

[44] McHorney CA, Ware JE, Jr., Raczek AE. The MOS 36-Item Short-Form Health Survey (SF-36): II. Psychometric and clinical tests of validity in measuring physical and mental health constructs. *Med. Care*. 1993;31:247-63.

[45] McHorney CA, Ware JE, Jr., Lu JF, Sherbourne CD. The MOS 36-item Short-Form Health Survey (SF-36): III. Tests of data quality, scaling assumptions, and reliability across diverse patient groups. *Med. Care*. 1994;32:40-66.

[46] Ware JE, Jr., Sherbourne CD. The MOS 36-item short-form health survey (SF-36). I. Conceptual framework and item selection. *Med Care* 1992;30:473-83.

[47] Brooks R. EuroQol: the current state of play. *Health Policy*. 1996;37:53-72.

[48] EuroQol Group. EuroQol--a new facility for the measurement of health-related quality of life. *Health Policy*. 1990;16:199-208.

[49] Pinto Prades JL. A European measure of health: the EuroQol. *Rev. Enferm*. 1993;16:13-6.

[50] Viana AA. Quality of life (EuroQol). *An. Med. Interna*. 1995;12:355.

[51] Gorsuch RL. Factor Analysis, 2nd ed. Hillsdale, NJ: Erlbaum, 1983.

[52] Tabachnick BG, Fidell LS. *Using Multivariate Statistics,* 3rd ed. New York: HarperCollins, 1996.

[53] Pagano IS, Gotay CC. Modeling quality of life in cancer patients as a unidimensional construct. *Hawaii Medical Journal*. 2006;65:76-85.

APPENDIX
EORTC QLQ-C30 ITEMS

	SUBSCALE
Do you have any trouble doing strenuous activities, like carrying a heavy shopping bag or a suitcase?	Physical
Do you have any trouble taking a long walk?	Physical
Do you have any trouble take a short walk outside of the house?	Physical
Do have to stay in bed or a chair for most of the day?	Physical
Do you need help with eating, dressing, washing yourself or using the toilet?	Physical
Are you limited in any way in doing either your work or doing household jobs?	Role
Are you completely unable to work at a job or to do household jobs?	Role
During the past week:	
Were you short of breath?	Dyspnea
Have you had pain?	Pain
10. Did you need rest?	Fatigue
11. Have you had trouble sleeping?	Insomnia
12. Have you felt weak?	Fatigue
13. Have you lacked appetite?	Appetite Loss
14. Have you felt nauseated?	Nausea
15. Have you vomited?	Nausea
16. Have you been constipated?	Constipation
17. Have you had diarrhea?	Diarrhea
18. Were you tired?	Fatigue
19. Did pain interfere with your daily activities?	Pain
20. Have you had difficulty in concentrating on things, like reading a newspaper or watching television?	Cognitive
21. Did you feel tense?	Emotional
22. Did you worry?	Emotional
23. Did you feel irritable?	Emotional
24. Did you feel depressed?	Emotional
25. Have you had difficulty remembering things?	Cognitive
26. Has your physical condition or medical treatment interfered with your family life?	Social
27. Has your physical condition or medical treatment interfered with your social activities?	Social
28. Has your physical condition or medical treatment caused you financial difficulties?	Financial
29. How would you rate your overall physical condition?	Global
30. How would you rate your overall quality of life?	Global

Notes. For items 1-7, a response of either "Yes" or "No" is possible. For items 8-28, four Likert-type responses are possible. A response of 1 reflects "Not at all," 2 "A little," 3 "Quite a bit," and 4 "Very Much." For items 29-30, seven Likert-type responses are possible, where 1 reflects "Very Poor" and 7 reflects "Excellent." The Subscale column indicates the subscales as specified in the QLQ-C30.

In: Psychological Tests and Testing Research Trends
Editor: Paul M. Goldfarb, pp. 39-54

ISBN: 978-1-60021-569-8
© 2007 Nova Science Publishers, Inc.

Chapter 2

THE PSYCHOLOGICAL VULNERABILITY MEASUREMENT: PSYCHOMETRIC CHARACTERISTICS AND VALIDATION IN NONCLINICAL POPULATION[1]

B. Rueda, A. M. Pérez-García, P. Sanjuán and M. A. Ruiz

Faculty of Psychology. Universidad Nacional
de Educación a Distancia. Madrid (Spain)

ABSTRACT

Cognitive vulnerability is considered as a factor predisposing an individual to depressive episodes. Measures of vulnerability have consistently emphasized perfectionism and dependence as the main factor on which vulnerability is based. Within this cognitive framework Sinclair and Wallston (1999) have proposed the Psychological Vulnerability Scale (PVS). This six-item self-report assesses a pattern of maladaptive beliefs, such as need for others´ approval, very stringent standards and negative attributions.

In this chapter we examined the psychometric properties of the PVS in a non-clinical population. We determined the construct validity of the PVS through correlations with perceived competence, hostility and affective states. We also investigated the predictive validity of the PVS regarding its contribution to alexithymia, health criteria and well-being.

The sample was composed by 436 participants (23% males and 77% females) with a mean age of 36. The PVS together with measures of perceived competence, hostility, affective states, alexithymia, health criteria and well-being were completed.

The scale showed adequate internal consistency (α = .76) and high temporal stability (3 months test-retest reliability = .70). Factor analysis revealed an unifactorial solution, accounting for 47% of the total variance. Item loadings were .58 and above. Construct

---

[1] This research was facilitated by grant support from the Spanish Ministry of Education and Science (reference: SEJ2004 – 03834).

validity was supported by the positive correlations with measures of hostility and negative affect, and by the negative correlations of the PVS with perceived competence and positive affect. Appropriate predictive validity of the scale was also found. It positively predicted alexithymia, and negatively predicted health behaviors and well-being. However, the contribution of the PVS to the symptoms was lower.

The results provided considerable evidence of the validation of the PVS in a non-clinical population. They also suggest that psychological vulnerability constitutes a maladaptive cognitive style with negative consequences in the physical and psychological domain.

INTRODUCTION

An essential theme in the literature about the cognitive processes related to emotional distress, is the role played by vulnerability. A number of investigations have shown a positive and consistent association between cognitive vulnerability and the onset and maintenance of depressive symptoms (Hankin, Abramson, Miller, and Haeffel, 2004; Hunt and Forand, 2005; Riso, Blandino, Penna, *et al.*, 2003; Roberts and Monroe, 1992; Zuroff, Igreja, and Mongrain, 1990). In the meta-analysis conducted by Nietzel and Harris (1990) to determine the magnitude of the relationship between vulnerability and depression, the mean effect size obtained ranged from .28 to .31. These authors also indicated that the highest effect sizes were obtained in studies using normal subjects, rather than in studies including pure patient samples or mixed samples.

From a clinical point of view, it thus appears that vulnerability may be regarded as a premorbid condition to depressive episodes. Vulnerability can also be considered as an important construct within the scope of personality psychology. Then, the issue of its validation and adequate assessment emerge as an important concern that requires a systematic investigation.

Conceptualization and Measurement of Vulnerability

Research on vulnerability has been developed around different conceptualizations and measures. Concepts such as Dependence-Self-Criticism (Blatt, D´Affiti and Quinlan, 1976), Sociotropy-Autonomy (Beck, 1983), Dysfunctional Attitudes (Beck, 1967; Weissman and Beck, 1978), Perfectionism (Frost, Marten, Lahart, and Rosenblate, 1990; Hewitt and Flett, 1991) and Depressogenic Attributions (Abramson, Metalsky, and Alloy, 1989) have been considered as vulnerability dispositions arising great interest in this field.

Some theories based on psychoanalytic and developmental grounds (Blatt and Zuroff, 1992; Blatt *et al.*, 1976; Blatt, Quinlan, Chevron, McDonald, and Zuroff, 1982) have emphasized two main personality configurations that can lead to depression.

The first configuration, called Anaclitic or Dependent, is characterized by feelings of loneliness, weakness and unassertiveness. Dependent people have intense needs to be loved and accepted by others in order to protect their fragile self-esteem. They also experience considerable fear of being abandoned and unprotected.

The second configuration style that predisposes an individual to depression is called Introjective or Self-Critical. Self-critical individuals are characterized by feelings of harsh self-scrutiny, inferiority, guilt and unworthiness. They strive for excessive achievement and perfection, and have a chronic fear of disapproval and criticism.

In order to assess dependent and self-critical personalities, Blatt and his colleagues developed the Depressive Experiences Questionnaire (DEQ) (Blatt, D´Affiti, and Quinlan, 1978). This 66-item questionnaire rates a range of experiences associated with depression, although they do not involve depressive symptoms. Preliminary factor analyses confirmed three internally consistent and stable factors. The Dependency factor was composed of items referred to concerns of feeling lonely and helpless, and the difficulty in expressing anger for fear of losing nurturance. The Self-Criticism factor was defined by items reflecting guilt, insecurity and critical toward the self for failing to meet high standards. The third factor identified was Efficacy, which consisted of items related to personal goals and responsibility.

Subsequent construct validation of the Dependency and Self-Criticism subscales (Zuroff, Moskowitz, Wielgus, Powers, and Franko, 1983) showed that both factors correlated positively with moral guilt and negatively with self-esteem. Dependency scale correlated positively with hostility guilt. And Self-Criticism in females was related to higher levels of Machiavellianism.

In a similar way, but from a cognitive perspective, Beck (1983) has described Sociotropy (social dependence) and Autonomy as two personality modes prone to depression. Sociotropic individuals are characterized by dependence on social feedback for gratification, whereas autonomous individuals are very concerned about personal failure and have a strong need to control the environment in order to avoid mistakes and criticism.

Beck and his colleagues (Beck, Epstein, Harrison, and Emery, 1983) developed the Sociotropy-Autonomy Scale (SAS) to assess these two dimensions. The SAS is a self-report questionnaire consisting of two 30-item scales: Sociotropy and Autonomy. High internal consistency and stability have been reported for both scales (Beck et al., 1983)

In a later factor analysis Bieling, Beck and Brown (2000) have found that the content of the items of both Sociotropy and Autonomy were better captured by two subfactors. Preference for Affiliation and Fear of Criticism and Rejection were the factors identified for Sociotropy. For Autonomy the two factors extracted were Independent for Goal Attainment and Sensitivity to Others´ Control. Positive correlations have been found between measures of psychopathology and the dimensions of Preference for Affiliation, Fear of Criticism and Rejection, and the Sensitivity to Others´ Control.

Beck's theory (1967) has also emphasized the role of dysfunctional attitudes in the onset of depressive episodes. Dysfunctional attitudes are defined as irrational cognitions that affect an individual's self-evaluation, for example the belief that self-worth and happiness depends on being perfect or on others´ approval. The Dysfunctional Attitude Scale (DAS) (Weissman and Beck, 1978) was developed to assess these cognitive-vulnerability assumptions. Although originally the instrument comprised 100 items, two parallel 40-item scale were created (DAS-A and DAS-B) following factor analyses (Weissman, 1979). The DAS-A is comprised by the Perfectionism and Need for Approval subscales, and is the form most widely used for research into cognitive vulnerability.

Another vulnerability factor predisposing to depression is Perfectionism. Excessive perfectionism is characterized by the setting of very high personal standards of performance and self-critical evaluations of one's own behavior. Perfectionist individuals strive for their goals by a fear of failure rather than by a need for achievement, and constantly seek approval by increasing their level of perfection.

For the measurement of perfectionism two multidimensional instruments have been generated. Frost et al. (1990) developed the Multidimensional Perfectionism Scale (MPS-F). This 35-item questionnaire contains six subscales: Concern over Mistakes, Personal Standards, Parental Expectations, Parental Criticism, Doubting of Actions and Organization. The total scale as well as its subscales have shown adequate internal consistency and reliability (Frost et al., 1990; Frost, Heimberg, Holt, Mattia, and Neubauer, 1993). Overall perfectionism and the subscales of Concern over Mistakes and Doubting of Actions are significantly associated with symptoms of psychopathology (Frost et al., 1990, 1993).

From a different conceptualization, Hewitt and Flett (1991) have suggested that perfectionism is composed of three separate dimensions: The Self-Oriented Perfectionism (SOP; setting high standards for oneself together with an intensive criticism), the Socially-Prescribed Perfectionism (SPP; the belief that others place unrealistic standards on one's behaviors), and the Other-Oriented Perfectionism (OOP; setting excessive expectations for others and evaluate them harshly). These authors (Hewitt and Flett, 1991) developed the Multidimensional Perfectionism Scale (MPS-H). It contains 45 items grouped under three 15-items subscales, designed to measure SOP, SPP and OOP. Empirical findings suggest that SOP and SPP are the dimensions more related to psychological distress (Enns, Cox, and Clara, 2005; Hewitt and Frost, 1991).

Finally, the hopelessness theory (Abramson et al., 1989; Alloy and Clements, 1998) points out depressogenic attributions as proximal causes of a subtype of depression, called "hopelessness depression". Depressogenic attributions are based on inferred stable and global causes of important negative life events, in combination with inferred negative consequences from the events and negative characteristics about the self.

To assess this type of cognitive vulnerability, the Cognitive Style Questionnaire was created (CSQ; Alloy, Abramson, Hogan et al., 2000). The CSQ is a modified version of the Attributional Style Questionnaire (ASQ; Seligman, Abramson, Semmel, and von Baeyer, 1979). It contains 12 hypothetical scenarios, each of which represents a negative event. The CSQ measures the internality, stability and globality of individuals´ attributions, together with inferences about the consequences and self-worth implications of the events. High scores on the CSQ has been related to onset and prospective depressive symptoms (Alloy and Clements, 1998).

Development of the Psychological Vulnerability Scale

Drawing upon these theoretical approaches and empirical findings, Sinclair and Wallston (1999) have designed a new measure of cognitive vulnerability, labeled Psychological Vulnerability Scale (PVS). This 6-item instrument screens for patterns of maladaptive beliefs related to feelings of dependence, perfectionism, need for external sources of approval, and generalized depressogenic attributions. The statements of the PVS are rated on 5-point scale, ranged from 1 ("does not describe me at all") to 5 ("describes me very well"). The PVS is a short instrument, easily administered.

To date the PVS has been mostly used in patients with chronic disease (Kneebone, Dunmore, and Evans, 2003; Sinclair and Wallston, 1999, 2001), and, to a lesser degree, with mixed samples composed of both clinical and healthy individuals (Selbie, Smith, Elliott et al.,

2004). In all these cases PVS has been applied in order to identify vulnerable individuals in whom psychotherapeutic interventions might be beneficial.

Preliminary psychometric data of the scale have been reported (Selbie *et al.*, 2004; Sinclair and Wallston, 1999) supporting adequate reliability. Internal consistency (Cronbach alpha) has ranged from .71 to .86 (Selbie *et al.*, 2004; Sinclair and Wallston, 1999), and test-retest correlations has been greater than .70 (Sinclair and Wallston, 1999). Furthermore, factorial analyses have obtained one single factor on which the items loaded above .30.

Construct validation of the scale has also been performed. Divergent validity has shown negative correlations between the PVS and personal coping resources, positive affect and physical well-being. In contrast, convergent validity has posited that the PVS was positively associated with helplessness, negative affect, depressive symptoms and health complaints (Selbie *et al.*, 2004; Sinclair and Wallston, 1999).

In spite of the empirical support for the adequacy of the PVS in clinical populations, little attention has been addressed to the properties of the scale in pure non-clinical populations. This aspect is important, not only because it allows the refinement of the instrument, but also because it permits clearer identification of individual differences in psychological vulnerability across the general population.

In this chapter we aimed at further understanding the reliability and construct validity of the PVS in a non-clinical population.

To evaluate the validity of the scale we determined its factor structure, and tested its association with other tools that measured different but related constructs. Consequently, we selected the measures of perceived competence, mood state, symptoms and well-being, since they have been extensively associated with vulnerability in the predicted direction (Bieling *et al.*, 2000; Bieling, Israeli, and Antony, 2004; Dunkley and Blankstein, 2000; Frost *et al.*, 1993; Martin, Flett, Hewitt, Krames, and Szanto, 1996; Sinclair and Wallston, 1999, 2001).

In addition, we tried to expand the understanding of the PVS by adding other aspects related to mental and physical health, such as hostility, health behaviors and alexithymia. According to the literature, individuals with vulnerable self-esteem tend to experience more ruminative anger and manage their anger in a non–constructive way (Mitchelson and Burns, 1998; Tangney, Wagner, Hill-Barlow, Marschall, and Gramzow, 1996). Likewise, they are more likely to perform risky behaviors, such as drinking, taking drugs or unhealthy eating habits (Crocker, 2002; McVey, Davis, Tweed, and Shaw, 2004).

With respect to alexithymia (Sifneos, 1972), research has suggested that this deficit in the identification and description of feelings is positively connected to perfectionist beliefs, feelings of inefficacy and social conformity (Havilan and Reise, 1996; Lundh, Johnsson, Sundqvist, and Olsson, 2002; Quinton and Wagner, 2005). Thus, it may be hypothesized that alexithymia could represent an appropriate outcome to provide some information about the predictive contribution of psychological vulnerability.

In summary, we expected that PVS was positively related to hostility (rumination and cynical hostility) and negative mood affect. These associations would support for the convergent validity of the scale. We also expected that PVS was negatively connected to perceived competence and positive mood affect, which would evidence the divergent validity of the instrument. Further, we proposed that PVS would be positively associated with the presence of symptoms and alexithymia, whereas it would be negatively connected with health behaviours and psychological well-being.

METHOD

Participants

Four hundred and thirty-six individuals (23% males and 77% females) participated in the study. The participants were enrolled in different courses administered by an Opening University. The age ranged from 17 to 63 years (Mean = 36; SD = 9.72).

The people who agreed to participate in the study were asked to complete a packet of questionnaires. This battery included measures of psychological vulnerability, perceived competence, hostility, affective states, health behaviors and alexithymia. Psychological vulnerability and other scales were also readministered three months following the first administration (Time 2).

At time 2 data collection, the sample was composed by 361 participants (23% males and 77% females), with an age ranged from 17 to 63 (Mean = 36; SD = 9.85).

Measures

The Psychological Vulnerability Scale (PVS; Sinclair and Wallston, 1999)
This is a 6-item scale measuring maladaptive cognitions related to dependence, perfectionism, need for external sources of approval, and generalized depressogenic attributions. Items were rated on a 5-point Likert scale. Thus, a high score indicates greater vulnerability.

The Perceived Competence Scale (PCS; Smith, Dobbins, and Wallston, 1991, Spanish Version of Fernández-Castro, Álvarez, Blasco, Doval, and Sanz, 1998)
This 8-item instrument measures the generalized expectancy of being capable of interacting with the environment effectively. Items were rated on a 5-point scale, being four items reversed-keyed. The total score reflects high level of perceived competence.

Previous investigations have yielded a high alpha reliability (Fernández-Castro *et al.*, 1998; Rueda and Pérez García, 2004; Rueda, Pérez García, and Bermúdez, 2005). For the present sample, internal consistency (α coefficient) was .80.

The Positive and Negative Schedule (PANAS; Watson, Clark, and Tellegen, 1988)
This 20-item measure has 2 dimensions: positive affect (10 items) and negative affect (10 items). The response scale was a 5-point Likert-type. Respondents were asked to report how they usually felt.

The PANAS has good psychometric properties in terms of reliability and validity (Watson *et al.*, 1988). In our study α coefficient was .84 for the positive affect subscale and .88 for the negative affect subscale.

The Dissipation-Rumination Scale (DRS; Caprara, 1986)
The DRS comprises 20 items. Five of them are control items and are not scored. In the present investigation we used the Spanish version of the scale which did not included these control items (Bermúdez, 1993). The rating scale ranged from 0 = extremely false to 6 =

extremely true. This self-report assesses the tendency toward an increasing desire for retaliation over time, in combination with the proneness to act aggressively following an interpersonal offence. A high score on the scale reflects greater rumination.

The DRS has been found a valid measure of hostility (Caprara, Manzi, and Perugini, 1992). The coefficient alpha obtained from our sample was .91.

The Hostility Scale: Cynicism Subscale (Ho; Cook Y. Medley, 1954; Spanish Version by Bermúdez, Fernández, and Sánchez-Elvira, 1992)

Cynicism reflects a generally negative view of humankind, depicting others as unworthy and selfish. This personality trait was measured by a subset of eight items derived of the Ho scale (Cook y Medley, 1954). The response format was a 6-point scale (from 0 = extremely false to 6 = extremely true). High scores depicted cynical hostility. Internal consistency (alpha coefficient) of the scale was .84.

A Brief Symptom Inventory

This inventory was developed to measure somatic symptoms (11 items). The participants were asked to state to what extent they usually experienced various physical complaints. The response format was 1 (no) and 2 (yes). The Cronbach´s alpha for the inventory was .64.

The Twenty-Item Toronto Alexithymia Scale (TAS-20; Bagby, Parker, and Taylor, 1994a; Bagby, Taylor, and Parker, 1994b)

This self-report measure contains 20 items using a five-point Likert scale. The scale is composed by three subscales: (a) difficulty in identifying feelings (7 items); (b) difficulty describing emotions to others (8 items); and (c) an externally oriented style of thinking (8 items). In the present investigation we used the total score on the TAS-20 as a measure of alexithymia. Internal consistency has be shown to be adequate (Bagby et al., 1994a). In our study alpha coefficient was .84.

The Healthy Behaviors Checklist

This 22-item inventory was developed to measure the extent to which the respondent performed a set of healthy behaviors. Ratings were made on a 5-point scale, being the score of four items reversed. The total of the scale was taken as an index of healthy behaviors. Alpha coefficient was .70.

The Hospital Anxiety and Depression Scale (HADS, Zigmond and Snaith, 1983)

The HADS is a 14-item questionnaire measuring anxious (7 items) and depressive (7 items) symptoms. Using a 5-point scale the respondents indicated the frequency of these symptoms during the past two weeks. In order to obtain a measure of psychological well-being the total score on the HADS was multiplied by minus 1. As a result, higher scores indicated greater psychological well-being. Good internal consistency has been reported for the HADS (Martin and Thompson, 2000). In our study Cronbach´s alpha was .88.

RESULTS

Psychometric Properties of the PVS

Reliability of the PVS consisted of Cronbach´s alpha to determine internal consistency, and test-retest correlation coefficients to establish the stability of the measure.

Cronbach´s alpha coefficients were adequate at both times of the research (α = .76 at Time 1; α = .82 at Time 2), being slightly higher at time 2. Test-retest correlation was performed with a subset of 361 participants over a 3-month period. The test-retest correlation was .70. The results revealed that the PVS was a measure internally consistent and stable over time.

Gender differences were not found in mean PVS scores at any time of the investigation. Possible differences in PVS between participants who continued in the research at both times, and those who dropped out were also examined. No significant differences emerged as a function of the participation versus non participation in the study

Factor Analysis of PVS

Means and standard deviations of the six items of the scale are reported in table 1. All the items had corrected item-total correlations higher than .30. The mean inter-item correlation was .35. This value did not exceed the cut-off point of .50, which could reflect that the scale items are overly redundant (Briggs and Cheek, 1986). Alpha coefficients if the items were deleted were also calculated. As shown in table 1, these coefficients decreased when each item was eliminated.

Table 1. Descriptive data and results of the Factor Analysis of the PV items

	M	SD	Corrected Item-Total Correlation	α if item deleted	Factor Loading
Item 1	2.69	1.03	.57	.71	.75
Item 2	2.12	.93	.45	.74	.62
Item 3	1.77	.89	.60	.71	.76
Item 4	2.83	1.04	.50	.73	.67
Item 5	2.40	.99	.51	.73	.69
Item 6	3.28	1.07	.42	.75	.58
Total α				.76	
Eigenvalue					2.81
% of Variance					47

Taking into account these preliminary results, we decided to retain all the items to replicate the factor structure of the scale found in previous studies (Selbie *et al.*, 2004; Sinclair and Wallston, 1999). A principal-components analysis was conducted and it confirmed that the scale consists of one large factor. The *eigenvalue* was 2.81 and 47% of the variance was explained by this sole factor. Item loadings ranged from .58 to .76 (see table 1).

Construct Validity

Construct validity was examined by linking PVS to measures of rumination, cynical hostility and negative mood affect (convergent validity), and to perceived competence and positive mood affect (divergent validity). As expected PVS was correlated positively with rumination and cynical hostility. A stronger and positive correlation was also found with negative mood affect. Conversely, PVS correlated negatively with perceived competence and positive mood affect. The association with this type of mood state was substantially weaker than the relation of the PVS with the negative mood affect (see table 2).

In sum, these patterns of associations provided extensive support for the construct validation of the PVS.

Table 2. Correlation of the PVS with measures of hostility, affective states, perceived competence and health outcomes

	Psychological Vulnerability
Rumination	.36***
Cynical Hostility	.39***
Negative Mood Affect	.58***
Perceived Competence	-.56***
Positive Mood Affect	-.29***
Symptoms	.27***
Alexithymia	.48***
Health Behaviors	-.24***
Well-Being	-.51***

***$p<.001$.

Predictive Validity

In order to examine the associations between PVS and the selected health criteria (symptoms, alexithymia, health behaviours and psychological well-being), we first obtained the correlations of the PVS with all these variables. The findings showed a considerable and negative association between PVS and well-being, and a positive association with alexithymia. The relation of PVS to the symptoms was moderately positive, whereas the connection with the health behaviors was negative (see table 2).

Taking into account that the negative affect is a factor of subjective distress that can bias the health-related self-reports (Watson and Pennebaker, 1989), a set of regression analyses in block were performed after controlling for the effect of the negative affective state. This strategy permitted to clarify the unique contribution of the PVS to the above-mentioned outcomes.

Table 3 summarizes the results of these analyses. PVS had a predictive and independent effect on most of all the outcomes. The contribution of the PVS was positive for alexithymia, and negative for health behaviors and well-being. In all these cases, after removing the negative affect, PVS remained significant. Only in the prediction of the symptoms, the contribution of the PVS was no longer significant when the negative affect was partial out.

Thus inspection of these results reveal great evidence for the predictive validity of the PVS in relation to health criteria, although the association of the PVS with the measure of symptoms seems to be mediated by the underlying negative mood state.

Table 3. Multiple Regression analysis predicting health outcomes

	R^2	$F_{(2,435)}$	β
Symptoms	.14	34.37***	
Psychological Vulnerability			.09
Negative Mood Affect			.31***
Alexithymia	.27	80.22***	
Psychological Vulnerability			.33***
Negative Mood Affect			.25***
Health Behaviors	.09	21.93***	
Psychological Vulnerability			-.11*
Negative Mood Affect			.22***
Well-Being	.39	140.42***	
Psychological Vulnerability			-.26***
Negative Mood Affect			-.44***

***$p<.001$; *$p<.05$.

CONCLUSION

The aim of the present chapter was to establish the psychometric properties and the construct validity of the PVS in a non-clinical population.

The results first confirmed that the PVS was a reliable measure to be applied in healthy populations, showing adequate internal consistency and stability over time. With respect to the construct validity, the factor analysis replicated previous findings (Selbie *et al.*, 2004; Sinclair and Wallston, 1999), showing that PVS contained an unidimensional structure, loading all the items ≥.58 on this sole factor.

We also determined the convergent and divergent validity of the PVS as a way to establish its construct validity. Consistent with previous empirical evidence (Martin *et al.*, 1996; Sinclair and Wallston, 1999, 2001), we found that PVS was negatively associated with perceived competence and positive affect. This pattern of relationships suggests that vulnerable individuals, whose self-worth is based on either stringent self-standards or social approval, feel less competent when dealing with environmental challenges. Consequently, these people tend to respond to threats in a more rigid way, underemphasizing their abilities and losing the sense of control (Niiya, Crocker, and Bartmess, 2004; Vohs and Heatherton, 2001).

Furthermore, PVS was positively linked to rumination, cynical hostility and negative affect, which is consistent with the literature (Bieling *et al.*, 2004; Frost *et al.*, 1993; Tangney *et al.*, 1996). These results are important because they evidence that rumination and a cynical outlook are potential cognitive correlates of vulnerability.

Additionally, we can also infer that psychological vulnerability may trigger, not only negative affective responses, but also hostile reactions and aggressive rumination in face of negative feedback. This point is illustrated by the content of the items 2 and 6 of the PVS ("I feel entitled to better treatment from others than I generally receive" and "I often feel resentful when others take advantage of me"), which reveals frustration and resentment regarding social relationships (Sinclair and Wallston, 1999). Likewise, self-criticism, which can be regarded as one hallmark of vulnerability, has been associated with aggression and submission in conflictive situations (Mongrain, Vettese, Shuster, and Kendal, 1998; Vettese and Mongrain, 2000). To the extent that self-critical individuals fail to assert themselves, they are more likely to feel helpless and direct their anger inward when coping with interpersonal conflicts.

Our analyses also provided considerable evidence for the predictive capacity of the PVS. Psychological vulnerability was positively related to alexithymia, and negatively associated with preventive behaviours and well-being. Importantly, even when the effect of the negative affect was controlled, the PVS accounted for unique variance in all these outcomes.

Although we can only speculate why these connections were so, we can suggest that, due to the high dependence on external sources and the excessive need for being perfect, vulnerable people could adopt more unhealthy lifestyles, such as stringent diets or excessively sunbathe (Crocker, 2002; McVey *et al.*, 2004). In addition, they could feel less capable of identifying and describing feelings for fear of perceiving rejection or criticism. Further, the contribution of the PVS to preventive behaviors and alexithymia is specially relevant since, to date, no study has examined the impact of the psychological vulnerability on these outcomes.

Finally the finding that the psychological vulnerability was unrelated to physical symptoms after removing the effect of negative affect, is consistent with the evidence that individual differences in negative affectivity underlie the correlations between self-reported measures of health (Brown and Moskowitz, 1997; Watson and Pennebaker, 1989; Williams, 2006). Thus, it is possible that vulnerable individuals perceive a great number of symptoms due to their selective attention to physical complaints. Another plausible explanation is that they focus more on these bodily sensations as a result of their difficulty in recognizing other inner responses. Research with more objective health indicators are required, to shed more light on the real association between psychological vulnerability and the presence of health complaints.

Although this study confirmed the psychometric adequacy and construct validity of the PVS in a non-clinical population, it contains some limitations that merit attention. Firstly, the current research was a cross-sectional design. Thus we cannot establish any causal influence of psychological vulnerability on the selected criteria. A longitudinal investigation would contribute to clarify whether the presence of vulnerability may prompt the onset of unhealthy behaviors, alexithymia and the reduction in well-being, or, conversely, the rise in these variables could result in greater vulnerability. Secondly, future studies testing the diathesis-stress model are needed. Such investigations would add more information about the predictive utility of psychological vulnerability when considered alone or in interaction with negative life events. Finally, although we focused on the validation of the PVS with a non-clinical sample, attempts to explore its psychometric properties in populations with a clinical diagnosis of depression would be highly valuable.

In conclusion, the present chapter provides additional support for the psychometric properties and construct validation of the PVS in a non clinical population. The instrument showed appropriate reliability and stability, together with good convergent and divergent validity. Considering the potential usefulness of the scale in non clinical settings, the findings also represent an impetus for future work in the prevention of affective disorders.

REFERENCES

Abramson, L. Y., Metalsky, G. I., and Alloy, L. B. (1989). Hopelessness depression: A theory-based subtype of depression. *Psychological Review, 96*, 358-372.

Alloy, L. B., and Clements, C. M. (1998). Hopelessness theory of depression: Tests of the symptom component. *Cognitive Therapy and Research, 22*, 303-335.

Alloy, L. B., Abramson, L. Y., Hogan, M. E., Whitehouse, W. G., Rose, D. T., Robinson, M. S. *et al.* (2000). The Temple-Wisconsin Cognitive Vulnerability to Depression (CVD) Project: Lifetime history of Axis I psychopathology in individuals at high and low cognitive risk for depression. *Journal of Abnormal Psychology, 109*, 403-418.

Bagby, R. M., Parker, J. D. A., and Taylor, G. J. (1994a). The twenty-item Toronto alexithymia scale-I. Item selection and cross-validation of the factor structure. *Journal of Psychosomatic Research, 41*, 23-32.

Bagby, R. M., Taylor, G. J., and Parker, J. D. A. (1994b). The twenty-item Toronto alexithymia scale-II. Convergent, discriminant, and concurrent validity. *Journal of Psychosomatic Research, 41*, 33-40.

Beck, A. T. (1967). *Depression: Clinical, experimental and theoretical aspects.* New York: Harper and Row.

Beck, A. T. (1983). Cognitive therapy of depression: New perspectives. In P. J. Clayton and J. E. Barrett (Eds.), *Treatment of depression: Old controversies and new approaches* (pp. 265-290). New York: Raven.

Beck, A. T., Epstein, N., Harrison, R. P., and Emery, G. (1983). *Development of the Sociotropy-Autonomy Scale: A measure of personality factors in psychopathology.* Unpublished manuscript. University of Pennsylvania: Philadelphia, PA.

Bermúdez, J. (1993). *Adaptación española de la escala de Disipación-Rumiación: Datos preliminares* [Spanish adaptation of the Dissipation-Rumination scale: Preliminary data]. Unpublished manuscript. UNED.

Bermúdez, J., Fernández, E., and Sánchez-Elvira, A. (1992). *La Escala de Hostilidad (Ho) de Cook-Medley para muestras españolas* [The Cook and Medley Hostility scale (Ho) for Spanish samples]. Unpublished manuscript. UNED.

Bieling, P. J., Beck, A. T., and Brown, G. K. (2000). The Sociotropy-Autonomy Scale: Structure and implications. *Cognitive Therapy and Research, 24*, 763-780.

Bieling, P. J., Israeli, A. L., and Antony, M. M. (2004). Is perfectionism good, bad, or both?. Examining the perfectionism construct. *Personality and Individual Differences, 36*, 1373-1385.

Blatt, S. J., D´Affiti, J. P., and Quinlan, D. M. (1976). Experiences of depression in normal young adults. *Journal of Abnormal Psychology, 85*, 383-389.

Blatt, S. J., D´Affiti, J. P., and Quinlan, D. M. (1978). *Depressive Experiences Questionnaire.* Unpublished manuscript. Yale University: New Haven, CT.

Blatt, S. J., Quinlan, D. M., Chevron, E. S., McDonald, C., and Zuroff, D. C. (1982). Dependency and self-criticism: Psychological dimensions of depression. *Journal of Consulting and Clinical Psychology, 150*, 113-124.

Blatt, S. J., and Zuroff, D. C. (1992). Interpersonal relatedness and self-definition: Two prototypes for depression. *Clinical Psychology Review, 12*, 527-562.

Briggs, S. R., and Cheek, J. M. (1986). The role of factor analysis in the development and evaluation of personality scales. *Journal of Personality, 54*, 106-148.

Brown, K. W., and Moskowitz, D. S. (1997). Does unhappiness make you sick?. The role of affect and neuroticism in the experience of common physical symptoms. *Journal of Personality and Social Psychology, 72*, 907-917.

Caprara, G. V. (1986). Indicators of aggression: The Dissipation-Rumination Scale. *Personality and Individual Differences, 6*, 763-769

Caprara, G. V., Manzi, J., and Perugini, M. (1992). Investigating guilt in relation to emotionality and aggression. *Personality and Individual Differences, 7*, 763-769.

Cook , W. W., and Medley, D. M. (1954). Proposed hostility and pharisaic-virtue scales for the MMPI. *Journal of Applied Psychology, 38*, 414-418.

Crocker, J. (2002). Contingencies of self-worth: Implications for self-regulation and psychological vulnerability. *Self and Identity, 1*, 143-149.

Dunkley, D. M., and Blankstein, K. R. (2000). Self-critical perfectionism, coping, hassles, and current distress: A structural equation modeling approach. *Cognitive Therapy and Research, 24*, 713-730.

Enns, M. W., Cox, B. J., and Clara, I. P. (2005). Perfectionism and Neuroticism: A longitudinal study of specific vulnerability and diathesis-stress models. *Cognitive Therapy and Research, 29*, 463-478.

Fernández-Castro, J., Álvarez, M.., Blasco, T., Doval, E., and Sanz, A. (1998). Validación de la Escala de Competencia Personal de Wallston: Implicaciones para el estudio del estrés. [Validation of the Wallston's Personal Competence Scale and its implication for the stress research]. *Ansiedad y Estrés, 4*, 31-41.

Frost, R. O., Heimberg, R. G., Holt, G. S., Mattia, J. I., and Nuebauer, A. L. (1993). A comparison of two measures of perfectionism. *Personality and Individual Differences, 14*, 119-126.

Frost, R. O., Marten, P., Lahart, C., and Rosenblate, R. (1990). The dimensions of perfectionism. *Cognitive Therapy and Research, 14*, 449-468.

Haviland, M. G., and Reise, S. P. (1996). A California Q-set alexithymia prototype and its relationship to ego-control and ego-resiliency. *Journal of Psychosomatic Research, 41*, 597-608.

Hewitt, P. L., and Flett, G. L. (1991). Perfectionism in the self and social contexts: Conceptualization, assessment, and association with psychopathology. *Journal of Personality and Social Psychology, 60*, 456-470.

Hankin, B. L., Abramson, L. Y., Miller, N., and Haeffel, G. J. (2004). Cognitive vulnerability-stress theories of depression: Examining affective specificity in the prediction of depression versus anxiety in three prospective studies. *Cognitive Therapy and Research, 28*, 309-345.

Hunt, M., and Forand, N. R. (2005). Cognitive vulnerability to depression in never depressed subjects. *Cognition and Emotion, 19*, 763-770.

Kneebone, I. I., Dunmore, E. C., and Evans, E. (2003). Symptoms of depression in older adults with multiple sclerosis (MS): Comparison with a matched sample of younger adults. *Aging and Mental Health, 7*, 182-185.

Lundh, L. G., Johnsson, A., Sundqvist, K., and Olsson, H. (2002). Alexithymia, memory of emotion, emotional awareness, and perfectionism. *Emotion, 2*, 361-379.

Martin, C. R., and Thompson, D. R. (2000). A psychometric evaluation of the hospital anxiety and depression scale in coronary care patients following acute myocardial infarction. *Psychology, Health and Medicine, 5,* 193-201.

Martin, T. R., Flett, G. L., Hewitt, P. L., Krames, L., and Szanto, G. (1996). Personality correlates of depression and health symptoms: A test of a self-regulation model. *Journal of Research in Personality, 31,* 264-277.

McVey, G. L., Davis, R., Tweed., S., and Shaw, B. F. (2004). Evaluation of a school-based program designed to improve body image satisfaction, global self-esteem, and eating attitudes and behaviors: A replication study. *International Journal of Eating Disorders, 36,* 1-11.

Mitchelson, J. K., and Burns, L. R. (1998). Career mothers and perfectionism: Stress at work and at home. *Personality and Individual Differences, 25,* 477-485.

Mongrain, M., Vettese, L. C., Shuster, B., and Kendal, N. (1998). Perceptual biases, affect, and behavior in the relationships of dependents and self-critics. *Journal of Personality and Social Psychology, 75,* 230-241.

Nietzel, M. T., and Harris, M. J. (1990). Relationship of dependency and achievement / autonomy to depression. *Clinical Psychology Review, 10,* 279-297.

Niiya, Y., Crocker, J., and Bartmess, E. N. (2004). From vulnerability to resilience: Learning orientations buffer contingent self-esteem from failure. *Psychological Science, 15,* 801-805.

Quinton, S., and Wagner, H. L. (2005). Alexithymia, ambivalence over emotional expression and eating attitudes. *Personality and Individual Differences, 38,* 1163-1173.

Riso, L. P., Blandino, J. A., Penna, S., Dacey, S., Grant, M. M., du Toit, P. L., Duin, J. S., Pacoe, E. M., and Ulmer, C. S. (2003). Cognitive aspects of chronic depression. *Journal of Abnormal Psychology, 112,* 72-80.

Roberts, J. E., and Monroe, S. M. (1992). Vulnerable self-esteem and depressive symptoms: Prospective findings comparing three alternative conceptualizations. *Journal of Personality and Social Psychology, 62,* 804-812.

Rueda, B., y Pérez-García, A. M. (2004). Análisis comparativo de la competencia percibida general y la específica de salud. [Comparative analyses of Perceived Competence and Perceived Health Competence]. *Ansiedad y Estrés, 10,* 127-139.

Rueda, B., Pérez García, A. M., and Bermúdez, J (2005). Estudio de la Competencia Percibida a partir de sus dos componentes: Expectativa de autoeficacia y expectativa de resultados. [Study of Perceived Competence based on its two components: Self-Efficacy Expectancy and Outcome Expectancy]. *Revista de Psicología General y Aplicada, 58,* 75-87.

Selbie, H., Smith, B. H., Elliott, A. M., Teunisse, S., Chambers, W. A., and Hannaford, P. C. (2004). A validation of the psychological vulnerability scale and its use in chronic pain. *The Pain Clinic, 16,* 153-162.

Seligman, M. E. P., Abramson, L. Y., Semmel, A., and von Baeyer, C. (1979). Depressive attributional style. *Journal of Abnormal Psychology, 88,* 242-247.

Sifneos, P. E. (1972). *Psychotherapy and emotional crisis.* Cambridge: Harvard University Press.

Sinclair, V. G., and Wallston, K. (1999). The development and validation of the Psychological Vulnerability Scale. *Cognitive Therapy and Research, 23,* 119-129.

Sinclair, V. G., and Wallston, K. A. (2001). Predictors of improvement in a cognitive-behavioral intervention for women with rheumatoid arthritis. *Annals of Behavioral Medicine, 23,* 291-297.

Smith, C. A., Dobbins, C. J. and Wallston, K. A. (1991). The mediational role of perceived competence in psychological adjustment to rheumatoid arthritis. *Journal of Applied Social Psychology, 21,* 1218-1247.

Tangney, J. P., Wagner, P. E., Hill-Barlow, D., Marschall, D. E., and Gramzow, R. (1996). Relation of the shame and guilt to constructive versus destructive responses to anger across the lifespan. *Journal of Personality and Social Psychology, 70,* 797-809.

Vettese, L. C., and Mongrain, M. (2000). Communication about the self and partner in the relationships of dependents and self-critics. *Cognitive Therapy and Research, 24,* 609-626.

Vohs, K. D., and Heatherton, T. F. (2001). Self-esteem and threats to self: Implications for self-construal and interpersonal perceptions. *Journal of Personality and Social Psychology, 81,* 1103-1118.

Watson, D., Clark, L. A., and Tellegen, A. (1988). Development and validation of brief measures of positive and negative affect: the PANAS scales. *Journal of Personality and Social Psychology, 54,* 1063-1070.

Watson, D., and Pennebaker, J. W. (1989). Health complaints, stress and distress: Exploring the central role of negative affectivity. *Psychological Review, 96,* 234-254.

Weissman, A. N. (1979). The Dysfunctional Attitude Scale: A validation study (Doctoral dissertation. University of Pennsylvania, 1979). *Dissertation Abstracts International, 40,* 1389-1390B.

Weissman, A. N., and Beck, A. T. (1978). *Development and validation of the Dysfunctional Attitude Scale: A preliminary investigation.* Paper presented at the meeting of the American Educational Research Association. Toronto, Ontario. Canada.

Williams, P. G. (2006). Personality and illness behavior. In M. E. Vollrath (Ed.), *Handbook of Personality and Health* (pp. 157-173). West Sussex, United Kingdom: Wiley.

Zigmond, A. S., and Snaith, R. P. (1983). The Hospital Anxiety and Depression Scale. *Acta Psychiatrica Scandinavica, 67,* 361-370.

Zuroff, D. C., Igreja, I., and Mongrain, M. (1990). Dysfunctional attitudes, dependency, and self-criticism as predictors of depressive mood states: A 12-month longitudinal study. *Cognitive Therapy and Research, 14,* 315-326.

Zuroff, D. C., Moskowitz, D. S., Wielgus, M. S., Powers, T. A., and Franko, D. L. (1983). Construct validation of the dependency and self-criticism scales of the depressive experience questionnaire. *Journal of Research in Personality, 17,* 226-241.

In: Psychological Tests and Testing Research Trends
Editor: Paul M. Goldfarb, pp. 55-81

ISBN: 978-1-60021-569-8
© 2007 Nova Science Publishers, Inc.

Chapter 3

CONSTRUCT AND CONCURRENT VALIDITY OF A SCREENING EXECUTIVE TEST: THE NINE-CARD SORTING TEST

Nora Silvana Vigliecca and Jorge Antonio Castillo

Consejo Nacional de Investigaciones Científicas y Técnicas de la Argentina (CONICET)
Centro de Investigaciones de la Facultad de Filosofía y Humanidades (CIFFyH) y
Servicio de Neurología y Neurocirugía del Hospital Córdoba, Córdoba, Argentina

ABSTRACT

Introduction: Considering that most of the card-sorting tasks are "one shot", developing tests which demand similar cognitive operations but different stimuli and instructions may be useful for longitudinal studies and for understanding specific components of problem solving ability and brain function. The nine-card sorting test (9CST) involves a purposive and interviewee-centered activity, which deals with three non-verbal sorting principles and their combination by pairs.

Objectives: 1) To study the validity of the 9CST by: a) its correlation with the WCST (construct validity) and b) its capacity to differentiate between frontal vs. non-frontal patients as well as frontal patients vs. healthy subjects (concurrent validity). 2) To study the test-retest and inter-scorer reliability on 40 healthy subjects.

Methods: Validity data were obtained from a sample of 106 volunteers: 32 patients with anterior (frontal) encephalic lesions (A), 30 patients with posterior (temporal, parietal or occipital) encephalic lesions (P) and 44 healthy (H) subjects. The three groups were matched by sex, age, educational background and manual preference and the two groups of patients, also by type of lesion, time since onset of condition and presence of other neurological risks. A neuropsychological battery complemented card-sorting evaluation.

Results: Significant differences were observed between the A and P patients in both card-sorting tests (and in an abbreviated version of the Raven test) but not in the rest of the neuropsychological tests administered considered as a whole. Three 9CST indexes correlated significantly with the WCST indexes of categories, errors and perseverative errors. Neither the WCST nor the 9CST differentiated the P patients from healthy subjects but the difference between A patients and healthy subjects became more evident with the 9CST. A very simple test of face recognition also differentiated betweend the A and P patients but in the opposite direction than the card sorting tests. Reliability coefficients were ≥0.79 for all the 9CST indexes. Practice effects were not observed in the 9CST number of categories completed.

Conclusion: This test of free distribution demonstrated a suitable validity and reliability. It can be a valid screening test to detect frontal impaired patients from healthy people. It also can be useful to detect frontal impaired patients when they are compared with patients impaired in posterior encephalic areas who have similar cognitive resources in alternative tasks such as attention, discrimination, memory, copy and verbal ability. An association between card sorting tests and intelligence, and a bias in sample selection favoring the more skillful non-frontal patients are discussed.

Frontal – Execution- Factor analysis- Internal consistency- Focal brain lesions- Mild cognitive impairment- Discriminant analysis- Face memory.

INTRODUCTION

Considering the conditions in which we, Argentine professionals, usually have to administer neuropsychological tests, particularly in public hospitals, it is urgent for us to construct brief, economical, comprehensive and valid tests.

Executive functions are high- level cognitive functions involved in the control and direction of lower-level functions. Although the terms "frontal" and "executive" have been used interchangeably when referring to a broad classification of tests (Stuss and Levine, 2002) the association between these terms should be demonstrated.

The Wisconsin card-sorting test (WCST) has been identified as a measure of executive function in neurologically impaired populations (which have included focal and diffuse brain damage, seizure disorders, Parkinson's disease and multiple sclerosis); it has also been identified by its relationship with some clinical entities such as schizophrenia and attention deficit disorder (Heaton, Chelune, Talley, Kay and Curtiss, 1993). Because of its apparent sensitivity to the effects of frontal lobe lesions, it is often referred to (simplistically, in the opinion of its authors) as a measure of "frontal" or "prefrontal" functioning.

Besides some doubts in relation to its validity as a frontal predictor (Anderson, Damasio, Jones and Tranel, 1991; Barcelo, 2001; Chase-Carmichael, Ris, Weber and Schefft, 1999), the WCST is somehow difficult to perform not only from the interviewee's point of view but also from the interviewer's point of view. In addition, as a neuropsychological tool it can: a) be difficult to be carried out by aphasics or left hemisphere impaired patients because it requires knowing the number notion and following verbally complex instructions, b) overlook important functions of the prefrontal cortex since it involves an interviewer- centered decision making (Goldberg and Podell, 2000), and c) be highly frustrating when patients can not find the sorting principle.

Finding the sorting principle, by the way, requires abstraction and concept formation, which are shared by most of the visual reasoning tasks. Although abstract reasoning and problem solving tasks may involve other areas besides the frontal lobe (Lezak, 1995), a selective recruitment of the lateral frontal cortex has been reported for this kind of tasks, some times referred to as general intelligence tasks (Duncan et al, 2000). Nevertheless, the peculiarity and main advantage of executive tests is that interviewers can see "the interviewee's thought *in actions"*, i.e., how the interviewee solves the problem, with his/her own difficulties, and not just the final result.

Moreover, and since most of the card- sorting tasks are "one shot" (i.e., they generally cannot be repeated because of the practice effects involved) developing tests which demand similar cognitive operations but employ different stimulus (and, preferably, a different stimulus organization to avoid procedural memory) may be useful for longitudinal studies. The longitudinal or repeated-measure approach can be necessary not only to infer changes in the patient's executive performance but it also serves other purposes such as rehabilitation exercises or psychometric studies. The consistency among cognitive tasks of similar nature may also help to understand specific components of problem solving ability and brain function.

The nine card sorting test (9CST) is an easy to administer executive test, which was developed by taking into account the cognitive demands of previous sort and shift tests, as described by Lezak (1995), as well as the pre-number notions (seriation, classification and correspondence) as set forth by Piaget (1990; 1991). It involves a comprehensive, purposive and novel activity, which deals with three non-verbal sorting principles and their combination in pairs.

Simultaneously, each sorting principle involves three variants, for example, the color criterion involves the categories of red, blue and green (figure 1). In order to use a fewer number of stimuli than previous card sorting tests the three sorting principles with their three variants were distributed throughout the nine cards by following the Latin square design[33]. This modification not only pointed at developing a briefer and more economical psychological instrument, by the use of fewer stimuli, but also at increasing the test difficulty by incorporating the ambiguity of having to disorder one criterion so as to order the remaining ones.

While in the WCST one sorting principle is required at one time, in the 9CST "classification" (for example by color or form) is required together with "correspondence" (for example the red circle corresponds to the red triangle) or "seriation" (for example the small circle goes before the middle circle and together with the small square) to solve the task. The better the problem solver, the more the alternative strategies he/ she will find. On the other hand, the sorting principle of number or quantity (as used in the WCST) was replaced in the 9CST by size, i.e., by a pre number serial notion (Piaget 1990; 1991). The lack of cards with verbal stimuli also differentiates the 9CST from the California card- sorting test (Crouch, Greeve and Brooks, 1996; Delis, Squire, Bihrle and Massman, 1992), which intentionally points at studying verbal and non-verbal abilities. Furthermore, as the 9CST is a logical construction task in which, in its paper version, the patient has to organize all the cards simultaneously on the table, the spatial component involved in perceptual organization and object assembly may be more necessary in the 9CST than in the WCST.

---

[33] This is an statistical resource which, in this case, reduces the hypothetical 27 combinations of these three factors to just 9. Consequently, each level of variation appears only once per row and per column.

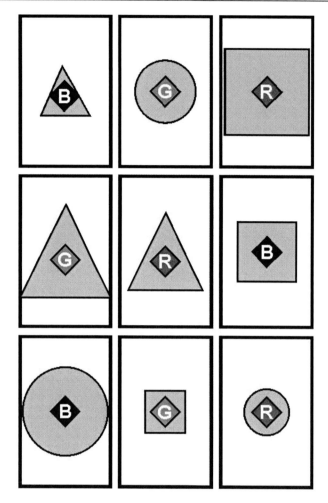

Figure 1. The Nine-Card Sorting Test (9CST) stimulus- cards in the initial position (to be ordered). The colors of the internal rhombi are blue (B), green (G) and red (R).

Similar to the WCST, in the 9CST the subject does not know "how" to order the cards. Unlike the WCST (but resembling other tests such as the Nelson's test, which is a modified version of the WCST (Nelson, 1976, Obonsawin, Crawford, Page, Chalmers, Low and Marsh, 1999), and the California Card Sorting Test (Crouch et al, 1996; Delis et al, 1992;) in the 9CST the interviewer does not induce the interviewee to begin with (and/ or to shift towards) a certain classification criterion, therefore, said criterion has to be inferred and chosen by the interviewee. There are many possible orderings but only the logically correct ones are reinforced. Stimulus ambiguity is present in the 9CST in a similar way as in the WCST, i.e., different classification criteria overlap in an item. So, subjects must single out the relevant attributes and ignore the irrelevant ones. The Latin Square design incorporates a second source of ambiguity since, in order to control the variation in two criteria, the interviewee has to avoid the remaining one. Hypothesis generation, testing, remembering the previously reached principles and the ability to abandon them (Lezak, 1995) are similar to the other card sorting tests.

The main advantage of this test is the simplicity of administration, which would allow researchers to infer abilities related to high-level functions with a minimum of stimulus, recording and scoring requirements. However, due to the fact that its primary dependent variable expresses the subject's performance through a narrow range of values, the 9CST should be considered in principle as a screening instrument and until more studies were developed on the matter. This new test does not intend to replace the other card sorting or executive tests but complement them. Taking into account the advantages and disadvantages of the different instruments, better inferences could be accomplished.

Previous studies with 167 healthy subjects indicated a poor but significant correlation between the WCST and the 9CST in the number of categories achieved (r .41) as well as a similar pattern of response (with coefficients of the same magnitude and direction) when demographic, intelligence and personality variables were considered. Significant correlations were observed with an abbreviated version of the Raven test (reduced to 9 cards) as well as with age, education and risk of neurological damage whereas non- significant correlations were obtained with the personality assessment screener test (PAS), sex and manual preference (Vigliecca, Argüello, Castillo, Fernandez and Ontivero, 2001a).

"According to current theories, the frontal lobes control: conceptualization and abstract reasoning, mental flexibility, motor programming and executive control of action, resistance to interference, self-regulation, inhibitory control, and environmental autonomy. Each of these processes is needed for elaborating appropriate goal directed behaviors and for adapting the subject's response to new or challenging situations" (Dubois, Slachevsky, Litvan and Pillon, 2000). Since most of these cognitive demands are theoretically involved in both the WCST and the 9CST, in the present study we examined if the 9CST can be considered a valid measure of frontal function in the same way as the WCST. Nevertheless, taking into account the intrinsic design differences between both tests we considered that it could be useful to study also their relationships with other cognitive tests in order to see how these characteristics are empirically expressed. This is particularly relevant since, as in most of the psychological tests, the final clinical interpretation is generally conducted within the context of a comprehensive evaluation with information from different sources.

Objectives

1. To study the validity of the 9CST by means of: a) its correlation with the WCST (construct validity); and b) its capacity to differentiate between frontal vs. non-frontal patients as well as frontal patients vs. the healthy subjects (concurrent validity).
2. To study the test-retest and inter-scorer reliability.
3. Complementarily, a) to analyze the relationship between both card sorting tests and other neuropsychological tests in the three samples studied to see convergent and divergent results that may help to explain aspects of content validity; and b) just with exploratory purposes and pointing at a potential use of the 9CST as part of bigger batteries, to study the capacity of this test together with other neuropsychological tests to discriminate simultaneously the frontal, the non-frontal and the healthy subjects.

There is a need for this kind of comprehensive neuropsychological studies in executive functions, particularly considering that the complementary neuropsychological information collected in previous card sorting studies has been provided as part of the "methodology" research section, i.e., as a sample parameter (Chase-Carmichael et al, 1999, Delis et al, 1992; Heaton et al, 1993) or as the criteria implemented to include or exclude subjects (Goldberg and Podell, 2000). For Spanish neuropsychological instruments this need is even more critical due to the lack of evidence- based studies on this matter.

METHODS

1. Validity

Data were obtained from a sample of 106 volunteers: 32 patients with anterior (frontal) encephalic lesions (A), 30 patients with posterior (temporal, parietal or occipital) encephalic lesions (P) and 44 healthy (H) subjects (adapted to daily life demands and without any known neurological or psychiatric disease). The three groups were matched by sex, age, educational background and manual preference (table 1). Subjects had to give their written informed consent to participate.

Table 1. Demographic data

GROUP	Age (Mean ± SD)	Education (%) 1st	2nd	3rd	Women (%)	Right- Handed Subjects (%)	N
Anterior	45.44 ± 14.77	50	44	6	44	90	32
Posterior	43.06 ± 13.98	40	53	6	43	90	30
Healthy	41.48 ± 16.44	38	47	13	48	91	44
Total	43.12 ± 15.23	42	48	9	45	90	106
	$F_{(2, 103)} = 0.62$, $p < 0.54$	$\chi^2 = 2.33$; df: 4; $p < 0.67$			$\chi^2 = 0.18$; df: 2; $p < 0.91$	$\chi^2 = 0.17$; df: 2; $p < 0.99$	
χ^2 : Chi square							

The sample of patients was made up of successive inpatients of the Cordoba Hospital-Neurology and Neurosurgery Service, a public hospital for adults. In order to be included in the neuropsychological study, in principle patients had to be alert, and willing to begin and finish the complete battery of tests, independently of their relative capacity or willingness to perform some of the subtests in particular. In order to be included specifically in the card sorting- study, patients had to begin and finish the first card- sorting test, which was initiated after the neuropsychological battery had been administered (see below). All the patients who will be described in the present study had only focal brain lesions confined to the anterior or the posterior areas (patients with anterior "and" posterior damage were excluded). Lesions were confirmed by CT scan and/or MRI techniques and independently of the neuropsychological study. Most of the lesions were also confirmed by anatomopathology.

The lesion laterality in function of the etiology is shown in table 2. Unfortunately, most of the bilateral focal brain lesions were frontal (12/14). Of the two subjects who presented posterior bilateral lesions, one of them had suffered from a head trauma and the other one, two strokes on different occasions (without other associated visible lesions). Consequently, the effect of the lesion laterality on the dependent variables was also controlled as an additional measure.

Table 2. Classification of the focal brain lesions in function of the etiology and laterality

ETIOLOGY	Lesion laterality					
	Left		Right		Bilateral	
	A	P	A	P	A	P
HEM STR	0	0	0	0	0	1
ISQ STR	0	0	1	0	0	0
HT	0	0	0	0	1	1
AVM	2	3	1	1	2	0
MAL TU	2	8	10	3	3	0
BEN TU	1	3	2	4	0	0
ANEU	0	0	0	0	4	0
OTHERS	1	2	0	4	2	0
Totals	6	16	14	12	12	2
χ^2 = df: 7	0.74; p=0.99		9.34; p=0.23		9.91; p=0.19	

HEM STR: Hemorrhagic stroke, ISQ STR. Ischemic stroke, HT: Head trauma, AVM: Arterio-venous malformation, MAL TU: Malignant tumor, BEN TU: Benign tumor, ANEU: Aneurysm. A: Anterior; P: Posterior. χ^2 : Chi square.

Both groups of patients did not differ either in their time (divided in months and recoded in four categories) since onset of condition (Chi square (χ^2) = 0.26; df: 3; p<0.97) or in the presence of other neurological risk (previous hypoxia, head trauma with loss of consciousness, malnutrition, drug abuse, etc.): χ^2 = 0.03; df: 1; p<0.86. Five patients of each group suffered from hemiparesis (brachial strength 4/5) and no one suffered from aphasia. All these patients had a score ≥ 90% in items of orientation (person, time and place) without differences between the A and P patients in these variables (personal orientation: (F (1, 60) = 0.55, p<0.46); time and place orientation: (F (1, 60) = 0.02, p<0.88)). All these patients were also able to identify four basic shapes (triangle, square, circle and cross) and four colors (blue, red, green and yellow), which were explored by "name" and "touch" items, for example, "Tell me what color is this" / "touch the color red".

Excluding the card sorting tests, the other cognitive tests that will be shown in this study were selected from a neuropsychological battery for Spanish speakers (Vigliecca and Aleman, 2000; Vigliecca, Martini, Aleman and Jaime, 2001b; Vigliecca, 2004), which included tasks of sustained and shifting attention, copy of alternating or repetitive graph patterns, verbal fluency, abstraction and calculations as well as tests on reading, writing and verbal and visual memory.

The complementary and coincident neuropsychological tests administered to the three samples of subjects were: Verbal auditory sustained attention (phonemic discrimination of the letter "A" (by tapping the desk) among a series of 60 letters said by the interviewer. Indexes: errors of commission (0-42) and errors of omission (0-18). Months forward (oral response). Indexes: number of errors (0-12) and time required to say the months in the usual order (maximum time of administration, i.e., maximum waiting time when inability was evident: 3

minutes). Months backward (oral response). Indexes: number of errors (0-12) and time required to say the months in reversed order (maximum time: 6 minutes). Constructional praxis (written response): copy of 4 graph sequences, each one scored from 0 to 3 (total 0-12) according to reproduction accuracy. Forward digit recall (repeating the digits said by the interviewer) (reproduction accuracy scored 0-9) and backward digit recall (repeating the digits said by the interviewer in reversed order) (reproduction accuracy scored 0-8). Written verbal fluency in one minute after a command ("*In one minute write as much as you can about what there is and what is happening in this room*"). Indexes: maximum number of words written, grapheme adequacy (scored 0-3 according to legibility) and syntactic complexity (scored from 0 to 3, which reads, 0: lack of expression, 1: enumerative, 2: enumerative with some narrative sentences, 3: all narrative)). Dictation of a sentence and two arithmetic operations: one addition and one subtraction (scored 0-3 according to reproduction accuracy and organization). Written arithmetic calculations (resolution of the previous dictated operations) each one scored from 0 to 3 (total 0-6) according to accuracy. Subtracting serial sevens from 100 to 30 (oral response). Indexes: Accuracy (0-10) and time required to do the task (maximum time: 6 minutes). Oral verbal fluency in one minute: Phonemic word association (maximum number of words, which started with "F"). Reading (a story). Indexes: Oral expression (scored 0-3) and comprehension/ abstraction (scored 0-3). Visual memory (recognition of only one face among six possible options): number of attempts (out of 3) necessary to recognize the previously seen target face (scored from 3 (one attempt) to 0). Visual memory: Retrieval (written response) of a complex figure (scored from 0 to 8 according to reproduction accuracy (number of elements and organization)). Paired associated words (delayed recall after three learning trials, which consists of remembering a list of 10 pairs of words by saying the second word after the first one has been given by the interviewer as a cue). Indexes: number of recalled easy pairs (0-5) number of recalled hard pairs (0-5). Semantic verbal memory: naming by picture confrontation (number of correct names out of 60).

Taking into account the motor and sensorial components of each task, the purest sensorial (visual) task of the battery was the face recognition, which required just pointing to the target stimulus as a motor component.

Additional measure: Considering that this study was part of a larger neuropsychological research and that more tests were administered to some patients (according to clinical needs) and to other groups of healthy subjects (according to research purposes), this information was also taken into account in the present study to get more and better interpretations. Specifically, and given that: a) in the clinical sample we administered nine Raven's matrices (Raven, 1997; 1999) to 74% of the patients, and b) we had another paired sample of 50 healthy subjects to whom this tests was administered, we decided to analyze if the studied samples differed also in this parameter which, in previous studies with healthy subjects turned out to be significantly correlated to the 9CST and the WCST performances (Vigliecca et al, 2001a). Although this task also required just pointing to the target stimulus as motor response, the underlying cognitive function could be, supposedly (Duncan et al, 2000), frontal convergent.

The Raven's paired sample of healthy subjects was (mean ± standard deviation) 44.8 ± 18.49 years old and was composed of: a) 54% of women, b) 50%, 44% and 6% of subjects with 1st, 2nd or 3rd level of education respectively, and c) 94% of right handed subjects. Non-significant differences were observed among the three groups studied in any of these sample variables according to parametric and non- parametric statistical analyses. (The Raven's paired sample was extracted from its own normative sample and was independent of the rest of the samples mentioned in the present study).

The order of presentation of the tests was as follows: the Spanish neuropsychological battery in first place, and then the two card sorting tests, which were interchanged in its order of presentation for each subject. When the Raven matrices were administered, they came in last place. Subjects who count on the necessary perceptual, motor and command understanding resources to carry out a card- sorting task participated of the study. Some patients (nine) who completed the 9CST were unable to complete the WCST, but not vice versa.

The WCST was administered in an abbreviated form with 64 cards but following standard procedures (Heaton et al, 1993).

The 9CST (figure 1) was administered in its paper version, which involved the organization of the nine cards on the table. The three sorting principles (form, size and color) could be organized in a simple or in a combined array. In the combined array, two of the visual attributes presented in the card figures should be organized in a row x column configuration (diagonal designs were not feasible). In an attempt to avoid, as much as possible, the interference of verbal conditionings, particularly in aphasic, pre- school, or poorly educated people, minimal verbal instructions were designed to guide the task. The primary commands were: "Order", "you can order better" (when the subject reached only a simple array) and "order in another way" (when the subject reached a combined array). The subject had to communicate his/her arrays to the interviewer so as to receive feedback. There were many possible responses but only three simple and three combined arrays were logically correct. These six logical arrays were reinforced. The reinforcements were "well done" and "very well done" for the successful simple and combined arrays respectively. When no array was reached, the command "order" was repeated or reformulated by a similar one such as "sort" or "you have to put the equal ones together".

The test lasted until the three combined arrays were reached or until the subject uttered (and it was evident that) he/she was not able to find another one (or any one at all). However, and as much as possible, the subject was stimulated to find the maximum number of arrays during seven minutes, which was the maximum time of administration when the failure was evident. If the subject was still working or trying to find a principle when the seven minutes had passed, the task was not interrupted.

In this chapter, only the number of correct combined arrays (from now on "categories") and the time required to reach those arrays were considered. One combined array (one category) was scored with one point. Consequently, in this study, the possible number of 9CST categories ranged from 0 to 3.

As this is a test of free distribution, the stimuli and details of administration and interpretation are available for all those professionals who request them.

2. Reliability

Test-retest (intra- scorer) and inter-scorer reliability data were obtained from a sample of 40 healthy volunteers. They were 18 female subjects and 22 male subjects of 29.62 ± 21.81 years of age (range: 6- 84; distribution: ≤ 10: 27%; 11-30: 25%; 31-50: 30%; ≥51: 18%) and

7.95 ± 4.77 years of education (range: 0- 18; distribution: first level of education: 62%; second level: 22%; third level or higher: 15%).

For the intra-scorer reliability study, the 40 volunteers were re evaluated (according to their accessibility) after an averaged inter- test interval of 10.30 ± 9.47 days (range: 4-30). These interval trends are very common in our clinical setting (particularly between pre and post surgical evaluations) according to institutional and patient's needs. The correlation between the inter-test interval length and the retest performance was also analyzed.

For the inter-scorer reliability study, two different trained examiners, acting independently, scored the data registered for the 40 subjects in the 9CST administration protocol.

3. Complementary Studies

a. The correlation between both card sorting tests and all the complementary neuropsychological tests administered was analyzed in the three samples studied.
b. Secondarily, and in order to show, with exploratory purposes, the capacity of the 9CST in conjunction with other neuropsychological tests to discriminate simultaneously the frontal, the non-frontal and the healthy subjects, several tests were incorporated into an evaluation model which analyzed the individual and common discrimination properties of each test[34]. With this purpose, not only the correlation between both card-sorting tests and the rest of neuropsychological tests was taken into account but also some previous findings. For example, and surely caused by the simultaneous participation of either anterior and posterior brain areas, the easy paired associated words demonstrated to be a good predictor of the differentiation of the A, P and H samples in a previous work of our laboratory (Vigliecca, 2004). Likewise, naming has been reported in the literature as a function associated to the temporal lobes (Hirono et al, 2001; Kemppainen et al, 2003; Watson, Welsh-Bohmer, Hoffman, Lowe and Rubin, 1999). As a poor performance was theoretically expected for the P patients in these two tasks, they were included into the discriminant model as equivalent variables. The combination of these two variables along with some 9CST indexes and other 9CST divergent variables, which would result from the analysis described in section 3a, was expected to produce a good discrimination among the three samples.

Statistical Analysis

Considering that the primary indexes of executive performance analyzed were the number of categories completed in the 9CST and the WCST, both with a narrow range of values, most of the statistical analyses were carried out with the Spearman rank correlation coefficient and the median test. For dependent observations, Wilcoxon matched pair test was used. The complementary neuropsychological evaluation, considered as whole, was analyzed by ANOVA. The median test and the discriminant analysis were carried out to analyze the

---

[34] Obviously this is just an example and other discriminative models can be constructed.

simultaneous discrimination of the three samples in section 3b. Since not all the subjects completed all the neuropsychological tests, the number of cases for each analysis was not homogeneous (missing cases deleted).

RESULTS

1. Validity

As the coincident neuropsychological tests administered to the A, P and H samples turned out to be internally consistent (standardized Cronbach´s alpha coefficients $\geq$ 0.85 for the subtests dealing with correct responses in any sample) these test scores were added as an index of global cognitive performance. Although the A group tended to show a better overall cognitive performance than the P group, non significant differences were observed between these two groups of patients according to a one way ANOVA (A: 6.35 ± 1.00; P: 5.71 ± 1.80; $F (1, 51) = 2.65$, p<0.11) [35]. As expected, by incorporating the H group (7.51 ± 0.99) to the ANOVA, results became highly significant ($F (2, 93) = 17.71$, p<0.000), thus indicating the sensitivity of this neuropsychological battery to detect brain lesions.

The Spearman rank correlation coefficients observed between the WCST and 9CST indexes are shown in table 3. The WCST indexes analyzed were: a) number of categories completed, b) number of errors, c) number of perseverative errors, and d) number of "other" errors (i.e., when the respond card did not match any dimension on the stimulus card). The 9CST indexes were: a) number of categories completed, b) total time elapsed until the last category was completed, c) averaged time required by category, and d) efficiency (i.e. number of categories completed as a function of the time required by category scored from 0 to 60. [36]). For each card-sorting test, only one factor was extracted by the principal component method, for these four indexes analyzed[37]. The factor loadings were 0.86 or over for the 9CST indexes, and 0.94 or over for the WCST indexes, except for the "other" errors in which the factor loading was of 0.34.

As can be seen in table 3, the 9CST total time elapsed did not correlate significantly with any of the WCST measures, and the WCST "other" errors only correlated significantly with the 9CST number of categories completed. The WCST number of categories completed, correlated significantly with all the 9CST performance measures except for the 9CST total time elapsed. Meanwhile, the 9CST number of categories completed, correlated significantly with all the WCST performance measures analyzed. Consequently, from now on we will only analyze the 9CST and the WCST number of categories completed unless otherwise indicated.

---

[35] By using z scores, results were identical.

[36] In this case, the number of categories was scored from 0 to 12, which is the scoring system applied when the simple arrays are considered, and the time required by category was recoded from 1 to 5 so that the smallest number indicated the poorest performance. Both indexes were multiplied to obtain efficiency.

[37] The 9CST was also internally consistent: By categorizing the 9CST time responses into five categories of performance, the internal consistency among these four 9CST indexes, expressed by the standardized Cronbach´s alpha coefficient, was 0.84.

Table 3. Correlation coefficients between the WCST and 9CST indexes

	WCST CATEGORIES	WCST ERRORS	WCST PERSEVERATIVE ERRORS	WCST "OTHER" ERRORS
9CST CATEGORIES	0.576	-0.606	-0.577	-0.226
	6.882	-7.439	-6.898	-2.266
	0.000*	0.000*	0.000*	0.025*
9CST TOTAL TIME	0.007	0.086	0.022	0.064
	0.069	0.839	0.214	0.629
	0.944	0.403	0.831	0.531
9CST TIME/CATEGORY	0.280	-0.203	-0.234	-0.079
	2.847	-2.021	-2.349	-0.777
	0.005*	0.046*	0.021*	0.439
9CST EFICIENCY	0.492	-0.492	-0.486	-0.174
	5.503	-5.503	-5.425	-1.724
	0.000*	0.000*	0.000*	0.088

From top to bottom, for each cell: Spearman rank correlation coefficient, t (N-2),
p-level (* significant correlations at 0.05 level).
9CST: Nine card sorting test; WCST: Wisconsin card sorting test. N=97.

The distributions of frequencies according to the common mean for the A, P and H samples in the number of categories completed in both card- sorting tests are shown in table 4. When considering only the performance differences between the A and P patients, the WCST (χ^2 = 6.47; df: 1; p<0.01) showed a trend to be a better predictor of this difference than the 9CST (χ^2 = 4.25; df: 1; p<0.04). On the contrary, when healthy subjects were incorporated to the analysis, results indicated that the 9CST was the best predictor of this difference, surely because 64% of the healthy subjects showed a score above the median in this test (χ^2 = 13.00; df: 1; p<0.0003) against a 45% in the WCST (χ^2 = 6.18; df: 1; p<0.0129). Both card sorting tests were useful to differentiate between the A patients from the other two groups but neither of them differentiated the P patients from the healthy subjects (9CST: χ^2 = 2.09; df: 1; p<0.147; WCST: χ^2 = 0.128; df: 1; p<0.719). As a result, the WCST did not differentiate the patients considered as whole from the healthy subjects (χ^2 = 1.82; df: 1; p<0.177) but the 9CST did so (χ^2 = 9.17; df: 1; p<0.002).

Table 4. Distributions of frequencies according to the median for the A, P and H samples in the number of categories completed in both card- sorting tests

Test	Sample	Median $\leq$	Median $>$	Chi square df = 2
9CST	A	25	7	13.001
	P	16	14	p = 0.001
	H	16	28	(Overall median: 1)
WCST	A	24	5	7.796
	P	12	12	p = 0.020
	H	24	20	(Overall median: 2)

9CST: Nine card sorting test; WCST: Wisconsin card sorting test.
A: Anterior; P: Posterior; H: Healthy.

Additional Measures

The A patients had a poorer performance than the P patients in the nine Raven's matrices analyzed by the median test ($\chi^2 = 4.11$; df: 1; p<0.042, median: 4). The A patients had also a poorer performance than the H subjects ($\chi^2 = 5,95$; df: 1; p<0,014, median 6) but the P patients did not statistically differentiate from the H subjects ($\chi^2 = 1.16$; df: 1; p<0.280, median 6). The abbreviated Raven's test correlated with both card- sorting tests. The correlation was positive for the categories completed in both card sorting tests and negative for time (in the 9CST) and errors (in the WCST). The 9CST total time elapsed and the WCST "other" errors did not correlate significantly with the Raven test (Spearman r = -0.34; t (47): -1.69; p<0.097 and Spearman r = -0.19; t (45): -1.34; p<0.186, respectively) but the rest of the 9CST and WCST indexes did so (Spearman r $\geq$ 0.43; t (47) $\geq$ 3.31; p$\leq$ 0.002 and Spearman r $\geq$ 0.45; t (45) $\geq$ 3.37; p$\leq$ 0.001).

Non significant differences were observed between patients with unilateral or bilateral lesions neither in the nine Raven's matrices ($\chi^2 = 0,00$; df: 1; p<0,988, median: 4) nor in the global cognitive performance (unilateral: 5.93 $\pm$ 1.52; bilateral: P: 6.52 $\pm$ 1.08; ANOVA (F (1, 51) = 1.57, p<0.21). As can be seen in table 5, and by excluding bilateral lesions, in this sample of patients there were no differences between left and right brain lesions in the number of categories completed according to the median for any of the card sorting tests (chi squares near zero for all the contingency tables). Besides, when considering only bilateral lesions, the performance in both the 9CST and the WCST was exactly the same: nine out of eleven patients showed a score below the median. Similarly, and according to the median test, non significant differences were observed between patients with unilateral or bilateral lesions neither in the 9CST ($\chi^2 = 1.25$; df: 1; p<0.263, median: 1) nor in the WCST ($\chi^2 = 0.36$; df: 1; p<0.550, median:2) [38].

Table 5. Card sorting performance and lesion laterality

Localization		Median	9CST	WCST
Anterior	Right	$\leq$	12	11
		>	3	2
	Left	$\leq$	4	5
		>	2	1
Posterior	Right	$\leq$	6	4
		>	5	4
	Left	$\leq$	8	7
		>	8	7
Totals			48	41

9CST: Nine card sorting test; WCST: Wisconsin card sorting test.

---

[38] Just for informative purposes, from the 9 patients who complete the 9CST but not the WCST, only one P patient (with a unilateral right lesion) showed a score above the median in the 9CST.

2. Reliability

Reliability coefficients for both intra and inter scorer evaluations were ≥0.79 for all the 9CST indexes (table 6). In the intra- scorer study, practice effects were only observed in those 9CST indexes involving response time (Wilcoxon Matched Pairs Test: z ≥ 2.71; N = 40; p≤0.006) but not in the number of categories completed (Wilcoxon Matched Pairs Test: z = 1.59; N = 40; p<0.109) (table 7). The correlations between the inter-test interval and the retest performance were not significant for all the 9CST indexes (Spearman r ≤ 0.16; t (38) ≤ 0.99; p≥0.326) except for the total time elapsed (Spearman r = 0.34; t (38): 2.20; p<0.034), which demonstrated a significant and positive correlation with the length of the inter-test interval (the longer the inter-test interval the longer the time required to do the retest). Non-significant differences were observed between the two scorers in any of the 9CST indexes (Wilcoxon Matched Pairs Test: z ≤ 0.81; N = 40; p≥0.423) (table 7).

Table 6. Correlation coefficients in reliability studies

	9CST CATEGORIES	9CST TOTAL TIME	9CST TIME/CATEGORY	9CST EFICIENCY
INTRA SCORERS	0.875	0.824	0.794	0.861
	11.177	8.957	8.065	10.442
	0.000*	0.000*	0.000*	0.000*
INTER SCORERS	0.975	0.988	0.986	0.975
	27.429	40.385	37.323	27.288
	0.000*	0.000*	0.000*	0.000*

From top to bottom for each cell: Spearman rank correlation coefficient, t (N-2), p-level (* significant correlations at 0.05 level). N=40.

Table 7. Score changes in reliability studies

9CST	CATEGORIES	TOTAL TIME (Sec)	TIME/ CATEGORY (Sec)	EFICIENCY (Categories)
INTRA SCORERS	0.15 ± 0.53	-90.80 ± 207.81*	-78.46 ± 190.65*	1.95 ± 3.80*
INTER SCORERS	0.00 ± 0.22	3.75 ± 26.67	0.25 ± 14.36	-0.15 ± 1.72

Mean ± SD of the difference between evaluations. * p<0.05 (t Student and Wilcoxon matched paired tests). N = 40.

3. Complementary Studies

A. Correlation between Both Card Sorting Tests and the other Neuropsychological Tests

Despite the similarities previously described between the two card sorting tests, there were some differences. The most interesting difference was the pattern of correlations with all the complementary neuropsychological tests administered, specifically for the A group of patients (table 8). While the 9CST correlated significantly with 46% of these subtests, the WCST only correlated significantly with the backward digit recall test.

For the rest of the groups analyzed, the performance of both tests was in most of the items coincident (tables 9 -10) and, considering the total sample (table 11), both tests correlated significantly with more than the 70% of the complementary neuropsychological tests administered. Consequently, the global index of cognitive performance turned out to be significantly correlated with both card sorting tests in all the groups analyzed except for the A sample with the WCST (table 12) [39].

The 9CST did not correlate with either face recognition or with months forward (errors) in any of the samples studied (tables 8-11). Neither did the 9CST correlate with written verbal fluency (tables 8-10) in the A, P and H samples considered separately (In spite of that, the index of number of words correlated with the 9CST in the total sample (table 11)). As a result face recognition, written verbal fluency and months forward were considered as 9CST divergent tasks for the A, P and H samples.

Table 8. Correlations between the two card sorting tests and all the subtests and indexes administered in the complementary neuropsychological evaluation in frontal patients

	WCST	9CST
1a. Verbal auditory sustained attention Errors of commission	-0.360	-0.410*
1b. Verbal auditory sustained attention: Errors of omission	-0.327	-0.447*
2a. Months forward: Errors	-0.036	0.198
2b. Months backward: Errors	-0.166	-0.439*
2c. Months forward: Time	-0.069	-0.333
2d. Months backward: Time	-0.150	-0.462*
3. Constructional praxis (copy of graph sequences)	0.059	0.105
4a. Forward digit recall	0.284	0.334
4b. Backward digit recall	0.423*	0.440*
5a. Written verbal fluency in one minute: Number of words	0.059	0.148
5b. Written verbal fluency in one minute: Grapheme adequacy	0.134	0.056
5c. Written verbal fluency in one minute: Syntactic complexity	-0.277	-0.088
6. Dictation	-0.109	0.359
7. Written arithmetic calculations	0.176	0.429*
8a. Subtracting serial sevens: Accuracy	0.173	0.387*
8b. Subtracting serial sevens: Time	-0.068	-0.469*
9. Oral verbal fluency/one minute: Phonemic word association	0.304	0.462*
10. Reading (expression)	0.098	0.358
11. Reading (comprehension/ abstraction)	0.269	0.465*
12. Visual memory (face recognition)	0.126	-0.110
13. Visual memory: Retrieval of a complex figure	0.209	0.087
14a. Paired associated words: easy pairs (delayed recall)	0.355	0.499*
14b. Paired associated words: hard pairs (delayed recall)	0.202	0.352
15. Semantic verbal memory: Naming by picture confrontation	0.121	0.292

WCST: Wisconsin card sorting test, N always $\geq$ 27; 9CST: Nine card sorting test, N always $\geq$ 29. Spearman rank correlation coefficients *p<0.05.

---

[39] In this last statistical analysis, the cases were deleted if only one item of the battery was not completed. When missing cases were replaced by the mean, results did not change.

Table 9. Correlations between the two card sorting tests and all the subtests and indexes administered in the complementary neuropsychological evaluation in temporal, parietal and occipital patients

	WCST	9CST
1a. Verbal auditory sustained attention Errors of commission	-0.228	-0.107
1b. Verbal auditory sustained attention: Errors of omission	-0.335	-0.451*
2a. Months forward: Errors	0.029	-0.161
2b. Months backward: Errors	-0.325	-0.584*
2c. Months forward: Time	-0.589*	-0.707*
2d. Months backward: Time	-0.548*	-0.513*
3. Constructional praxis (copy of graph sequences)	0.419*	0.595*
4a. Forward digit recall	0.562*	0.393*
4b. Backward digit recall	0.479*	0.474*
5a. Written verbal fluency in one minute: Number of words	0.275	0.287
5b. Written verbal fluency in one minute: Grapheme adequacy	0.178	0.192
5c. Written verbal fluency in one minute: Syntactic complexity	0.353	0.150
6. Dictation	0.170	0.351
7. Written arithmetic calculations	0.173	0.222
8a. Subtracting serial sevens: Accuracy	0.252	0.302
8b. Subtracting serial sevens: Time	-0.216	-0.219
9. Oral verbal fluency/one minute: Phonemic word association	0.335	0.456*
10. Reading (expression)	0.468*	0.399*
11. Reading (comprehension/ abstraction)	0.445*	0.301
12. Visual memory (face recognition)	0.593*	0.254
13. Visual memory: Retrieval of a complex figure	0.543*	0.557*
14a. Paired associated words: easy pairs (delayed recall)	-0.052	0.350
14b. Paired associated words: hard pairs (delayed recall)	0.143	0.274
15. Semantic verbal memory: Naming by picture confrontation	0.350	0.447*

WCST: Wisconsin card sorting test, N always $\geq$ 21; 9CST: Nine card sorting test, N always $\geq$ 27. Spearman rank correlation coefficients *$p<0.05$.

Table 10. Correlations between the two card sorting tests and all the subtests and indexes administered in the complementary neuropsychological evaluation in healthy subjects

	WCST	9CST
1a. Verbal auditory sustained attention Errors of commission	0.143	0.116
1b. Verbal auditory sustained attention: Errors of omission	-0.158	0.049
2a. Months forward: Errors [1]	-------	-------
2b. Months backward: Errors	-0.104	-0.114
2c. Months forward: Time	-0.153	-0.194
2d. Months backward: Time	-0.121	-0.011
3. Constructional praxis (copy of graph sequences)	0.318*	0.358*
4a. Forward digit recall	0.267	0.134
4b. Backward digit recall	0.273	0.210
5a. Written verbal fluency in one minute: Number of words	0.351*	0.199
5b. Written verbal fluency in one minute: Grapheme adequacy	0.298	0.265
5c. Written verbal fluency in one minute: Syntactic complexity	0.244	0.092
6. Dictation	0.238	0.369*
7. Written arithmetic calculations	0.027	0.265
8a. Subtracting serial sevens: Accuracy	0.145	0.374*
8b. Subtracting serial sevens: Time	-0.152	0.069
9. Oral verbal fluency/one minute: Phonemic word association	0.138	0.141
10. Reading (expression)	0.687*	0.443*
11. Reading (comprehension/ abstraction)	0.290	0.125
12. Visual memory (face recognition)	0.125	-0.047
13. Visual memory: Retrieval of a complex figure	0.283	0.250
14a. Paired associated words: easy pairs (delayed recall)	0.495*	0.405*
14b. Paired associated words: hard pairs (delayed recall)	0.694*	0.441*
15. Semantic verbal memory: Naming by picture confrontation	0.204	0.333*

WCST: Wisconsin card sorting test; 9CST: Nine card sorting test, N always $\geq$ 43. Spearman rank correlation coefficients *p<0.05. [1] Months forward: Errors: 0 mean, 0 variance.

Table 11. Correlations between the two card sorting tests and all the subtests and indexes administered in the complementary neuropsychological evaluation in the total sample

	WCST	9CST
1a. Verbal auditory sustained attention Errors of commission	-0.073	-0.084
1b. Verbal auditory sustained attention: Errors of omission	-0.256*	-0.311*
2a. Months forward: Errors	-0.032	-0.064
2b. Months backward: Errors	-0.201*	-0.375*
2c. Months forward: Time	-0.281*	-0.453*
2d. Months backward: Time	-0.261*	-0.319*
3. Constructional praxis (copy of graph sequences)	0.338*	0.451*
4a. Forward digit recall	0.380*	0.368*
4b. Backward digit recall	0.407*	0.414*
5a. Written verbal fluency in one minute: Number of words	0.297*	0.315*
5b. Written verbal fluency in one minute: Grapheme adequacy	0.193	0.149
5c. Written verbal fluency in one minute: Syntactic complexity	0.071	0.005
6. Dictation	0.131	0.369*
7. Written arithmetic calculations	0.147	0.305*
8a. Subtracting serial sevens: Accuracy	0.244*	0.398*
8b. Subtracting serial sevens: Time	-0.192	-0.204*
9. Oral verbal fluency/one minute: Phonemic word association	0.312*	0.428*
10. Reading (expression)	0.462*	0.399*
11. Reading (comprehension/ abstraction)	0.342*	0.283*
12. Visual memory (face recognition)	0.243*	0.096
13. Visual memory: Retrieval of a complex figure	0.353*	0.385*
14a. Paired associated words: easy pairs (delayed recall)	0.368*	0.436*
14b. Paired associated words: hard pairs (delayed recall)	0.443*	0.375*
15. Semantic verbal memory: Naming by picture confrontation	0.240*	0.373*

WCST: Wisconsin card sorting test, N always ≥ 92; 9CST: Nine card sorting test, N always ≥ 100. Spearman rank correlation coefficients *p<0.05.

Table 12. Card sorting performance and global index of cognitive performance

	9CST	WCST
A	0.475	0.272
	2.808	1.413
	0.009*	0.169
	29	27
P	0.594	0.461
	3.466	2.268
	0.002*	0.035*
	24	21
H	0.386	0.441
	2.680	3.148
	0.010*	0.003*
	43	43
Total	0.526	0.416
	6.000	4.314
	0.000*	0.000*
	96	91

From top to bottom, for each cell: Spearman rank correlation coefficient, t (N-2), p-level (*significant correlations at 0.05 level) and N. 9CST: Nine card sorting test; WCST: Wisconsin card sorting test. A: Anterior; P: Posterior; H: Healthy.

B. Simultaneous Discrimination of the Frontal, Non-Frontal and Healthy Subjects

The 9CST divergent tests (face recognition and months forward) were incorporated into a model of analysis together with: a) the 9CST number of categories completed, b) the 9CST time required by category, c) the naming test and e) the delayed recall of the easy paired associated words.

As can be seen in table 13, more than 80% of the A patients had a score above the median in face recognition (table 13). Probably for this reason, face recognition was not associated with any of the two card sorting tests in the A group (table 8). Considering just the sample of patients in table 13, the difference between the A and P patients in face recognition was statistically significant ($\chi^2 = 4.70$; df.: 1; p<0.030). Considering the P patients and H subjects, the difference between these two groups was also statistically significant ($\chi^2 = 10.31$; df.:1; p<0.001). In other words, this very simple test of visual memory turned out to be useful to differentiate the P patients from the other two groups.

Naming showed a discrimination pattern, which resembled that of face recognition (having the P group the lowest score (table 13)). Conversely, written verbal fluency and easy-paired associated words, significantly discriminated the H group from the other two groups (table 13). Although 55% of the A patients (vs. 44% of the P patients) showed a score above the median in the easy paired associated words and 40% of the A patients (vs. 61% of the P patients) showed a score above the median in written verbal fluency, the difference between A and P patients did not reach significance in these tasks (table 13). The very simple test of months forward, significantly differentiated the H group (100% accuracy) from the P group (89% accuracy) ($\chi^2 = 4.64$; df: 1; p<0.031), but the H and A subjects (who were 93% accurate) ($\chi^2 = 2.85$; df: 1; p<0.091) and the P and A subjects did not differ in this parameter ($\chi^2 = 0.29$; df: 1; p<0.586).

Consistently, a discriminant analysis indicated, for this model of evaluation, a percentage of correctly predicted cases of 83% for the A lesions, 73% for the P lesions and 81% for the H group.

Table 13. Distributions of frequencies according to the median for the A,
P and H samples on naming, written verbal fluency and delayed
recall of easy paired associated words

Test	Sample	Median ≤	Median >	Chi square df = 2
Face Recognition	A	5	26	11.475
	P	12	17	p = 0.003
	H	4	39	(Overall median: 3)
Naming	A	13	18	12.429
	P	19	9	p = 0.002
	H	11	32	(Overall median: 43)
Written Verbal Fluency	A	18	12	14.949
	P	11	17	p = 0.001
	H	7	36	(Overall median: 14)
Easy Paired Associated Words	A	14	17	14.774
	P	18	9	p = 0.001
	H	9	34	(Overall median: 3)

CONCLUSION

Present results demonstrate that the 9CST can be a very useful screening test to detect frontal impaired patients when they are compared with healthy people. 9CST also can be a useful tool to detect frontal impaired patients when they are compared with patients impaired in posterior encephalic areas who have similar cognitive resources in alternative tasks such as attention, discrimination, memory, copy and verbal ability. In addition, the 9CST was correlated to the WCST, which has been reported as a valid test for the discrimination of frontal neurological impaired patients (Heaton et al, 1993, Stuss and Levine, 2002). The 9CST also demonstrated a suitable reliability as indicated by intra and inter scorer reliability coefficients.

Unexpectedly, since we were working with a supposed "one shot" test and with a rather short inter-test interval, in the intra-scorer study, practice effects were only observed in those 9CST indexes involving response time but not in the number of categories completed. So, we could affirm that at least the cognitive organization of the stimuli by rows and columns (i.e., the number of categories completed by the combined arrays) constituted a stable parameter in the present sample and that executive performance could reliably be studied in longitudinal approaches by means of this 9CST index. Conversely, the total time elapsed until the last category was completed was sensitive even to the inter-test interval variations.

Lesions of the frontal lobes do not to disrupt cognitive functions as obviously as do postcentral lesions (Lezak, 1995; Vigliecca 2004). Rather, frontal lobe damage may be conceptualized as disrupting reciprocal relationships between the major functional systems

(Lezak, 1995). The frontal functions depend on the distinct connections of the various sectors of the frontal cortex with posterior association cortex (Jacobs, 2004; Petrides, 2005). For example, posterior damage can affect WCST performance and both frontal and posterior activations have been reported in WCST-functional neuroimaging studies (Stuss and Levine, 2002). As well, from the WCST original study (Heaton et al, 1993), we could affirm that as much a frontal as a non- frontal lesion may cause an impaired performance on this task.

Theoretically speaking, although not all the patients with posterior lesions will have perceptual or memory problems, when they do have these problems, they can be expected to have secondary problems in executive tests involving these cognitive resources (Slomine et al, 2002). But some persons may have problems in executive functioning when their posterior cortex and/or its functions are preserved, i.e., when those persons know exactly what to do but are not able to do it. In fact, this seems to be the case for the patients of the present study: Apparently all of them shared almost the same ability to understand the situation but only some of them (most of whom were P patients) were able to consciously build a plan and execute it. These P patients were similar in their card sorting performance to the H subjects. What will happen with the card sorting performance when the P patients have a poorer general cognitive ability than the A ones is a question that remains to be answered in future studies.

In the present study as well as in the WCST original one (Heaton et al, 1993), the non-frontal patients showed a significant higher performance than the frontal patients in intelligence or reasoning measures, as indicated by the nine Raven's matrices in the present study and, apparently, by the WAIS full scale IQ in the WCST one. But in the WCST adult study, the non- frontal patients significantly differentiated from healthy subjects in card sorting performance while in the current study they did not. Coincidentally, in the WCST study the non-frontal patients significantly differentiated from healthy subjects in the full scale IQ while in the present one they did not differentiate in the nine Raven's matrices. So it is possible that in conjunction with a bias in sample selection (favoring the most skillful non-frontal patients) there can also be an association between executive and intelligence functions.

If intelligence has to do with the capacity to solve problems purposefully, effectively and plastically, hardly can the frontal function be distinguished from the intellectual one, if that difference exists at all (De Zubicaray 1998; Duncan et al, 2000; Gambini, Campana, Garghentini and Scarone, 2003; Obonsawin et al, 1999). By the way, the nine Raven's matrices in this work correlated with both the 9CST and WCST (see below). Likewise, when a sample of 55 high school students from 12 to 17 years old were evaluated by the neuropsychological battery for Spanish speakers (including 40 subtests plus the WCST, the 9CST and the nine Raven's matrices), one of the tests which demonstrated the best and more encompassing correlation with academic achievement was the 9CST (Vigliecca, Castillo and Ontivero, 2002). Although that result could indicate a predictive and ecological validity of the 9CST in school settings, the meaning of this finding (as a manifestation of intelligence, executive function or prefrontal function) cannot be elucidated at present.

As regards the differences observed between the original WCST study (Heaton et al, 1993) and the present one, the number of cases, the sample characteristics and the matching variables cannot be discarded as explanations. Depending on how much the number of card sorting studies and cases increases, the differences among the samples studied and the causes of these differences will become clearer. Nevertheless, if researchers intentionally match groups (i.e. A and P patients) that are naturally different in their reasoning or cognitive ability (we still do not know in what direction) any result in card sorting performance will be doubtful. It would be ideal if we could take the intellectual function (or any eventual other cognitive measure that the researchers may want to analyze) only as a dependent variable (which, in fact is) and not as a sample variable or, what is worse, as a matching or a selection criterion to include or exclude subjects.

Kurtz, Wexler and Bell (2004) have taken a step forward in this kind of executive function approach, which contemplates other cognitive variables of analysis as dependent variables. Nevertheless, except for the divergent test of face memory (administered, apparently, only to healthy people), the other tests they used with schizophrenic patients did not coincide with the ones we used in the present study. In order to get more precise inferences from the independent and the dependent variables analyzed by the different laboratories, and the convergent and divergent results obtained, other authors should proceed in the same way.

Further research should be also carried out to study if the lack of differences between the P patients and healthy subjects and between the right and left hemisphere brain damaged patients in the present study were due to the fact that, in general, patients able to complete both card sorting tests participated in the study, specially considering that the WCST turned out to be, apparently, a restrictive recruitment factor.

At least 70% of the complementary neuropsychological tests administered correlated significantly with the number of categories completed in both card sorting tests, thus confirming the cognitive complexity of executive tests, involving the action of many more elemental functions such as attention, sensation, motor coordination, etc. Besides, nearly 50% of these neuropsychological tests correlated with the 9CST for the A group. These were tests of vigilance and reversing serial order, calculation, abstraction, verbal fluency and paired associated words (many of them usually associated with "frontal" function in the literature (Dubois et al, 2000; Duchek and Balota, 2005; Jacobs, 2004; Lezak, 1995; Stuss and Levine, 2002; Vigliecca, 2004, Wildgruber, Dkischka, FaBbender and Ettlin, 2000). Consequently, the 9CST could be considered a representative or valid index of the universe of these more basic or complementary situations explored. However, we cannot say the same for the WCST, which correlated significantly with only one of those subtests in frontal patients. These findings certainly indicate some kind of content difference between both card- sorting tests, which can be valuable at the time of making comparative inferences.

The face recognition task was not significantly related to the 9CST in any of the samples studied and almost the same proportion of frontal patients who showed a poor performance on the 9CST had; on the other hand, a good performance on face recognition. This result would be coincident with previous findings in which face recognition has been described as a highly temporal lobe dependent cognitive function (Kleinschmidt and Cohen, 2006; Nichols, Kao, Verfaellie and Gabrieli, 2006). Besides, patients with frontal brain damage have been described as having an excellent performance on memory tests of recognition (Lezak, 1995).

On the other hand, both the card sorting and the face recognition tests showed similar patterns of response for the P patients since near 50% of them scored above (and below) the median on these tests[40]. Nevertheless, although in the opposite direction, both card sorting

---

[40] Taking into account that memory and cognition are logically organized in the brain by categories of similar content, either verbal or non-verbal, we can not consider the card sorting performance independent of this process of conceptualization, mediated to a large extent by posterior areas.

and face recognition tests were sensitive to the discrimination of the A and P patients. Naming also discriminate A and P patients but the vast majority of the P patients showed a score below the median in this task. In other words, when considering only neurological patients, it could be easier to discriminate the A and P ones by means of other and simpler tests than the executive tasks, for example, the test of face recognition, which does not take more than 30 seconds to be administered and it is viable to be administered even in the most impaired patients (including the aphasic ones), or the naming test, which requires, in healthy subjects, approximately 3 minutes to be administered (Vigliecca and Aleman, 2007). In addition, the use of only one executive test, such as the 9CST, could represent a time saving procedure when just the discrimination of the A patients from the healthy subjects is at stake. But, in order to get sensitivity and specificity, the neuropsychological challenge is to differentiate at once among the two groups of patients *and* the healthy subjects, something that can be optimally reached theoretically with a heterogeneous combination of instruments.

From previous studies of our laboratory (Vigliecca, 2004) we have demonstrated that the incorporation of non- executive tests (such as very simple discrimination, memorization and construction tasks) to the batteries designed to study frontal functioning is absolutely necessary to obtain better discriminations among all the comparison groups and to get better inferences among the multiple factors involved in brain function. In other words, and in order to discriminate frontal patients, a battery of tests should be made up not only of those tests usually considered as indicative of frontal function but also of other tests which will contribute to the double dissociation with the rest of the groups analyzed.

Unfortunately, in the present and previous studies with card sorting tests, the non-frontal patients were similar to the frontal patients in most of the complementary neuropsychological information collected. Nevertheless, in this study we can affirm that, at least in part, the differences between the A and P patients in card sorting performance may have been due to the differences observed between these two groups on the nine Raven's matrices, which were convergent with card sorting performances. These results were also coincident with previous findings in healthy people (Vigliecca et al, 2001a). If similar evidence is confirmed by other laboratories, the Raven test could be considered an alternative option to evaluate frontal function, particularly for those cases in which the patients had a limited motor response.

By incorporating the more 9CST divergent tests plus some of the 9CST convergent ones into a discriminant analysis, a percentage of correctly predicted cases of 83% for the A lesions, 73% for P lesions and 81% for the H group was obtained. This result demonstrated that the 9CST together with some complementary neuropsychological tests such as face recognition, written verbal fluency in one minute, naming, months forward and easy-paired associated words can represent a valid tool for the discrimination of these three groups.

Yet, we are convinced that if we had incorporated more "non-frontal" tests to the battery administered to the healthy subjects, the discrimination of the three groups but particularly of the P group would have been more precise. When we designed the battery and collected the data for the healthy subjects taking part in the current study, we did not consider the result obtained with the whole original Spanish battery regarding its capacity to differentiate between A, P and H samples (Vigliecca, 2004) because, unfortunately, those results had still not been processed at that moment. As a consequence, we designed the tasks taking into account the assessments and the conceptual trends usually proposed in the literature as representative of "frontal function" without incorporating a similar number of tests sensitive to detect also posterior lesions. Anyway, some few complementary tests on reading, writing and verbal and visual memory were included in the present battery and finally we could observe that, beyond the executive and intellectual impairments, the A patients showed a better performance than the P patients in memory tests such as naming and face recognition. Nevertheless, the A patients showed a poorer performance than the H subjects in written verbal fluency and easy paired associated words. Alternatively, the A patients were similar to the H subjects in naming and face recognition as well as in the verbal automatism of months forward and the P patients were similar to the H subjects in executive and intellectual tasks but inferior in the rest of the functions evaluated in the discriminant model.

All these findings are, in general terms, coincident with the current paradigm about frontal and non-frontal functions (Duchek and Balota, 2005; Lezak, 1995; Petrides, 2005; Stuss and Levine, 2002; Vigliecca, 2004): The P patients showed the greatest number of elemental functions affected and most of these functions were, in this model, related to declarative memory. Conversely, the A patients showed the greatest number of comprehensive functions affected and these functions were related to executive control or intelligence.

The differences observed between A and P patients in the easy paired associated words and in written verbal fluency also followed the expected pattern of the present theory. Nevertheless, these differences were not enough to be significant. Although the first task requires the simple recall of words in the same way as naming (and, consequently, the posterior areas), it also requires the frontal control to track two series of stimulus simultaneously and to inhibit the interference between items of similar semantic category which were present in both the easy and hard pairs of this Spanish version of the test (for example, "book- page", "school- vegetable", "pumpkin- pen"). Correspondingly, although written verbal fluency requires active and self regulated syntactic and semantic verbal organization and the fine motor control of writing (functions that can be considered as frontal), it also requires visuospatial coding, recognition of previously learned material, naming and long term memory storage, which are controlled to a great extent by posterior areas[41]. In sum, the lack of difference between the A and P patients in these tasks may have been due to the fact that both groups had, for different reasons and compared with healthy subjects, an impairment in the underlying brain functions, which involve surely both anterior and posterior encephalic areas.

Finally, and in order to see if the present results may be generalized to other samples and situations, the 9CST is freely offered for research by requesting it from the author. Regarding the potential use of this test for different psychological purposes it can be interesting to add that the same nine-card configuration could be used for other categories of stimuli. Besides, by simply adding some new commands or instructions, the same stimuli could be used to study most of the components of problem solving ability.

---

[41] Besides, in written verbal fluency the "frontal" cognitive demands were not as critical as in the 9CST since the subjects were able to choose the easiest command and the easiest organization of words (i.e., they were free to write in the enumerative way, which was coincident with the first part of the command: "*write about what there is in this room*") to carry out the task.

ACKNOWLEDGEMENTS

This study was supported by funds from the CONICET. Special thanks to the desinterested cooperation of the medical doctors of the Cordoba Hospital Neurosurgery Service for the realization of this research: Arneodo, M.; Barbeito, P.; Berra, J.; Campana, J; Mezzano, E.; Olocco, R.; Papalini, F.; and Velázquez, D.

REFERENCES

Anderson, S. W., Damasio, H., Jones, R. D., and Tranel, D. (1991). Wisconsin Card Sorting Test performance as a measure of frontal lobe damage. *Journal of Clinical and Experimental Neuropsychology, 13*, 909-922.

Barcelo, F. (2001). Does the Wisconsin card sorting tests measure prefrontal function? *Spanish Journal of Psychology, 4*, 79-100.

Chase-Carmichael, C. A., Ris, M. D., Weber, A. M., and Schefft, B. K. (1999). Neurologic validity of the Wisconsin card- sorting test with a pediatric population. *Clinical Neuropsychology, 13*, 405-413.

Crouch, J. A., Greeve, K. W., and Brooks, J. (1996). The California Card Sorting Test may dissociate verbal and non-verbal concept formation abilities. *The British Journal of Clinical Psychology, 35*, 431-434.

Delis, D. C., Squire, L. R., Bihrle, A., and Massman, P. (1992). Componential analysis of problem-solving ability: performance of patients with frontal lobe damage and amnesic patients on a new sorting test. *Neuropsychologia, 30*, 683-697.

De Zubicaray, G. I., Smith, G. A., Chalk, J. B., and Semple, J. (1998). The Modified Card Sorting Test: test-retest stability and relationships with demographic variables in a healthy older adult sample. *The British Journal of Clinical Psychology, 37*, 457-466

Dubois, B., Slachevsky, A., Litvan, I., and Pillon, B. (2000). The FAB: A frontal assessment battery at bedside. *Neurology, 55*, 1621-1626.

Duchek, J. M. and Balota, D. A. (2005). Failure to control prepotent pathways in early stage dementia of the Alzheimer's type: evidence from dichotic listening. *Neuropsychology, 19*, 687-695.

Duncan, J., Seitz, R. J., Kolodny, J., Bor, D., Herzog, H., Ahmed, A., Newell, F. N., and Emslie, H. (2000). A neural basis for general intelligence. *Science, 289*, 457-460.

Gambini, O., Campana, A., Garghentini, G., and Scarone S. (2003). No evidence of a homogeneous frontal neuropsychological profile in a sample of schizophrenic subjects. *The journal of neuropsychiatry and clinical neurosciences. 15*, 53-57.

Goldberg, E., and Podell, K. (2000). Adaptative decision making, ecological validity, and the frontal lobes. *Journal of Clinical and Experimental Neuropsychology, 22*, 56-68.

Heaton, R. K., Chelune, G. J., Talley, J. L., Kay, G. G., and Curtiss, G. (1993) *Wisconsin card sorting test*. Odessa, Florida: Psychological Assessment Resources.

Hirono, N., Mori, E., Ishii, K., Imamura, T., Tanimukai, S., Kazui, H., Hashimoto, M., Takatsuki, Y., Kitagaki, H., and Sasaki, M. (2001). Neuronal substrates for semantic memory: a positron emission tomography study in Alzheimer's disease. *Dementia and Geriatric Cognitive* Disorders, 12, 15-21.

Jacobs, D. H. (2004). Frontal lobe syndromes. EMedicine, from WebMD. URL (last visit October 23, 2006): *http://www.emedicine.com/NEURO/topic436.htm*; Contact list: *http://www.emedicine.com/contactus.shtml*

Kemppainen, N., Laine, M., Laakso, M. P., Kaasinen, V., Nagren, K., Vahlberg, T., Kurki, T., and Rinne, J. O. (2003). Hippocampal dopamine D2 receptors correlate with memory functions in Alzheimer's disease. *European Journal Neuroscience, 18,* 149-154.

Kleinschmidt, A., Cohen, L. (2006). The neural bases of prosopagnosia and pure alexia: recent insights from functional neuroimaging. *Current Opinion in Neurology, 19,* 386-391.

Kurtz, M. M., Wexler, B. E., and Bell, M. D. (2004). The Penn Conditional Exclusion Test (PCET): relationship to the Wisconsin Card Sorting Test and work function in patients with schizophrenia. *Schizophrenia Research, 68,* 95-102.

Lezak, M. D. (1995). *Neuropsychological Assessment.* (3rd ed). New York: Oxford University Press.

Nelson, H.E. (1976). A modified card sorting test sensitive to frontal lobe defects. *Cortex, 12,* 313-324.

Nichols, E. A., Kao, Y. C., Verfaellie, M., and Gabrieli, J. D. (2006). Working memory and long-term memory for faces: Evidence from fMRI and global amnesia for involvement of the medial temporal lobes. *Hippocampus, 16,* 604-616.

Obonsawin M. C., Crawford J. R., Page J., Chalmers P., Low G. and Marsh P. (1999). Performance on the Modified Card Sorting Test by normal, healthy individuals : Relationship to general intellectual ability and demographic variables. *The British Journal of Clinical Psychology, 38,* 27-41.

Petrides, M. (2005). Lateral prefrontal cortex: architectonic and functional organization. *Philosophical transactions of the Royal Society, Series B Biological Sciences, 360,* 781-795.

Piaget, J. (1991). *Psicología de la inteligencia.* Buenos Aires: Siglo veinte.

Piaget, J. (1990). *Seis estudios de psicología.* Barcelona: Ariel.

Raven, J. C. (1997). *Test de matrices progresivas. Escalas coloreada.* Buenos Aires. Paidos.

Raven, J. C. (1999). *Test de matrices progresivas. Escalas general.* Buenos Aires. Paidos.

Slomine, B. S., Gerring, J. P., Grados, M. A., Vasa, R., Brady, K. D., Christensen, J. R., Denckla, M. B. (2002). Performance on measures of executive function following pediatric traumatic brain injury. *Brain Injury, 16,* 759-772.

Stuss, D. T., and Levine, B. (2002). Adult Clinical Neuropsychology: Lessons from Studies of the Frontal Lobes. *Annual Review of Psychology,* 43, 401-433.

Vigliecca, N. S., and Aleman, G. P. (2007). Adaptation and validation of a naming test in Spanish speakers. Do demographic variables show the pattern of evolution towards Alzheimer disease? *Neurología,* 22, 285-291.

Vigliecca, N. S., and Aleman, G. P. (2000). Neuropsychological tests abbreviated and adapted for Spanish speakers: Factor analysis and age correlation. *Revista latina de pensamiento y lenguaje. Neuropsicología latina,* 8, 65-85.

Vigliecca, N. S., Argüello, N. L., Castillo, J. A., Fernandez, M. S., and Ontivero, K. E. (2001a). Development and validation of abbreviated neuropsychological tests: Execution, intelligence and personality. *Revista latina de pensamiento y lenguaje. Neuropsicología latina, 9* (Suppl. 2): 65-66.

Vigliecca, N. S., Castillo, J. A., and Ontivero, K. E. (2002). Tests neuropsicológicos abreviados y adaptados para hispanoparlantes: aplicación en escuelas secundarias y relación con el rendimiento académico. Graduate Thesis. Facultad de Psicología. Universidad Nacional de Córdoba.

Vigliecca, N. S., Martini, M. A., Aleman, G. P., and Jaime, M. P. (2001b). Neuropsychological tests abbreviated and adapted for Spanish speakers: Reliability and validity studies for the discrimination of patients with unilateral brain lesions. *Revista latina de pensamiento y lenguaje. Neuropsicología latina, 9,* 223-244.

Vigliecca, N. S. (2004). Neuropsychological tests abbreviated and adapted to Spanish speakers: Review of previous findings and validity studies for the discrimination of patients with anterior vs. posterior lesions. *Revista de Neurología, 39,* 205-212.

Watson, M. E., Welsh-Bohmer, K. A., Hoffman, J. M., Lowe, V., and Rubin, D. C. (1999). The neural basis of naming impairments in Alzheimer's disease revealed through positron emission tomography. *Archives of clinical neuropsychology, 14,* 347-357.

Wildgruber, D., Dkischka, U., FaBbender, K., and Ettlin, T. M. (2000). The frontal lobe score: part II: evaluation of its clinical validity. *Clinical Rehabilitation, 14,* 272-278.

In: Psychological Tests and Testing Research Trends
Editor: Paul M. Goldfarb, pp. 83-110

ISBN: 978-1-60021-569-8
© 2007 Nova Science Publishers, Inc.

Chapter 4

GIFTED WITH DYNAMIC INTELLIGENCE TEST MEASURES AND NORMAL WITH STATIC INTELLIGENCE TEST MEASURES: WHAT DOES IT MEAN? [*]

Rosa Angela Fabio

Department of Psychology, Faculty of Formation Science,
Catholic University of Milan, Italy

ABSTRACT

In the first part of this chapter, differences and similarities between static and dynamic measures of intelligence are presented and analysed. Static measures of intelligence are generally obtained by testing either a ratio of mental age to chronological age or a score of deviation from age norm. Dynamic measures of intelligence are generally obtained by administrating novel problem solving tasks to the subjects, supplying them with gradual and balanced assistance that progressively disclose the solution of the problem, and determining the amount of aid the learner needs to be able to solve the problem. The amount of aid is inversely proportional to the modifiability index. The modifiability index is the general propensity to change, and can better measure intelligence.

In the second part of this chapter it is hypothesized that some subjects can obtain a normal score with static test measures and a giftedness score with dynamic test measures. Two experiments were conducted to examine the relationship between dynamic measures and static measures of intelligence in low socio-economic background subjects and in ADHD subjects. In the first experiment 24 subjects with either high (12) or low (12) level of socio-economic background were trained to master problem solving tests with dynamic and static measures of intelligence. In the second experiment 57 subjects, 10 with ADHD-IA, 10 with ADHD-HI, 10 with ADHD-C and 27 controls were trained to master problem solving tests with dynamic and static measures of intelligence. The results showed that subjects with ADHD-C and Controls scored similarly on dynamic and

[*] This research and its publication was partially funded by the Catholic University of Milan under the program of promotion and diffusion of scientific research.

static measure, but subjects with ADHD-HI and subjects with a low level of socio-economic background had lower scores with static test measures and higher scores with dynamic test measures. Results are discussed in terms of their implications for intelligence tests.

Key words: dynamic measures, intelligence, potential, gifted, adhd.

INTRODUCTION

Although definitions of human intelligence vary, the views of most theorists cluster around a few common perspectives. The most common is to think of intelligence as being the ability to successfully operate in an uncertain environment through learning and adapting based on experience (Legg and Hunter, 2006); another definition refers to intelligence as the ability to effectively adapt to the environment, either by changing oneself, changing the environment, or finding a new environment. In any case, intelligence is based upon cognitive processes, including perception, memory, reasoning, and problem-solving. Intelligence is not a single cognitive or mental process, but instead the combination of these processes that we use to adapt to our environment. Since it is related to the individual's learning ability, the change processes, and the modifiability or plasticity of cognitive processes, it is based on a dynamic and not a static concept. In the first part of this chapter, static and dynamic measure of intelligence will be considered.

Static vs Dynamic Measures of Intelligence

Static measures of intelligence are generally obtained by testing either a ratio of mental age to chronological age or a score of deviation from age norm. Dynamic measures of intelligence are generally obtained by administrating novel problem solving tasks to the subjects, supplying them with gradual and balanced assistance that progressively disclose the solution of the problem, and determining the amount of aid the learner needs to be able to solve the problem. The amount of aid is inversely proportional to the modifiability index. The modifiability index is the general propensity to change, and can better measure intelligence.

Static Measure of Intelligence

Intelligence tests come in many forms, and some tests use a single type of item or question. Most tests of this type yield both an overall score and individual subtest scores. Regardless of design, all IQ tests attempt to measure the same general intelligence. Their components test are generally designed and selected because they are found to be predictive of later intellectual development, such as educational achievement. IQ also correlates with job performance, socioeconomic advancement, and social pathologies.

Among intelligence tests, one test currently dominates the field: the Wechsler Intelligence Scale for Children Revised (WISC-R; Wechsler, 1974) and the Wechsler Adult Intelligence Scale (WAIS; Wechsler, 1974).

In recent years, new static measures of intelligence have been proposed. As Benson (2006) stated, since the 1970s intelligence researchers have been trying to preserve the usefulness of intelligence tests. They have done so in a number of ways, including updating the Wechsler Intelligence Scale for Children (WISC) and the Stanford-Binet Intelligence Scale so they better reflect the abilities of test-takers from diverse cultural and linguistic backgrounds. They have developed new, more sophisticated ways of creating, administering and interpreting those tests, and they have produced new theories and tests that broaden the concept of intelligence beyond its traditional boundaries. As a result, many of those biases identified by critics of intelligence testing have been reduced, and new tests are available that, unlike traditional intelligence tests are based on modern theories of brain function.

Examples of this new generation of static IQ tests are the K-ABC (Kaufman Assessment Battery for Children) and the KAIT (Kaufman Adolescent and Adult Intelligence Test) of Kaufman and Kaufman (1983; 1993). The Kaufman Assessment Battery for Children (K-ABC; Kaufman and Kaufman, 1983) measures the intelligence of 2½- to 12½-year-olds via the sequential-simultaneous processing model associated with the Luria-Das model (Das, Kirby, and Jar man, 1979; Luria, 1973) and cerebral specialization theory (Sperry, 1968). The KAIT (Kaufman Adolescent and Adult Intelligence Test; Kaufman and Kaufman, 1993) assesses intelligence of individuals with ages ranging from 11 years to more than 85 years old and is based on the Cattell-Horn theory of fluid and crystallized intelligence (Horn and Cattell, 1966; 1967; Horn, 1985, 1989). Crystallized intelligence (Gc) corresponds to the type of problem solving that depends on schooling and is influenced by one's formal education and training, by reading books, magazines, and newspapers, and by watching television, and generally by participating fully in one's environment. Fluid intelligence (Gf) reflects the ability to solve new problems with adaptability and flexibility; the emphasis is on reasoning ability rather than visuospatial ability, and this type of intelligence can be tested both auditory and visually as well as verbally and nonverbally.

Also Das (2002) and Das, Naglieri and Kirby (1994) have developed the planning, attention, simultaneous, and successive (PASS) theory as an alternative to the conceptualization of intelligence as a general mental ability. Specifically the PASS theory refers to intelligence as composed of multiple interdependent cognitive processes. From this perspective follows the Das-Naglieri Cognitive Assessment System (CAS; Naglieri and Das, 1997) that measures the PASS processes. This assessment can help educators to design interventions that will actually improve children's learning; can distinguish between children with different conditions, such as a learning disability or attention deficit disorder; and will accurately measure the abilities of children from different linguistic and cultural backgrounds.

So far, only single or dual factor tests have been considered. However, other theories oppose traditional methods that view intelligence as unitary, and perceive intelligence as multifaceted. For example Gardner's Multiple Intelligence Theory describes IQ as containing seven distinct domains. These domains include: linguistic intelligence, logical-mathematical intelligence, spatial intelligence, musical intelligence, bodily-kinaesthetic intelligence, intrapersonal intelligence, interpersonal intelligence. Linguistic intelligence is the ability to use language to excite, please, convince, stimulate or convey information; Logical-mathematical intelligence is the ability to explore patterns, categories, and relationships by manipulating objects or symbols, and to experiment in a controlled orderly way; Spatial intelligence is the ability to perceive and mentally manipulate a form or object, and to perceive and create tension, balance, and composition in a visual or spatial display; Musical intelligence is the ability to enjoy, perform, or compose a musical piece; Bodily-kinaesthetic intelligence is the ability to use fine and gross motor skills in sports, the performing arts, or arts and craft production; Intrapersonal intelligence is the ability to gain access to and understand one's inner feelings, dreams, and ideas; and interpersonal Intelligence is the ability to get along and understand others. (Hatch and Gardner, 1988, cited in Vialle 1999). This formulation has had little impact on testing, in part because the lack of quantitative factor-analytic studies that might validate the theory.

Also Sternberg (1995) has taken a more direct approach to changing the practice of testing. His Sternberg Triarchic Abilities Test (STAT) is a battery of multiple-choice questions that tap into the three independent aspects of intelligence —analytical, practical, and creative—each of which is itself divided into verbal, quantitative, and figural sections. The STAT test items differ from conventional test items in their emphasis on ability to learn rather than on what has been learnt. Some items are measured by learning from context. For example, verbal skill is measured by learning from context, not by vocabulary (which represents the product rather than the processes of learning). The STAT also measures skills for coping with novelty, whereby the examinee must imagine a hypothetical state of the world and then reason as though this state of the world were true. Finally the STAT also measures practical abilities, such as reasoning about advertisements and political slogans, not just about decontextualized words or geometric forms. These are only a few of the differences that separate this test from its predecessors. However, the STAT is not immune to effects of prior learning, nor is it "culture-free." Sternberg suggests that it is impossible to create a test that is genuinely immune to effects of prior experience or that is culture-free, because intelligence cannot be tested outside the boundaries of a culture. Intelligence is always used in some context, and must be measured in some context. The test, however, seems broader and more comprehensive than other existing tests, and hence allows for more diversity in backgrounds than would be true of typical tests. Other reformers have expressed more fundamental criticisms of traditional IQ measurement like Goleman (1995) who suggests that emotional intelligence (EQ) is more important than IQ.

According to Thorndike (1997), IQ tests have changed little since their inception. They are psychometrically more sophisticated, and have correlations with information processing theories but continue to include items that involve such activities as naming objects, recreating designs with patterned blocks and remembering numerical sequences (Elliot, 2003). However, researchers have come to recognise the many limitations in IQ measures; their tendency to lack an empirically supported theoretical framework (Flanagan and McGrew, 2000), the limited relationship between scores and instructional practices (Reschly, 1997), their emphasis upon products rather than psychological processes (Sternberg, 1995; Wagner and Sternberg, 1984), their tendency to linguistic and cultural bias (Lopez, 1997) and their inability to guide clinicians in deriving specific interventions for educational difficulties (Fuchs et al., 1987; McGrew, 1994).

Dynamic Measures

Since the concept of intelligence is referred to as dynamic cognitive process and since the word "adapting" refers to a dynamic quality, a new perspective on the assessment of intelligence is through dynamic measures. For this reason dynamic measures of intelligence can better address dynamic and adaptive behaviour (Fabio, 2005; Sternberg, 2006).

As Elliot (2003) and Lidz and Elliott (2000) point out dynamic assessment is an umbrella term used to describe a heterogeneous range of approaches that are linked by a common element, c.f. instruction and feedback, that are built into the testing process and are differentiated on the basis of an individual's performance. Thus the amount of assistance provided is directly contingent upon the testee's performance and modifiability. In contrast, static measures require limited instruction, usually involving initial guidance, and contingent feedback from the tester is actively discouraged on the grounds that it will damage test standardisation. Behind this common ground there are some differences between leading proponents about core constructs, purposes, methodologies and implications (Sternberg and Grigorenko, 2002; Elliot, 2003).

In some dynamic testing models, a pretest–intervene–retest procedure is used to measure the breadth of the zone of proximal development. The procedure is based on the assumption that the best way to help a child learn is to explore the teaching strategies to which that child is most responsive (Berk, 2001). The theoretical foundations of dynamic measures are derived from the sociocultural theory of Vygotskij (1978)—in particular, the Zone of Proximal Development (ZPD) concept—and Feurstein's Mediated Learning Experience (MLE; Feurstein et al., 1979). Vygotskij believed that a great deal of development was mediated by social interaction. The ZPD refers to the distance between the level of performance a child can reach unaided and the level of participation a child can accomplish when guided by someone more knowledgeable in that domain. Therefore, it refers to a range of tasks that the child cannot yet handle alone but can do with the help of more skilled partners (Vygotskij). As Campione, Brown, Ferrara, and Bryant (1984) have pointed out, the breadth of the zone varies across individuals and across domains of learning within an individual. For one child in a particular domain, the zone may be narrow, indicating that the child is not yet ready to master tasks beyond his or her unaided performance. For another child in the same domain or the same child in a different domain, the zone may be broader, suggesting that the child can perform at a higher level than the current performance indicates with the help of a more expert partner. Other researchers have found that the zone tends to be broader or narrower in a great variety of tasks (Fabio, 1999; Fabio, 2001; Fabio and Mancuso, 1995; Vygotskij, 1978).

Another way in which Vygotskij (1978) used the zone of proximal development was to test the child's readiness, or intellectual maturity, in a specific domain (Brown and Campione, 1984). As such, he was using it as an individual-difference metric. He argued that if we measure the IQ of two children with the same chronological and mental age (8 years), then we cannot make assumptions on the course of their future mental development and school performance. On the contrary, if we consider their IQ measures as starting points and not as definite (static) measurements and we give them new problems, then they will be able to handle problems above their starting level. If the children solve problems with adult assistance, and one child attains an IQ of a mental age of 9 years and the second child an IQ of a mental age of 12 years, then the difference between 9 and 8 or between 12 and 8 is the zone of proximal development. "It is the distance between the actual development level as determined by independent problem solving and the level of potential development as determined through problem solving under guidance of persons who know more" (Vygotskij, pp. 85–86). The other theoretical foundation of dynamic measures is the mediated learning experience, which describes a special quality of interaction between a learner and a person, whom we shall call a mediator. The function of a mediator is to observe how the learner approaches problem solving. The problem at hand is a ruse for the mediator to be able to observe the learner's thinking process (Feuerstein, Rand, Hoffman, and Miller, 1980).

Dynamic Tests Used in this Study

The dynamic tests that have been used in the present study come from balanced and standardized works on subjects of three different age level: 212 kindergarten children (mean age = 5 years 3 months; range 4 years 10 months to 5 years 11 months), 308 primary school children , (mean age = 8 years 2 months, range from 6 to 11 years) and 170 teenager (mean age = 18 years 7 months; range 17 years 10 months to 18 years 11 months) (Fabio and Mancuso, 1995; Fabio, 1999; Fabio, 2001; Fabio, 2003).

The rationale of these studies is that flexible access to information and transfer can be used as an index of plasticity and modifiability. As a consequence indexes of dynamic assessment measure problem solving ability in two phases:

- in the learning phase, when the subject faces new problem solving;
- in the transfer phase, when the subject generalises what he has learnt in the learning phase to new, more complex problem solving.

This type of measure consists of submitting the learners to more difficult problem solving that is more difficult than the level indicated by their basic ability, in supplying them with gradual and balanced assistance, progressively disclosing the solution of the problem submitted and determining the aid level adopted by the learner in solving the problem. The aid level is inversely proportional to the modifiability index.

In the following section some examples of dynamic tests used in the three age levels are presented: kindergarten, primary and secondary dynamic tests.

Kindergarten Dynamic Test

The test was applied to and standardized with kindergarten children (Fabio and Mancuso, 1995). In its final form consists of 16 items, 8 of which are related to the learning stage and 8 to the transfer stage. The latter contain the same problem solving rules as those in the learning stage plus one new rule that must interact with the other items in order for the child to be able to find the solution.

The items, derived from the piagetian's theory about the cognitive stage, are the following:

1. conservation of length concept
2. conservation of liquid surface concept
3. simultaneity
4. conservation of substance and weight concept

5. class inclusion
6. transitivity
7. sequentiality
8. bi-univocal (one-to-one) correspondence.

The important focus in this approach to dynamic measures is the standardization of the step-by-step aids supplied to the child for problem solving. There are five identified steps to attain the solution of the problem. They range from the most generic attention to the most central one, where the child is taught how to solve the problem:

1. general attention advice: encouraging the child to a higher attention level;
2. selective attention aid: guiding the child's analytical attention, preventing his making mistakes in task analysis;
3. aid in the presentation of the partial rule: containing a description of some of the rules leading to item solution;
4. aid in the presentation of the global rule: containing all the rules on which the solution of the item is based;
5. execution aid: the mediator teaches the child the strategy needed to attain the solution and helps him to make use of it operatively.

Once the correct solution of the first item was achieved, the same procedure was followed for all the other items: learning items first and then transfer ones. The mediator marked down how many aids had been requested by the child to achieve the correct solution and attributed relevant scores. Scores were established as the inverse of the number of aids required, i.e. when the child solved the task with 1 aid only, he was assigned 5 points; with 2 aids 4 points; with 3 aids 3 points, with 4 aids 2 points and with 5 aids 1 point. Summing up the scores in the learning stage we have the Learning Modifiability Index (LMI), summing up the scores in the transfer stage we have the Transfer Modifiability Index (TMI), the sum of the two indexes gives the General Modifiability Index (GMI: ranging from 16 to 80).

Examples of items are:

- Learning item 1 and transfer item 1: conservation of length concept

Concerning the acknowledgement of length as an invariable value. In the test item sheet there are two trees having the same length and coincident ends. The examinee is told that they have the same length. Then another sheet is shown to him where the trees are no longer aligned. In the transfer item the child is shown a third sheet with three non-aligned strokes (length and colour are still the same). Each time the child is required to tell whether the strokes have the same length.

For example, the aid sequence in this transfer item is:

1. Pay attention; look well at the three trees;
2. Observe the length of the three trees;
3. Place the trees as if they were aligned;
4. Place them on the same line, the starting points are different; and they seem to have different length.

5. Examples.

- Learning item 2 and transfer item 2: conservation of liquid surface concept

Figure 1. Learning item 1 and transfer item 1.

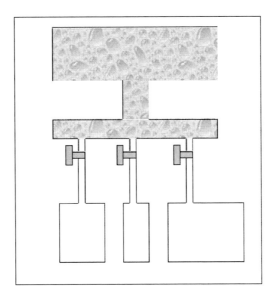

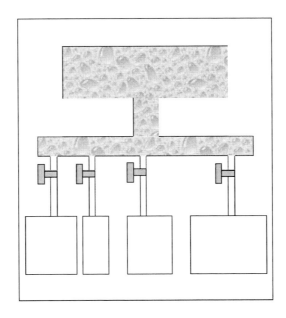

Figure 2. Learning item 2 and transfer item 2.

Concerning the acknowledgement of simultaneity of starting and ending of two dynamic processes. In the test item there is a sheet with a tap with three identical water pipes. Under the water pipes there are three different containers. The examinee is told that tap contains some water and that when it is opened water come down in the same quantity in all the three containers. In the test item the examinee is required to tell what of the containers will become full before. In the transfer items the tap has four identical water pipes. Under the water pipes there are three different types of containers. The examinee is required to tell what of the containers will become full before.

Primary School Dynamic Test

The test was standardized with primary school children (Fabio, 2001) in its final form contains 14 items, 7 items are related to the learning phase, 7 items to the transfer phase. The latter contain the same rules for problem solving as the items related to the learning phase plus a new rule that must interact with the others for the child to be able to find the solution. The items are as follows:

1. completion of a series of letters
2. completion of a series of numbers
3. completion of geometrical figures
4. perceptive difference
5. mental image superimposition
6. chain of words
7. simultaneous coordination of information.

After the first item is presented, the procedure of giving gradual and standardized aids begins.

Once the correct solution of the first item had been achieved, the same procedure was followed for all the other items: learning items first and then transfer ones. The mediator marked down how many aids had been requested by the child to achieve the correct solution and attributed relevant scores. As in the kindergarten test, scores were inverted, i.e. when the child solved the task with 1 aid only, he was assigned 5 points; with 2 aids 4 points; with 3 aids 3 points, with 4 aids 2 points and with 5 aids 1 point. Summing up the scores in the learning stage we once more have the learning modifiability index (LMI), summing up the scores in the transfer stage we have the transfer modifiability index (TMI), the sum of the two indexes gives the general modifiability index (GMI: ranging from 14 to 70).

Examples of items are:

- Learning item 2 and transfer item 2: completion of a series of numbers

The item is concerned with inductive reasoning in completing a series of numbers. In both stages of the test the child is given a sheet with some numbers: they are in groups of three and are placed one after the other according to a logical criterion. In the learning stage the series of three numbers follow this rule: the first and second figure increase by 1 unit, while the third one decreases by 1 unit. In the transfer stage the rule is: the first figure decreases by 2 units, while the second one increases by 1 and the third one by 2. The child must say in both stages which will be the numbers in the following series of three.

For example, the aid sequence in transfer item 2 was:

1. pay much attention to the relationship between the numbers;
2. the relationship between the numbers refers to the sequence of the series of three numbers;
3. inside each series of three numbers the first figure decreases by 2 units, look at the other two figures;

4. look at the other two figures: the second one increases by 1 unit while the third one increases by 2;

5. example.

- Learning item 5 and transfer item 5

135 244 353 _____

921 733 545 ____

Figure 3. Learning item 2 and transfer item 2.

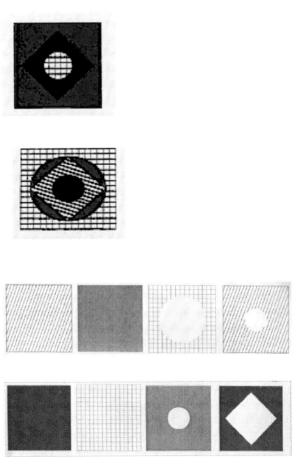

Figure 4. Learning item 5 and transfer item 5.

The item is concerned with the ability to mentally over impose images (Feuerstein, 1979). The child is given two sheets: in the first thee are eight different figures; in the second some of the precedent figures are over imposed to create a complex one. Specifically for learning item three images are over imposed, for transfer item four images are over imposed. The examinee is required to tell which one of the eight figures has to be over imposed both in the learning and in the transfer phase.

Secondary School Dynamic Test

The test applied and standardized with teenagers (Fabio, 1999) in its final form consists of 12 items, 6 items refer to the learning stage and 6 items refer to the transfer stage. As in the previous tests, the same rules for problem solving in the learning stage apply also to the transfer stage, plus one new rule that must interact with the other items to allow the examinee to achieve the solution. The items are as follows:

1. deductive reasoning, conditional type;
2. deductive reasoning with crypto arithmetic problems;
3. inductive reasoning in completing a series of letters;
4. inductive reasoning in completing a series of numbers;
5. problem solving of a graphic-perceptive mathematic type;
6. problem solving of a graphic-perceptive type on the clock .

After the first item is presented, the procedure of giving gradual and standardized aids begins.

Once the correct solution of the first item was achieved, the same procedure was followed for all the other items: learning items first and then transfer ones. The mediator marked down how many aids had been requested by the subject to achieve the correct solution and attributed relevant scores. Scores were established as the inverse of the total number pf aids given, i.e. when the child solved the task with 1 aid only, he was assigned 5 points; with 2 aids 4 points; with 3 aids 3 points, with 4 aids 2 points and with 5 aids 1 point. Summing up the scores in the learning stage we have the learning modifiability index (LMI), summing up the scores in the transfer stage we have the transfer modifiability index (TMI), the sum of the two indexes gives the general modifiability index (GMI: ranging from 12 to 60).

Examples of items are:

• Learning item 1 and transfer item 1: deductive conditional reasoning

It consists of the following sentence, "If there is the book, then the triangle is there, too," followed by four questions:

There is the book, what follows?
The book is not there, what follows?
There is the triangle, what follows?
The triangle is not there, what follows?

In this case the possible answers are: 1) It's there, 2) It's not there, 3) no conclusion can be made. The sequence of the five suggestions leading to the solution of the conditional assertion was:

1. Pay much attention to the relation contained in the sentence.
2. The relation only tells you that if the book is there then also the triangle is there. Not the other way round.
3. There might be other objects too, for example, a table or a square and the triangle.
4. It could be that the book is not there and nonetheless the triangle may or may not be there.
5. Since it is implied in the relation that if there is the book then the triangle is there, other objects might also be present and amongst them the triangle. The answers to this problem are: 1) the triangle is there; 2) nothing can be said about the triangle; 3) nothing can be said about the book; 4) the book is not there.

Learning item 5 and transfer item 5: problem solving of a graphic-perceptive mathematic type

The item is concerned with inductive reasoning in completing a graphic-perceptive mathematic type problem. The subject is presented a series of squares that contain some arrows with specific directions. In the test item the examinee is required to tell which (if one) arrow has to be put in the last square. In the transfer item the examinee is required to make the same thing, but he has to reason with a higher number of squares.

"If there is the book, then the triangle is there, too,"

There is the book, what follows?
The book is not there, what follows?
There is the triangle, what follows?
The triangle is not there, what follows?

Possible answers are: 1) It's there, 2) It's not there, 3) no conclusion can be made.

"If there is the lamp and the book, then the circle is there"

There is the book and the lamp, what follows?
The book is not there, what follows?
There is the circle, what follows?
The circle is not there, what follows?

Possible answers are: 1) It's there, 2) It's not there, 3) no conclusion can be made.

Figure 5. Learning item 1 and transfer item 1.

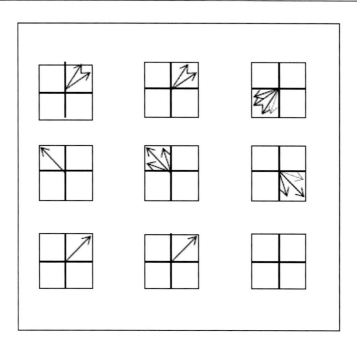

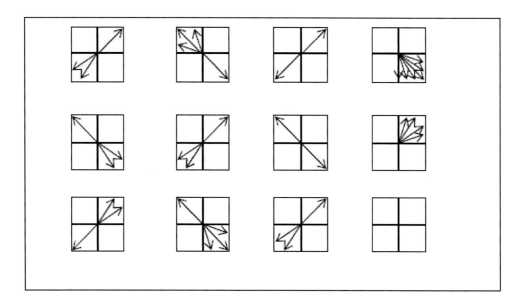

Figure 6. Learning item 2 and transfer item 2.

In a recent work Fabio (2005) studied the validity and reliability of dynamic measures related to the tests presented above. The aims that were addressed in that study were: 1. to evaluate whether the modifiability index was specific in the various contexts or whether it could be considered as a general ability to learn and transfer. Because the tests propose several items outlining various types of logical processes, it was important to determine whether there was coherence within the test, that is, whether it was possible to find similar results in the modifiability indexes of the various items; 2. to investigate the validity of dynamic measures in relation to various indexes: the correlations between dynamic testing and some cognitive variables such as the level of selective attention, the global attention level, and overall school performances in language and mathematics; 3. to point out the relationship between dynamic testing and static testing. Three studies investigated the relationship between dynamic measures and the following factors: a) static measures of intelligence (Raven Test, D48) and b) codifying speed, codifying accuracy and school performance. The three studies examined kindergarten children (N=150), primary school children (N=287) and young adult students (N=198) who were trained to master problem solving tests with dynamic measures of intelligence. Static measures of intelligence, codifying speed, codifying accuracy and school performance measures were included in all the studies. Results showed that internal coherence indexes, measured with Cronbach Alpha, were very high. Such data, which have been confirmed in the three age groups, suggest that there is a single latent ability in the performance of the various tasks that can be seen as a general propensity to change. With reference to the correlations between dynamic testing and some cognitive variables such as selective attention level, global attention level (as evaluated by the teacher) and school performances in language and mathematics, the individuals with high modifiability indexes showed higher global attention level (as measure evaluated by the teachers), their codification systems were faster (positive correlation between correct answers in selective attention and index of General Modifiability) and more accurate (negative correlation with omitted answers). These individuals also showed a higher level of school performance. The static indexes of I.Q. were also correlated with the above mentioned cognitive variables, but to a lesser extent, and they were not correlated with the accuracy of codification.

The results regarding the correlation with the various cognitive variables can be seen as the indexes of the external validity of dynamic testing. Through these studies we have come to beleive that dynamic indexes, although partially correlated to static ones, are qualitatively superior to the latter since they are capable of measuring a concept that is closer to the definition of intelligence as adaptability or modifiability.

Finally, dynamic testing proved to be only partially correlated with static testing. The correlation coefficients between the scores obtained with static testing (Raven Matrices) and dynamic indexes were $r(150)= .58$, $p< .01$, $r(287) = .48$, $p < .01$ and $r(190) = .48$, $p< .01$, respectively for kindergarten children, primary school children and teenagers. Figures 7, 8, 9 show these correlations in a more analytical way.

For the definition of static testing categories we took into account the subjects who had achieved the worst (13%) and the best (13%) scores, in the Raven Matrices test. Subjects who had the worst scores and were defined as children with "low static measures", those who achieved standard scores were defined as subjects with "medium static measures" while those with best scores were defined as having "high static measures" . In the same way, to define low and high dynamic indexes we found those who had achieved the worst (13%) and the best (13%) performance in the modifiability indexes. The percentage of individuals in each category is presented in the figures shown below. These results show that subjects with "low static measures" lack high modifiability indexes, while most of the children with "high static measures" show high modifiability indexes and only a small little percentage of them show a low modifiability indexes.

By combining static and dynamic testing the following profiles emerge:

1. individuals with low static indexes and a low or medium modifiability level
2. individuals with medium static indexes and a low, medium or high modifiability level
3. individuals with high static indexes and a medium or high modifiability level.

In the present work the focus is understanding the nature of the subjects that come into the joint classes of lower static measures and higher dynamic measures (see figures 7, 8, 9).

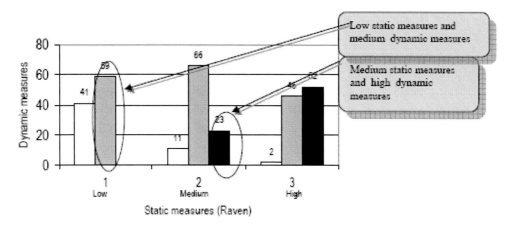

Figure 7. Relation between Static and Dynamic Testing in Kindergarten children.

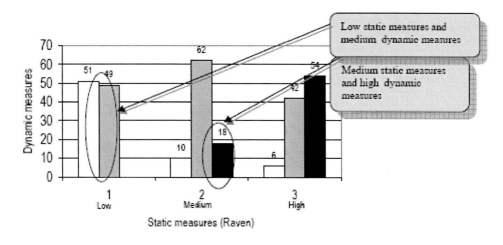

□ low modifiability ▨ medium modifiability ■ high modifiability

Figure 8. Relation between Static and Dynamic Testing in primary school children.

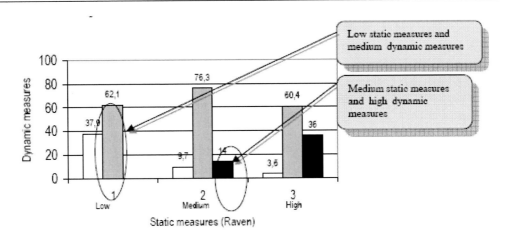

Figure 9. Relation between Static and Dynamic Testing in teenagers.

Rationale of the Present Study

The enhanced subjects of the figures 7, 8 and 9 with lower static indexes and a higher modifiability level are those who perform poorly when left on their own and often perform substantially better when given appropriate instructional intervention; conceptually it may be that the measurement of the 'product' flowing into the static index is likely to include the dynamic type index, i.e. the changing capability of the individual. However these subjects show high latent abilities and expertise that more conventional measures fail to tap. It may be that subjects are underestimated (like the underachievers). This underestimate may come from two lines: from low socio-economic background subjects and from ADHD subjects.

For the first group, the rationale is that dynamic measures can add predictive information because instructed tasks are somewhat beyond the learner's competence, hence, requiring modification of existing knowledge or skills dynamic indexes of intelligence, and so are not related to low sociocultural background.

Low-socioeconomic status children may demonstrate a large difference between actual and potential development (Missiuna and Samuels, 1989). They can perform poorly on static measures but better on dynamic measures. Because cognitive modifiability indexes measure the potential intelligence of the individual, the influence of an individual's sociocultural background may not be significant at all (Tzuriel and Kaufman, 1999). Also Vialle (1999) notes the under representation of disadvantaged students in educationally gifted programs and suggests the cause of this under representation of disadvantaged students lies in the traditional approach, whereby a narrow set of identification procedures– usually an IQ test– is used to identify gifted students who are then placed in a program that may or may not be specifically designed to meet their intellectual strengths.

For the second group the rationale is that static measures of intelligence, because they reveal the product of learning and not the process, may underestimate gifted ADHD students. Disruptive behaviours of gifted ADHD students can emerge and fail to see indicators of high ability.

Some studies (Kalbfleisch, 2000; Kaufmann, Kalbfleisch, and Castellanos, 2000; Moon, 2001; Moon, Zentall, Grskovic, Hall, and Stormant, 2001; Zentall, Moon, Hall, and Grskovic,

2001; Moon, 2002) suggest that identified gifted ADHD children are more impaired than other ADHD children, suggesting the possibility that we are missing gifted children with milder forms of ADHD and that high ability can mask ADHD, and attention deficits and impulsivity tend to depress the test scores as well as the high academic performance that many schools rely on to identify giftedness. Hyperactive is a word often used to describe gifted children as well as children with ADHD. As with attention span, children with ADHD have a high activity level, but this activity level is often found across situations (Barkley, 1997). A large proportion of gifted children are highly active too. As many as one-fourth may require less sleep; however, their activity is generally focused and directed (Clark, 1992; Webb, Meckstroth, and Tolan, 1982), in contrast to the behaviour of children with ADHD. Bright children are referred to psychologists or paediatricians because they exhibited certain behaviours (e.g., restlessness, inattention, impulsivity, high activity level, day-dreaming) commonly associated with a diagnosis of ADHD.

First Study

As expressed above children who perform similarly on static pretests sometimes respond quite differently to instruction (e.g., Brown and Barclay, 1976; Brown, Campione, and Barclay, 1979; Vygotsky, 1978), suggesting that dynamic measures can provide information over and above that available from static tests. May be that dynamic measures more consistently tap fluid abilities, whereas many static tests tend to tap primarily crystallized ability (Lohman, 1993).

Hypotheses

The prediction is that children with low socioeconomic status perform worse in static intelligence measures than children with high socioeconomic status, but they perform equally well on dynamic measures of intelligence with respect to children with high socioeconomic status.

METHOD

Participants

24 subjects with either high (12) or low (12) level of socio-econonomic background.

The descriptive characteristics of the sample are provided in table I. Socioeconomic status was assessed using the Duncan Socioeconomic Index (SEI; Duncan 1961; Stevens and Cho, 1985; Lynch and Kaplan, 2000). The ethnic composition of the overall sample was 100% White. The participants in this study were selected from a database containing 210 children attending public primary schools in a district in Lombardy (Italy). All girls and boys were eligible for inclusion in this study, no child had a history of brain damage, epilepsy, psychosis or anxiety disorder.

Table 1. Demographic statistics

Group	Measures	
Children with Low Socioeconomic status	N of boys/girls	6/6
	Age (mean (SD))	8.2 (1.2)
	SEI[1]	24.3 (11.3)
Children with High Socioeconomic status	N of boys/girls	6/6
	Age (mean (SD))	8.3 (1.3)
	SEI	67.3 (16.3)

[1] SEI is Duncan Socioeconomic Index. Scores range from 0-99.

Procedure

Participants were assessed during school lessons. Static I.Q. was assessed using the WISC-R for each subject, in a silent classroom. The dynamic test applied and standardized with primary school children (Fabio, 2001) was also administered. Description of the procedure was as described above. Parents completed consent forms prior to participation in the study.

Results

The aim of the study was to identify the influence of the 'socio-cultural background' variable on dynamic testing. Table 2 show means, standard deviations and statistical significance related to each scale and subscales of static and dynamic measures.

Table 2. Means. standard deviations and statistical significance related to each scale and subscales

	Children with Low Socioeconomic status Mean Std Dev.		Children with High Socioeconomic status			
	Mean	Std Dev.	Mean	Std. Dev.	t	p
Static intelligence test - QI	93.60	10.59	105.44	17.59	7.82	.001
Verbal	87.50	18.76	110.37	20.48	13.87	.001
Information	8.60	3.50	10.85	3.51	6.88	.001
Similarities	10.80	2.90	11.03	4.66	1.81	.23
Arithmetic	9.80	3.21	9.55	2.91	1.88	.44
Vocabulary	7.10	6.24	12.44	2.10	18.32	.001
Comprehension	9.70	2.98	10.88	3.66	4.21	.06
Performance	99.70	15.84	100.59	14.25	2.15	.105
Picture Completion	10.40	2.45	10.00	2.51	0.81	.32
Picture Arrangement	10.60	4.69	10.56	3.43	1.08	.362
Block Design	9.80	3.96	10.03	4.01	0.89	.450
Object Assembly	9.80	2.61	11.81	2.61	1.73	.170
Symbols copy	10.10	2.60	11.48	2.76	1.53	.021
Dynamic intelligence test	48.70	9.69	49.90	7.88	1.62	.19
Learning phase	24.90	4.86	24.13	3.95	0.62	.53
Transfert phase	23.80	5.28	25.77	4.50	1.10	.46

The results showed that subjects with a low level of socio-economic background had lower scores with static test measures than subjects with high socio-economic background. Considering dynamic test measures, subjects with a low level of socio-economic background had the same scores of subjects with high socio-economic background . The socio-cultural background was not significant with respect to dynamic measures, but it was significant in relation to static ones. This is in agreement with the results of previous studies on dynamic indexes and once again stresses the fact that dynamic indexes measure something different about the culture of an individual, they measure his propensity to change (Tzuriel, 1997; Tzuriel and Kaufman, 1999).

Second Study

As described in the rationale of the two studies, the second one was related to one particular category of subjects that may be underestimated in cognitive functioning: ADHD. The Diagnostic and Statistical Manual of Mental Disorders-IV (DSM-IV; APA, 1994) defines ADHD based on elevations of two separate but correlated symptom dimensions, those of inattention (IA) and hyperactivity/impulsivity (H/I). Children meet criteria for the disorder by having six or more symptoms of either IA or of H/I, or both. Hence, DSM-IV describes three diagnostic subtypes of ADHD based on differential elevations of symptoms on these two dimensions. The first is Predominantly Inattentive subtype (ADHD-IA), in which children have six or more symptoms of IA but fewer than six symptoms of H/I, the second is Predominantly Hyperactive/Impulsive subtype (ADHD-HI), in which children have six or more symptoms of H/I but fewer than six symptoms of IA, and the third is Combined subtype (ADHD-C), in which children show elevations of six or more symptoms on both dimensions. Sets of symptoms are diagnosed with ADHD, combined type (ADHD-C). The combined type group is the most common, occurring in 61% of identified cases compared to 30% for the inattentive type and 9% for the hyperactive impulsive type. It is possible that the dimensions of IA and H/I are each associated with unique neuropsychological impairments. For instance, as Barkley (1997) proposes and some previous studies support, the dimension of H/I may be associated with deficits in behavioral inhibition. In contrast, some studies suggest that the dimension of IA may be associated with general deficits in processing speed and vigilance. Characteristics of ADHD that are similar (or overlap) with giftness are as follows:
Behaviors Associated with ADHD (Barkley, 1997)

1. Poorly sustained attention in almost all situations
2. Diminished persistence on tasks not having immediate consequences
3. Impulsivity, poor delay of gratification
4. Impaired adherence to commands to regulate or inhibit behavior in social contexts
5. More active, restless than normal children
6. Difficulty adhering to rules and regulations

Behaviors Associated with Giftedness (Webb, 1993)

1. Poor attention, boredom, daydreaming in specific situations
2. Low tolerance for persistence on tasks that seem irrelevant

3. Judgment lags behind development of intellect
4. Intensity may lead to power struggles with authorities
5. High activity level; may need less sleep
6. Questions rules, customs and traditions

Particular characteristics of ADHD-HI, such as boredom, high activity level, low lack of attention are mainly associated with gifted children.

Hypotheses

The prediction is that children with ADHD-C can show similar results on static and dynamic measures of intelligence, ADHD-HI will have similar results on static measure but may exhibit giftness results dynamic measures of intelligence.

METHOD

Participants

The descriptive characteristics of the sample are provided in table 3. All the subjects of the groups did not differ in socioeconomic status or ethnicity; the ethnic composition of the overall sample was 100% White. The participants in this study were selected from a database containing 1020 children attending public primary schools in a district in Lombardy (Italy). All 1020 9- and 10- year girls and boys were eligible for inclusion in this study, no child had a history of brain damage, epilepsy, psychosis or anxiety disorder.

The final sample included 57 children, 10 with ADHD-IA (3 female, 7 males), 10 with ADHD-HI (1 female, 9 males), 10 with ADHD-C (1 female, 9 males), and 27 controls children (8 female, 19 males).

Children belonging to these groups were tested for ADHD using an Italian version of parents' interview, the Deficit Attention Parent Scale (SDAG) and an Italian version of teachers interview, the Deficit Attention Teacher Scale (SDAI), of Marzocchi and Cornoldi (2000), following DSM-IV (APA, 1994) criteria. The Deficit Attention Teacher Scale (SDAI) is composed of 18 items, corresponding to the symptom domain of ADHD, as described in the DSM-IV (APA, 1994). The items provide an ADD index: nine of them overlap with the hyperactivity index (even items) and nine overlap with distractibility or attention problems (odd items). Inclusion in the clinical group was based also on clinical assessment by a specialized psychologist.

Children with symptoms of ADHD were included in the ADHD group, whilst children with symptoms of Conduct Disorder (CD) or ADHD with Oppositional Deviant Disorder (ODD) were excluded to maintain a more homogeneous subject population. In order to confirm this diagnosis, the Italian version of Disruptive Behaviour Disorder Rating Scale (SCOD) of Marzocchi, Oosterlaan, De Meo, Di Pietro, Pezzica, Cavolina, Sergeant and Zuddas (2001), was completed by parents and teachers. On the bases of the number of symptoms recorded in the SCOD - the psychologist used the six symptoms criterion to decide whether the child had a disorder which was pervasive (both at school and at home) and chronic (over 6 months period disorder). Children were categorized as ADHD-HI if they had six or more symptoms of H/I but fewer than six symptoms of IA; as ADHD-C if they showed elevations of six or more symptoms on both dimensions IA and H/I; and as ADHD-IA if they showed elevations of six or more symptoms of IA and fewer than six symptoms of H/I. The groups were matched for gender and for age.. Control children were recruited from the same school of the two clinical groups. Demographic and clinical characteristics of ADHD and control children are summarized in table 3.

Table 3. Demographic statistics

Group	Measures	
ADHD-IA	N of boys/girls	9/1
	Age (mean)	8.9
	IQ (mean)[1]	86.4
	SDAI - distractibility (mean)[2]	18
	SDAI - hyperactivity (mean)	3.7
ADHD-C	N of boys/girls	7/3
	Age (mean)	8.8
	IQ (mean)	98.3
	SDAI - distractibility (mean)	15.8
	SDAI - hyperactivity (mean)	16.5
ADHD-HI	N of boys/girls	7/3
	Age (mean)	8.9
	IQ (mean)	115.6
	SDAI – distractibility (mean)	1.9
	SDAI - hyperactivity (mean)	15
CONTROL	N of boys/girls	18/9
	Age (mean)	9.03
	IQ (mean)	103.44
	SDAI - distractibility (mean)	3.29
	SDAI - hyperactivity (mean)	2.6

Note: IQ was estimated from WISC-R (1994). Distractibility and hyperactivity indicies were estimated from SDAI (Marzocchi and Cornoldi, 2000). The SDAI is composed of 18 items, corresponding to the symptom domain of ADHD, as described in the DSM-IV (APA, 1994). The items provide an ADD index: nine of them overlap with the hyperactivity index (even items) and nine overlap with distractibility or attention problems (odd items). The cut-off criterion for both subscales is 14.

Procedure

Participants were assessed during school lessons. Parents completed consent forms prior to participation in the study. The IQ measure was administered by WISC-R for each subject, in a silent classroom. The dynamic test applied and standardized with primary school children (Fabio, 2001) was also administered. Description of the procedure for presentation of the dynamic test can be found above.

Table 4. Means. standard deviations and statistical significance related to each scale and subscales

	ADHD-IA		ADHD-C		ADHD-HI		CONTROL		F	p
	Mean	Std Dev.	Mean	Std Dev.	Mean	Std Dev.	Mean	Std Dev.		d.f.(3, 53)
Static intelligence test - QI	85.40	9.68	98.30	8.65	115.60	18.59	103.44	17.59	6.22	.001
Verbal	74.70	10.31	98.30	6.68	113.50	18.76	98.37	20.48	8.87	.001
Information	4.30	1.76	7.80	2.09	11.60	3.50	8.85	3.51	9.88	.001
Similarities	6.90	5.13	12.30	2.26	15.80	2.69	12.03	4.66	7.81	.001
Arithmetic	7.40	1.07	9.60	2.11	10.80	3.32	9.55	2.91	2.88	.044
Vocabulary	3.60	3.34	8.40	4.45	12.10	6.24	8.44	7.10	3.32	.026
Comprehension	7.20	4.26	10.70	2.83	10.70	2.98	9.88	3.66	2.21	.097
Performance	101.60	12.21	99.50	17.48	114.70	15.84	108.59	14.25	2.15	.105
Picture Completion	7.90	3.87	9.00	1.82	11.40	2.45	10.00	2.51	3.16	.032
Picture Arrangement	11.80	2.52	11.70	5.16	13.60	4.69	11.00	3.43	1.08	.362
Block Design	11.70	3.05	10.10	4.14	12.80	3.96	12.03	4.01	0.89	.450
Object Assembly	11.70	2.90	10.30	1.05	12.80	2.61	11.81	2.61	1.73	.170
Symbols copy	8.90	2.42	8.70	3.40	10.10	2.60	11.48	2.76	3.53	.021
Dynamic intelligence test	47.20	4.61	48.00	6.21	67.70	9.69	52.70	7.88	7.62	.001
Learning phase	25.20	1.87	25.50	2.59	32.90	4.86	26.11	3.95	3.62	.06
Transfert phase	22.00	4.02	23.50	3.97	34.80	5.28	26.59	4.50	5.00	.004

Data Analyses

One way ANOVA with "subjects" (ADHD-IA, ADHD-HI, ADHD-C and Controls) as independent variable. The dependent variables were the measures derived from static and dynamic general scale and subscales. Post hoc t-test were used to make paired comparisons of the groups.

Results

Table 4 show means, standard deviations and statistical significance related to each scale and subscale of static and dynamic measures.

The results showed that subjects with ADHD had lower scores (subtype IA and C) with static test measures than controls. Considering dynamic test measures, subjects with ADHD had the same scores as controls subjects. In the case of ADHD-HI subjects scored better than controls. With reference to static measure they present just one S.D.'s over the medium (100 ± 15), but with reference to dynamic measures they present two S.D.'s over the medium ($48,4 \pm 9.3$), showing gifteness.

Although this is beyond the aim of this study, it is interesting to note that static results of ADHD-IA were the worse. The reason may be that subjects with ADHD-IA had very high level of comorbidity with learning disabilities and this can result in low static measures. In any case, dynamic measure of these subjects become normal.

CONCLUSION

Dynamic testing reduces the possibility that a child who can profit from instruction mediation is denied opportunities to learn because of a poor score on a static assessment. On the other hand, children who perform similarly on static pretests sometimes respond quite differently to instruction (e.g., Brown and Barclay, 1976; Brown, Campione, and Barclay, 1979; Vygotsky, 1978), suggesting that dynamic measures can provide information over and above that available from static tests. Perhaps dynamic measures add predictive information because instructed tasks are somewhat beyond the learner's competence and, hence, require modification of existing knowledge or skills. The present results are emphasizing two important issues: the first one is that dynamic tests don't discriminate against minorities and individuals whose backgrounds are not middle and upper-middle class; the second one is that dynamic measures are able to underline subjects with latent giftness like the subjects that lie in the overlapping area between ADHD-HI and giftness. Returning to the title of this work "Gifted with dynamic intelligence test measures and normal with static intelligence test measures: what does it means?", the reply may be that the meaning lies in the possibility that dynamic assessment better measure intelligence.

REFERENCES

Barkley, R.A. (1997). Attention deficit hyperactivity disorder: A handbook for diagnosis and treatment. New York, NY: Guilford Press.

Benson, J.C. (2006). IQ Test: How It Works and Why Its Used. http://www.articles2k.com/article.

Berk, L. E. (2001). Development through the lifespan. *Elmsford,* NY: Pearson.

Bolig, E. and Day, J. (1993). Dynamic Assessment of Giftedness: The Promise of Assessing Training Responsiveness. *Roper Review,* 16, 110- 113.

Brown, A. L., and Campione, J. C. (1984). Three faces of transfer: Implication for early competence, individual differences and instruction. In M. Lamb, A. Brown, and B. Rogoff (Eds.), *Advances in developmental psychology.* (143–192). Hillsdale, NJ: Erlbaum.

Brown, A.L., Campione, J.C. and Barclay, C.G. (1979). Training Self-Checking Routines for Estimating Test Readiness: Generalization from List Learning to Prose Recall. *Child Development,* 50, 501-512

Budoff, M. (1987). Measures for assessing learning potential. In C. S. Lidz (Ed.), Dynamic assessment: *An interactional approach to evaluating learning potential.* (pp. 173–195). New York: Guilford.

Campione, J. C., Brown, A. L., Ferrara, R. A., and Bryant, N. R. (1984). The zone of proximal development: Implications for individual differences and learning. In B. Rogoff and J. V. Wertsch (Eds.), *New directions for child development* (77–91). San Francisco: Jossey-Bass.

Clark, B. (1992). Growing Up Gifted. New York: Merrill.

Das, J. P. (2002). A better look at intelligence. *Current Directions In Psychological Science, 11,* 28-33.

Das, J. P., Naglieri, J. A., and Kirby, J. R. (1994). *Assessment of cognitive processes.* Boston: Allyn and Bacon.

Das, J.P., Kirby J., and Jarman, R.F. (1979). Simultaneous and Successive Cognitive Processing, New York, Academic Press.

Duncan, O.D. (1961). A socioeconomic index for all occupations. In A., Jr., Reiss: *Occupations and Social Status.* New York: Free Press.

Elliot, J. (2003). Dynamic Assessment in Educational Settings: realising potential. *Educational Review,* 55, 221-231.

Eysenck, H. (1982). A Model for Intelligence. New York: Springer-Verlag.

Fabio, R. A. (1999). Costruzione di un test di misura dell'intelligenza potenziale. *Giornale Italiano di Psicologia,* 1, 125–146.

Fabio, R. A., (2001). L'intelligenza potenziale: Strumenti di misura e di riabilitazione. Milano: Angeli ed.

Fabio, R. A., (2003). La modificabilità cognitiva nella scuola elementare. *Età evolutiva,* 59, 69–78.

Fabio, R. A., (2005). Dynamic assessment of intelligence is a better reply to adaptive behaviour and cognitive plasticity. *Journal of General Psychology,* 132, 41-64.

Fabio, R. A., and Mancuso, G. (1995). La valutazione degli indici dinamici in bambini in età prescolare. *Psicologia e Scuola,* 76, 46–57.

Feuerstein, R., Rand, Y., and Hoffman, M. B. (1979). The dynamic assessment of retarded performers: The learning potential assessment device-theory, instruments, and techniques. Baltimore, MD: University Park Press.

Feuerstein, R., Rand, Y., Hoffman, M. B., and Miller, R. (1980). *Instrumental enrichment.* Baltimore, MD: University Park Press.

Flanagan, D. P., McGrew, K. S., and Ortiz, S. O. (2000). The Wechsler Intelligence Scales and Gf-Gc theory: A contemporary approach to interpretation. Boston: Allyn and Bacon.

Gardner, H. (2006). Intelligence in Seven Steps. http://www.newhorizons.org/ crfut_gardner.html.

Gardner, M. F. (1979). Expressive One-Word Picture Vocabulary Test. Novato, CA: Academic Therapy Publications.

Gardner, M. F. (1990). Expressive One-Word Picture Vocabulary Test-Revised. Novato, CA: Academic Therapy Publications.

Goleman, D. P. (1995). *Emotional Intelligence: Why It Can Matter More Than IQ for Character, Health and Lifelong Achievement.* Bantam Books, New York.

Hatch, T., and Gardner, H. (1988). From testing intelligence to assessing competencies: A pluralistic view of intellect. *Roeper Review,* 8, 147-150.

Hatch, T., and Gardner, H. (1989). Multiple Intelligences Go to School: Educational Implications of the Theory of Multiple Intelligences. *Educational Researcher,* 18, 4-10.

Horn, J. L., and Cattell, R. B. (1965). Vehicles. ipsatization, and the multiple method of measurement of motivation. *Canadian Journal of Psychology,* 19, 265-279.

Horn, J. L., and Cattell, R. B. (1966). Refinement and test of the theory of fluid and crystallized general intelligences. *Journal of Educational Psychology, 57,* 253-270.

Horn, J. L., and Cattell, R. B. (1967). Age differences in fluid and crystallized intelligence. *Acta Psychologica, 26,* 107-129.

Kalbfleisch, M.L. (2000). Electroencephalographic differences between males with and without ADHD with average and high aptitude during task transitions. Unpublished doctoral dissertation, University of Virginia, Charlottesville.

Kaufman, A. S., and Kaufman, N. L. (1983). Kaufman Assessment Battery for Children. Circle Pines, MN: American Guidance Service.

Kaufmann, F., Kalbfleisch, M. L., and Castellanos, F. X. (2000). Attention deficit disorders and gifted students: What do we really know? Storrs, CT: Connecticut University Press.

Kaufmann, F.A., and Castellanos, F.X. (2000). Attention-deficit/hyperactivity disorder in gifted students. In K.A. Heller, F.J. Monks, R.J. Sternberg, and R.F. Subotnik (Eds.), *International handbook of giftedness and talent.* (621-632). Amsterdam: Elsevier.

Legg, S. and Hutter, M. (2006). A Formal Measure of Machine Intelligence, IDSIA. Annual Ma chine Learning Conference of Belgium and The Netherlands. http://www.idsia.ch/ marcus.

Lidz, C. Y., ELLIOT, J. (2000). Introduction to dynamic assesment. En: Advances in Cognition and Educational Practice, vol. 6: Dynamic Assesment: Prevailing Models and Application. *Editado por Carol Lidz y Julian Elliott.* Elseiver Science.

Luria, A. R. (1966). *Human brain and psychological processes.* New York: Harper and Row.

Lynch, J., Kaplan, G. (2000). Socioeconomic Postion. In B. L.F., Kawachi: Social Epidemiology. New York: Oxford University Press, 2000.

Marzocchi, G. M., and Cornoldi, C. (2000). Una scala di facile uso per la rilevazione dei comportamenti problematici dei bambini con Deficit di Attenzione e Iperattività [A scale to identify behavioural problems in ADHD children]. *Psicologia Clinica dello Sviluppo,* 4, 43-62.

Marzocchi, G. M., Oosterlaan, J., De Meo, T., Di Pietro, M., Pizzica, S., Cavolina, P., Sergeant J. A., and Zuddas A. (2001), Disruptive Behaviour Disorder Rating Scale for teacher (Italian version). *Giornale di Neuropsichiatria dell'Età Evolutiva,* 21, 378-393.

Missiuna, C., Samuels, M. (1989). Dynamic assessment: review and critique. *Special Services in the schools,* 5, 23-28.

Moon, S. (2002). Gifted children with attentio. deficit/hyperactivity disorder. In M. Neihart, S. Reis, N. Robinson, S. Moon (Eds.). The social and emotional development of gifted children: What do we know? (pp. 193-204). Waco, TX: Prufrock Press.

Moon, S.M., Zentall, S.S., Grskovic, J.A., Hall, A. and Stormont, M. (2001). Emotional, social, and family characteristics of boys with AD/HD and giftedness: A comparative case study. *Journal for the Education of the Gifted,* 24, 207-247

Naglieri, J. A. and Das, J. P., and (1997). Naglieri-Das Cognitive Assessment System. Chicago: Riverside.

Naglieri, J. A., and Das, J. P. (1988). Planning-Arousal-Simultaneous-Successive (PASS): A Model for Assessment. *Journal of School Psychology, 26,* 35-48.

Sternberg, R. J. (1986) Advances in the Psychology of Human Intelligence. Vol. 3. New Jersey: Lawrence Erlbaum Associates, Publishers.

Sternberg, R. J. (2006). International Handbook of Intelligence. Connecticut: Yale University.

Sternberg, R. J., and Grigorenko, E. L. (2002). Difference scores in the identification of children with learning disabilities: It's time to use a different method. *Journal of School Psychology,* 40(1), 65-83.

Sternberg, R. J., and Grigorenko, E. L. (2002). Dynamic testing. New York: Cambridge University Press.

Sternberg, R. J., and Grigorenko, E. L. (Eds.). (2002). The general factor of intelligence: How general is it?. Mahwah, NJ: Lawrence Erlbaum Associates..

Stevens, G., and Cho, J. H. (1985). Socioeconomic indexes and the new 1980 census occupational classification scheme. *Social Science Research,* 14, 142-168

Thorndike, R. L., Hagen, E. P., and Sattler, J. M. (1986). Stanford-Binet Intelligence Scale (4th ed.). Chicago, IL: Riverside.

Thorndike, R. M. (1997). The early history of intelligence testing. In D. P. Flanagan, J. L. Genshaft, and P. L. Harrison (Eds.), *Contemporary intellectual assessment: Theories, tests, and issues.* Chicago, IL: Riverside.

Tzuriel, D. (2000). Dynamic assessment of young children: Educational and intervention perspectives. *Educational Psychology Review,* 12, 385–435.

Tzuriel, D., and Kaufman, R. (1999). Mediated learning and cognitive modifiability: dimension and current research. *Educational and Child Psychology,* 14, 83–108.

Tzuriel, D., and Klein, P. (1985). Analogical thinking modifiability in disadvantaged, regular, special education, and mentally retarded children. *Journal of Abnormal Child Psychology,* 13, 539–552.

Tzuriel, D., and Klein, P. (1987). Assessing the young child: Children's analogical thinking modifiability. In C. S. Lidz (Ed.), Dynamic assessment: An interactional approach to evaluating learning potential (pp. 268–287). New York: Guilford.

Vialle, W. (1999). Identification of giftedness in culturally diverse groups. *Gifted Education International,* 13, 250 - 257.

Vygotskij, L. S., (1978). Mind in society: The development of higher psychological processes. Cambridge, MA: Harvard University Press.

Vygotsky, L. S. (1986). Thought and language. Cambridge, MA: MIT Press.

Webb. J.T. (2001). Mis-diagnosis and dual diagnosis of gifted children: Gifted and LD, ADHD, OCD, oppositional defiant disorder. N. Hafenstein and F. Rainey (Eds.), Perspectives in gifted education: Twice exceptional children (pp. 23-31). Denver: Ricks Center for Gifted Children, University of Denver.

Wechsler, D. (1974). Wechsler intelligence scale for children-Revised edition. San Antonio, TX: The Psychological Corporation.

Wechsler, D. (1997). Wechsler adult intelligence scale–Third edition. San Antonio, TX: The Psychological Corporation.

Wielkiewicz, R. M. (1990). Interpreting low scores on the WISC–R third factor: It's more than distractibility. *Journal of Consulting and Clinical Psychology,* 2 (1), 91-97.

Zentall, S.S., Moon, S.M., Hall, A.M., and Grskovic, J.A. (2001). Learning and motivational characteristics of boys with AD/HD and/or giftedness. *Exceptional Children,* 67, 499-519.

In: Psychological Tests and Testing Research Trends
Editor: Paul M. Goldfarb, pp. 111-139

ISBN: 978-1-60021-569-8
© 2007 Nova Science Publishers, Inc.

Chapter 5

THE SELF-INJURY QUESTIONNAIRE - TREATMENT RELATED (SIQ-TR): CONSTRUCTION, RELIABILITY, AND VALIDITY IN A SAMPLE OF FEMALE EATING DISORDER PATIENTS

Laurence Claes and Walter Vandereycken

Department of Psychology, Catholic University of Leuven, Belgium

ABSTRACT

Self-injurious behaviour (SIB) refers to the direct and deliberate damage of one's own body surface without suicidal intent. This is a considerable health problem occurring at a high frequency in psychiatric inpatients units. In order to design specific therapeutic interventions, the primary diagnostic task is to identify the current external and internal stimulus conditions that contribute directly to the instigation of SIB. But for that purpose we do not have good assessment instruments and therefore we developed a new self-reporting questionnaire: the Self-Injury Questionnaire - Treatment Related (SIQ-TR; see Appendix A) which not only assesses the taxonomic specifications of SIB (e.g., type, frequency, duration), but also the affective antecedents and consequences as well as the functions of each type of SIB separately. A validation study in 273 female eating disorder patients showed that we were able to construct four reliable and valid Emotions Scales (Positive/Negative Affectivity Before/After SIB) and three Functionality Scales (Positive Social Reinforcement, Automatic Positive/Negative Reinforcement). Convergent and divergent validity of the SIB characteristics, the Emotion Scales and the Functionality Scales were calculated by correlating the SIQ-TR with the Self-Harm Inventory, the Self Expression and Control Questionnaire and the Symptom Checklist. Finally, we discuss how the SIQ-TR can be used to plan the therapeutic management of SIB.

INTRODUCTION

Unlike the more general concept of self-harm, including indirect self-damaging behavior and suicidal attempts, self-injurious behaviour (SIB) refers to the direct and deliberate damage of one's own body surface without suicidal intent (Favazza, 1998). Since only a small proportion is really "mutilating" we avoid the term self-mutilation. Moreover, we restrict our clinical target by excluding self-injury in organic mental disorders, psychotic patients and mentally retarded people. SIB is a serious health problem occurring at a rate of 4% in the general adult population and 21% in adult clinical populations (Briere and Gil, 1998). Adolescence is a period of increased risk for SIB, as is evidenced by rates of 14 to 39% in community samples of adolescents (Ross and Heath, 2002) and 40 to 61% in adolescent psychiatric inpatient samples (Darche, 1990; Diclemente, Ponton, and Hartley, 1991). The high rate of SIB, certainly within psychiatric settings, and the psychological dysfunctioning often linked to such behaviors (Claes, Vandereycken, and Vertommen, 2003; Nock and Kazdin, 2002), underscore the need for a better understanding and treatment of these behaviors (Nock and Prinstein, 2004; 2005).

SIB has many forms together with a great diversity in meanings. In order to develop an individually tailored treatment plan, the primary diagnostic task is to pinpoint the behavior and its current developmental process, i.e. identifying the external (e.g., reduced social attention) and internal (e.g., anxiety, anger) stimulus conditions that contribute directly to the instigation of SIB. Hence, a treatment-related assessment seeks to determine the motives, purposes or functions of SIB (Gardner and Sovner, 1994). Though there are several assessment instruments, only a few measures systematically focus on the internal and external antecedents of SIB (for an overview see Claes, Vandereycken, and Vertommen, 2005). Faced with a growing number of female eating disorder patients showing SIB, we were challenged to design appropriate treatment plans (see Vanderlinden and Vandereycken, 1997). But the existing assessment tools were either too restricted or unreliable. Therefore, we developed a new self-reporting questionnaire, the Self-Injury Questionnaire -Treatment Related (SIQ-TR), to asses not only the taxonomic specifications of SIB (e.g., type, frequency, duration, and intensity), but also the affective antecedents/consequences and the functions of each type of SIB separately. In the remainder of this article, we describe the construction, reliability and validity of the SIQ-TR, as we have developed and studied it in a large group of female eating disorder patients.

CONSTRUCTION OF THE SIQ-TR

As mentioned above, we have clearly delineated SIB from other forms of self-harm and define it as any socially nonaccepted self-inflicted damage of the body surface without suicidal intent (no wish to die). One of the first features we wanted to specify is the *type of action* employed in SIB. Ross and McKay (1979) have used a behavioral-descriptive approach distinguishing nine categories: cutting, biting, abrading, severing, inserting, burning, ingesting or inhaling, hitting and constructing. We limited the assessment to five types of SIB which were frequently reported in our eating disorder samples: scratching, bruising, cutting, burning, and biting oneself; additionally the subject can specify another type of SIB. For each type we asked how long ago the patient had displayed this form of SIB. If it was less than a month ago, the subject had to fill out different questions concerning the taxonomy and functionality of that particular SIB.

A second feature to assess is the *localisation of SIB* on the body. Some assessment instruments use rather vague terms to describe the body parts involved (e.g., head, extremities) while others specify this in detail (e.g., left upper arm, right forearm). Another way is the use of localisation sheets on which one can point out which body part has been injured. We have chosen to let the subject indicate which of five body regions were mostly injured: (1) head, neck; (2) arms, hands, fingers, nails; (3) torso, belly, buttock; (4) legs, feet, toes; and (5) breasts or genitals.

The third feature is the *frequency of SIB during a specific period of time*. We gave the subject the opportunity to indicate how many days SIB did occur during the last month (between 1-5, 6-10, 11-15, more than 15 days). When multiple episodes are present, one can also specify – as fourth feature - the *frequency distribution of SIB during a specific period of time* (less than 1, 1 to 2, 3 to 4, more than 5 acts per day).

The fifth feature to be assessed is the *frequency of pain experience during SIB* (never, now and then, often, always); and the sixth feature refers to the *intensity of pain experience during SIB* (none, mild, moderate, strong, very strong). These questions are important because roughly one third of our SIB patients do not feel pain while injuring themselves, possibly due to a dissociative state a the moment of self-injury (Claes, Vandereycken, and Vertommen, 2001).

The seventh characteristic is an *attitudinal* one, assessed in four questions: (a) whether the SIB was planned, (b) whether the subject knows how the SIB came about, (c) whether the subject took care of the wounds, and (d) whether the subject did hide the self-inflicted wounds. Own research (Claes, Vandereycken, and Vertommen, 2001, 2003) showed that most acts of SIB are not planned, that wounds are seldom taken care of and are often concealed.

Next (eight and ninth feature), the *affective antecedents and consequences* of SIB were assessed. The emotion list referrred to four basic emotions (Magai and McFadden, 1995): happiness (specified as glad, relieved), sadness (sad, guilty), anger (angry at myself, angry at other), and anxiety (nervous, bored, anxious), and one alternative of choice. These different affective states are supposed to merge on a higher order level into two affective clusters, a positive and negative affect (Frijda, 1993). For each of these emotions, the subject was asked to indicated on a 5-point Likert scale in which degree (not at all, a bit, moderately, much, very much) each of these affects were absent or present before and after SIB.

Finally, the *functionality* of each type of SIB (feature 10) was investigated by offering 11 possible functions (motives, reasons, purposes) and one free choice item: the subject had to indicate to which degree each of these functions were playing a role during SIB. The list of possible functions was based on the existing literature (Vanderlinden and Vandereycken, 1997; Suyemoto, 1998; Brown, Comtois, and Linehan, 2002; Herpertz, 1995). Vanderlinden and Vandereycken (1997) have proposed a functional scale according to the direct consequence of the SIB upon the psychological state of the patients, ranging from a highly rewarding effect to a highly destructive impact: relaxation (enjoying pain, diminishing tension, diverting attention, inducing dissociation); attention (obtaining self-affirmation, getting protection); stimulation (feeling one's body or identity, escaping from dissociation); punishment (e.g., because of guilt feelings, for being weak, undisciplined), and self-destructiveness (becoming unattractive, a parasuicidal act). More recently, Nock and Prinstein (2004, p. 886) proposed and evaluated four primary functions of SIB that differ along two dichotomous dimensions: "(1) contingencies that are automatic versus social, and (2) reinforcement that is either positive (i.e., followed by the presentation of a favorable stimulus) or negative (i.e., followed by the removal of an aversive stimulus). Automatic-negative refers to an individual's use of SIB to achieve a reduction in tension or other negative affective states. In automatic-positive reinforcement, individuals engage in SIB to create a desirable physiological state. Social-negative reinforcement refers to SIB as a means to escape from interpersonal task demands. Social-positive reinforcement for SIB involves gaining attention from others or gaining access to materials".

VALIDATION STUDY: METHOD

The SIQ-TR as well as other questionnaires (measuring convergent and divergent constructs) were administered to a group of female eating disorder (ED) patients. Only the patients who admitted to have injured themselves "during the last week or month" were included in the study.

Participants

Participants were 273 female patients admitted to two specialized inpatient ED units in Belgium. Overall, 30.4% (N=83) of them admitted to have performed at least one type of SIB since less than a month. The mean age of the self-injurers was 24.8 years (SD=8.2). Of these patients, 54.2% finished primary and/or secondary education, 30.1% higher education and 12.0% university (3.6% missing).

Procedure

Data were obtained during a comprehensive evaluation routinely carried the first days of admission in the inpatient unit. The use of data from each patient's clinical record was approved for research purposes by the hospital's and university's institutional review boards. Patients with active psychosis or mental retardation were excluded. Beside the SIQ-TR patients filled out the following self-reporting questionnaires.

Measures

The *Self-Harm Inventory* (SHI-22; Sansone, Wiederman, and Sansone, 1998) is intent to assess the extent to which psychiatric patients report engaging in SIB. Items were collected from the literature and the clinical experience of the authors and their associated multidisciplinary treatment teams. Patients are asked to indicate if they have ever intentionally engaged in any of the 22 examples of SIB ("yes" or "no"). Sample items include: "overdosed", "cut yourself on purpose", "burned yourself on purpose", "hit yourself on purpose", "banged your head on purpose", and "driven recklessly on purpose". A total SHI score is computed as the number of SIB that the patient reported (total of "yes" responses).

Finally, there is an area for respondents to write down any SIB that was not specifically addressed in the questionnaire. SHI scores of 5 or greater were found to be indicative of borderline personality disorder and a score of 5 did accurately classify nearly 84% of individuals with and without borderline personality disorder (Sansone et al., 2000).

The *Self-Expression and Control Scale* (SECS; van Elderen, et al., 1996) measures internalization of anger (Anger-in), externalization of anger (Anger-Out), control of internalization of anger (Control Anger-In), and control of externalization of anger (Control Anger-Out). The internalization of anger (10 items; $\alpha=0.87$) refers to the frequency of experienced feelings of anger, which feelings are internalized or directed inwardly. The externalization of anger refers to the frequency of experienced feelings of anger, which feelings are externalized or directed outwardly (10 items; $\alpha=0.89$). Control of internalization of anger (10 items; $\alpha=0.91$) refers to the frequency of attempts or behaviors to control inwardly directed feelings or expressions of anger; and control of externalization of anger (10 items; $\alpha=0.90$) refers to the frequency of attempts or behaviors to control outwardly directed feelings or expressions of anger. Subjects can respond by rating themselves on a four-point frequency scale (1=almost never, 2=sometimes, 3=often, 4=always). The four subscales have shown high internal consistency coefficients; additionally, the intersubscale correlations were low enough to justify different, albeit related concepts and, as such, different subscales (van Elderen et al., 1996).

The *Symptom Checklist* (SCL-90, Dutch version: Arrindell and Ettema, 1986) is a well-known measure for the assessment of a wide array of psychiatric symptoms. It comprises 90 items (symptoms) to be rated on a five-point scale ranging from "not at all applicable" to "strongly applicable". Along with a global measure for psychoneuroticism ($\alpha=0.97$), it measures complaints of general and phobic anxiety ($\alpha=0.88$/$\alpha=0.87$), depression ($\alpha=0.91$), somatization ($\alpha=0.88$), obsessions/compulsions ($\alpha=0.84$), paranoid ideation and interpersonal sensitivity ($\alpha=0.92$), hostility ($\alpha=0.84$), and sleeplessness ($\alpha=0.82$). The validity studies of the SCL-90 demonstrated levels of concurrent, convergent, discriminant and construct validity from good to very good (see Arrindell and Ettema, 1986).

Analyses

We used descriptive statistics to examine the frequency of different SIB actions as well as related characteristics of SIB. Various data-analytic procedures were used to evaluate the reliability (e.g., internal consistency coefficient or alpha coefficient), the construct validity (factor analysis) and convergent and divergent validity (Pearson correlation coefficient) of the SIQ-TR.

VALIDATION STUDY: RESULTS

Table 1. Frequencies, percentages and correlations of different types of SIB as measured with the SIQ-TR and correlations between the SIQ-TR (SIB during last week/month) and SHI (SIB during last year)

					SHI		
SIQ-TR	N	%	1	2	3	4	5
1. Scratching	44	53	(0.43**)	0.34**	0.37**	0.06	0.28**
2. Bruising	28	33.7		(0.53**)	0.31**	0.23**	0.23**
3. Cutting	44	53			(0.71**)	0.26**	0.15**
4. Burning	11	13.3				(0.75**)	0.19**
5. Biting	15	18.1					-- °

° SHI has no item referring to "biting oneself"; Above the diagonal correlations between the SIBs as measured by the SIQ-TR; on the diagonal (between brackets) correlations between SIQ-TR and SHI; ** $p < 0.01$.

Types of SIB

Overall, 30.4% (N=83) of the 273 female ED patients admitted to have injured themselves since less than a month: 55.4% (N=46) performed one type of SIB, 25.3% (N=21) two types, 14.5% (N=12) three types, 4.8% (N=4) four or more types of SIB. Of the 83 self-injurers 53% scratched themselves, 33.7% bruised, 53% cut, 13.3% burned, and 18.1% bit themselves.

The correlations between the different types of SIB are shown in table 1, and range from 0.06 to 0.37. The alpha coefficient of the five different types of SIB is 0.62, meaning that they are related but separate constructs that need to be analyzed separately. The correlations between the different acts of SIB as assessed by the SIQ-TR (during the last week/month) and the same acts assessed by the SHI (during the last year) are in line with the expectations.

Characteristics of SIB

Table 2 shows the frequencies and cumulative percentages of the different categorically scored characteristics of each type of SIB separately. Overall, the "arms, hands, and/or nails" are the most frequently injured body parts. SIB occurs on average "1 to 5 times a month", and "less than once a day". Most patients admit that they feel "now and then" some "mild" pain during SIB. The means and the standard deviations of the dimensionally scored SIB characteristics are shown in table 3. Most patients admit that their SIB was seldomly planned ("never" or "sometimes"), that they "sometimes" realize how their SIB came about, that they "sometimes take care" of their wounds (except for bruising probably because this act doesn't cause bleeding wounds), and that they "often" concealed their wounds.

Table 2. Frequencies (N) and cumulative percentages (C%) of characteristics of different types of SIB

	Scratching (N_{max}=44)		Bruising (N_{max}=28)		Cutting (N_{max}=44)		Burning (N_{max}=11)		Biting (N_{max}=15)	
	N	C%	N	C%	N	C%	N	C%	N	C%
Body parts injured										
Head										
No	28	65.1	14	50.0	43	97.7	6	100	14	93.3
Yes	15	100	14	100	1	100	0	100	1	100
Arms, hands, nails										
No	7	16.3	12	42.9	6	13.6	1	9.1	0	0
Yes	36	100	16	100	38	100	10	100	15	100
Torso, belly, buttock										
No	35	81.4	21	75	38	86.4	5	83.3	15	100
Yes	8	100	7	100	6	100	1	100	0	100
Legs, feet, toes										
No	32	74.4	20	71.4	31	70.5	5	71.4	15	100
Yes	11	100	8	100	13	100	2	100	0	100
Breasts, genitals										
No	40	93.0	27	96.4	42	95.5	6	100	15	100
Yes	3	100	1	100	2	100	0	100	0	100
Frequency (days/month)										
1-5	23	52.3	19	67.9	28	65.1	8	80	8	53.3
6-10	11	77.3	2	75	7	81.4	2	100	3	73.3
10-15	3	84.1	3	85.7	3	88.4	0	100	1	80
>15	7	100	4	100	5	100	0	100	3	100
Frequency (times/day)										
< 1	20	45.5	13	48.1	25	56.8	9	81.8	6	40
1-2	19	88.6	8	77.8	17	95.5	2	100	6	80
3-4	2	93.2	4	92.6	2	100	0	100	0	80
≥ 5	3	100	2	100	0	100	0	100	3	100
How often pain										
Never	11	25	6	21.4	11	25	4	36.4	4	28.6
Now and then	26	84.1	13	67.9	22	75	3	63.6	5	64.3
Often	6	97.7	7	92.9	6	88.6	2	81.8	2	78.6
Always	1	100	2	100	5	100	2	100	3	100
Degree of pain										
None	8	18.2	5	17.9	10	22.7	4	36.4	3	20.0
Mild	26	77.3	14	67.9	18	63.6	3	63.6	5	53.3
Moderate	8	95.5	7	92.9	10	86.4	4	100	5	86.7
Strong	2	100	2	100	6	100	0	100	2	100
Very strong	0	100	0	100	0	100	0	100	0	100

Table 3. Means (M) and standard deviations (SD) of characteristics of different types of SIB

	Scratching (N_{max}=44)		Bruising (N_{max}=28)		Cutting (N_{max}=44)		Burning (N_{max}=11)		Biting (N=15)	
Characteristics[a]	M	SD	M	SD	M	SD	M	SD	M	SD
Planned	1.5	(0.7)	1.7	0.8	1.8	0.8	1.5	0.9	1.3	0.8
Not dissociated	2.2	(1.0)	2.4	0.8	2.3	0.9	2.3	0.9	1.7	1.0
Wound Care	2.5	(1.1)	1.5	0.9	2.6	1.1	2.3	1.1	2.0	1.1
Hiding Wounds	3.0	(0.9)	3.0	0.9	3.2	0.8	2.9	0.9	2.8	1.1

[a] Scored on a 4-point Likert scale: 1=never; 2=sometimes; 3=often; 4=always.

The significant relations between the characteristics of SIB were all in the expected direction: the frequency of SIB per month and the frequency of SIB per day are positively correlated (r=0.54, p<0.001), as well as the frequency of pain and the intensity of pain (r=0.71; p<0.001). Furthermore, the injuring of the arms and hands was positively associated with the planning of SIB (more planning; r=0.31, p<0.05) and the hiding of SIB (more hiding; r=0.32, p<0.05) and negatively with taking care of SIB (less wound care; r=-0.41, p<0.05). The frequency of SIB per month was negatively correlated with taking care of the wound (the more SIB, the less taking care of SIB; r=-0.35, p<0.05) as was the correlation between the frequency of pain and the hiding of SIB (the more frequent pain was experienced during SIB, the less the SIB was hidden; r=-0.29, p<0.05), probably because the SIB needed to be taken care of.

**Table 4. Principal component analysis with varimax rotation
of reported feelings before/after SIB**

	Feelings before SIB		Feelings after SIB	
Feelings	Component 1 Neg-B[a]	Component 2 Pos-B	Component 1 Neg-A	Component 2 Pos-A
Glad	-[b]	0.79	-	0.51
Relieved	-	0.66	-	0.72
Nervous	0.44	-	0.62	
Bored	-	0.49	-	0.59
Angry Self	0.68	-	0.75	-
Angry Other	0.36	-	0.59	-
Anxious	0.88	-	0.80	-
Sad	0.67	-	0.78	-
Guilty	0.77	-	0.78	-

[a] Neg-B=Negative Emotions before SIB Scale; Pos-B=Positive Emotions before SIB Scale; Neg-A=Negative Emotions after SIB Scale; Pos-A=Positive Emotions after SIB Scale;
[b] Component loadings smaller than 0.35 are not mentioned.

Affective Antecedents/Consequences

For each type of SIB, the patients were asked to indicate to which degree each of nine affects preceded and followed the act of self-injuring. To assess construct validity, we performed a component analysis on both the preceding feelings and the consequent feelings (see table 4). The component structure that was most stable for both the preceding and the consequent feelings was the two factor solution, which accounts for 43.6% of the variance of the preceding feelings and 55.1% of the variance of the consequent feelings. In both solutions, the first component is labelled "negative affect" and the second component "positive affect".

The internal consistency of the four emotion scales was evaluated with Cronbach's alpha coefficients (table 5). The alpha coefficient of the original "Negative Emotions before SIB Scale" was 0.47; after elimination of the item "Nervous" the alpha coefficient increased up to 0.61. Compared with the other items of the "Negative Emotions before SIB Scale", the item "Nervous" is less intense than other emotions, such as anger, anxiousness, sadness and guilt.

The alpha coefficient of the "Positive Emotions before SIB Scale" was 0.14; however, after elimination of the negative affect "bored", the alpha coefficient increased to 0.78. The alpha coefficient of the original "Negative Emotions after SIB Scale" was 0.89; after elimination of the item "Nervous" the alpha coefficient slightly increased up to 0.89. The alpha coefficient of the "Positive Emotions after SIB Scale" was 0.51; after elimination of the negative affect "bored", the alpha coefficient remained 0.51. Although the increase in internal consistency is small for the "Negative/Positive Emotions after SIB Scales", we decided to eliminated the items because the emotion scales before and after SIB are comparable. The resulting alpha coefficients (presented in table 5) ranged from 0.51 to 0.89, which suggests moderate to very good internal consistency reliability for each subscale. The fact that the "Positive Emotion Scales before/after SIB" have lower internal consistency coefficients than the "Negative Emotions Scales" is due to the fact that the number of items of the Positive Emotion Scales is much smaller (and the alpha coefficient depends on the number of items in the scale).

The correlations between the "Negative Emotion Scales" (before/after SIB) and the "Positive Emotion Scales" (before/after SIB) are negative, and the negative correlation is strongest after the act of SIB. Furthermore, the correlation between the "Positive Emotions before SIB Scale" and the "Positive Emotions after SIB Scale" is positive, as well as the correlation between the "Negative Emotions before SIB Scale" and the "Negative Emotions after SIB Scale" (see table 5). We checked by means of an dependent sample t-test whether the negative and positive emotion scales changed significantly before and after SIB. We found a significant decrease in negative emotions and a significant increase in positive emotions from pre- to post-SIB for scratching [Negative Affect: $t(42)=3.62$, $p<0.001$; Positive Affect: $t(43)=-6.22$, $p<0.0001$], bruising [Negative Affect: $t(25)=2.99$, $p<0.01$; Positive Affect: $t(24)=-6.26$, $p<0.0001$], cutting [Negative Affect: $t(40)=3.64$, $p<0.001$; Positive Affect: $t(42)=-7.34$, $p<0.0001$], and burning [Negative Affect: $t(9)=2.42$, $p<0.05$; Positive Affect: $t(9)=-2.86$, $p<0.01$]. For biting [Negative Affect: $t(12)=4.45$, $p<0.001$; Positive Affect: $t(12)=0.37$, $p=0.771$] we only found a decrease in negative affect, but no increase of positive affect.

Finally, we correlated the four emotion scales with the SECS and the SCL-90 (particularly the anxiety, depression, and hostility subscales). The findings (see table 6) show a positive correlation between SECS "anger-in" and SIQ-TR "negative affect before SIB" and "positive affect after SIB". Furthermore, the "Anxiety", "Depression" and "Hostility" (Anger) Scales of the SCL-90 were positively related with SIQ-TR "Negative Emotions before SIB" and "Negative Emotions after SIB" (except for hostility) and negatively with "Positive Emotions Before/After SIB".

Table 5. Means (M), standard deviations (SD), correlations and alpha coefficients for the Positive/Negative emotions before/after SIB scales

Subscales	Scratching (N_{max}=44)		Bruising (N_{max}=28)		Cutting (N_{max}=44)		Burning (N_{max}=11)		Biting (N_{max}=15)		Correlations (Overall)			
	M	(SD)	M	(SD)	M	(SD)	M	SD	M	SD	1	2	3	4
1. Neg-B	3.6	(0.9)	3.9	(0.8)	3.6	(0.9)	3.4	(1.1)	3.6	(0.7)	0.61	-0.05	0.42**	0.07
2. Pos-B	1.1	(0.3)	1.0	(0.2)	1.0	(0.3)	1.0	(0.0)	1.3	(0.6)		0.78	-0.06	0.15
3. Neg-A	2.9	(1.0)	3.2	(1.1)	2.9	(1.1)	2.9	(1.0)	2.8	(1.0)			0.89	-0.35**
4. Pos-A	2.1	(1.1)	2.2	(0.9)	2.4	(1.2)	1.9	(0.9)	1.3	(0.3)				0.51

Numbers on the diagonal are alpha coefficients; ** $p<0.01$.

Table 6. Correlations between the Emotions Before/After SIB Scales (SIQ-TR) and the Self-Expression Questionnaire and the Symptom Checklist Scales

	Feelings Before/After SIB Scales			
	Neg-B	Pos-B	Neg-A	Pos-A
Self-Expression Questionnaire				
Anger In	0.40**	-0.07	0.18	0.39**
Anger Out	-0.16	0.02	-0.07	-0.04
Anger In Control	-0.23	0.09	0.07	-0.11
Anger Out Control	0.04	0.13	-0.04	0.04
Symptom Checklist (SCL-90)				
Anxiety	0.17	-0.14	0.28*	-0.20
Depression	0.37**	-0.16	0.28*	-0.03
Hostility	0.26*	-0.24	0.09	0.00

** $p<0.01$.

Functions of SIB

For each type of SIB, the patient was asked to indicate to which degree each of eleven functions (reasons, motives, purposes) did play a role in the coming about of the particular SIB. Instead of analyzing each function of SIB separately, we performed a factor analysis on the eleven functions of SIB, to create separate function scales. Research by Nock and Prinstein (2004; 2005) supported the structural validity and reliability of a four-function model, with patients reporting engaging in SIB for automatic reinforcement (e.g., to stop bad feelings), automatic positive reinforcement (e.g., to feel something, even if it is pain), social negative reinforcement (e.g., to avoid doing something unpleasant you do not want to do) and social positive reinforcement (e.g., to get attention). Because we did not include "social negative reinforcement functions" in our list, we expected to find three function scales: (1) automatic reinforcement, (2) automatic positive reinforcement, and (3) social positive reinforcement.

The results of our principal component analysis (table 7) show that three components have an eigenvalue greater than one and account for 56% of the variance. The first component can be labelled "(social) positive reinforcement" as the functions with the highest loading refer to "show others how strong I am" and "get attention", while the other two functions also refer to getting a positive effect of SIB (being strong, feel pleasure). The notion that patients sometimes engage in SIB to gain attention or to manipulate others is often discussed in the clinical literature, yet like the other proposed functions, this notion has received little empirical support (Nock and Prinstein, 2004). The second component can be labelled as "automatic positive reinforcement", since individuals engage in SIB to create a desirable physiological state (e.g., to feel something, even if it's pain). The third component is labelled "automatic negative reinforcement" referring to an individual's use of SIB to achieve a reduction in tension or other negative affective states (e.g., to stop bad feelings).This function is the most commonly invoked in the clinical literature and there is some empirical evidence supporting the automatic reinforcing properties of SIB (Nock and Prinstein, 2004).

**Table 7. Principal component analysis with varimax rotation
of reported functions for engaging in SIB**

Functions	Component 1 S-PR	Component 2 A-PR	Component 3 A-NR
To show others how strong I am	0.87	-	-
To get attention from others	0.71	-	-
To show myself how strong I am	0.64	-	-
To feel some pleasure	0.61	-	-
To make myself unattractive	-[*]	0.77	-
To punish myself	-	0.71	-
To avoid or suppress suicidal thoughts	-	0.69	-
To escape from a twilight or numb state	-	0.53	-
To avoid or suppress negative feelings	-	-	0.83
To avoid or suppress painful images or memories	-	-	0.74
To get into a twilight or numb state	-	-	0.72

S-PR=Social Positive Reinforcement; A-PR=Automatic Positive Reinforcement; N-PR=Automatic Negative Reinforcement; [*] Component loadings smaller than 0.22 are not mentioned.

Table 8 shows the alpha coefficients, the means, standard deviations and correlations for each of the three function scales. The internal consistency of the three scales was evaluated with Cronbach's alpha coefficients. The resulting alpha coefficients ranged from 0.65 to 0.70 (the alpha coefficient of A-PR increased to 0.69 after removal of the item "escape from dissociation"), which suggests moderate internal consistency reliability for each scale. The three subscales were significantly correlated. The magnitude of these correlations (0.17-0.30) indicates shared variance between 2.8% and 9% among the subscales. This supports the hypothesis that, although related, the three functions represent distinct constructs. The social positive reinforcement of SIB is scored lowest, followed by automatic positive reinforcement and automatic negative reinforcement for each type of SIB separately.

Table 8. Means (M), standard deviations (SD), correlations and alpha coefficients for the Functions of SIB Scales

Subscales	Scratch (N_{max}=44)		Bruise (N_{max}=28)		Cut (N_{max}=44)		Burn (N_{max}=11)		Bite (N_{max}=15)		Correlations (Overall)		
	M	(SD)	M	(SD)	M	(SD)	M	SD	M	SD	1	2	3
1. S-PR	1.3	(0.4)	1.7	(0.8)	1.7	(0.8)	1.8	(1.1)	1.4	(0.6)	0.68	0.17*	0.20*
2. A-PR	2.5	(1.1)	2.5	(0.7)	2.5	(0.9)	2.7	(1.4)	2.0	(0.8)		0.65	0.30**
3. A-NR	3.0	(1.2)	3.0	(1.1)	3.1	(1.1)	3.0	(1.3)	2.7	(0.9)			0.70

S-PR=Social Positive Reinforcement; A-PR=Automatic Positive Reinforcement; N-PR=Automatic Negative Reinforcement; Numbers on the diagonal are alpha coefficients; *p<0.05, **p<0.01.

Table 9. Correlations between the Functions of SIB Scales and the Emotions Before/After SIB scales and the Self-Expression Questionnaire

	Functions of SIB		
	S-PR	A-PR	A-NR
Emotions Before/After SBI			
Neg-B	0.04	0.38**	0.40**
Pos-B	0.28**	0.05	0.17
Neg-A	0.05	0.33**	0.32**
Pos-A	0.32**	0.11	0.33**
Self-Expression Questionnaire			
Anger-in	0.07	0.32*	0.43**
Anger-out	0.42**	-0.13	-0.25
Anger-in-control	-0.06	-0.05	-0.14
Anger-out-control	-0.12	0.05	0.01
SIQ-TR			
"Planned SIB"	0.21*	-.016	-0.05
"Hiding Wounds"	-0.21*	0.22*	0.12

*p<0.05, **p<0.01.

The three functions of SIB were correlated with the SIQ-TR "Emotion before/after SIB" scales, the SECS, and the SIQ-TR items "Hiding SIB" and "Planning SIB (table 9). On theoretical basis, one would expect that the "Social Reinforcement Function Scale" has a positive correlations with "anger out" (showing that something is wrong) and "Planning SIB" (when others are present) and a negative correlation with the item "hiding SIB". The "Automatic Positive/Negative Reinforcement Function Scales" are hypothesized to correlated negative with "anger out" and positive with "anger in" (not showing to others that something is wrong) and positively with the item "hiding SIB". "Social Positive Reinforcement" is significantly positively correlated with "positive feelings before/after SIB", "anger-out", and "planning SIB", and negatively with "hiding wounds". "Automatic Positive/Negative Reinforcement" is positively linked with "negative feelings before/after SIB" and "hiding wounds" and negatively associated with "anger out" and "planning of SIB" (a function called automatic is of course expected to correlate negatively with planned SIB). As can be seen in table 9, the "Social Positive Reinforcement Function" has the opposite correlation pattern of the "Automatic Positive/Negative Reinforcement Function Scales".

DISCUSSION

We have examined SIB using a functional rather than a syndromal approach. Whereas the latter focuses on the assessment and treatment of behaviors according to their static (momentary) and structural (topographic, nosologic) characteristics, a functional approach refers to the dynamic processes and developmental factors that produce and maintain these behaviors (antecedent and consequent influences). Nevertheless we designed a new self-reporting measure (SIQ-TR) that starts with the assessment of the taxonomic features of different types of SIB (e.g., frequency, duration, pain experience) but expands the scope to get a better insight in the emotional antecedents and consequences, as well as the functionality of SIB. The results of our study in a large sample of female ED patients show that we were able to develop reliable and valid scales for these purposes.

The principal component analysis revealed a two component solution as the most stable for both the preceding and consequent affects of SIB. The emotion scales confirm the hypothesis of the affect regulation function of SIB which is described as the most important in the clinical literature (e.g., Suyemoto, 1998; Brown, Comtois, and Linehan, 2002). A pre/post-SIB comparison clearly shows, as expected, an increase in positive affectivity and a decrease in negative affectivity. Furthermore, the results of our functionality scales are completely in line with the findings of Nock and Prinstein (2004), supporting the structural validity and reliability of a four-function model of SIB: patients engage in SIB for automatic negative reinforcement (e.g., to stop bad feelings), automatic positive reinforcement (e.g., to feel something, even if it is pain), social negative reinforcement (e.g., to avoid doing something unpleasant you do not want to do) and social positive reinforcement (e.g., to get attention). Because we did not include "social negative reinforcement" in our function list, we expected and confirmed three function scales: (1) Automatic Negative Reinforcement, (2) Automatic Positive Reinforcement, and (3) Social Positive Reinforcement. The correlation pattern of the Social Reinforcement Scale and the two Automatic Reinforcement Scales was the opposite of each other: the Social Reinforcement Function was positively correlated with Anger-Out (SECS), Positive Affectivity, and Planning SIB, and negatively with Hiding Wounds; the Automatic Reinforcement Scales were positively correlated with Anger-In (SECS), Negative Affectivity, Non-planning SIB, and positively with Hiding Wounds.

The variety of functions suggests that different learning experiences may be involved in the development of SIB. Hence, for each individual patient, clinicians should consider appropriate therapeutic approaches related to the identified function of SIB (therefore our questionnaire is called "treatment related"). Interventions may be most effective if aimed at replacing SIB with functionally equivalent but adaptive behaviors (Linehan, 1993; Nock and Prinstein, 2004, p.889). The SIQ-TR may be used then as one of the instruments in the judgment of evolution during and after treatment.

Our instrument requires more investigation because of some limitations of the existing research. Future studies should include male patients and other psychiatric disorders. Our method of assessment relied exclusively on self-report at one time point. Future research can be improved by using multiple informants, performance-based assessment methods, and the collection of data over several time points to ensure the validity and reliability of observed results (for an extensive overview, see Prinstein, Nock, Spirito, and Grapentine, 2001). But, on the other hand, making use of self-reports allows for an examination of reinforcement that is automatic thus less detectable by external informants as well as an assessment of SIB that occurs in situations where no one else is present (Nock and Prinstein, 2004, 2005). Anyhow, a reliable and clinically useful self-reporting instrument is indispensable, and we hope the SIQ-TR will fulfill these expectations.

REFERENCES

Arrindell, W.A., and Ettema, J.H.M. (1986). *SCL-90: Handleiding bij een multidimensionele psychopathologie-indicator.* Lisse: Swets and Zeitlinger.

Briere, J. and Gil, E. (1998). Self-mutilation in clinical and general population samples: Prevalence, correlates, and functions. *American Journal of Orthopsychiatry, 68*, 609-620.

Brown, M.Z., Comtois, K.A., and Linehan, M.M. (2002). Reasons for suicide attempts and nonsuicidal self-injury in women with borderline personality disorder. *Journal of Abnormal Psychology, 111*, 198-202.

Claes, L., Vandereycken, W., and Vertommen, H. (2001). Self-injurious behaviors in eating-disordered patients. *Eating Behaviors, 2*, 263-272.

Claes, L., Vandereycken, W., and Vertommen, H. (2002). Therapy-related assessment of self-harming behaviors in eating disordered patients: A case illustration. *Eating Disorders: The Journal of Treatment and Prevention, 10*, 269-279.

Claes, L., Vandereycken, W., and Vertommen, H. (2003). Eating disordered patients with and without self-injurious behaviours: A comparison of psychopathological features. *European Eating Disorders Review, 11*, 379-396.

Claes, L., Vandereycken, W., and Vertommen, H. (2005). Clinical assessment of self-injurious behaviors: An overview of rating scales and self-reporting questionnaires. In A. Colombus (Ed.), *Advances in Psychology Research. Volume 36* (pp. 183-209). New York: Nova Science Publishers.

Darche, M.A. (1990). Psychological factors differentiating self-mutilating and non-self-mutilating adolescent inpatient females. *Psychiatric Hospital, 21*, 31-35.

DiClemente, R.J., Ponton, L.E., and Hartley, D. (1991). Prevalence and correlates of cutting behavior: Risk for HIV transmission. *Journal of the American Academy of Child and Adolescent Psychiatry, 30*, 735-739.

Favazza, A.R. (1998). The coming of age of self-mutilation. *Journal of Nervous and Mental Disease, 186*, 259-268.

Frijda, N.H. (1993). Moods, emotion episodes, and emotions. In M. Lewis, and J.M. Haviland (Eds.), *Handbook of emotions* (pp. 381-403). New York: Guilford Press.

Gardner, W.I., and Sovner, R. (1994). *Self-injurious behaviours: Diagnosis and treatment. A multimodal functional approach.* USA: Vida Publising.

Herpertz, S. (1995). Self-injurious behaviour: Psychopathological and nosological characteristics in subtypes of self-injurers. *Acta Psychiatrica Scandinavica, 91*, 57-68.

Linehan, M.M. (1993). *Cognitive-behavioral treatment of borderline personality disorder.* New York: Guilford Press.

Magai, C., and McFadden, S. (1995). *The role of emotions in social and personality development: History, theory, and research.* New York: Plenum Press.

Nock, M.K., and Kazdin, A.E. (2002). Examination of affective, cognitive, and behavioral factors and suicide-related outcomes in children and young adolescents. *Journal of Clinical Child and Adolescent Psychology, 31*, 48-58.

Nock, M.K., and Prinstein, M.J. (2004). A functional approach to the assessment of self-mutilative behavior. *Journal of Consulting and Clinical Psychology, 72*, 885-890.

Nock, M.K., and Prinstein, M.J. (2005). Contextual features and behavioral functions of self-mutilation among adolescents. *Journal of Abnormal Psychology, 114*, 140-146.

Prinstein, M.J., Nock, M.K., Spirito, A., and Grapentine, W.L. (2001). Multimethod assessment of suicidality in adolescent psychiatric inpatients: Preliminary results. *Journal of the American Academy of Child and Adolescent Psychiatry, 40*, 1053-1061.

Ross, S., and Heath, N. (2002). A study of the frequency of self-mutilation in a community sample of adolescents. *Journal of Youth and Adolescence, 31*, 67-77.

Sansone, R.A., Wiederman, M.W., and Sansone, L.A. (1998). The self-harm inventory (SHI): Development of a scale for identifying self-destructive behaviors and borderline personality disorder. *Journal of Clinical Psychology, 54*, 973-983.

Sansone R.A., Wiederman, M.W., Sansone, L.A., and Monteith, D. (2000). Patterns of self-harm behavior among women with borderline personality symptomatology: Psychiatric versus primary care settings. *General Hospital Psychiatry, 22*, 174-178.

Suyemoto, K.L. (1998). The functions of self-mutilation. *Clinical Psychology Review, 18*, 531-554.

Vanderlinden, J., and Vandereycken, W. (1997). *Trauma, dissociation, and impulse dyscontrol in eating disorders*. New York-London: Brunner/Mazel - Taylor and Francis.

Van Elderen, T., Verkes, R.J., Arkesteijn, J., and Komproe, I. (1996). Psychometric characteristics of the Self-Expression and Control Scale in a sample of recurrent suicide attempters. *Personality and Individual Differences, 21*, 489-496.

APPENDIX A.
SELF-INJURY QUESTIONNAIRE TREATMENT RELATED (SIQ-TR)

Self-injurious behavior refers to various kinds of deliberate self-inflicted damage of one's own body surface (e.g., cutting oneself, burning oneself) but without suicidal intent (no wish to die).

In this questionnaire, five types of self-injurious behaviors are checked: scratching, bruising, cutting, burning, and biting oneself.

Each time you will be asked whether you have displayed a particular type of self-injury and, if so, to give more information about it (frequency, feelings, thoughts, etc.).

If you display a form of self-injury that is not mentioned in this questionnaire (e.g., serious hair pulling), you can specify it on the last page.

Thank you for your collaboration.

A1 How long ago did you SCRATCH yourself until it bleeded

a week	(-> go to question A2)
a month	(-> go to question A2)
several months	(-> go to question B1)
more than a year	(-> go to question B1)
never	(-> go to question B1)

A2 Which body parts did you injure most of the time?

O head, neck
O arms, hands, fingers, nails
O torso, belly, buttocks
O legs, feet, toes
O breasts, genitals

A3 On how many days did this occur during the last month?

O from 1 to 5 days
O between 6 and 10 days
O between 11 and 15 days
O more than 15 days

A4 How many times a day did this occur on average?

O less than 1 time a day
O 1to 2 times a day
O 3 to 4 times a day
O 5 or more times a day

A5 How often did you feel pain during this act?

O never
O now and then
O often
O always

A6 To what degree did you feel pain during this act?

O none
O mild
O moderate
O strong
O very strong

A7 When this act occurred, then …				
1=never 2=sometimes 3=often 4=always				
It had been clearly planned beforehand	1	2	3	4
I realized how it had come about	1	2	3	4
I took care of the wound(s)	1	2	3	4
I hid the act from other people	1	2	3	4

1 = Not at all 2 = A bit 3 = Moderately 4 = Much 5 = Very much

A8 How did you feel shortly BEFORE this act occurred?					
Glad	1	2	3	4	5
Relieved	1	2	3	4	5
Nervous	1	2	3	4	5
Bored	1	2	3	4	5
Angry at myself	1	2	3	4	5
Angry at others	1	2	3	4	5
Anxious	1	2	3	4	5
Sad	1	2	3	4	5
Guilty	1	2	3	4	5
Other feeling (describe): ……………..	1	2	3	4	5

A9 How did you feel shortly AFTER this act occurred?					
Glad	1	2	3	4	5
Relieved	1	2	3	4	5
Nervous	1	2	3	4	5
Bored	1	2	3	4	5
Angry at myself	1	2	3	4	5
Angry at others	1	2	3	4	5
Anxious	1	2	3	4	5
Sad	1	2	3	4	5
Guilty	1	2	3	4	5
Other feeling (describe): ……………..	1	2	3	4	5

A10 Why did you perform this act?					
To feel some pleasure	1	2	3	4	5
To avoid or suppress negative feelings	1	2	3	4	5
To avoid or suppress painful images or memories	1	2	3	4	5
To get into a twilight or numb state	1	2	3	4	5
To get attention from others	1	2	3	4	5
To escape from a twilight or numb state	1	2	3	4	5
To punish myself	1	2	3	4	5
To make myself unattractive	1	2	3	4	5
To avoid or suppress suicidal thoughts	1	2	3	4	5
To show myself how strong I am	1	2	3	4	5
To show others how strong I am	1	2	3	4	5
To avoid doing something unpleasant, you don't want to do	1	2	3	4	5
To avoid school, work, or other activities	1	2	3	4	5
To avoid being with people	1	2	3	4	5
Another reason (describe): …………	1	2	3	4	5

B1 How long ago did you <u>BRUISE</u> yourself?

O a week	(-> go to question B2)
O a month	(-> go to question B2)
O several months	(-> go to question C1)
O more than a year	(-> go to question C1)
O never	(-> go to question C1)

B2 Which body parts did you injure most of the time?

O head, neck
O arms, hands, fingers, nails
O torso, belly, buttocks
O legs, feet, toes
O breasts, genitals

B3 On how many days did this occur during the last month?

O from 1 to 5 days
O between 6 and 10 days
O between 11 and 15 days
O more than 15 days

B4 How many times a day did this occur on average?

O less than 1 time a day
O 1to 2 times a day
O 3 to 4 times a day
O 5 or more times a day

B5 How often did you feel pain during this act?

O never
O now and then
O often
O always

B6 To what degree did you feel pain during this act?

O none
O mild
O moderate
O strong
O very strong

B7 When this act occurred, then …				
1=never 2=sometimes 3=often 4=always				
It had been clearly planned beforehand	1	2	3	4
I realized how it had come about	1	2	3	4
I took care of the wound(s)	1	2	3	4
I hid the act from other people	1	2	3	4

1 = Not at all 2 = A bit 3 = Moderately 4 = Much 5 = Very much					
B8 How did you feel shortly BEFORE this act occurred?					
Glad	1	2	3	4	5
Relieved	1	2	3	4	5
Nervous	1	2	3	4	5
Bored	1	2	3	4	5
Angry at myself	1	2	3	4	5
Angry at others	1	2	3	4	5
Anxious	1	2	3	4	5
Sad	1	2	3	4	5
Guilty	1	2	3	4	5
Other feeling (describe): ……………..	1	2	3	4	5
B9 How did you feel shortly AFTER this act occurred?					
Glad	1	2	3	4	5
Relieved	1	2	3	4	5
Nervous	1	2	3	4	5
Bored	1	2	3	4	5
Angry at myself	1	2	3	4	5
Angry at others	1	2	3	4	5
Anxious	1	2	3	4	5
Sad	1	2	3	4	5
Guilty	1	2	3	4	5
Other feeling (describe): ……………..	1	2	3	4	5

B10 Why did you perform this act occurred?					
To feel some pleasure	1	2	3	4	5
To avoid or suppress negative feelings	1	2	3	4	5
To avoid or suppress painful images or memories	1	2	3	4	5
To get into a twilight or numb state	1	2	3	4	5
To get attention from others	1	2	3	4	5
To escape from a twilight or numb state	1	2	3	4	5
To punish myself	1	2	3	4	5
To make myself unattractive	1	2	3	4	5
To avoid or suppress suicidal thoughts	1	2	3	4	5
To show myself how strong I am	1	2	3	4	5
To show others how strong I am	1	2	3	4	5
To avoid doing something unpleasant, you don't want to do	1	2	3	4	5
To avoid school, work, or other activities	1	2	3	4	5
To avoid being with people	1	2	3	4	5
Another reason (describe): …………	1	2	3	4	5

C1 How long ago did you CUT yourself?

O a week   (-> go to question C2)
O a month   (-> go to question C2)
O several months   (-> go to question D1)
O more than a year   (-> go to question D1)
O never   (-> go to question D1

C2 Which body parts did you injure most of the time?

O head, neck
O arms, hands, fingers, nails
O torso, belly, buttocks
O legs, feet, toes
O breasts, genitals

C3 On how many days did this occur during the last month?

O from 1 to 5 days
O between 6 and 10 days
O between 11 and 15 days
O more than 15 days

C4 How many times a day did this occur on average?

O less than 1 time a day
O 1to 2 times a day
O 3 to 4 times a day
O 5 or more times a day

C5 How often did you feel pain during this act?

O never
O now and then
O often
O always

C6 To what degree did you feel pain during this act?

O none
O mild
O moderate
O strong
O very strong

C7 When this act occurred, then …				
1=never 2=sometimes 3=often 4=always				
It had been clearly planned beforehand	1	2	3	4
I realized how it had come about	1	2	3	4
I took care of the wound(s)	1	2	3	4
I hid the act from other people	1	2	3	4

1 = Not at all 2 = A bit 3 = Moderately 4 = Much 5 = Very much					
C8 How did you feel shortly BEFORE this act occurred?					
Glad	1	2	3	4	5
Relieved	1	2	3	4	5
Nervous	1	2	3	4	5
Bored	1	2	3	4	5
Angry at myself	1	2	3	4	5
Angry at others	1	2	3	4	5
Anxious	1	2	3	4	5
Sad	1	2	3	4	5
Guilty	1	2	3	4	5
Other feeling (describe): ………….....	1	2	3	4	5

C9 How did you feel shortly AFTER this act occurred?					
Glad	1	2	3	4	5
Relieved	1	2	3	4	5
Nervous	1	2	3	4	5
Bored	1	2	3	4	5
Angry at myself	1	2	3	4	5
Angry at others	1	2	3	4	5
Anxious	1	2	3	4	5
Sad	1	2	3	4	5
Guilty	1	2	3	4	5
Other feeling (describe): ………….....	1	2	3	4	5

C10 Why did you perform this act?					
To feel some pleasure	1	2	3	4	5
To avoid or suppress negative feelings	1	2	3	4	5
To avoid or suppress painful images or memories	1	2	3	4	5
To get into a twilight or numb state	1	2	3	4	5
To get attention from others	1	2	3	4	5
To escape from a twilight or numb state	1	2	3	4	5
To punish myself	1	2	3	4	5
To make myself unattractive	1	2	3	4	5
To avoid or suppress suicidal thoughts	1	2	3	4	5
To show myself how strong I am	1	2	3	4	5
To show others how strong I am	1	2	3	4	5
To avoid doing something unpleasant, you don't want to do	1	2	3	4	5
To avoid school, work, or other activities	1	2	3	4	5
To avoid being with people	1	2	3	4	5
Another reason (describe): …………	1	2	3	4	5

D1 How long ago did you BURN yourself?

O a week   (-> go to question D2)
O a month   (-> go to question D2)
O several months   (-> go to question E1)
O more than a year   (-> go to question E1)
O never   (-> go to question E1)

D2 Which body parts did you injure most of the time?

O head, neck
O arms, hands, fingers, nails
O torso, belly, buttocks
O legs, feet, toes
O breasts, genitals

D3 On how many days did this occur during the last month?

O from 1 to 5 days
O between 6 and 10 days
O between 11 and 15 days
O more than 15 days

D4 How many times a day did this occur on average?

O less than 1 time a day
O 1to 2 times a day
O 3 to 4 times a day
O 5 or more times a day

D5 How often did you feel pain during this act?

O never
O now and then
O often
O always

D6 To what degree did you feel pain during this act?

O none
O mild
O moderate
O strong
O very strong

D7 When this act occurred, then ...				
1=never 2=sometimes 3=often 4=always				
It had been clearly planned beforehand	1	2	3	4
I realized how it had come about	1	2	3	4
I took care of the wound(s)	1	2	3	4
I hid the act from other people	1	2	3	4

1 = Not at all 2 = A bit 3 = Moderately 4 = Much 5 = Very much

D8 How did you feel shortly BEFORE this act occurred?					
Glad	1	2	3	4	5
Relieved	1	2	3	4	5
Nervous	1	2	3	4	5
Bored	1	2	3	4	5
Angry at myself	1	2	3	4	5
Angry at others	1	2	3	4	5
Anxious	1	2	3	4	5
Sad	1	2	3	4	5
Guilty	1	2	3	4	5
Other feeling (describe):	1	2	3	4	5

D9 How did you feel shortly AFTER this act occurred?					
Glad	1	2	3	4	5
Relieved	1	2	3	4	5
Nervous	1	2	3	4	5
Bored	1	2	3	4	5
Angry at myself	1	2	3	4	5
Angry at others	1	2	3	4	5
Anxious	1	2	3	4	5
Sad	1	2	3	4	5
Guilty	1	2	3	4	5
Other feeling (describe):	1	2	3	4	5

D10 Why did you perform this act?					
To feel some pleasure	1	2	3	4	5
To avoid or suppress negative feelings	1	2	3	4	5
To avoid or suppress painful images or memories	1	2	3	4	5
To get into a twilight or numb state	1	2	3	4	5
To get attention from others	1	2	3	4	5
To escape from a twilight or numb state	1	2	3	4	5
To punish myself	1	2	3	4	5
To make myself unattractive	1	2	3	4	5
To avoid or suppress suicidal thoughts	1	2	3	4	5
To show myself how strong I am	1	2	3	4	5
To show others how strong I am	1	2	3	4	5
To avoid doing something unpleasant, you don't want to do	1	2	3	4	5
To avoid school, work, or other activities	1	2	3	4	5
To avoid being with people	1	2	3	4	5
Another reason (describe):	1	2	3	4	5

E1 How long ago did you BITE yourself?

O a week   (-> go to question E2)
O a month   (-> go to question E2)
O several months   (-> go to question F1)
O more than a year   (-> go to question F1)
O never   (-> go to question F1)

E2 Which body parts did you injure most of the time?

O head, neck
O arms, hands, fingers, nails
O torso, belly, buttocks
O legs, feet, toes
O breasts, genitals

E3 On how many days did this occur during the last month?

O from 1 to 5 days
O between 6 and 10 days
O between 11 and 15 days
O more than 15 days

E4 How many times a day did this occur on average?

O less than 1 time a day
O 1to 2 times a day
O 3 to 4 times a day
O 5 or more times a day

E5 How often did you feel pain during this act?

O never
O now and then
O often
O always

E6 To what degree did you feel pain during this act?

O none
O mild
O moderate
O strong
O very strong

E7 When this act occurred, then …				
1=never 2=sometimes 3=often 4=always				
It had been clearly planned beforehand	1	2	3	4
I realized how it had come about	1	2	3	4
I took care of the wound(s)	1	2	3	4
I hid the act from other people	1	2	3	4

1 = Not at all 2 = A bit 3 = Moderately 4 = Much 5 = Very much					
E8 How did you feel shortly BEFORE this act occurred?					
Glad	1	2	3	4	5
Relieved	1	2	3	4	5
Nervous	1	2	3	4	5
Bored	1	2	3	4	5
Angry at myself	1	2	3	4	5
Angry at others	1	2	3	4	5
Anxious	1	2	3	4	5
Sad	1	2	3	4	5
Guilty	1	2	3	4	5
Other feeling (describe): ………….....	1	2	3	4	5
E9 How did you feel shortly AFTER this act occurred?					
Glad	1	2	3	4	5
Relieved	1	2	3	4	5
Nervous	1	2	3	4	5
Bored	1	2	3	4	5
Angry at myself	1	2	3	4	5
Angry at others	1	2	3	4	5
Anxious	1	2	3	4	5
Sad	1	2	3	4	5
Guilty	1	2	3	4	5
Other feeling (describe): ………….....	1	2	3	4	5

E10 Why did you perform this act?					
To feel some pleasure	1	2	3	4	5
To avoid or suppress negative feelings	1	2	3	4	5
To avoid or suppress painful images or memories	1	2	3	4	5
To get into a twilight or numb state	1	2	3	4	5
To get attention from others	1	2	3	4	5
To escape from a twilight or numb state	1	2	3	4	5
To punish myself	1	2	3	4	5
To make myself unattractive	1	2	3	4	5
To avoid or suppress suicidal thoughts	1	2	3	4	5
To show myself how strong I am	1	2	3	4	5
To show others how strong I am	1	2	3	4	5
To avoid doing something unpleasant, you don't want to do	1	2	3	4	5
To avoid school, work, or other activities	1	2	3	4	5
To avoid being with people	1	2	3	4	5
Another reason (describe): …………	1	2	3	4	5

F1 OTHER form of self-injury : ………………………… (specify)
How long ago did you display this behavior?

O a week   (-> go to question F2)
O a month   (-> go to question F2)
O several months   (-> end of questionnaire)
O more than a year   (-> end of questionnaire)

F2 Which body parts did you injure most of the time?

O head, neck
O arms, hands, fingers, nails
O torso, belly, buttocks
O legs, feet, toes
O breasts, genitals

F3 On how many days did this occur during the last month?

O from 1 to 5 days
O between 6 and 10 days
O between 11 and 15 days
O more than 15 days

F4 How many times a day did this occur on average?

O less than 1 time a day
O 1to 2 times a day
O 3 to 4 times a day
O 5 or more times a day

F5 How often did you feel pain during this act?

O never
O now and then
O often
O always

F6 To what degree did you feel pain during this act?

O none
O mild
O moderate
O strong
O very strong

F7 When this act occurred, then …				
1=never 2=sometimes 3=often 4=always				
It had been clearly planned beforehand	1	2	3	4
I realized how it had come about	1	2	3	4
I took care of the wound(s)	1	2	3	4
I hid the act from other people	1	2	3	4

1 = Not at all 2 = A bit 3 = Moderately 4 = Much 5 = Very much					
F8 How did you feel shortly BEFORE this act occurred?					
Glad	1	2	3	4	5
Relieved	1	2	3	4	5
Nervous	1	2	3	4	5
Bored	1	2	3	4	5
Angry at myself	1	2	3	4	5
Angry at others	1	2	3	4	5
Anxious	1	2	3	4	5
Sad	1	2	3	4	5
Guilty	1	2	3	4	5
Other feeling (describe): ………….....	1	2	3	4	5
F9 How did you feel shortly AFTER this act occurred?					
Glad	1	2	3	4	5
Relieved	1	2	3	4	5
Nervous	1	2	3	4	5
Bored	1	2	3	4	5
Angry at myself	1	2	3	4	5
Angry at others	1	2	3	4	5
Anxious	1	2	3	4	5
Sad	1	2	3	4	5
Guilty	1	2	3	4	5
Other feeling (describe): ………….....	1	2	3	4	5

F10 Why did you perform this act?					
To feel some pleasure	1	2	3	4	5
To avoid or suppress negative feelings	1	2	3	4	5
To avoid or suppress painful images or memories	1	2	3	4	5
To get into a twilight or numb state	1	2	3	4	5
To get attention from others	1	2	3	4	5
To escape from a twilight or numb state	1	2	3	4	5
To punish myself	1	2	3	4	5
To make myself unattractive	1	2	3	4	5
To avoid or suppress suicidal thoughts	1	2	3	4	5
To show myself how strong I am	1	2	3	4	5
To show others how strong I am	1	2	3	4	5
To avoid doing something unpleasant, you don't want to do	1	2	3	4	5
To avoid school, work, or other activities	1	2	3	4	5
To avoid being with people	1	2	3	4	5
Another reason (describe): …………	1	2	3	4	5

In: Psychological Tests and Testing Research Trends   ISBN: 978-1-60021-569-8
Editor: Paul M. Goldfarb, pp. 141-149   © 2007 Nova Science Publishers, Inc.

Chapter 6

SCREENING OF EATING DISORDERS IN THE GENERAL POPULATION

*Einar Vedul-Kjelsås**

Department of Neuroscience; Faculty of Medicine, Norway; and St. Olavs University
Hospital; Division of Psychiatry, Department of Research and Development; Norway

ABSTRACT

Objective: This chapter examines the measurement of eating disorders in the general population using the Survey for eating disorders (SEDs, Götestam and Agras, 1995, Ghaderi, 2002). The chapter is based on a prevalence study of eating disorders in the general female population in Norway.

Method: A total number of 3500 women, representatively recruited from the Norwegian female population, were sent a self-report questionnaire in 2004, including the SEDs, including both DSM-III-R and DSM-IV criteria for eating disorders. Among those, 1521 subjects (45.8%) returned completed forms.

Results: The point prevalence of eating disorders was found to be 2.6%, using DSM-IV. Using DSM-III-R, the point prevalence was 3.6%.

Discussion: The two different versions of the DSM-system gave different results. Methodological issues are discussed focusing on similarities and differences between DSM-III-R and DSM-IV. In addition, a discussion in light of DSM-V for eating disorders is provided.

An eating disorder (ED) is commonly described as a persistent disturbance of eating behaviour that is not secondary to a general medical condition or another psychiatric disorder. According to the Diagnostic and statistic manual of mental disorders, 4th edition (DSM-IV) [1] there are three established types of eating disorders, anorexia nervosa (AN) and bulimia nervosa (BN) being the most widely recognized. A third diagnostic category is "eating disorders not otherwise specified" (EDNOS), a group of disorders that do not meet all the

---

* Address for correspondence: Department of Neuroscience; Faculty of Medicine, NTNU; N-7006 Trondheim, Norway; and St. Olavs University Hospital; Division of Psychiatry, Department of Research and Development; N-7006 Trondheim, Norway; e-mail: kjein@ntnu.no

criteria for AN or BN. EDNOS is the most common category of eating disorders seen in outpatient settings, yet it has received almost no research attention [2]. The prevalence of EDNOS is not clear, partly because there are no positive diagnostic criteria for the diagnosis. Consequently, there is no agreed way of determining what constitutes a "case" [2]. Additionally, binge eating disorder (BED) is proposed to constitute a fourth diagnosis due to its differences in characteristics compared to the other three categories.

Studies of the epidemiology of eating disorders are contradictory because of different selection criteria for populations and use of methods. Additionally, two specific problems are the low prevalence of eating disorders in the general population and the tendency of eating disorders subjects to conceal their illness. These factors make it necessary to study a large number of the general population to achieve enough differential power [3].

There have been few studies on the prevalence of eating disorders in the general population. Most studies examine groups of the population like college women, psychiatric inpatients or certain age groups. Additionally, most studies have focused on only AN, BN or BED only.

A frequently cited study by Götestam and Agras from 1994 [4] examined the prevalence of eating disorders among the general female population in Norway. Based on a self-report questionnaire the point prevalence of AN, BN, EDNOS and BED was 0.3%, 0.7%, 1.3% and 1.5%, respectively. The total point prevalence of eating disorders was found to be 3.8%. The study was based on the DSM-III-R diagnostic categorization, and the questionnaire provided full diagnosis of AN, BN, BED and EDNOS. In this chapter, we find it to be natural to do some specific comparisons with Gøtestam and Agras [4], as both studies includes Norwegian women, collected in 1991 and 2004.

Ghaderi and Scott used questionnaires on two occasions to evaluate a random sample of 1157 females in the Swedish population [5]. Their study revealed a total prevalence of eating disorder of 3.15% according to DSM-IV. The prevalence of AN was 0.1%, BN 1.3% and BED 1.2%. The prevalence of EDNOS was found to be 0.5%. In 1998, Nobakht and Dezhkam examined the prevalence of AN and BN among Iranian schoolgirls aged 15-18 years. Their findings, 0.9% for AN and 3.2% for BN, suggested the comparability to prevalence rates reported in studies in Western societies. A two-stage approach was the method of choice in this study [6]. A two-stage approach was also used in an epidemiological study on Swiss adolescent girls between 14 and 17 years. A prevalence rate of 0.7% was found for AN and 0.5% for BN [7]. A more recent study from Spain investigated the epidemiology of the general population between 18-25 years using a structured clinical interview for DSM-IV. The lifetime prevalence of AN, BN, EDNOS and BED was 2.0%, 4.6%, 4.7% and 0.6%, respectively [8].

Several reviews have been published on the epidemiology of eating disorders. One of the most recent, estimated the prevalence of eating disorders based on a selection of the literature on epidemiology and updates [3]. Only studies that used a strict definition of AN and BN as defined by the American Psychiatric Association and the World Health Organization was considered. According to the review, the average prevalence for AN was found to be 0.3% for women while the prevalence rates for BN were 1% and 0.1% for young women and men, respectively. The estimated prevalence of BED was at least 1%. The review focused on prevalence studies using a two stage case identification procedure in the general population. This two-stage screening approach is the most widely accepted procedure for the identification of prevalent cases.

METHODS

Self-Report

The questionnaire used in the present chapter was a modified version of the Survey for Eating Disorders (SEDs) [9]. This modification was carried out to meet the current DSM-IV-criteria. The SEDs was also the questionnaire of choice in the study by Götestam and Agras. The version of SEDs used in this chapter consists of 40 questions [9], 18 of which are necessary for full SEDs-based diagnoses of AN, BN, BED and EDNOS based on the DSM-III and the DSM-IV-criteria. Demographic characteristics were provided through seven questions concerning age, education, civil status, work and BMI. An additional 33 questions were given on eating behaviour and eating problems. In this chapter, only figures on point prevalence (current SEDs-based eating disorders) are presented. Categorization of the different types of eating disorders is merely based on self-report (SEDs).

SEDs was developed by Götestam and Agras in 1994 to give DSM-III-R-based diagnoses of AN, BN, BED and EDNOS, and to address shortcomings of current questionnaires [10]. SEDs has been used in several population-based studies [4, 5, 11, 12] and has been found to be a sensitive instrument with high positive predictive value [10].

Participants

A total of 3500 women aged 18-65, representatively recruited from the Norwegian female population, were sent the questionnaire. All non-responders were sent a second questionnaire along with a reminding letter to increase the response rate.

Among the 3500, 178 participants could not be traced due to unknown address, giving a total number of possible respondents of 3322. Among these, 1521 individuals (45.8%) returned completed forms.

RESULTS

Demographic Characteristics Based on DSM-IV

Demographics for the sample without a current eating disorder (n = 1481) and for those indicating a DSM-IV-based current eating disorder (n= 40) are shown in table 1.

Women with a current eating disorder tended to be younger and more obese than those without an eating disorder. In addition, fewer in the eating disorders sample were married, and the majority lived alone.

Götestam and Agras (1995) [4] found that the eating disorder sample had a higher education than the comparing sample. In this chapter, however, individuals with or without an eating disorder showed similar patterns of education.

Table 1. Demographic characteristics according to DSM-IV

Variable	Total sample (I) (n=1521)		No ED sample (II) (n=1481)		ED sample (III) (n=40)		Significance (II - III)
Age, years (SD)	40.4	(12.7)	40.7	(12.7)	29.6	(8.7)	t=5.4***
Body mass index (kg/m²), M (SD)	24.4	(4.1)	24.4	(4.0)	25.2	(5.8)	t=-1.2^{ns}
Civil status (%)							x^2=24.2***
Married	777	(51.1)	741	(53.3)	8	(20.0)	
Living together	316	(20.8)	283	(20.3)	8	(20.0)	
Separated/divorced	124	(8.2)	110	(7.9)	6	(15.0)	
Alone	292	(19.2)	246	(17.7)	18	(19.3)	
Education (%)							x^2=7.5^{*ns}
Primary school	200	(13.1)	201	(13.6)	9	(22.5)	
High school	344	(22.6)	334	(22.6)	10	(25.0)	
Vocational education	324	(21.3)	313	(21.1)	11	(27.5)	
University/college	623	(41.0)	613	(41.4)	10	(25.0)	
Work situation (%)							x^2=13.0*
Working	1011	(66.5)	991	(66.9)	20	(50.0)	
Student/school	175	(11.5)	164	(11.1)	11	(27.5)	
Homework/housewife	78	(5.1)	77	(5.2)	1	(2.5)	
Unemployed	26	(1.7)	26	(1.8)	0	0	
Sicklisted or other	135	(8.9)	131	(8.8)	4	(10.0)	
Body mass index class (%)							
Underweight	42	(2.8)	39	(2.7)	3	(8.1)	x^2 = 6.7^{ns}
Average weight	858	(56.4)	839	(58.6)	19	(51.4)	
Overweight	438	(28.8)	429	(30.0)	9	(24.3)	
Obese	130	(8.5)	124	(8.7)	6	(16.2)	

Eating Disorder Diagnosis Based on DSM-IV

The point prevalence of eating disorders found in this chapter based on DSM-IV, is presented in table 2. The total point prevalence was 2.6%. The point figures of AN was 0%, BN 0.9 % and BED 0.3 %. EDNOS had a point prevalence of 1.5%.

Current eating disorders were most common among the youngest women, with exception of binge eating disorder which was found to be most common among the oldest women.

Eating Disorder Diagnosis Based on DSM-III-R

According to the DSM-III-R, the total point prevalence was 3.6%. The point prevalence of AN was found to be 0.3 %, BN 1.4% and EDNOS 1.8%. BED was not suggested as a diagnostic category in DSM-III-R.

Age specific point prevalence figures were for the most part in accordance with DSM-IV numbers (table 3). However, more older women were categorized with an eating disorder.

Compared to Götestam and Agras, (1995) [4], an increase in the point prevalence was found for BN and EDNOS, in contrast to AN where the point prevalence was identical to that found in 1994.

Table 2. Point prevalence of AN, BN, BED and EDNOS according to DSM-IV according to age cohorts

Age groups	AN (%)	BN (%)		BED (%)		EDNOS (%)		Eating disorder (%)		Total sample
18-29	0	8	(2.3)	2	(0.6)	12	(3.4)	22	(6.2)	355
30-39	0	4	(1.0)	1	(0.3)	7	(1.8)	12	(3.1)	389
40-49	0	1	(0.3)	1	(0.3)	4	(1.2)	6	(1.7)	343
50-59	0	0		0		0		0		318
60-66	0	0		0		0		0		110
Age missing	0	0		0		0		0		6
Sum	0	13	(0.9)	4	(0.3)	23	(1.5)	40	(2.6)	1521

Table 3. Point prevalence of AN, BN, BED and EDNOS according to DSM-III-R according to age cohorts

Age groups	AN (%)		BN (%)		EDNOS (%)		Eating disorder (%)		Total sample
18-29	3	(0.8)	10	(2.8)	14	(3.9)	27	(7.6)	355
30-39	2	(0.5)	7	(1.8)	7	(1.8)	16	(4.1)	389
40-49	0	0	3	(0.9)	2	(0.6)	5	(1.5)	343
50-59	0	0	1	(0.3)	3	(0.9)	4	(1.3)	318
60-66	0	0	0	(0.8)	2	(1.8)	2	(1.8)	110
Age missing	0	0	0		0		0		6
Sum	5	(0.3)	21	(1.4)	28	(1.8)	54	(3.6)	1521

Crossover Categorization between DSM-III-R and DSM-IV

The two women categorised with a SEDs-based AN in DSM-III-R, had moved to the EDNOS category in DSM-IV. Of the 18 women categorized with BN in DSM-III-R, one moved to BED, and four moved to EDNOS. Of the 19 EDNOS in DSM-III-R, two moved to BED.

DISCUSSION

Interpretation of the Results

The results in this chapter provide information about the point prevalence of eating disorders based on the DSM-III-R and the DSM-IV-criteria. According to DSM-IV, the total point prevalence was 2.6%. Corresponding figures for AN was 0%, BN 0.9 % and BED 0.3 %. EDNOS had a point prevalence of 1.5%. According to DSM-III-R, the total point prevalence was 3.6%. Corresponding numbers for AN was 0.3 %, BN 1.4% and EDNOS 1.8%. BED was not suggested as a diagnostic category in DSM-III-R.

These results show an expected point prevalence of eating disorders among the general female population and are also similar to results presented in other studies [3, 4]. However, it may be noted that these surveys differ in choice of instruments and selection of populations.

Compared to the study by Götestam and Agras, this chapter, according to DSM-IV, did not find a significant increase in the total point prevalence of eating disorders. On the contrary, using DSM-IV point prevalence figures, we found a decrease in this chapter compared to Gøtestam and Agras [4]. According to DSM-III-R standards, the total point prevalence was nearly identical, 3.8% in Gøtestam and Agras and 2.6% in this chapter.

Compared to DSM-III-R, DSM-IV introduced more strict criteria making it even "harder" to be diagnosed with an eating disorder. In other words, diagnoses are more specified as diagnostic system develops. Consequently, some individuals that were diagnosed according to DSM-III-R would not be diagnosed with an eating disorder based on today's standard, or would have moved from one category to another. This may be seen in our results, as figures for AN and BN have decreased from DSM-III-R to DSM-IV, while the EDNOS category has increased. The same trend may be seen if we compare with Gøtestam and Agras [4], who based their analyses on DSM-III-R. For instance, women that do not fulfil the strict criteria of AN, BN or BED in DSM-IV, but still have an eating disorder of clinical severity fall into the large EDNOS group.

An increase in the prevalence of eating disorder may be due to an even greater exposure to thin models in the media, increased negative attitudes towards fatness, and the belief of dieting as a normal means of weight control. However, according to the DSM-IV, the point prevalence was in fact decreased in this chapter compared to Gøtetstam and Agras [4], suggesting a positive trend over the last 13 years concerning the degree of environmental influences and other risk factors associated with eating disorders. However, comparing DSM-III-R figures in this chapter with Gøtestam and Agras, is suggesting neither a positive nor a negative trend.

In today's society, there seem to be better knowledge among teenagers, parents, teachers and health workers resulting in an earlier identification and intervention of individuals with eating problems. However, the development of eating disorders is still a challenge, both in terms of prevention and management.

The age-specific point prevalence found in this chapter revealed that eating disorders are most common among women aged 18-29, regardless of which version of DSM being used. This result is in accordance with studies shown that eating disorders mainly affect young adult females. Among the eating disorder categories, EDNOS was the most common diagnosis, underlining that most individuals with a clinical severe eating disturbance do not fulfil the strict criteria of AN, BN or BED. Anorexia nervosa was as expected a rare disorder with a point prevalence of 0% using DSM-IV, and 0.3% using DSM-III-R. Interestingly, the two women with a SEDs based AN according to DSM-III-R, moved to the EDNOS category in DSM-IV. This may raise doubts about the usefulness and applicability of the present diagnose system.

In this chapter, we revealed that marriage was less common in the eating disorder sample, a feature also found by Götestam and Agras. This may suggest that living with a partner creates an environment that inhibits dieting and extreme weight concern through factors like promotion of self-esteem and psychological support.

Average BMI was calculated based on the subjects' self-reported height and weight. These numbers revealed that the eating disorder sample was similar to the no eating disorder sample, which suggests that BMI is not a satisfactory measure for identifying possible eating disorders in the general population.

Overweight and obese individuals are more likely to develop an eating disorder because they may be less satisfied with their body image, and more involved in dieting and weight control. One could also suggest that overweight and obesity may lead to low self-esteem, dissatisfaction and depression, characteristics that could contribute to the developing of an eating disorder.

Methodological Concerns

Some potential limitations in this chapter should be noted. Questionnaire-based studies of eating disorders have been criticized for several reasons. One major problem is that some items may be interpreted differently by different populations. A second problem is the relatively low positive prediction value of some screening questionnaires. The questionnaire of choice in this chapter, however, has been constructed to meet these potential shortcomings.

The SEDs have been found to have a high predictive value as well as good validity and reliability. A recent publication in the International Journal of Eating Disorders [14], concludes that self-report forms are satisfactory tools in screening for eating disorders, when compared to clinical interviews.

Today, there is a problem with the diagnose system, as too many fall into the 'not otherwise specified group - EDNOS'. Hopefully, the forthcoming DSM-V adopts a different structure for the eating disorders, a more transdiagnostic perspective, as suggested by Fairburn and Harrison [15], and Fairburn and Bohn [2].

Another limitation in this chapter is that our findings are limited to the adult population aged 18 to 65. Consequently, the point prevalence of other age groups was not found. As eating disorders are strongly associated with young girls, it would have been of interest to study females below the age of 18. However, the age limit of 18 years was chosen of practical reasons, as girls under 18 would need approval from their parents.

In the study in this chapter, a total number of 3500 women were sent the questionnaire. Compared to the study by Götestam and Agras, this was an increase of 1000 individuals. However, only 45.8 % returned completed forms, compared to 74.9% in Gøtestam and Agras [4]. This decrease in respondents could be due to the increased number of studies today and consequently fewer may find it interesting or exciting to participate.

Another explanation could be that some participants thought the questionnaire was addressed to individuals with an eating disorder. In fact, we received some blank questionnaires with this explanation. In general, it could also be argued that some individuals that suffer from an eating disorder may avoid participating despite that they can not be identified. It has been shown that eating disorders were more common among a non-respondent group compared to a respondent group with a prevalence of 5.1% and 2.5%, respectively [3]. This may be due to several reasons; some individuals, in particularly AN-patients, do not recognize their illness or wish to conceal it.

Additionally, eating disorder may be considered taboo and related to shame and guilt, a feature shared by many psychiatric diseases. Furthermore, for some individuals, it may be painful to answer personal questions. Another concern is that the respondents may answer incorrectly to the questions. This may be the result of misunderstandings, but could also be due to an unconscious or conscious act.

CONCLUSION

Conclusively, the two different versions of the DSM-system gave different point prevalence figures. It is a methodological challenge in eating disorder research that the diagnostic system is changing, and the diagnoses are specified to a greater extent. To compare recent studies with earlier ones, one should definitively include items according to the version of DSM used in the older studies. Very few instruments include both DSM-III-R and DSM-IV, as SEDs do.

The drafts on DSM-V are currently in progress, and it will be very interesting to see how the eating disorder diagnoses appear in this forthcoming DSM version. It may be likely that we will see a more transdiagnostic structure, as may also be the case for other groups of psychiatric disorders.

REFERENCES

[1]   American Psychiatric Association. (1994). *Diagnostic and statistic manual of mental disorders* (4th ed.). Washington, DC: Author.
[2]   Fairburn, C.G., Bohn, K. (2004). Eating disorder NOS (EDNOS): An example of the troublesome "not otherwise specified" (NOS) category in DSM-IV. *Behaviour Research and Therapy*, in press.
[3]   Hoek, H.W. and von Hoeken, D. (2003). Review of the prevalence and incidence of eating disorders. *International Journal of Eating Disorders, 34*, 383-396.
[4]   Götestam, K.G., Agras W.S. (1995). General population-based epidemiological study of eating disorders in Norway. *International Journal of Eating Disorders, 18*, 119-126.
[5]   Ghaderi, A., Scott, B. (2001). Prevalence, incidence and prospective risk factors for eating disorders. *Acta psychiatrica scandinavica, 104*, 122-130.
[6]   Nobakht, M., Nezhkam, M. (2000). An epidemiological study of eating disorders in Iran. *International Journal of eating disorder, 28*, 265-271.

[7]   Steinhausen, H.C., Winkler, C., Meier, M. (1997). Eating disorders in adolescents in a Swiss epidemiologic study. *International Journal of Eating Disorders, 22, 147-151.*

[8]   Favaro, A., Ferrara, S., Santonastaso, P. (2003). The spectrum of eating disorders in young women: A prevalence study in a general population sample. *Psychosomatic Medicine, 65, 701-708.*

[9]   Ghaderi, A., Scott, B. *Survey for Eating Disorders* (SEDs).

[10]   Ghaderi, A., Scott, B. (2002). The preliminary reliability and validity of the Survey for Eating Disorders (SEDs): A self-report questionnaire for diagnosing eating disorders. *European Eating Disorders Review, 10, 61-76.*

[11]   Ghaderi A, Scott B. 1999. Prevalence and psychological correlates of eating disorders among women 18-30 years in the general population. *Acta Psychiatrica Scandinavica* 99, 261-266.

[12]   Taraldsen K, Götestam, K.G, Eriksen L. (1996). Prevalence of eating disorders among Norwegian women and men in a psychiatric outpatient unit. *International Journal of Eating Disorders 20, 185-190.*

[13]   Råstam, M., Gillberg, C., Garton, M. (1989). Anorexia nervosa in a Swedish urban region: A population-based study. *British Journal of Psychiatry, 155, 642-646.*

[14]   Rahkonen, A.K., Sihvola, S., Raevuori, A,. Kaukoranta, J., Bulik, C.M., Hoek, H.W,. Rissanen, A., Kaprio, J. (2006). Reliability of self-reported eating disorders: Optimizing population screening. *International Journal of Eating Disorders, 39 (8), 754-762.*

[15]   Fairburn, C.G., Harrison, P.J. (2003). Eating disorders. *The Lancet, 361, 407-416.*

In: Psychological Tests and Testing Research Trends
Editor: Paul M. Goldfarb, pp. 151-171

ISBN: 978-1-60021-569-8
© 2007 Nova Science Publishers, Inc.

Chapter 7

A COMPARATIVE NEUROPSYCHOLOGICAL APPROACH TO COGNITIVE ASSESSMENT IN CLINICAL POPULATIONS

*Isabelle Boutet[*1], Cary Kogan[1] and Norton W. Milgram[2]*

[1] School of Psychology, University of Ottawa,
125 University St, Ottawa, Ontario, Canada, K1N 6N5
[2] Division of Life Sciences, University of Toronto at Scarborough,
1265 Military Trail, Scarborough, Ontario, Canada, M1C 1A4

ABSTRACT

Comparative neuropsychology refers to a line of research where tests originally developed to investigate cognitive processes in animals are modified for use with humans. We have used a comparative neuropsychological approach to develop a new test battery specifically for use with clinical populations. The new battery evaluates object discrimination, egocentric spatial abilities, visual and spatial working memory, and cognitive flexibility. We have investigated the usefulness of this battery in two clinical groups: in a geriatric population and in patients with Fragile-X syndrome (FXS), a genetic condition associated with mental retardation. Our results in geriatric participants indicate age differences on tasks that evaluate egocentric spatial abilities, cognitive flexibility, and object recognition. Our results with FXS patients indicate strengths in egocentric spatial abilities and visual working memories alongside weaknesses in object discrimination, cognitive flexibility, and spatial working memory. These studies illustrate the utility of comparative neuropsychology to the study of cognition in normal and clinical populations. Future directions for novel test development and translation to the clinic are discussed within the comparative framework.

[*] Corresponding author: Isabelle Boutet, PhD; School of Psychology; University of Ottawa; 125 University St.; Ottawa, Ontario; K1N 6N5; Tel: 613-562-5800 x2612; Fax ; 613-562-5150; *Email:iboutet@uottawa.ca*

INTRODUCTION

Comparative neuropsychology refers to a domain of research in which procedures originally developed to investigate cognitive processes in animals are modified for use with human subjects (Oscar-Berman and Zola-Morgan, 1980). The terminology was coined in the context of neuropsychological studies aimed at identifying, based on behavioral performance, areas of the brain that are affected in different conditions and populations. For example, Freedman and Oscar-Berman (1986) compared the performance of patients with Alzheimer's disease (AD) to those with Parkinson's disease (PD) on visual and spatial learning as well as reversal tasks to reveal the unique pattern of deficits associated with each diagnosis. The data suggest that AD patients maintain selective damage to the orbitofrontal system. The adaptation of animal tasks to humans is not new. In the 1960s, a line of research had investigated animal tasks in humans in order to further delineate learning mechanisms in adults (Levine, 1963) and children (Kendler and D'Amato, 1995). For example, Levine examined the ability of human participants to associate a card with a reward with the objective of testing the notion that humans learn simple discrimination tasks using hypothesis testing rather than stimulus-reward (S-R) reinforcements.

Earlier adaptations of animal tasks to study learning and memory in humans made little or no attempt to utilize comparable testing procedures across animal and human participants; rather, it was assumed that animal tasks had to be significantly modified to offer a level of complexity suitable for the study of learning and memory in humans. In a comparative neuropsychology approach, a guiding principle deems that it is crucial to maintain testing procedures as similar as possible to those employed with animals in order to make appropriate inferences about affected brain regions in humans based on known findings from lesion studies in animals. The underlying assumption is that by keeping testing procedures comparable, the same cognitive processes as those evaluated in animals can be investigated in humans. For example, Freedman and Oscar-Berman (1989) used an object discrimination reversal task to investigate perseverative responding in patients with AD and PD. Reversal discrimination tasks are traditionally used in animals to investigate perseverative responding and cognitive flexibility. Reversal discrimination tasks are administered following training on a simple discrimination learning task where the animal is trained to associate one of two stimulus with a reward. Once learning is established according to a criterion of correct responses on the simple task, researchers reverse the S-R contingencies and the previously unrewarded stimulus is now rewarded. Learning the reversal rule is typically acquired at a much slower rate than is the original discrimination learning. An analysis of overall response patterns (Jones and Mishkin, 1972) suggest that the increased difficulty is a result of perseverative responding in primates. That is, non-human primates tend to persist in responding to the previously rewarded stimulus. Freedman and Oscar-Berman (1989) found that patients with AD were significantly impaired on object discrimination learning as compared to patients with PD, even though both groups were equated for severity of dementia. Considering that selective orbitofrontal system lesions impair performance on object reversal tasks in primates (Jones and Mishkin, 1972), the authors concluded that the pattern of deficits observed in AD is indicative of damage to the orbitofrontal system.

This study conducted by Freedman and Oscar-Berman (1989) illustrates one of the main advantages of comparative neuropsychology. Extensive lesion experiments in non-human primates have resulted in a comprehensive literature on the precise brain regions underlying successful performance on the comparative tasks. This allows researchers to make inferences about affected brain regions on the basis of the performance of humans on these same tasks. This feature affords an advantage over traditional neuropsychological tasks where clear brain-behavior relationships have not been established. For example, whereas the sub-tests in the standardized instruments for assessing intelligence (e.g., Wechsler instruments) correlate with specific general abilities (e.g., short-term memory, executive functions, etc.), they do not allow for relationships to be drawn between performance and regional brain function.

Comparative neuropsychology offers several other distinct advantages over traditional standardized neuropsychological measures. First, performance deficits for specific neuropsychological tasks are often difficult to interpret because they engage multiple cognitive functions that cannot always be identified or dissociated. Performance on a given task may be influenced by impairments in the cognitive function of interest but may also be the result of the generalized effects of mental retardation, senility, poor attention, etc. A corollary to this argument is that two neuropsychological tasks that are thought to probe similar cognitive functions may yield inconsistent results (e.g., Munir, Cornish and Wilding, 2000). Comparative neuropsychological tasks are advantageous because they require equivalent cognitive demands from participants because the instruction set remains constant across tasks (e.g., to find the reward). Furthermore, each task is based on a simple rule that targets a single well-delineated cognitive function. Finally, constellations of performance on various combinations of tasks can be used to infer specific impairments. For example, intact performance on an object discrimination learning task together with impaired performance on the DNMS tasks might suggest memory deficits alongside preserved visual discrimination abilities.

Second, many traditional neuropsychological tasks cannot be administered to patients with severe cognitive and language deficits because the global cognitive demands of standardized tests are often too high. By contrast, comparative neuropsychological procedures can be used with a broad range of individuals including those with poor language production as well as those who suffer from impaired cognitive abilities as a result of senility or mental retardation. The tasks are simple because the same instructions are valid for all the tasks administered. They are also motivating because immediate feedback is provided to participants through reinforcements contingent on correct answers. Moreover, the procedure is 'non-verbal' in the sense that the verbal instructions are nominal and performance is not evaluated on the basis of verbal answers but rather on the basis of overt non-verbal behaviour.

Third, comparative neuropsychology enables one to directly compare the performance of animals with that of humans. This may be particularly useful in diseases that exist in both humans and animals (e.g. AD). Furthermore, researchers are increasingly relying on animal models to develop pharmacological therapies for human populations. Most traditional neuropsychological tasks do not offer the opportunity for translational research because the tasks employed in humans present a much higher level of complexity, making it difficult to claim that the same cognitive functions are being evaluated in animals and in humans. By contrast, comparative neuropsychology allows for the direct comparison of humans and animals on virtually identical tasks.

A final advantage of the comparative neuropsychological approach is its ability to make direct comparisons of performance between different clinical conditions. Freedman and Oscar-Berman (1989), for example, compared the performance of patients with AD and PD on visual and spatial learning as well as reversal tasks, allowing these researchers to establish a more precise profile of strengths and weaknesses in the two populations. The ability to directly compare clinical populations stems from the other advantages discussed above. Populations with different levels of language development can be compared because the receptive language demands of the tasks are very low. Similarly, the overall cognitive requirements of the tasks are sufficiently basic that it is possible to compare populations of individuals with intellectual deficit to those with average intellectual abilities.

This chapter further explores applications of the comparative neuropsychological approach to compare cognitive performance between normal and clinical populations. We describe two such studies. In the first study, we measured the performance of healthy adults aged 65 and over on a battery of comparative neuropsychological tasks in order to (1) identify normative age-associated deficits, and (2) compare these deficits with those observed in patients with AD as well as in older animals. Our goal was to determine whether the cognitive impairments inherent to AD are qualitatively or quantitatively different from those seen in normative aging. Furthermore, we compared our results with those obtained from animal studies in order to evaluate the validity of these animal models.

The second study describes preliminary data from a series of experiments aimed at detailing the strengths and weaknesses in individuals suffering from Fragile-X syndrome, a genetic condition that results in significant developmental delays. The goals of the study were to (1) examine the feasibility of using the novel test battery in this population, (2) to further characterize the cognitive profile of FXS males and (3) to make inferences about affected brain regions in FXS.

We begin with a detailed description of the procedures and test battery used in both studies. The results of the study on normative aging and the study on FXS are presented in turn below. Finally, we review the potential utility of the comparative neuropsychology approach in view of the results obtained in these studies. We also discuss other avenues of translational research.

RESEARCH METHODOLOGY: A DESCRIPTION OF THE NOVEL TEST BATTERY

Participants were tested using a modified version of the Wisconsin Test Apparatus developed in our laboratory (Figure 1). The investigator and the subject sit facing each other across a table and separated by a wooden apparatus. The apparatus consists of a vertical panel and a horizontal box with a sliding tray. The tray contains three reinforcement wells. The vertical panel has a tray opening that allows the investigator to move the tray towards the subject. When the tray opening is closed, the subject cannot see the tray or the investigator. The vertical panel also has a one-way mirror window that allows the investigator to see the subject and that can be opened to allow the investigator and subject to communicate.

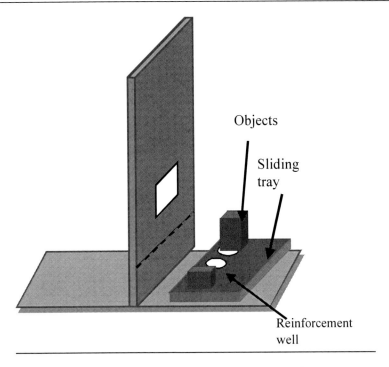

Figure 1. A schematic illustration of the apparatus used to administer the test battery.

The participant was given the following original instructions before the commencement of the testing session:

> "This is a type of game. I am going to show you different objects on a tray. One of the objects always hides a nickel. I want you to try and find the nickel every time I push the tray towards you. Okay? Remember, your job is to try and get the nickel every time."

Verbal feedback was given throughout the experiment (e.g., "*Good, you found the nickel*" or "*That's okay. You're doing fine. Keep trying.*").

On all tasks, participants were tested until they obtained a criterion of 9 correct answers within a block of 10 trials or until a maximum of 50 trials were administered. Performance on the following test battery was measured.

Object Discrimination Learning (ODL)

Participants were presented with two different objects, one object is rewarded and the nickel was always placed under that object. The objects were randomly placed over the left, right and center wells. The purpose of this task is to assess the ability to learn to associate an object with a reward.

Object Discrimination Reversal (ODR)

Immediately after completion of the ODL task, the ODR task was administered. The same two objects were used but the nickel was placed under the previously unrewarded object. Subjects were rewarded for responding to the previously incorrect object. The purpose of this task is to assess the ability to inhibit a previously learned response. Reversal learning is regarded as a measure of cognitive flexibility where difficulty in switching is indicative of perseverative behaviour. The ODL and ODR tasks have been widely used in primates (e.g., Lai et al., 1995; Tsuchida, Kubo and Kojima, 2002; canines: Christie et al., 2005), canines (Milgram, Head, Weiner and Thomas, 1994; Tapp et al., 2003), and felines (Moore and McCleary, 1976).

Egocentric Discrimination Learning (EDL)

This task followed the same general procedure as the ODL task except that the correct response is based on a spatial rule. Two identical objects were employed and the rule was to select the object farthest to the right, or farthest to the left. The two objects were randomly presented over the left, right, and center wells. For example, if participants were being taught to associate 'leftmost' as a correct answer, a nickel was placed under the object that is in the leftmost position of the tray (e.g. nickel under the center well and no nickel under the right well). The purpose of the EDL task is to evaluate the ability to associate an egocentric spatial rule with a reward.

Egocentric Discrimination Reversal (EDR)

Immediately following the completion of the EDL task, the EDR task was administered. For this task, the rule to be learned was reversed from the Original Learning task (e.g. learn 'leftmost' in the Original learning task, learn 'rightmost' in the Reversal task). As in the ODL task, the purpose of the reversal component is to evaluate the ability to inhibit a previously learned response.

Delayed-Non-Match-to-Sample (DNMS)

In this task, participants were first presented with a sample object on top of the center well, which was rewarded with a nickel. The object was then removed and after a delay (5, 10 or 20 seconds), two objects were shown on the left and right wells. One object was the sample, the other was a new object under which a nickel is positioned. The participant had to learn to choose the object that does not match the sample. The sample and new object were chosen from a pool of 100 common household items. The purpose of this task is to evaluate visual working memory.

Delayed-Non-Match-to-Position (DNMP)

This task followed the same procedure as the DNMS task except that the correct response was based on a spatial rule and two identical objects are used. Participants were first presented with an object (sample) on top of one well, which was rewarded with a nickel. The tray with the object was removed and after a delay (5, 10 or 20 seconds), participants were shown two objects identical to the sample. One was located at the same location as the sample and the other at a different location. The object presented at the new location was rewarded with a nickel (e.g. sample in the center, rewarded object on the left well). The purpose of this task is to evaluate spatial working memory.

STUDY 1: COGNITIVE DECLINE AND HUMAN AGING

In this study, we compared performance of younger and healthy older adults aged 65 and over on the six tasks comprising the battery. In the past, comparative neuropsychology has been primarily used to investigate individuals suffering from degenerative disorders (Blanchet et al., 2000; Freedman and Oscar-Berman, 1986; 1987; 1989; Irle, Kessler, Markowitsch and Hofmann, 1987; Sahakian et al., 1988; Sahgal et al., 1992). Very few studies have used this approach to investigate non-pathological aging (Lamar and Resnick, 2004; Mell et al., 2005; Rogers, Keyes and Fuller, 1976). This is surprising because it is likely that the results obtained with animals reflect a mix of pathological and non-pathological aging processes. Indeed, because no behavioral diagnostic test exists to detect dementia in animals, whether age differences in animals are due to pathological vs. non-pathological aging can only be assessed from brain tissue post-mortem. Our goal was to compare age-associated cognitive impairments in healthy older adults with those seen in AD and aged animals. Identification of commonalities between animals and humans is important because preclinical screening of protective agents in humans is often driven by studies demonstrating positive outcomes in animal models. This research also allowed us to examine whether similar cognitive functions are affected in normal aging and AD. Recent studies suggest that it is the extent of neuropathology, and not the specific region affected, that distinguishes normal from pathological aging (Galvan, David, Delacourte, Luna and Mena, 2001; Delacourte et al., 1999), suggesting that the profile of cognitive impairments seen in AD should be qualitatively similar to that those seen in normal aging, but with a quantitatively more severe decline in the latter case.

To the best of our knowledge, only two studies have examined the effect of normal human aging on reversal learning (Mell et al., 2005; Rogers et al., 1976), both using procedures that differ considerably from those traditionally employed in aged animals and in patients suffering from AD. Based on the presence of neuropathology in the orbitofrontal cortex of healthy older adults (Delacourte et al., 1999; Galvan et al, 2001; Salat, Kaye and Janowsky, 2002) and on the presence of impairments on visual on visual reversal tasks (humans: Freedman and Oscar-Berman, 1989; non-human primates: Anderson, de Monte and Kempf, 1996; Bartus, Dean and Fleming, 1979; Herndon, Moss, Rosene and Killiany, 1997; Lai, Moss, Killiany, Rosene and Herndon, 1995; Rapp, 1990; Voytko, 1999; canines: Milgram, Head, Weiner and Thomas, 1994; Tapp et al., 2003) and spatial reversal tasks (humans: Freedman and Oscar-Berman, 1989; non-human primates: Lai et al., 1995; Tsuchida, Kubo and Kojima, 2002; canines: Christie et al., 2005) in AD and aged animals, we predicted that older adults would display signs of impairments on both reversal learning tasks.

AD patients (Irle et al., 1987) and aged animals (non-human primates: Herndon et al., 1997; Moss, Rosene and Peters, 1988; Presty et al., 1987; Rapp and Amarall, 1991; Walker et al., 1988; canines: Milgram et al., 1994) also display deficits on delayed non-matching to sample (DNMS) tasks. As far as we know, only one study has examined the effects of normal aging using the DNMS task. Lamar and Resnick (2004) found significant differences between healthy older adults and younger adults on a DNMS task with recurring complex stimuli. In the present study, we developed a trial-unique DNMS task in which completely new objects were presented at each trial. This procedure is easier and more similar to that used in animals (Milgram et al., 1994; Moss et al., 1988; Presty et al., 1987) and in patients with AD (Irle et al., 1987). Based on the findings of impaired DNMS performance in healthy older adults (Lamar and Resnick, 2004), in patients with AD (Irle et al.; 1987), and in older animals (non-human primates: Herndon et al., 1997; Moss et al., 1988; Presty et al., 1987; Rapp and Amarall, 1991; Walker et al., 1988; canines: Milgram et al., 1994), we predicted that healthy older adults would show signs of impairments on this task.

AD patients and aged animals also show deficits in delayed-response (DR) tasks that evaluate spatial working memory (humans: Freedman and Oscar-Berman, 1986; Sahakian et al., 1988; primates: Bachevalier et al., 1991; Presty et al., 1987; Rapp, 1990). In canines, age-associated deficits have been observed in the DNMP tasks, which is conceptually comparable to DR tasks. No study has examined the effect of normal aging on DR or DNMP tasks. We predicted that older adults would show impairments on the DNMP task because DR tasks, which are conceptually similar to the DNMP task, are impaired in AD patients (Freedman and Oscar-Berman, 1986) and in aged primates (Bachevalier et al., 1991). Moreover, aged canines show deficits on the DNMP (Adams, Chan, Callahan and Milgram, 2000).

To summarize, we used a comparative neuropsychological approach to examine whether tasks that are sensitive to neuropathology in AD and in aged animals are also sensitive to normal aging in humans. Based on previous results obtained with AD patients and aged primates and canines, we predicted that older adults would display some signs of impairment on reversal tasks, the DNMS task, and the DNMP task as compared to younger adults.

Participants

Results from 29 older adults (OA) (22 females) and 29 younger adults (YA) (22 females) are described in this chapter. The mean age for OA was 75 (range 65 to 86 years old) and for YA it was 21 (range 19 to 23 years old). The mini-mental state examination (MMSE) (Folstein, Folstein and McHugh, 1975) was used to evaluate mental status. The mean score for OA was 28.4 (SD: 1.54), which is considered within the normal range. Participants suffering from any disorder, mental health, or physical health problems that could confound the results of the study were excluded.

Results and Discussion

The results reviewed in this chapter focus on group comparisons between OA and YA. We looked at both number of trials to attain criterion and number of errors as dependent variables (see Figure 2). The results obtained with these two measures were generally consistent and only number of errors will be reported here. Because the distribution of the data violated the assumption of homogeneity of variance, independent group t-tests were performed on a square-root transformation of the data (Winer, 1971). Because we were looking for signs of cognitive impairments in OA, we divided the data in three categories: comparisons associated with p values smaller than .05 were considered highly suggestive of age differences; comparisons associated with p values smaller than .10 suggested a trend for OA to perform more poorly than YA; comparisons with p values greater than .10 suggested no age differences.

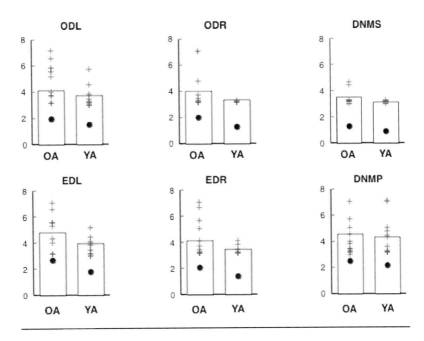

Figure 2. Mean trials (bars) and errors (filled circles) for older adults (OA) and younger adults (YA) for the six tasks employed. The graphs illustrate the square-root transformed data. Gray crosses represent individual trial scores.

Group comparisons for the ODR, DNMS, EDL, and EDR tasks were highly suggestive of age differences. The ODL and DNMP tasks were not sensitive to age differences.

As predicted, both reversal tasks and the DNMS task revealed age differences. Evidence from lesion studies in primates (Bachevalier and Mishkin, 1986; Jones and Mishkin, 1972; Mahut, 1971; Mahut and Zola, 1973; Meunier, Bachevalier and Mishkin, 1997; Spiegler and Mishkin, 1981) and from imaging studies in humans (Elliott and Dolan, 1999; Lamar, Yousem and Resnick, 2004; Remijnse, Nielen, Uylings and Veltman, 2005) suggests that the oritofrontal cortex is implicated in visual and spatial reversal task as well as in the DNMS task. Our finding of age differences for tasks that are subserved by the orbitofrontal cortex is consistent with mounting evidence that this region is one of the first frontal lobe regions to show both physiological and functional vulnerability with increased age in healthy individuals (Convit et al., 2001; Lamar et al., 2004; Lamar and Resnick, 2004; Raz, 2000).

We also found evidence of age differences on the EDL task, which was contrary to our original prediction. Our initial hypothesis, however, was based on evidence that position discrimination tasks are not sensitive to aging in monkeys (Lai et al., 1995; Tsuchida et al., 2002; Voytko, 1999) or to neuropathology in patients with AD (Freedman and Oscar-Berman, 1989). It is important to note that the EDL is a new task developed in our laboratory to replace traditional position discrimination learning tasks because these tasks can be acquired using a stimulus-association strategy (Christie et al., 2005). Hence, we cannot rule out the possibility that the EDL task utilizes different cognitive strategies than those used in position discrimination learning. It should be noted that further analyses revealed that the EDL task was the only task to correlate with education level. Although education level was on average equivalent across the two groups, it is possible that individual differences in education level confounded the results obtained on the EDL task.

Also contrary to our predictions was the absence of group differences on the DNMP task. The DNMP task is also a novel task that was developed to evaluate spatial working memory using a procedure comparable to the DNMS task. The high degree of variability in both YA and OA on the DNMP task may in part explain why we failed to find differences in this task.

Our results highlight many of the advantages of the comparative neuropsychological approach. First, our results demonstrate that despite their apparent simplicity, the tasks we used are sufficiently sensitive to detect cognitive decline in healthy older adults. Second, our findings were on the whole consistent with those reported in animal studies and hence provide some evidence that animal models of human aging are valid. Third, the deficits we found in healthy older adults parallel those found in patients with AD, with a quantitatively more severe decline in the latter case. Finally, comparing our results with imaging studies in humans and lesion studies in primates allows us to provide additional support for the notion that to the orbitofrontal system is particularly vulnerable to the aging process.

STUDY 2: PROFILING STRENGTHS AND WEAKNESSES IN FRAGILE-X SYNDROME

The second study presented in this chapter reviews preliminary results obtained from a group of male participants affected by Fragile-X syndrome. Fragile-X syndrome (FXS) is the most common form of heritable mental retardation (Morton et al., 1997). The syndrome arises from a cytogenetic abnormality on the X chromosome resulting in a set of physical, cognitive, and behavioural features (DeVries, Halley, Oostra and Niermeijer, 1994; Wiegers, DeVries, Curfs and Fryns, 1993). Of particular interest to the present chapter is the fact that males with FXS have significant learning disabilities with intelligence quotients in the moderate to severe retardation range. The FXS phenotype is characterized by weak attentional control (Cornish, Munir and Cross, 2001; Wilding, Cornish and Munir, 2002), poor short-term memory (Jakala et al., 1997; Schapiro et al., 1995), and linguistic processing deficits (Belser and Sudhalter, 2001). In addition to mental retardation, affected males often present with psychiatric symptoms including autistic features, anxiety, aggression, and inattention (Hagerman and Hagerman, 2002). These characteristics make evaluating cognitive function in FXS males particularly challenging. We felt that the comparative neuropsychology approach would be ideal for this population and thus, we set out to examine the feasibility of using our test battery in this population. We also sought to characterize the cognitive profile of FXS males.

A profile of strengths and weaknesses is beginning to emerge from studies that employed either traditional neuropsychological tasks (e.g., Backes et al., 2000; Curfs, Borghgraef, Wiegers, Schreppers-Tijdink and Fryns, 1989; Kemper, Hagerman and Altshul-Stark, 1988) or customized computer tasks (Cornish et al., 2001; Kwon et al., 2001) to evaluate traditional domains of cognitive abilities (e.g., aspects of attention, visual cognition, and motor development) in affected individuals. However, these earlier studies suffer from the same limitations of traditional neuropsychological tasks as outlined above. Specifically, these tasks and tests often exclude lower functioning individuals from participating thereby producing a skewed sample of results that include only the highest functioning individuals affected by FXS. Furthermore, the traditional neuropsychological tasks employed require a variety of cognitive functions for successful performance thereby obscuring the true source of any observed deficit. This particular limitation applies equally to the customized computer tasks developed for this population. In addition, the traditional neuropsychological measures used to date have not been correlated with brain function from animal studies, limiting the ability to draw conclusions about putatively affected brain areas. Finally, the computerized tasks used in the past were developed specifically to investigate FXS and therefore comparative data from individuals affected by other forms of developmental delay do not exist. Comparative neuropsychological tasks can address each of these limitations and provide a clearer understanding of the strengths and weaknesses in cognition associated with FXS.

Participants

Preliminary results from 15 males affected by FXS aged 11 to 23 are described in this chapter. The FXS group was compared to 15 normally developing individuals matched for equivalent mental age (MA group). The ages of the CA group ranged from 15 to 22 and the ages in the MA group ranged form 4 to 9 years. The Peabody Picture Vocabulary Test (Dunn and Dunn, 1981) was used to evaluate mental age in all groups. The average mental age of the FXS group did not significantly differ from the average mental age of the MA group.

Results

The results reviewed in this chapter will focus on group comparisons between FXS and MA (Figure 3). A MA group was used as comparison for FXS because the overall cognitive level of the two groups is equivalent, allowing us to identify strengths and weaknesses without the confound of mental retardation. We performed the same analyses as in Study 1. Comparisons at the $p < .05$ level were considered significant. In addition, we analyzed the relative difficulty of the six tasks across the two age groups separately using the Friedman test applied to the raw data (Figure 4).

FXS individuals were found to be impaired relative to MA controls on the ODL, ODR, and DNMP tasks. The groups did not significantly differ on the EDL and EDR tasks, and on the DNMS task with a delay of 5 s. Fewer FXS individuals than MA individuals were able to reach criterion with longer delays (10 and 20 s) on the DNMS task. Analyses related to task difficulty were significant for both the FXS and MA group. The task difficulty analysis generally supports the group comparisons by revealing a profile of strengths in the egocentric tasks and weaknesses in object discrimination tasks in the FXS group in comparison with the MA group.

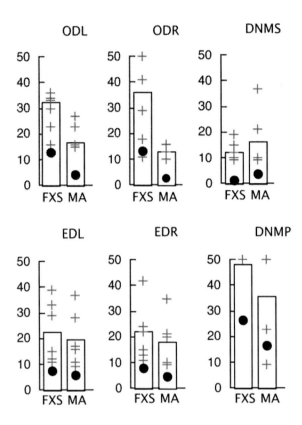

Figure 3. Mean trials (bars) and errors (filled circles) for patients with fragile-X syndrome (FXS) and mental age matched controls (MA) for the six tasks employed. Gray crosses represent individual trial scores.

These results indicate that FXS individuals have relative strengths in egocentric spatial abilities and object recognition at short delays, alongside weaknesses in acquisition of new stimulus-reward associations, in inhibiting a previously learned stimulus-reward association, and in visual-spatial working memory. Poorer performance on the object recognition task at longer delays likely reflects the inability in this population to maintain attention on relevant information (Munir et al., 2000; Wilding et al., 2002). The weaknesses observed in FXS are consistent with known abnormalities of the amygdala (Mazzocco, Freund and Baumgardner,1995; Spiegler and Mishkin, 1981) and orbitofrontal cortex (Guerreiro et al, 1998; Tamm, Menon, Johnston, Hessl and Reiss, 2002; Meunier et al., 1997). The data presented here are also consistent with the findings of Munir et al. (2000) who describe a generalized deficit in working memory for the visual-spatial sketchpad according to the Baddely and Hitch model.

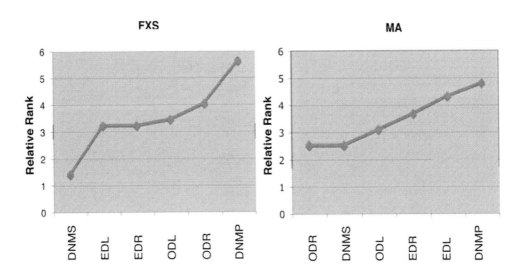

Figure 4. Relative ranking of the six tasks for Fragile-X participants (FXS) and mental age matched controls (MA) as a function of number of trials.

One surprising result was the finding of impaired reversal learning in the visual domain (ODR) alongside spared performance in the reversal learning in the spatial domain (EDR). The lack of impairment in the egocentric reversal task is inconsistent with previous studies indicating that individuals with FXS have difficulty in tasks that require cognitive flexibility (Munir et al., 2000). This discrepancy illustrates the utility of the test battery in allowing comparison of equivalent tasks across the visual and spatial domain. Whereas it was concluded that individuals with FXS have generalized impairment in cognitive flexibility, our results suggest that this impairment is limited to the visual domain. This result is an example of how the comparative neuropsychological approach can assist in better characterizing strengths and weaknesses in cognitive abilities.

Our preliminary results also illustrate the feasibility of administering this novel test battery to individuals with development delays, language impairments, and psychiatric features. We were able to obtain data from all the affected individuals who participated in the study. Finally, the comparative neuropsychological approach allowed us to make inferences about affected brain regions in FXS. This is of great advantage because of a longstanding limitation in the FXS literature on brain-behavior relationships as assessed with functional imaging. No study to date has been able to successfully collect data from affected males because of their inability to tolerate the procedure. The study described here is still in progress. We are currently obtaining test-retest reliability data in FXS on the same test battery as well as data from other genetic conditions such as Down syndrome in order to partial out the generalized effects of mental retardation.

CONCLUSION

Taken together, the results of the studies reviewed in this chapter provide further support for utilizing a comparative neuropsychological approach to evaluate cognition in normal and clinical populations. As mentioned in the Introduction, comparative neuropsychology rests on the assumption that by administering identical testing procedures, researchers can make inferences about implicated brain areas in humans on the basis of the knowledge accrued from lesion studies in non-human primates. It should be noted that this assumption has not been thoroughly validated. On one hand, comparison of the patterns of performance of humans and animals suggests that the two species use the same strategies to perform these tasks (Boutet, Kulaga, Ryan, Freedman and Milgram, 2004; Kessler, Irle and Markowitsch, 1986). On the other hand there is evidence that animals and humans perform reversal tasks differently. In animals, learning of reversal tasks requires many more trials than learning the original S-R association. In contrast, fewer trials are required to pass criterion on the reversal tasks than on the original learning task in humans. One possible interpretation for the difference between the acquisition of reversal tasks in animals and humans is that they employ different strategies to solve tasks in the WGTA. Levine (1966) has provided convincing evidence that humans formulate *a priori* hypotheses to solve the rule governing S-R type tasks. He proposed that humans and animals possess both associative and cognitive systems for processing information and that humans rely more heavily on cognitive strategies than on associative strategies. Hence, once humans become aware of the relevant S-R association in the original discrimination tasks (i.e., that the correct response depends on selecting one of the two stimulus), they can quickly switch to the opposite association in the reversal task. In contrast, animals' poor performance in reversal tasks (e.g., Lai et al., 1995; Rapp, 1990; Voytko, 1999) is largely attributable to perseverative responding, a clear indication that they are solving the task using an associative learning system.

The possibility that animals and humans solve tasks in the WGTA using different strategies is problematic for comparative neuropsychology because it raises the possibility that different brain regions are triggered when the same tasks are performed. It is important to note that this possibility remains speculative and that finding different pattern of results in animals and in humans does not necessarily mean that different brain regions are implicated. In fact, converging evidence from lesion studies in animals, studies of brain-damaged patients in humans, and imaging studies in humans point to common brain mechanisms for some of the tasks employed in comparative neuropsychology. The delayed-matching-to-sample (DNMS) task, for example, has been used to investigate visual working memory. Lesion studies in monkeys indicate that a number of isolated brain regions and combined regions are involved in performance on DNMS tasks including the orbitofrontal cortex (Bachevalier and Mishkin, 1986; Meunier et al., 1997). Similarly, patients with AD, a condition which is associated with damage to the orbitofrontal system (e.g. Chetelat et al., 2005; Lerch et al., 2005), show deficits in DNMS tasks (Irle et al., 1987; Sahakian et al, 1988). Furthermore, imaging studies in normal adults indicate that this same region is activated during performance of DNMS tasks (Elliott and Dolan, 1999). Hence, it appears that certain comparative neuropsychological tasks can be used to make inferences about affected brain regions. However, caution must be exercised until convergent data from multiple methods is available for all the tasks employed.

Although further studies are needed to demonstrate that similar cognitive abilities and brain regions are triggered by the entire array of tasks we employed, we feel that our results illustrate the utility of these tasks in investigating cognition in older adults and participants with limited intellectual and language abilities. An accounting of studies that have employed the comparative neuropsychological approach reveals a recent increased interest in this methodology to evaluate clinical populations (Table 1). We believe that this approach has great potential to advance our understanding of brain-behaviour relationships in humans and animals.

Future Directions

The present chapter outlines a variety of comparative neuropsychological tasks that have been used successfully in research on aging and developmental delay. Many of the tasks employed in humans have also been used pervasively in animal research to reveal the brain areas associated with successful task performance. The future success of the comparative neuropsychology approach will depend on a concerted effort to identify the brain areas involved in each of the tasks described in this chapter. Functional imaging technology is sufficiently advanced to resolve the details of which neural networks are critical to the functions measured by these tasks. This information will facilitate cognitive profiling of clinical populations.

The tasks described here were all administered in the WGTA. Additional tasks could be developed to examine a variety of other cognitive abilities using the WGTA. Furthermore, the animal literature is rife with examples of tasks that have the potential of being translated for use in humans. For example, a recent publication by Shore, Stanford, MacInnes, Klein and Brown (2001) describes a computerized version of a set of Hebb-Williams three-dimensional mazes that afford researchers the ability to compare mouse and human performance. This task was developed in recognition of the exponential increase in genetically modified mouse strains (i.e., knock-outs) that serve as models of human diseases.

Another important area of development will be to bring these experimental tasks out of the lab and in to the clinic. By collecting normative data on these tasks it will be possible to use these simple and practical tasks to identify individual patients' performance as well as to track their progress following intervention. Few good measures are available that can accurately track the natural course of conditions (e.g., stroke, brain injury, and degenerative diseases) that affect cognitive function across a broad range of populations. We hope that with more research, these measures will become more precise in describing the profile of strengths and weaknesses in various populations.

**Table 1. Clinical populations previously investigated
using comparative neuropsychology**

Population	Tasks Employed	Source
Korsakoff's	Spatial and object discrimination learning and reversal	Oscar-Berman and Zola-Morgan, 1980
	Concurrent object discrimination	Kessler et al., 1986
Bilateral frontal lobe disease	Delayed response and Delayed alternation	Freedman and Oscar-Berman, 1986
Senile Dementia of the Lewy Body Type	Matching to Sample	Sahgal et al., 1992
Down syndrome	Same test battery as described in this chapter	Nelson et al., 2005
	DNMS	Dawson et al., 1998, 2001
Alzheimer's	Delayed response	Freedman and Oscar-Berman, 1986
	Spatial and object discrimination learning and reversal	Freedman and Oscar-Berman, 1989
	Tactile discrimination learning and reversal	Freedman and Oscar-Berman, 1987
	Delayed matching to sample (DMS)	Sahakian et al., 1988
	DNMS	Irle et al., 1987
	Concurrent object discrimination	Irle et al., 1987
	Matching to sample	Sahgal et al., 1992
Parkinson's	Delayed response	Freedman and Oscar-Berman, 1986
	Spatial and object discrimination learning and reversal	Freedman and Oscar-Berman, 1989
	Tactile discrimination learning and reversal	Freedman and Oscar-Berman, 1987
	DMS	Sahakian et al., 1988
	DNMS	Blanchet et al., 2000
Autism	DNMS	Dawson, Meltzoff, Osterling and Rinaldi, 1998; Dawson, Osterling, Rinaldi, Carver and McPartland, 2001
	Delayed response	Dawson et al., 1998
Substance Abuse	DNMS	Bechara and Martin, 2004; Martin, Pilon-Kacir and Wheeler, 2006

REFERENCES

Adams, B., Chan, A., Callahan, H., and Milgram, N. W. (2000). The canine as a model of human cognitive aging: recent developments. *Prog. Neuropsychopharmacol Biol. Psychiatry, 24*(5), 675-692.

Anderson, J. R., de Monte, M., and Kempf, J. (1996). Discrimination learning and multiple reversals in young adult and older monkeys (Macaca arctoides). *Q. J. Exp. Psychol. B, 49*(3), 193-200.

Bachevalier, J., Landis, L. S., Walker, L. C., Brickson, M., Mishkin, M., Price, D. L., et al. (1991). Aged monkeys exhibit behavioral deficits indicative of widespread cerebral dysfunction. *Neurobiol. Aging, 12*(2), 99-111.

Bachevalier, J., and Mishkin, M. (1986). Visual recognition impairment follows ventromedial but not dorsolateral prefrontal lesions in monkeys. *Behav. Brain Res, 20*(3), 249-261.

Backes, M., Genc, B., Schreck, J., Doerfler, W., Lehmkuhl, G., and von Gontard, A. (2000). Cognitive and behavioral profile of fragile X boys: correlations to molecular data. *Am. J. Med. Genet, 95*(2), 150-156.

Bartus, R. T., Dean, R. L., 3rd, and Fleming, D. L. (1979). Aging in the rhesus monkey: effects on visual discrimination learning and reversal learning. *J. Gerontol, 34*(2), 209-219.

Bechara, A., and Martin, E. M. (2004). Impaired decision making related to working memory deficits in individuals with substance addictions. *Neuropsychology, 18*(1), 152-162.

Belser, R. C., and Sudhalter, V. (2001). Conversational characteristics of children with fragile X syndrome: repetitive speech. *Am. J. Ment. Retard, 106*(1), 28-38.

Blanchet, S., Marie, R. M., Dauvillier, F., Landeau, B., Benali, K., Eustache, F., et al. (2000). Cognitive processes involved in delayed non-matching-to-sample performance in Parkinson's disease. *Eur. J. Neurol, 7*(5), 473-483.

Boutet, I., Kulaga, V., Ryan, M., Freedman, M., and Milgram, N. (2004). Age-associated cognitive deficits in dogs and humans: a comparative approach. *34th meeting of the Society for Neuroscience*.

Chetelat, G., Eustache, F., Viader, F., De La Sayette, V., Pelerin, A., Mezenge, F., et al. (2005). FDG-PET measurement is more accurate than neuropsychological assessments to predict global cognitive deterioration in patients with mild cognitive impairment. *Neurocase, 11*(1), 14-25.

Christie, L. A., Studzinski, C. M., Araujo, J. A., Leung, C. S., Ikeda-Douglas, C. J., Head, E., et al. (2005). A comparison of egocentric and allocentric age-dependent spatial learning in the beagle dog. *Prog. Neuropsychopharmacol Biol. Psychiatry, 29*(3), 361-369.

Convit, A., Wolf, O. T., de Leon, M. J., Patalinjug, M., Kandil, E., Caraos, C., et al. (2001). Volumetric analysis of the pre-frontal regions: findings in aging and schizophrenia. *Psychiatry Res, 107*(2), 61-73.

Cornish, K. M., Munir, F., and Cross, G. (2001). Differential impact of the FMR-1 full mutation on memory and attention functioning : a neuropsychological perspective. *J. Cogn. Neurosci, 13*(1), 144-150.

Curfs, L. M., Borghgraef, M., Wiegers, A., Schreppers-Tijdink, G. A., and Fryns, J. P. (1989). Strengths and weaknesses in the cognitive profile of fra(X) patients. *Clin Genet, 36*(6), 405-410.

Dawson, G., Meltzoff, A. N., Osterling, J., and Rinaldi, J. (1998). Neuropsychological correlates of early symptoms of autism. *Child Dev, 69*(5), 1276-1285.

Dawson, G., Osterling, J., Rinaldi, J., Carver, L., and McPartland, J. (2001). Brief report: Recognition memory and stimulus-reward associations: indirect support for the role of ventromedial prefrontal dysfunction in autism. *J. Autism Dev. Disord, 31*(3), 337-341.

Delacourte, A., David, J. P., Sergeant, N., Buee, L., Wattez, A., Vermersch, P., et al. (1999). The biochemical pathway of neurofibrillary degeneration in aging and Alzheimer's disease. *Neurology, 52*(6), 1158-1165.

DeVries, L., Halley, D., Oostra, B., and Niermeijer, J. (1994). The fragile-X syndrome: a growing gene causing familial intellectual disability. *Journal of Intellectual Disabilities Research*. (38), 1-8.

Dunn, L. M., and Dunn, L. M. (1981). *Peabody picture vocabulary test-revised*. Minnesota.

Elliott, R., and Dolan, R. J. (1999). Differential neural responses during performance of matching and nonmatching to sample tasks at two delay intervals. *J. Neurosci, 19*(12), 5066-5073.

Folstein, M. F., Folstein, S. E., and McHugh, P. R. (1975). "Mini-mental state". A practical method for grading the cognitive state of patients for the clinician. *J. Psychiatr. Res, 12*(3), 189-198.

Freedman, M., and Oscar-Berman, M. (1986). Selective delayed response deficits in Parkinson's and Alzheimer's disease. *Arch. Neurol, 43*(9), 886-890.

Freedman, M., and Oscar-Berman, M. (1987). Tactile discrimination learning deficits in Alzheimer's and Parkinson's diseases. *Arch. Neurol, 44*(4), 394-398.

Freedman, M., and Oscar-Berman, M. (1989). Spatial and visual learning deficits in Alzheimer's and Parkinson's disease. *Brain Cogn, 11*(1), 114-126.

Galvan, M., David, J. P., Delacourte, A., Luna, J., and Mena, R. (2001). Sequence of neurofibrillary changes in aging and Alzheimer's disease: A confocal study with phospho-tau antibody, AD2. *J. Alzheimers Dis, 3*(4), 417-425.

Guerreiro, M. M., Camargo, E. E., Kato, M., Marques-de-Faria, A. P., Ciasca, S. M., Guerreiro, C. A., et al. (1998). Fragile X syndrome. Clinical, electroencephalographic and neuroimaging characteristics. *Arq. Neuropsiquiatr, 56*(1), 18-23.

Hagerman, R., and Hagerman, P. (2002). *Fragile X syndrome: diagnosis, treatment and research* (3rd edn. ed.). Baltimore (MD): The Johns Hopkins University Press.

Herndon, J. G., Moss, M. B., Rosene, D. L., and Killiany, R. J. (1997). Patterns of cognitive decline in aged rhesus monkeys. *Behav. Brain Res, 87*(1), 25-34.

Irle, E., Kessler, J., Markowitsch, H. J., and Hofmann, W. (1987). Primate learning tasks reveal strong impairments in patients with presenile or senile dementia of the Alzheimer type. *Brain Cogn, 6*(4), 429-449.

Jakala, P., Hanninen, T., Ryynanen, M., Laakso, M., Partanen, K., Mannermaa, A., et al. (1997). Fragile-X: neuropsychological test performance, CGG triplet repeat lengths, and hippocampal volumes. *J. Clin. Invest, 100*(2), 331-338.

Jones, B., and Mishkin, M. (1972). Limbic lesions and the problem of stimulus-- reinforcement associations. *Exp. Neurol, 36*(2), 362-377.

Kemper, M. B., Hagerman, R. J., and Altshul-Stark, D. (1988). Cognitive profiles of boys with the fragile X syndrome. *Am. J. Med. Genet, 30*(1-2), 191-200.

Kendler, H. H., and D'Amato, M. F. (1995). A comparison of reversal shifts and nonreversal shifts in human concept formation behavior. *Journal of Experimental Psychology*. (49), 165-174.

Kessler, J., Irle, E., and Markowitsch, H. J. (1986). Korsakoff and alcoholic subjects are severely impaired in animal tasks of associative memory. *Neuropsychologia, 24*(5), 671-680.

Kwon, H., Menon, V., Eliez, S., Warsofsky, I. S., White, C. D., Dyer-Friedman, J., et al. (2001). Functional neuroanatomy of visuospatial working memory in fragile X syndrome: relation to behavioral and molecular measures. *Am. J. Psychiatry, 158*(7), 1040-1051.

Lai, Z. C., Moss, M. B., Killiany, R. J., Rosene, D. L., and Herndon, J. G. (1995). Executive system dysfunction in the aged monkey: spatial and object reversal learning. *Neurobiol. Aging, 16*(6), 947-954.

Lamar, M., and Resnick, S. M. (2004). Aging and prefrontal functions: dissociating orbitofrontal and dorsolateral abilities. *Neurobiol. Aging, 25*(4), 553-558.

Lamar, M., Yousem, D. M., and Resnick, S. M. (2004). Age differences in orbitofrontal activation: an fMRI investigation of delayed match and nonmatch to sample. *Neuroimage, 21*(4), 1368-1376.

Lerch, J. P., Pruessner, J. C., Zijdenbos, A., Hampel, H., Teipel, S. J., and Evans, A. C. (2005). Focal decline of cortical thickness in Alzheimer's disease identified by computational neuroanatomy. *Cereb. Cortex, 15*(7), 995-1001.

Levine, M. (1963). Mediating responses in humans at the outset of discrimination-learning. *Psychological Review*(70), 254-276.

Levine, M. (1966). Hypothesis behavior by humans during discrimination learning. *J. Exp. Psychol, 71*(3), 331-338.

Mahut, H. (1971). Spatial and object reversal learning in monkeys with partial temporal lobe ablations. *Neuropsychologia, 9*(4), 409-424.

Mahut, H., and Zola, S. M. (1973). A non-modality specific impairment in spatial learning after fornix lesions in monkeys. *Neuropsychologia, 11*(3), 255-269.

Martin, P. M., Pilon-Kacir, C., and Wheeler, M. (2006). Interdisciplinary service learning and substance abuse screening in free clinic settings. *Subst. Abus, 26*(3-4), 49-52.

Mazzocco, M. M., Freund, L., and Baumgardner, T. L. (1995). The neurobehavioral and neuroanatomical effects of the *FMR1* full mutation: Monozygotic twins discordant fragile X syndrome. *Neuropsychology, 9*, 470-480.

Mell, T., Heekeren, H. R., Marschner, A., Wartenburger, I., Villringer, A., and Reischies, F. M. (2005). Effect of aging on stimulus-reward association learning. *Neuropsychologia, 43*(4), 554-563.

Meunier, M., Bachevalier, J., and Mishkin, M. (1997). Effects of orbital frontal and anterior cingulate lesions on object and spatial memory in rhesus monkeys. *Neuropsychologia, 35*(7), 999-1015.

Milgram, N. W., Head, E., Weiner, E., and Thomas, E. (1994). Cognitive functions and aging in the dog: acquisition of nonspatial visual tasks. *Behav. Neurosci, 108*(1), 57-68.

Moore, D. T., and McCleary, R. A. (1976). Fornix damage enhances successive, but not simultaneous, object-discrimination learning in cats. *J. Comp. Physiol. Psychol, 90*(1), 109-118.

Morton, J. E., Bundey, S., Webb, T. P., MacDonald, F., Rindl, P. M., and Bullock, S. (1997). Fragile X syndrome is less common than previously estimated. *J. Med. Genet, 34*(1), 1-5.

Moss, M. B., Rosene, D. L., and Peters, A. (1988). Effects of aging on visual recognition memory in the rhesus monkey. *Neurobiol. Aging, 9*(5-6), 495-502.

Munir, F., Cornish, K. M., and Wilding, J. (2000). A neuropsychological profile of attention deficits in young males with fragile X syndrome. *Neuropsychologia, 38*(9), 1261-1270.

Nelson, L., Johnson, J. K., Freedman, M., Lott, I., Groot, J., Chang, M., et al. (2005). Learning and memory as a function of age in Down syndrome: a study using animal-based tasks. *Prog. Neuropsychopharmacol Biol. Psychiatry, 29*(3), 443-453.

Oscar-Berman, M., and Zola-Morgan, S. M. (1980). Comparative neuropsychology and Korsakoff's syndrome. I.--Spatial and visual reversal learning. *Neuropsychologia, 18*(4-5), 499-512.

Presty, S. K., Bachevalier, J., Walker, L. C., Struble, R. G., Price, D. L., Mishkin, M., et al. (1987). Age differences in recognition memory of the rhesus monkey (Macaca mulatta). *Neurobiol. Aging, 8*(5), 435-440.

Rapp, P. R. (1990). Visual discrimination and reversal learning in the aged monkey (Macaca mulatta). *Behav. Neurosci, 104*(6), 876-884.

Rapp, P. R., and Amaral, D. G. (1991). Recognition memory deficits in a subpopulation of aged monkeys resemble the effects of medial temporal lobe damage. *Neurobiol. Aging, 12*(5), 481-486.

Raz, E. (2000). The function and regulation of vasa-like genes in germ-cell development. *Genome Biol, 1*(3), REVIEWS1017.

Remijnse, P. L., Nielen, M. M., Uylings, H. B., and Veltman, D. J. (2005). Neural correlates of a reversal learning task with an affectively neutral baseline: an event-related fMRI study. *Neuroimage, 26*(2), 609-618.

Rogers, C. J., Keyes, B. J., and Fuller, B. J. (1976). Solution shift performance in the elderly. *J. Gerontol, 31*(6), 670-675.

Sahakian, B. J., Morris, R. G., Evenden, J. L., Heald, A., Levy, R., Philpot, M., et al. (1988). A comparative study of visuospatial memory and learning in Alzheimer-type dementia and Parkinson's disease. *Brain, 111 (Pt 3)*, 695-718.

Sahgal, A., Galloway, P. H., McKeith, I. G., Lloyd, S., Cook, J. H., Ferrier, I. N., et al. (1992). Matching-to-sample deficits in patients with senile dementias of the Alzheimer and Lewy body types. *Arch. Neurol, 49*(10), 1043-1046.

Salat, D. H., Kaye, J. A., and Janowsky, J. S. (2002). Greater orbital prefrontal volume selectively predicts worse working memory performance in older adults. *Cereb. Cortex, 12*(5), 494-505.

Schapiro, M. B., Murphy, D. G., Hagerman, R. J., Azari, N. P., Alexander, G. E., Miezejeski, C. M., et al. (1995). Adult fragile X syndrome: neuropsychology, brain anatomy, and metabolism. *Am. J. Med. Genet, 60*(6), 480-493.

Shore, D. I., Stanford, L., MacInnes, W. J., Klein, R. M., and Brown, R. E. (2001). Of mice and men: virtual Hebb-Williams mazes permit comparison of spatial learning across species. *Cogn. Affect. Behav. Neurosci, 1*(1), 83-89.

Spiegler, B. J., and Mishkin, M. (1981). Evidence for the sequential participation of inferior temporal cortex and amygdala in the acquisition of stimulus-reward associations. *Behav. Brain Res, 3*(3), 303-317.

Tamm, L., Menon, V., Johnston, C. K., Hessl, D. R., and Reiss, A. L. (2002). fMRI study of cognitive interference processing in females with fragile X syndrome. *J. Cogn. Neurosci, 14*(2), 160-171.

Tapp, P. D., Siwak, C. T., Estrada, J., Head, E., Muggenburg, B. A., Cotman, C. W., et al. (2003). Size and reversal learning in the beagle dog as a measure of executive function and inhibitory control in aging. *Learn Mem, 10*(1), 64-73.

Tsuchida, J., Kubo, N., and Kojima, S. (2002). Position reversal learning in aged Japanese macaques. *Behav. Brain Res, 129*(1-2), 107-112.

Voytko, M. L. (1999). Impairments in acquisition and reversals of two-choice discriminations by aged rhesus monkeys. *Neurobiol. Aging, 20*(6), 617-627.

Walker, L. C., Kitt, C. A., Struble, R. G., Wagster, M. V., Price, D. L., and Cork, L. C. (1988). The neural basis of memory decline in aged monkeys. *Neurobiol. Aging, 9*(5-6), 657-666.

Wiegers, A. M., DeVries, L. B., Curfs, L. M., and Fryns, J. P. (1993). Identical psychological profile and behaviour pattern in different types of mutation in the FMR-1 region. *Clin. Genet, 43*(6), 326-327.

Wilding, J., Cornish, K., and Munir, F. (2002). Further delineation of the executive deficit in males with fragile-X syndrome. *Neuropsychologia, 40*(8), 1343-1349.

Winer, B. J. (1971). *Statistical principles in experimental design.* New York: McGraw-Hill.

In: Psychological Tests and Testing Research Trends
Editor: Paul M. Goldfarb, pp. 173-189

ISBN: 978-1-60021-569-8
© 2007 Nova Science Publishers, Inc.

Chapter 8

DEVELOPING AND VALIDATING PSYCHOLOGICAL TESTS

Robert J. Craig[*]
Roosevelt University, Chicago, IL, USA

ABSTRACT

This chapter describes the development, test construction, and validation of psychological tests. We describe item generation and selection, testing for content validity, developing a standardization sample, testing for reliability (internal consistency, test-retest), assessing for internal test bias, determining the factor structure of a test, and finally testing both the convergent validity and discriminant validity of tests. We demonstrate these principles by contrasting the application of these processes with a recently published scale and with a newly developed measure for the assessment of personality disorders.

In this chapter I will describe how we currently develop and validate psychological tests, emphasizing the development and validation of personality tests. However, this overview is not fundamentally different for developing other kinds of tests, such as ability tests, achievement tests, and tests of intelligence. For each major section, I will describe how authors used the processes described here to develop a brief screening measure of Acute Stress Disorder (Bryant, Moulds, and Guthrie,2000), and I will also describe how these procedures were used to develop a new screening measure for the assessment of personality disorders, called the *Personality Disorder Adjective Check List (PDACL)* (Craig, In Press).

---

[*] Address correspondence concerning this manuscript to Rjcraig41@comcast.net

TEST DEVELOPMENT AND TEST CONSTRUCTION

As little as 80 years ago, tests were developed merely by selecting the items, establishing a scoring system, and then finding a publisher. These items usually had what is referred to as "face validity". In other words, they looked valid. For example, suppose we were interested in creating a test that would diagnoses a narcissistic personality disorder. In the pre-scientific era, we would have consulted dictionaries and the psychiatric literature to learn what traits and behaviors characterized people who were considered narcissistic.

Next, the author would select a test format that best measured the desired construct. The test format could be questionnaires with a true/false format, (as in most personality tests), multiple choice (as in achievement tests), a selection format (as in an ability test), or even a production format (as in the Thematic Apperception Test, which requires a respondent to tell a story to pictures). The format might even require computations, as in mathematical ability tests. Finally, the author would then make up the items in the chosen format that might best measure the construct under study (2).

For a test of Narcissism using a true/false format, the questions might look something like this: (In parentheses is the answer that is scored if so endorsed)

- I am entitled to everything I can get. (T)
- People have not recognized my true brilliance. (T)
- I should have to stand in line like everyone else. (F)
- My ideas are ahead of the times. (T)

Next, a scoring key would be developed by the author by some arbitrary method and scores above the designated threshold purportedly reflect Narcissism. Sometimes a retest reliability study was conducted – sometimes it wasn't. Finally, the author would then seek a publisher.

But, wait a minute! What's missing here? How do we know this test validly assesses narcissism? The items "look" valid, but that does not mean they work (i. e., actually tap narcissistic behaviors and traits). In order to demonstrate validity, we would need to collect of group of respondents that we know to be really narcissistic and a group of respondents known to be self-deprecating or at least non-narcissistic. These two groups would be given the test and, hopefully, the known narcissists would score higher on our test, thereby demonstrating that it is valid. This seems quite obvious to us today, but it was not until the appearance of the Minnesota Multiphasic Personality Inventory (MMPI) (Hathaway and McKinley, 1941) that tests were validated prior to publication.

SCALE CONSTRUCTION TECHNIQUES: ITEM DEVELOPMENT AND GENERATION

There are four basic methods for constructing scales. This is true whether the test has a single focus or a narrow band test and hence has only one scale or whether it is an omnibus or broad band instrument with several scales. These are (1) intuitive-rational or logical criterion keying, (2) intuitive-theoretical, (3) factor analytic, and (4) empirical group discrimination.

In the intuitive-rational or *logical criterion keying* approach, the researcher develops items based on what is already known about the construct to be measured. In the example cited above, the researcher has used this method to develop the items to measure narcissism. If we were to construct a test for clinical depression, we would generate items based on what is known about the manifestations of clinical depression. Thus, we would write items that pertain to dysphoric mood, problems with energy, eating, sleep, and loss of interests along with questions dealing with suicidal ideation. The items on most psychological tests continue to be generated based on this method. It is called logical criterion keying because the item, if answered in the endorsed direction, is keyed (i.e., placed) on that scale.

In the *rational-theoretical* approach, the items are stilled generated from a rational approach and the logical criterion keying method is used to place an item on the scale but the item itself is derived based on someone's theory associated with the construct. For example, Millon believes that the antisocial personality disorder is motivated primarily by a fear of being dominated. According to Millon a person with this disorder behaves in such a way as to dominate others before they are dominated themselves (Millon and Davis,1996). Given this theoretical notion, Millon then developed items for his Antisocial Personality Disorder scale based on DSM criteria of the disorder (APA, 1983, 1987, 1994) but also based on his theory as to what motivates the antisocial style. So the scale would have items that tap official criteria (i.e., "When I was a teenager I got into a lot of trouble with the law" – not an actual item but used for illustrative purposes), but contain items that tap his theory as to the antisocial personality disorder's motivation to remain independent at all costs (i.e., "I won't let myself be tricked by family members who ask me for help" – again., not an actual MCMI item).

In this approach, experts are often used to judge the degree of correspondence of the item to a theory. As an example, Williams and Williams (1980) asked experts to nominate adjectives from the Adjective Check List test (Gough, and Heilbrun, 1983) that corresponded to the five transactional analysis ego states. This generated a list of adjectives that were subsequently determined to be reliably associated with these ego states. The researchers then went out and validated the scales by giving it to patients who the transactional analyst therapists indicated were operating primarily out of one of these ego states.

The Myers-Briggs Type Indicator (Myers and McCauley, 1985) is a frequently used personality test that is an operational measure of Carl Jung's theory of psychological types. Jung believed there were four preferences" (extroversion/introversion, sensing/intuiting, thinking/feeling, and judgment/perception) that results in eight basic psychological types. The items were then generated that tap the basic preference or style For example, if we were to develop an item that would tap the introversion/extroversion preference using a forced choice format, perhaps the item would ask "Do you (a) find it easy to speak in front of a large audience, or (b) prefer to speak when not much attention is focused on you". If you endorse choice "a" then you would get one point on the extroversion preference scale; if you endorsed "b" you would get one point on the introversion scale.

Few items from psychological tests are generated using the intuitive theoretical approach, due to its inherent difficulties. Most items are still generated using the rational-intuitive method with logical criterion keying.

A third way to develop a scale is by factor analysis. In this method, the test developer inter-correlates all the items and then conducts a factor study to ascertain the basic dimensions underlying the scale or test. Cattell developed the *Sixteen Personality Factor*

Questionnaire (16PF) by exclusively using the factor analytic method. He factored thousands of adjectives until he determined that all of personality could be described by 16 basic dimensions (Cattell, Eber, and Tatsuoka, 1970). Referring back to our scale for clinical depression, we might learn that our items reflect one of three factors, Cognitive Depression, Vegetative Depression, and Suicidal Ideation. The author may choose to publish the test as a single scale with three factors or publish the test with three scales that represent the major dimensions associated with the construct measured by the test. Today almost no test can be published without having a factor analytic study in the test manual that would report on the underlying dimensions in the test.

When using the questionnaire method, phrasing the question is critical. For example, true or false "I came to work sober yesterday". That is poorly phrased because we are uncertain what a "true" endorsement means. Does it reflect prior difficulties with alcohol or merely reliable attendance? Another example: "My use of drugs has caused a problem for my family." If false, does it mean that the use of drugs has not caused a problem in the family or does it mean the respondent does not use drugs? Confusion and double meanings need to be excised from questionnaire-based tests.

Constructs can be assessed directly ("I am an extroverted person") or indirectly ("I would like to be a singer). In the latter case, we are not interested in whether or not the respondent would like to be a singer but rather whether s/he has extroverted traits. Asking a respondent "I use alcohol to excess" may result in a false response based on denial or a wish to cover up a problem, so an author may screen for alcohol abuse by asking questions about traits commonly seen in substance abusers ("I like to try dangerous activities").

Another problem is the issue of social desirability. This is the tendency to answer an item in the socially desirable direction rather than actually what is true or false for the respondent. As an example, let us assume that an applicant for a sales position in insurance is given the personnel test with a forced choice format. One of the questions is as follows: Would you rather (a) go to party or (b) milk a cow? Now let us further suppose that nothing is more enjoyable for the respondent than milking a cow. However, where is s/he more likely to sell insurance – at a party or in barn? The socially desirable answer is obviously at a party. Many personality tests provide data on the social desirability of test items. However, just because an item is often answered in a socially desired direction does not mean that a particular respondent did answer it in this manner.

MODEL OF TEST DEVELOPMENT

The process of developing and validating tests is well understood but often not followed (Butcher, 1999; Haynes, Nelson, and Blaine, 1999). There are at least 36 steps involved in a developing, standardizing, and validating a test, although, depending on circumstances, not all of these steps need to be followed (Haynes, Richard and Kubany (1995).

Loevinger (1957) has presented a model of test development where test validation is an on-going iterative and sequential process. The model consists of three stages of test development and test validation. In the first phase of test construction – the *Stage of Substantive Validity* - a test's item pool is generated according to a theoretical model of the construct(s) measured by the test, or according to what has been empirically determined to be the domain of the construct(s). Experts may also be used at this stage to judge the initial items for conformance to the criterion or to the theoretical model. We would then pilot test the items on the planned population and refine the items as necessary. The item pool is then reduced on rational grounds, but empiricism is often used in the process. The final item pool is established and we would conduct a content validity study and finally develop the standardization sample. The model remained somewhat dormant until Ted Millon used it to develop the *Millon Clinical Multiaxial Inventory* (Millon, 1983). The model is becoming more popular and was the model selected in developing the *Personality Adjective Check List* (Strack,1987), and the *Personality Disorder Adjective Check List* (Craig, In Press).

For the Acute Stress Disorder scale (Bryant, Moulds, and Guthrie,2000) , the authors consulted DSM-IV criteria (APA, 1994) and asked six experienced clinical psychologists to provide items that they believed diagnosed Acute Stress Disorder. The authors selected 19 items that they believed encompassed the symptoms nominated by the clinicians.

Two general approaches have been used to assess personality disorders. Authors have developed structured or semi-structured diagnostic interview schedules (Rogers, 2001), or have employed self-report methodology to develop inventories, such as the Millon Clinical Multiaxial Inventory (MCMI-III) (Millon, Millon and Davis, 1994) using the questionnaire method with a true/false format, although Q-Sort methodology has also been tried (Shedler and Westen, 1998). One problem with these approaches is that both interviews and self-report questionnaires can take up to two hours (Widiger, 1995) to complete, with an average administration time of about 45 minutes across the various measures.

I was seeking a method that would be short, reliable, valid, focused, and clinically useful. Using an adjective check list method could fulfill these criteria. It had previously been shown that use of adjectives could tap the interpersonal domain seen in patients with personality disorders (Craig and Olson, 2001). In this method the respondent is given a list of adjectives and is asked to endorse (i.e., place a check next to the adjective if it described them and to omit it (i.e. leave the item unanswered) if it did not. This methodology is useful because respondents feel they are actually communicating specific aspects of themselves to the examiner. These tests tend to be relatively brief, with good reliability, and minimal problems in administration and scoring. They have high face validity and little patient resistance (Craig, 2005a). Furthermore, the adjective check list method had been successfully used to develop a test for normal personality styles (Strack, 1985).

Now that the test methodology had been selected, I needed to begin to select the items. I used a hybrid method incorporating many of the scale construction techniques previously discussed. Generating the items for the PDACL occurred as follows: First, I consulted previous reviews on assessing personality disorders (Baldassanni, Finklestein, and Arana, 1983; Bossuyt, Reitsma, Bruns, Gatsonis, Glasziou, Irvig, et al.2003; Burisch, 1984; Farmer, 2000; Goldsmith, Jacobsberg, and Bell, 1989; Haynes, and Lench, 2003; Perry, 1992; Widiger, and Frances,1987; and Zimmerman, 1994). Second, I reviewed major texts dealing with personality disorders in general or books devoted to a specific personality disorder. Next I reviewed various journal articles about each personality disorder. Whenever an author used an adjective to describe the disorder, that adjective was placed in a list of adjectives for that disorder. From this procedure, a preliminary list of over 900 adjectives was obtained for fourteen personality disorders.

Adjectives were placed in alphabetical order within each disorder and a group 25 nationally recognized experts, who have published on personality disorders, and clinicians, who devote a large part of their practice to evaluate and/or treat personality disorders, were invited to participate in the next phase. Of the 25 invitees, 19 replied and responded to the survey. They were given the list of the over 900 adjectives and asked to place a check in the designated spaces if they believed the adjective was essentially, moderately, weakly, or unrelated to the disorder. In order to reduce the item pool only items that the experts designated as essentially or moderately related to the disorder were retained. The item pool now totaled 571. These were further reduced based on rational grounds – primarily be eliminating synonyms for a given adjectives – leaving a total of 469.

This draft of the initial 469-item experimental version of the PDACL was given to over 200 African American male and female substance abusers in both inpatient and outpatient settings. This was done because it is important to validate a test with the population with whom it is intended to be used. However, it is also important to use the test with other populations to ensure that items selected are infrequently endorsed by populations known not to have the traits or disorders measured by the test. Hence, three community samples were also given the initial experimental version. These consisted of 76 students at a community college who took the test as part course requirements, 185 adults in non-clinical, community settings and 44 graduate students in clinical psychology. Adjective endorsement frequencies were then determined for both clinical patients and non-clinical groups. Finally, items in the experimental version were also correlated with scales from the MCMI-III (Craig and Olson, 2001) and with each other and a final decision was made as to which items to include in the final version of the test.

The final item pool of the PDACL was based on 5 principles: (1) item endorsement frequencies by clinical and non-clinical populations, (2) correlations of an individual item with the MCMI-III (Millon, Millon, and Davis, 1994) corresponding scales on which the scale is placed, (3) item intercorrelations with each other, (4) internal consistency considerations of the resulting scales, and (5) rational considerations as well.

CONTENT VALIDITY

After the items have been selected, the next step is to conduct a content validity study of the items. The method most often used here is to ask experts to judge the degree of fit of the item to the construct being measured. For the Acute Stress Disorder scale (Bryant, Moulds, and Guthrie,2000), the authors had expert on traumatic stress disorders to rate each item. For the PDACL, I had pared the item pool down to 187 adjectives and this list was given to 7 national experts, 11 practicing clinical psychologists, and 8 doctoral students in clinical psychology. They represented a range of experience with psychological testing and in diagnosing personality disorders.

The participants were given a rating sheet with the adjectives listed alphabetically on the vertical axis and the 14 personality disorder designations listed across the horizontal axis. They were asked to place a check in the column representing the personality disorder(s) in which they believed the adjective belonged. A Chi Square analysis indicated that 90% of the adjectives were accurately placed and this placement did not differ by experience level in assigning a particular adjective to a specific personality disorder. Nineteen items did differ and when differences occurred the national experts were more accurate in terms of item placement. Fourteen items did not achieve content validity and were eliminated. Two non-sense items were added, used as a rough screen for random responding, poor reading ability, and confusion, resulting in a 175-item test with 14 personality disorder scales averaging about 15 items per scale.

ITEM REDUNDANCY

For items on a personality test, it is psychometrically undesirable to have too many items scored on more than one scale, because item overlap distorts the factor structure of the test since the forced similarity between scores artificially elevates the inter-scale correlations and hence distorts the factor structure (Gibertini and Retzlaff, 1988.). However, some personality traits and characteristics are associated with more than one disorder in nature, so that item overlap cannot be totally avoided. However, of the 175 items on the PDACL 28 or only 16%, are scored on more than one scale.

STANDARDIZATION SAMPLE

Tests should be standardized on the population on which it is to be used. For the Acute Stress Disorder Scale (Bryant, Moulds, and Guthrie,2000), the authors gave the items to 99 patients who were referred to a PTSD hospital unit after experiencing a motor vehicle accident, nonsexual assault, or industrial accidents. They had a mean age of 31.59 years. Most were white.

For the PDACL, the population of choice was patients with personality disorders or those patients who were receiving mental health services where a personality disorder might be present. However, this kind of test should also be given to non-clinical patients to ensure that item endorsement rates do not exceed those of a clinical sample. Accordingly, we tested both types of populations.

With the help of over 54 psychologists, I was able to collect PDACL tests from patients receiving mental health services in nine states (California, Illinois, Indiana, Louisiana, Michigan, Missouri, New Jersey, New York, and Wisconsin). The total standardization sample consisted of 1134 participants, 332 non-clinical and 802 clinical subjects. The clinical sample was tested in a variety of inpatient and outpatient mental health contexts and all were receiving mental health services. Participants in the non-clinical group were all volunteers and were tested in a variety of community contexts. Participants ranged in age from 18 to 79 with a mean of 34.86; average educational level of the entire sample was 13.90.

TRANSFORMED SCORES

Almost all tests require a standardization sample whose raw score is transformed to a standardized score which allows the psychologist to compare an individual's score with that of the standardization sample. The Acute Stress Disorder (Bryant, Moulds, and Guthrie,2000) scale did not provide a discussion on transformed scores. In the PDACL raw scores are converted to a Base Rate (BR) score. We could not use a typical standardized score because personality disorders are not normally distributed and this is a fundamental assumption when converting raw scores to , it is inappropriate to convert raw scores to a transformed score that assumes an underlying normal distribution (i.e., T Scores, Standard Scores, etc.). Instead we use BR scores where a BR score >84 represents that point in the distribution of raw scores where 80% (or more, depending on the scale) scored at or above that raw score among patients with that clinical diagnosis. A BR score of 60 represents the average score on that scale for psychiatric patients and a BR score of 30 is the average raw score on that scale among non-clinical population.

EXPLORING FOR TEST BIAS

The most common way researchers assess for test bias is to compare the means of two groups on a given scale. When there is a statistically significant difference between means, there is suspicion of test bias. However, this design does not rule out an alternative hypothesis - that the test is detecting true differences between groups. Another way to assess for test bias is to examine two forms of error – slope bias and intercept bias.

Slope bias of a test is present when the validity coefficient for one group differs from the validity coefficient form another group. Intercept bias is present when a test systematically under-predicts or over-predicts for one group compared to another group on a relevant criterion. It is difficult and expensive to test for these forms of test error. Instead, most researchers study a test's factor structure across different samples. Any differences in the factor structure across different ethnic or gender groups, for example, increase the probability that slope or intercept bias is present when these scale scores are evaluated against an external criteria. If the factor structure is comparable, then it probably suggests the absence of slope bias (Nunnally and Bernstein, 1994).

One advantage of Loevinger's model of test development is that test validation is an on-going process prior to the publication of the test. If there is evidence of test bias, then we can make corrections early in the process and thereby avoid problems later. The authors of the Acute Stress Disorder (Bryant, Moulds, and Guthrie,2000) did not discuss possible test bias in their report. Evidence of test bias in the PDACL might be shown by differential endorsement rates of items, scales, or factor structure. Only 7 adjectives were differentially endorsed by gender in the non-clinical group (4 by men and 3 by women). In contrasts, there were a large number of adjectives differentially endorsed by men and by women in the clinical sample. These largely appeared on scales known to be more frequent among men (Antisocial, Aggressive) or women (Dependent).

We further expected that scale intercorrelations would be higher in the non-clinical sample than in the clinical sample. This is because personality is more integrated in non-patient samples. The results confirmed our expectations.

The last step in Loevinger's Stage 2 model is to conduct a factor analytic study to ascertain the major factors in the test. In the Acute Stress Disorder study (Bryant, Moulds, and Guthrie,2000), the authors conducted a principal component analysis with varimax rotation solutions. They found three main factors associated with their scale. Factor I was labeled Dissociation, Factor II was called Intrusion-Arousal and Factor II was called Reactivity. These three factors accounted for 74% of the total variance.

For the PDACL, I conducted a principal component analysis with oblique rotation and Kaiser normalization. We used a scree plot as a visual aid to determine the number of components to extract and found three factors accounting for 67.87% of the variance. Factor I was labeled "General Maladjustment", Factor II was labeled "Acting Out, Negativistic and Paranoid", AND Factor III was called "Less Severe Personality Pathology" and contained items mostly from the Histrionic, Narcissistic, and Compulsive personality scales. I conducted another factor analysis separately for whites, blacks and Hispanics. The same three main factors were identified in the total sample were also found in the separate analyses. I redid the analysis with a varimax rotation and attained similar results. We concluded that the factor structure of the PDACL is the same for whites, blacks and Hispanics. I also conducted factor studies for each PDACL scale and found anywhere from two to five factors for each scale.

From the analysis of the internal structure of the PDACL, it was concluded that separate norms for gender or race was considered unwarranted since there seems to be no evidence of internal test bias by race or gender.

VALIDITY SCREENS

If a respondent answers "true" to the question "My father was a good man", how do we know that he was a god man? Maybe he wasn't such a good man but the respondent may feel it is none of our business so s/he does not answer truthfully. Tests of personality have to include ways to assess whether or not the respondent is telling the truth. Having self knowledge, a willingness to report it, and answering questions with an open and honest approach will lead to the most accurate test findings. However, there are other options. Besides lying, there is the test-taking attitude of faking. By test-taking attitude, we mean the manner of approach that the respondent brings to the test session.

There are two kinds of faking: Faking Good or Faking Bad. This does not mean how well or how poorly one fakes a test response. Faking good means that the person answers the test questions by denying, under-reporting or minimizing problems one might have. Faking bad means that the person is exaggerating or endorsing problems one does not have. When personality tests are used in employment screening, one would expect a certain amount of faked-good responses. Endorsing a lot of problems could lead to not receiving a job offer. Similarly, in custody evaluations, we expect a parent to put up their best face in order to convince the psychologist that they should be awarded custody of the children. Conversely, there are circumstances when answering in a faked-bad direction might be construed by respondents to be in their best interest. Examples of this might include forensic evaluations where the legal plea is one of insanity and evaluations for disability where the respondent might (incorrectly) believe that the more problems the better their chances of getting money. All modern personality tests have scales that assess the extent to which respondents are faking good or faking bad.

The Acute Stress Disorder Scale (Bryant, Moulds, and Guthrie,2000),did not provide evidence of scales that assess faking. This is unfortunate because the PTSD literature is replete with evidence that exaggeration does occur when patients are seeking money for PTSD (Craig, 2005b).

The PDACL has six scales that assess response sets for profile validity. The number of endorsed adjectives acts as a control for under or over-endorsement. Endorsing an insufficient number of adjectives results in no scale elevations whereas endorsing too many words results in many scales being elevated. The number of positively endorsed items screens for faking good and the number of negatively endorsed items screens for faking bad. A validity index consisting of adjectives that are non-sense words checks for random responding and two scales checks for consistent responding. These scales screen pairs of adjectives to make sure that respondent is not checking pairs of trait words in a consistent (if "suspicious" is checked, then "paranoid" should also be checked or in an inconsistent manner (if "dependent" is endorsed, then "independent" should not be endorsed). Cutting-off scores for profile invalidity based on random responses, confused responding or faking would be established by pilot studies prior to engaging in the validity studies.

TEST RELIABILITY

Once the items have been established, content validity determined to be acceptable, and little or no evidence of test bias within the internal structure of the test, an additional task in Loevinger's Stage 2 model of test development is to test for reliability. There are two commonly used measures of reliability, *internal consistency* and *test-retest*. The internal reliability of a scale assess whether or not the items on the scale cohere as a group. The statistic *alpha* tells us if the items are internally consistent by comparing every possible group of items on the scale with every other possible group of items. Among ability and achievement tests, researchers often assess the *split-half reliability* by correlating the first half of the items with the second half of the items in the scale. This is rarely able to be done on personality tests because the first half of the items are not necessarily meant to be the same as the bottom half of the items.

For the Acute Stress Disorder (Bryant, Moulds, and Guthrie,2000) scale, the internal consistency was reported to be .96 for the total score, .84 for scale Dissociation, .87 for scale Re-experiencing, and .93 for scale Arousal. The internal consistency estimates of the PDACL ranged from .78 (Narcissistic) to .94 (Passive-Aggressive/Negativistic) with a median of .88 for 14 scales. Thus all scales exceeded the >.70 value considered as desirable alpha scores (Nunnally, and Bernstein, 1994; Streiner, 2003a,b).

The second measure of reliability is *test-retest reliability*. Here the measure is given at time 1 and then re-administered at time 2. A week's re-test interval is the most often reported interval for retesting personality tests. One has to be careful not to re-administered a test in too short a time, which then may tap memory traces of how the respondent answered the question upon initial administration. Also, for tests of clinical disorders, waiting too long for re-testing may introduce treatment effects which lower the scores and makes the scale falsely appear unreliable.

The test-retest reliability of the Acute Stress Disorder Scale (Bryant, Moulds, and Guthrie,2000) was .94 for the total score although the retest interval was not specified. Retest reliability was .85 for Dissociation, .94 for Re-experiencing, .89 for Avoidance and .94 for

Arousal. The retest reliability for the PDACL after one week retest interval ranged from .70 (Self-Defeating) to .91 (Aggressive) with a median reliability estimate of .82.

CONVERGENT VALIDITY

Loevinger's Stage 3 model of test development and validation (*external* validity) requires the author to study the test's convergent and divergent validity. This is done by correlating the test with similar or dissimilar measures. For example, if one test is measuring an avoidant personality disorder, then it should positively correlate with measures of shyness, submissiveness and social anxiety, since these are part of the avoidant personality style (convergent validity), and negatively correlate with measures of sociability, dominance and well-being (divergent validity).

For the Acute Stress Disorder (Bryant, Moulds, and Guthrie,2000) scale, the authors correlated it with the Depressive Experiences Scale, with the Intrusion and Avoidance scales from the Impact of Event scale, and the Arousal scale was correlated with the Beck Anxiety Inventory. Their scale was statistically associated with these similar instruments in the expected directions.

The PDACL underwent extensive convergent and divergent validity studies, correlating it with symptom scales, measures of psychopathology, measures of normalcy, and with two other inventories measuring personality disorders.

The PDACL was correlated with the Beck Depression Index (Beck and Steer, 1987). The PDACL tended to obtained significant associations with the Beck Depression Index on scales where an affective component is generally associated with the syndrome, and correlated negatively or at levels that were not statistically significant with scales where an affective disorder is generally not present.

Next the PDACL was correlated with the SCL-90-R. There were a significant number of correlations among with PDACL scales that suggested convergent validity with relevant symptom scales. For example, the Schizotypal Personality Disorder scale correlated highest with SCL-90-R Psychoticism and the Borderline Personality Disorder scale correlated highest with SCL-90-R Anxiety and Hostility.

Overall, these results demonstrated that the PDACL significantly correlates with similar symptom measures in a manner that is logically related to the meaning of the underlying construct associated with each personality disorder.

Next, the PDACL was correlated with a measure of psychopathology – the Minnesota Multiphasic Personality Inventory – (MMPI-2) (Butcher, Dahlstrom, Graham, Tellegen, and Kaemmer, 1989).The PDACL scales were significantly associated with several MMPI-2 Clinical, Content and Supplemental Scales. For example, Schizoid was positively associated with Hypochondriasis (Hs), Depression (Dep), Fears (FRS), Social Discomfort (SOD), and Maladjustment (Mt), Avoidant was negatively associated with K and Responsibility (Re) and positively associated with F, Anxiety (ANX), Obsessive Thinking (OBS), Depression (DEP), Cynicism (CYN), Low Self Esteem (LSE), Work Interference (WRK), Negative Treatment Indicators (TRT), Factor A, Responsibility (Re), Maladjustment (Mt), Marital Distress Scale (MDS), and Hostility (Ho). The Self-Defeating Personality Disorder scale was positively associated with Depression (Dep), Psychasthenia (Pt), Anxiety (ANX), Obsessive Thinking

(OBS), Depression (DEP), Low Self Esteem (LSE), Work Interference (WRK), Negative Treatment Indicators (TRT), and Maladjustment (Mt). The magnitude of these correlations ranged from for mid .40s to the high .60s.

We then correlated with PDACL with the factor scales of the Sixteen Personality Factors Questionnaire (16 PF) (Russell, Karol, Cattell, Cattel, and Catell, 1994 - 5th edition). This study was used both as a measure of convergent and divergent validity. The resulting correlations were in line with expectations. For example, Factor A (Warmth) showed negative correlations with PDACL scales where serious interpersonal deficits and withdrawal behaviors are part of the syndrome (e.g., Schizoid, Avoidant, Depressive, Schizotypal, etc.) and slightly positive values in disorders which rely on others (e.g., Dependent) or which use others (e.g., Antisocial). The presence high scores on Factor C (Emotionally Stable) in a profile is generally a sign of positive adjustment and so we would expect a negative correlation with most PDACL scales. This was, in fact, the pattern of correlations. The overall pattern of correlations between the 16 PF and the PDACL were consistent with expectations and provide evidence both convergent and divergent validity of the PDACL.

The PDACL was correlated with Strack's (1987) Personality Adjective Checklist (PACL) test. Strack's test was designed to assess Millon's theoretical model of personality classification in a normal population. We found a number of significant positive and negative correlations between the PDACL and the PACL in the expected direction. For example, the Dependent Personality Disorder scale negatively correlated with PACL Sociable (-.42), the Histrionic Personality Disorder scale positively correlated with PACL Sociable (.69) and Confidant (.57), the Antisocial Personality Disorder Scale positively correlated with PACL Confidant (.56) and negatively with PACL Cooperative (-.52). Once again, the pattern of correlations between the PDACL and the PACL were consistent with expectations and evidence both convergent and divergent validity.

These initial studies were quite promising but next we needed to correlate the PDACL with other tests measuring personality disorders. First we correlated the PDACL with the MCMI-III (Millon, Millon, Davis, 1994) among 176 patients who were receiving outpatient mental health services. The results showed that the PDACL scales significantly correlated with its MCMI-III counterpart scales at P<.005. The correlations were generally in the .40s and .50s. Next we correlated the PDACL with scales from the Coolidge Assessment Battery, (Coolidge and Merwin, 1992) a self-report measure of Axis-II disorders. The PDACL significantly correlated with nine CAB Personality Disorder scales with correlations ranging from -.12 (Compulsive) to .61 (Schizotypal) with a median correlation of .51.

Overall, these results indicated that the PDACL scales, for the most part, were significantly related to other measures of the same construct.

An additional PDACL discriminant validity study was conducted by correlating the PDACL with the NEO-PI-R (Costa and McCrae, 1992). This test is an operational measure of the Five-Factor model of personality classification. These five factors are Neuroticism, Extroversion, Openness to Experience, Agreeableness, and Conscientiousness. It was expected that most PDACL scales would negatively correlate with the NEO-PI-R scales, except Neuroticism, where a positive correlation (convergent validity) was expected. Results were within expectations. PDACL Antisocial Personality Disorder scale as well as the Aggression Personality Disorder scale correlated lowest with the Agreeableness factor. Results were also in line with facet subscales of the parent Factor. For example, PDACL Borderline Personality Disorder scale positively correlated with the Neuroticism Facet scales of Anxiety (N1), Angry Hostility (N2), Depression (N3) and Vulnerability (N6). PDACL Histrionic Personality Disorder scale positively correlated with the Extraversion facet scales of Warmth (E1), Gregariousness (E2), Assertiveness (E3), Activity (E4), Excitement (E5) and Positive emotions (E6).

Overall, these results suggest good convergent and divergent validity for the PDACL compared to symptom scales, to measures of personality traits and to other measures of personality disorders.

DIAGNOSTIC POWER

If one were developing an IQ test or tests of ability or achievement, the author would now conduct a predictive validity study and see how well the test predicts criterion. For diagnostic tests, we need to take an additional step. That is because the accuracy of a diagnostic test becomes far more complicated than merely demonstrating its convergent and divergent validity It is well and good that a test shows good reliability and good convergent validity. But does it "work". The crux of a diagnostic test is its diagnostic power. This is sometimes referred to as the "operating characteristics" of diagnostic tests (Gibertini, Brandenburg, and Retzlaff, 1986; Streiner, 2003b) or at other times is called the "diagnostic power" of tests (Baldassanni, Finklestein, and Arana, 1983). These characteristics are not unique to psychological tests, but are characteristic of any diagnostic tool, whether it is a blood test to detect pregnancy, a histology test to detect cancer, or a psychological test to detect personality disorders..

There are five critical values to a test's diagnostic power. *Sensitivity* is the probability that the patient has the disorder if the test scores are positive for the disorder. *Specificity* is the probability that the patient does not have the disorder if the test scores are negative for the disorders. *Positive Predictive Power* is the probability that the test will show positive if it is known that the patient has the disorder. *Negative Predictive Power* is the probability that the test will show negative if it is known that the patient does not have the disorder. *Diagnostic Power* is the overall probability of accurate diagnoses (both positive and negative) of the test.

If the test has eight scales, then these five operating characteristics need to be established for each of these eight scales. Furthermore subsequent research then needs to determine the test's operating characteristics with different populations. A test might "work" with one population (patients with depression), but perform poorly with another (patients with psychosis). Also, individual scales might work across all populations while others perform poorly across the board.

Since there is no gold standard in determining the presence of a personality disorder, most researchers use clinical diagnosis as the criteria against which to explore the operating characteristics of diagnostic tests of personality disorders. Across the 14 PDACL scales, sensitivity ranged from .67 (Depressive) to .95 (Schizoid) with a median of .83. Specificity ranged from .91 (Schizoid) to .99 (several scales) with a median of .97. Positive Predictive Power ranged from .45 (Schizotypal) to .93 (Antisocial) with a median of .74. Negative predictive power had a median level of .99 and Diagnostic Power had a median of .97. Note, that both sensitivity and positive predictive power of the PDACL scales are substantially higher than the base rate for those disorders in the standardization sample, suggesting strong incremental validity over base rate performance (Haynes and Lench, 2003).

CROSS-VALIDATION

The last step in test development is to cross-validate the results on an independent sample in order to demonstrate that your earlier results were not sample-dependent. In the Acute Stress Disorder (Bryant, Moulds, and Guthrie,2000), scale, the authors cross-validated their results but used 77% of the original participants. For the PDACL an independent sample of 127subjects was used to cross-validate these results. Upon cross-validation, there was some shrinkage in diagnostic power, as was expected. However, in a few scales the diagnostic power actually was higher with the independent sample. Also, as expected, the specificity and negative predictive power was higher than it was for sensitivity and positive predictive power

In summary, the PDACL demonstrated good internal consistency estimates, correlated significantly and moderately with other tests measuring the same constructs (personality disorders), and with measures of symptoms and psychopathology and demonstrated good convergent and divergent power. Finally the test's diagnostic power showed incremental validity over the prevalence rates for those disorders.

The author's of the Acute Stress Disorder scale (Bryant, Moulds, and Guthrie,2000), did not report on the total amount of time it took to develop this scale, but it took me ten years to produce a finished product. Then I was ready to (hopefully) find a publisher. Some authors have preliminary data and then seek a publisher. I chose to have the product finished before sending it out for review. Most publishers have an outline they ask authors for prior to making a decision on publication. By having the product finished, it could become immediately available to the market and this is an inducement for publishers to take a closer look at the product.

If the reader takes anything away from this chapter, I hope it is a greater appreciation of the difficulty and time-consuming effort it takes to develop and validate a psychological test. Compromises have to be made all along the way. For example, it was my intention to have a standardization sample of over 2000. After eight years I had just over a thousand. If I had waited to acquire the remainder, it is likely this test would never have been completed. Also, despite my closest sincerity and scrutiny, some of the PDACL scales did not work as well as expected. The Compulsive Personality Disorder scale did not show good convergent validity. Please understand the difficulties involved when evaluating tests and measures in psychology. It is far easier to criticize than to create.

ACKNOWLEDGEMENTS

There was even a period of time where authors selected items from previously published tests and placed them on their new test. The original California Psychological Inventory chose 150 items from the original Minnesota Multiphasic Personality Inventory as part of this new test. This was done because intellectual property laws and copyrights were often not pursued or enforced. Today, such practices are deemed unethical and unlawful.

REFERENCES

American Psychiatric Association (1983). *Diagnostic and statistical manual of mental disorders. 3rd ed.* Washington, DC: Author

American Psychiatric Associatiosn (1987). *Diagnostic and statistical manual of mental disorders. Rev. ed.* Washington, DC: Author

American Psychiatric Association (1994). *Diagnostic and statistical manual of mental disorders. 4th ed.* Washington, DC: Author

Baldassanni, R. J., Finklestein, S., and Arana, G. W. (1983). The prediction power of diagnostic tests and the effect of prevalence of illness. *Archives of General Psychiatry.* 40, 569-573.

Beck, A. T., and Steer, R. A. (1987). *Beck Depression Inventory manual*: San Antonio, Tx: The Psychological Corporation.

Bossuyt, P., Reitsma, J. B., Bruns, D. E., Gatsonis, C. A., Glasziou, P. P., Irvig, L. M. et al. (2003). Towards complete and accurate reporting of studies of diagnostic accuracy: The STARD initiative. *Annals of Internal Medicine*, 138, 40-44.

Burisch, M. (1984). Approaches to personality inventory construction. *American Psychologist*, 39, 14-227.

Butcher, J. N. Research designs in objective personality assessment. In P. C. Kendall, J. N. Butcher, and G. N. Holmbeck (Eds.). (1999) *Handbook of research methods in clinical psychology* (2nd ed.). NY: John Wiley and Sons (pp 155-182).

Butcher, J. N., Dahlstrom, W. G., Graham, J. R., Tellegen, A., and Kaemmer, B. (1989). *Minnesota Multiphasic Personality Inventory-2: Manual for administration and scoring.* Minneapolis: University of Minnesota Press.

Bryant, R. A., Moulds, M. L., and Guthrie, R. M. (2002). Acute Stress Disorder scae: A self-report measure of Acute Stress Disorder. *Psychological Assessment*, 12, 61-68.

Cattell, R. B., Eber, H. W., and Tatsuoka, M. M. (1970). *Handbook for the 16PF.* Champaign, IL: Institute for Personality and Ability Testing.

Coolidge, F. L., and Merwin, M. M. (1992). Reliability and validity of the Coolidge Axis II Inventory: A new inventory for the assessment of personality disorders. *Journal of Personality Assessment*, 59, 223-238.

Costa, P. T., and McCrae, R. R. (1992). *NEO-PI-R: Professional manual.* Odessa, Fl: Psychological Assessment Resources.

Craig, R. J. (In Press). *The Personality Disorder Adjective Check List: A screening inventory for Axis II syndromes.* Odessa, FL: Psychological Assessment resources.

Craig, R. J. (2005a). Assessing personality and mood with adjective check list methodology: A review. *International Journal of Testing*, 5, 177-196.

Craig, R. J. ((2005b). *Personality-guided forensic psychology.* Washington, DC: American Psychological Association.

Craig, R. J., and Olson, R. E. (2001). Adjectival descriptions of personality disorders: A convergent validity study of the MCMI-III. *Journal of Personality Assessment*, 77, 259-271.

Farmer, R. F. (2000). Issues in the assessment and conceptualization of personality disorders. *Clinical Psychology Review*, 7, 823-851.

Gibertini, M., Brandenberg, N., and Retzlaff, P. (1986). The operating characteristics of the Millon Clinical Multiaxial Inventory. *Journal of Personality Assessment.* 50, 554-567.

Gibertini, M., and Retzlaff, P. D. (1988). Factor invariance of the Millon Clinical Multiaxial Inventory. *Journal of Psychopathology and Behavioral Assessment.* 10, 65-74.

Goldsmith, S. J., Jacobsberg, L. B., and Bell, R. (1989). Personality disorder assessment. *Psychiatric Annals,* 19, 139-142.

Gough, H. G., and Heilbrun, A. G. (1983). *The Adjective Check List manual: 1983 edition.* Palo Alto, CA: Consulting Psychologists Press.

Haynes, S. N., and Lench, H. C. (2003). Incremental validity of new clinical assessment measures. *Psychological Assessment,* 15, 456-466.

Haynes, S. N., Richards, D. C., and Kubany, E. S. (1995). Content validity in psychological assessment: A functional approach to concepts and methods. *Psychological Assessment* 7, 238-247.

Hanyes, S. N., Nelson, K., and Blaine, D. D. Psychometric issues in assessment research. In P. C. Kendall, J. N. Butcher, and G. N. Holmbeck (Eds*.). Handbook of research methods in clinical psychology* (2nd ed.). NY: John Wiley and Sons (pp 123-154).

Hathaway, S. R., and McKinley, J. C. (1941). *Minnesota Multiphasic Personality Inventory.* Minneapolis: University of Minnesota Press.

Loevinger, J. (1957). Objective tests as instruments of psychological theory. *Psychological Reports,* 3, 635-694.

Millon, T. (1983). *Millon Clinical Multiaxial Inventory.* Minneapolis: National Computer Systems.

Millon, T. with Davis, R. (1996), Disorders of personality: DSM-IV and beyond. NY: John Wiley and Sons.

Millon, T., Millon, C., and Davis, R. D. (1994). *Millon Clinical Multiaxial Inventory -III.* Minneapolis: National Computer Systems.

Myers, I. B., and McCaulley, M. H. (1985). *Manual: A guide to the development and use of the Myers-Briggs Type Indicator*: Palo Alto, CA: Consulting Psychologists Press.

Nunnally, J. C., and Bernstein, I. H. (1994). *Psychometric theory* (3rd ed.). New York: McGraw Hill.

Perry, J. C. (1992). Problems and considerations in the valid assessment of personality disorders. *American Journal of Psychiatry,* 149, 1645-1653.

Rogers, R. (2001). *Handbook of diagnostic and structured interviewing.* New York: Guilford Press.

Russell, M., Karol, D., Cattell, R. B., Cattell, A. K., and Cattell, H. E. (1994). *16 PF (5th ed). Administrator's manual.* Champaign, IL: Institute for Personality and Ability Testing.

Shedler, J., and Westen, D. (1998). Refining the measurement of Axis II: A q-sort procedure for assessing personality pathology. *Assessment.* 5, 333-353.

Strack, S. N. (1987). Development and validation of an adjective check list to assess the Millon personality types in a normal population. *Journal of Personality Assessment.* 51, 572-587.

Streiner, D. L. (2003a). Being inconsistent about consistency: When coefficient alpha does and doesn't matter. *Journal of Personality Assessment,* 80, 217-222.

Streiner, D. L. (2003b). Diagnosing tests: Using and misusing diagnostic and screening tests. *Journal of Personality Assessment,* 81, 209-219.

Widiger, T. A., and Frances, A. (1987). Interviews and inventories for the measurement of personality disorders. *Clinical Psychology Review*, 7, 49-75.

Widiger, T. A. (1995). *Personality Disorder Interview for DSM-IV: A semi-structured interview for the assessment of personality disorders.* Odessa, FL: Psychological Assessment Resources.

Williams, K. B., and Williams, J. S. (1980). The assessment of transactional analysis ego states via the Adjective Check List. *Journal of Personality Assessment*, 4, 120-129.

Zimmerman, M. (1994). Diagnosing personality disorders: A review of issues and research models. *Archives of General Psychiatry*, 51, 225-245.

In: Psychological Tests and Testing Research Trends   ISBN: 978-1-60021-569-8
Editor: Paul M. Goldfarb, pp. 191-209   © 2007 Nova Science Publishers, Inc.

Chapter 9

THE HOOKED ON NICOTINE CHECKLIST: A MEASURE OF DIMINISHED AUTONOMY OVER TOBACCO

Joseph R. DiFranza[1] and Robert J. Wellman[2]

[1] Department of Family Medicine and Community Health;
University of Massachusetts Medical School; Worcester, Massachusetts;
[2] Behavioral Sciences Department; Fitchburg State College; Fitchburg, Massachusetts;
and Department of Family Medicine and Community Health University
of Massachusetts Medical School Worcester, Massachusetts

How can you tell if a person is addicted to tobacco? When does addiction to tobacco begin and how might it be measured? These questions have bedeviled clinicians and researchers for years. The current situation might be likened to the dilemma faced by the U.S. Supreme Court when it tried to define hardcore pornography. As Justice Potter Stewart famously declared, "I shall not today attempt further to define the kinds of material I understand to be embraced within that shorthand description; and perhaps I could never succeed in intelligibly doing so. But I know it when I see it…"[1] Although clinicians may know it when they see it, there is no recognized 'gold standard' for defining addiction to tobacco. Traditional approaches to defining tobacco addiction have failed to produce a consensus. Experts do not agree on a single list of the essential features of tobacco addiction. Should we talk of nicotine addiction, or tobacco addiction? Is the addiction caused by just nicotine alone, or in combination with other substances in tobacco? Some feel that 'addiction' and 'dependence' are synonyms, while others make distinctions between these terms. On top of the lack of consensus on how to define addiction, and what to call it, there is controversy about identifying its onset. Some have argued that addiction begins only when a minimum of three symptoms are present as required to make a diagnosis of nicotine dependence under the criteria of the Diagnostic and Statistical Manual of Mental Disorders (DSM) or the International Statistical Classification of Diseases (ICD).[2, 3] But then, what do we call the process that causes the first two symptoms? Is that not addiction? If so, could a smoker have two symptoms of addiction but not be addicted?

How can we hope to diagnose and measure addiction if experts cannot agree on what it is? The first author was interested in identifying the first symptoms of addiction in novice smokers so that these might be matched to early neurophysiologic alterations in the brain produced by nicotine. However, the idea of studying the onset of addiction was met with a barrage of criticism from grant and manuscript reviewers because, no matter how the author redefined addiction or dependence, it was impossible to placate every reviewer. There was always one reviewer who thought that the offered definition was wrong. It appears that in the current state of affairs, the number of opinions on the definition of addiction approaches the number of experts in the field. If addiction and dependence mean something different to each of us, is the meaning in the eye of each beholder? If so, do these terms have any meaning at all? Stymied, the first author hit upon a new strategy to get past this minefield: avoid any mention of addiction or dependence.

In search of an alternative to the quagmire of addiction and dependence, the first author borrowed upon the wisdom of the uninitiated. Lay audiences often want to know what it takes to become "hooked." Unlike 'addiction' and 'dependence' which have been precisely defined so many times that we no longer know what these terms mean, 'hooked' carries the advantage of being slang and undefined as a scientific term. Its common usage indicates that, like a fish on a hook, a person is addicted when they lose autonomy over their drug use. This reflects a different perspective on addiction from those that define it in relation to self-harm or the inability to meet culturally-defined responsibilities. To those who are free from the need to make a diagnosis, addiction means, simply, a loss of autonomy. In this chapter, we describe the Hooked on Nicotine Checklist as a measure of autonomy and discuss its development, theoretical foundation and psychometric properties.

WHAT IS THE RECEIVED WISDOM ABOUT TOBACCO ADDICTION?

Until quite recently, commonly held ideas about tobacco addiction were heavily influenced by the notions that (1) pleasurable drug effects motivate smoking; (2) tolerance to the pleasurable effects of nicotine drives an escalation to moderate daily levels of consumption; (3) through countless repetitions, the act of smoking becomes an ingrained habit; (4) withdrawal symptoms are triggered when daily nicotine intake exceeds a certain undefined level, marking the transformation from habit to addiction, (5) and that the process of moving from an 'experimental' to an 'established' (i.e., dependent) smoker took about two years.[5] These ideas have been challenged by recent data showing that novice adolescent smokers experience withdrawal symptoms (i.e., physical dependence) long before they smoke daily.[6-16] In prospective studies adolescents have reported experiencing symptoms of tobacco addiction within weeks after they began smoking, at a point when their consumption averaged two cigarettes per week,[8, 9] long before they satisfied the ICD diagnostic criteria.[2, 17]

AUTONOMY OVER TOBACCO

One drawback to diagnostic criteria for nicotine dependence, as offered by the ICD or DSM, is that a tobacco user must have a cluster of at least three symptoms before a diagnosis can be made. This leaves open the question as to why novice smokers report difficulty quitting prior to meeting these criteria,[17] and implies that the criteria themselves are artificial. Measures of autonomy over tobacco capture individuals who travel beneath the radar of the diagnostic criteria.

A person is fully autonomous over tobacco if he or she can stop using without incurring any cost in the way of effort or discomfort, and conversely, has diminished autonomy to the extent that quitting requires effort or produces discomfort.[18] Thus, the loss of full autonomy marks the point at which a person becomes hooked, the point at which the consequences of use, either physical or psychological, present a barrier to becoming and remaining abstinent. Full autonomy would be regained and addiction dispelled when maintaining abstinence no longer required effort – i.e., when all symptoms had resolved. Having diminished autonomy does not imply that quitting is impossible, only that it requires an effort, or that there is a price to pay in terms of discomfort. Nor is autonomy the only factor influencing the success of a quit attempt. Other factors such as motivation and support are also important.

This approach to addiction is very different from that represented in either the DSM or the ICD, both of which rely on evidence that the drug use is a self-destructive behavior, and attempt to be non-judgmental because of the great stigma attached to being an addict. In contrast, under the notion of diminished autonomy addiction begins when the user loses complete freedom over his or her own actions. The word 'addiction' is derived from the Latin word *addictus* indicating an obligation assigned by a judge against the person who lost a legal challenge. In this sense, addiction is a loss of freedom, not an act of self-destruction. Thus, the autonomy concept holds to the original etymology.

A major advantage conferred by the term autonomy is that, unlike dependence or addiction, there is a consensus as to its meaning. This allows it to serve as a gold standard; autonomy over tobacco use can be measured without first coming to consensus on a definition of dependence or addiction and without a priori assumptions about their nature. Although autonomy does not measure every facet of addiction, at least we know what we are measuring.

THE SENSITIZATION-HOMEOSTASIS THEORY

A unique feature of the autonomy concept is that it is married to a theory of how nicotine acts on the brain to cause a loss of autonomy. No other definition or measure of dependence or addiction is tied to a specific theory of how nicotine causes addiction.

The central tenet of the sensitization-homeostasis theory is that nicotine's addiction liability derives from its ability to stimulate neural pathways that are responsible for the suppression of craving.[19] Sensitization occurs when subsequent doses of a drug produce a larger response than the initial dose. As a result of sensitization, the craving suppression produced by nicotine is magnified to super-physiologic levels. The over-inhibition of neurons responsible for craving initiates compensatory homeostatic measures that stimulate the craving pathways and result in their autonomous activation when nicotine is absent. When the craving-generating neurons function autonomously, the smoker loses autonomy over tobacco. Separate homeostatic mechanisms cause withdrawal symptoms when nicotine is withdrawn and these also contribute to a loss of autonomy.

AUTONOMY IS MULTI-DIMENSIONAL

Through thousands of interviews with young smokers, we have identified three distinct mechanisms through which autonomy can be diminished:

- *Cravings*, elicited by external or internal cues and mediated by neurophysiological processes
- *Withdrawal symptoms*, elicited by curtailing or ceasing tobacco use
- Learned psychological dependence on tobacco.

Cravings are urges that may be regular, intense, intrusive, disruptive or persistent.

Withdrawal includes irritability, nervousness, anxiety, restlessness, or difficulty concentrating during abstinence or when tobacco use is reduced significantly.

Psychological dependence includes (1) relying on smoking to cope with stress or boredom; (2) relying on smoking to perform demanding tasks; and (3) learned helplessness over nicotine (e.g., "I couldn't live without my cigarettes").

These three mechanisms are not behaviors, but processes that diminish autonomy. They can be viewed as the engine that drives and shapes the behavior of smokers. An analogy may be helpful.

- Infection with the influenza virus is the mechanism that *causes* the flu.
- Behaviors such as nose blowing, coughing and shivering are the *result* of the infection.
- These behaviors *indicate* that the flu is present.
- People who have the flu also use more cold remedies and miss work. These behaviors are associated with the flu, but do not directly indicate the presence of an infection. Although they are *descriptive* of the behavior of flu victims, they are not part of the disease.

In regard to diminished autonomy over tobacco use:

- Cravings, withdrawal and psychological dependence *cause* diminished autonomy over tobacco use.
- Certain behaviors such as a failed cessation attempt are the *result* of diminished autonomy and *indicate* that autonomy is diminished.
- Other behaviors are *descriptive* of the actions of hooked smokers but are not part of the disease.

Examples of behaviors that indicate diminished autonomy:

- The use of tobacco to relieve or avoid withdrawal symptoms
- Failed attempts to maintain abstinence
- Tolerance, as defined by the need to smoke more frequently to cope with cravings or withdrawal (e.g., smoking within five minutes of awakening)

The following items indicate diminished autonomy *only* if they result from an inability to maintain abstinence:

- Tobacco is used in larger amounts or over a longer period than was intended
- A great deal of time is spent in activities necessary to obtain or use tobacco
- Continued tobacco use despite harm
- Smoking when sick in bed
- Important social, occupational, or recreational activities are given up or reduced because of smoking

Behaviors that merely describe the actions of smokers but are unrelated to autonomy:

- A narrowing of the repertoire of use (e.g., smoking one brand)
- Stereotypy in the mechanics of smoking (e.g., smoking the same amount of each cigarette)
- The use of brands with higher nicotine or tar levels
- Tolerance as manifested in the ability to withstand higher doses of nicotine before experiencing discomfort
- Smoking for pleasure
- Requiring a higher dose of nicotine to achieve the same effect

HOW CAN DIMINISHED AUTONOMY BE MEASURED?

The Hooked on Nicotine Checklist (HONC) is a ten-item questionnaire designed to measure diminished autonomy over tobacco use. Each item was chosen for its face validity as an indicator of diminished autonomy. Table 1 presents the HONC items.

Table 1. The Hooked on Nicotine Checklist

	NO	YES
Have you ever tried to quit, but couldn't?		
Do you smoke *now* because it is really hard to quit?		
Have you ever felt like you were addicted to tobacco?		
Do you ever have strong cravings to smoke?		
Have you ever felt like you really needed a cigarette?		
Is it hard to keep from smoking in places where you are not supposed to?		
When you haven't used tobacco for a while … OR When you tried to stop smoking …		
did you find it hard to concentrate because you couldn't smoke?		
did you feel more irritable because you couldn't smoke?		
did you feel a strong need or urge to smoke?		
did you feel nervous, restless or anxious because you couldn't smoke?		

HOW ARE INDIVIDUAL HONC ITEMS INTERPRETED?

An autonomous smoker can quit without effort or discomfort, for example, with no more effort than it takes to stop eating carrots for a day. Autonomy is diminished when there is an obstacle to overcome or a price to be paid for quitting.

1. Have you ever tried to quit, but couldn't?

A failed cessation attempt is an obvious indication of diminished autonomy. It doesn't matter how hard or how sincerely the person tried to quit. The key is the desire to quit. If quitting took no effort, the person would no longer be smoking.

2. Do you smoke *now* because it is really hard to quit?

The same rationale applies here. This item is included to capture those who do not want to smoke, but have not made an "official" effort to quit, often out of fear of failure. Since they are doing something they don't want to, their autonomy is diminished.

3. Have you ever felt like you were addicted to tobacco?

A person who has full autonomy over his or her use of tobacco does not feel addicted. We are not asking people to self-diagnose addiction.

4. Do you ever have strong cravings to smoke?

Strong cravings make quitting difficult and unpleasant.

5. Have you ever felt like you really needed a cigarette?

Smokers feel they really need a cigarette because of cravings, withdrawal symptoms, or psychological dependence. Whatever the reason, quitting becomes more difficult.

6. Is it hard to keep from smoking in places where you are not supposed to?

An autonomous smoker would have no difficulty refraining from smoking, especially where it is forbidden.

When you haven't used tobacco for a while … OR When you tried to stop smoking …

7. did you find it hard to concentrate because you couldn't smoke?
8. did you feel more irritable because you couldn't smoke?
9. did you feel a strong need or urge to smoke?
10. did you feel nervous, restless or anxious because you couldn't smoke?

Withdrawal symptoms make quitting unpleasant and more difficult.

HOW IS THE HONC SCORED?

The HONC is scored by tallying the number of "yes" responses. Scores may be used either dichotomously, to indicate whether a person has any symptom of diminished autonomy, or continuously, to indicate the number of symptoms and therefore the degree to which autonomy is diminished.

Dichotomous scoring– The HONC as an indicator of diminished autonomy.

Individuals who score zero on the HONC by answering NO to all ten questions enjoy full autonomy over their use of tobacco. Because each of the ten symptoms measured by the HONC has face validity as an indicator of diminished autonomy, a smoker has lost full autonomy if any symptom is endorsed.

In schools and clinics, smokers who have scores above zero can be told that they are already hooked. Many youths become hooked before they even consider themselves to be smokers, because they don't smoke every day. In research, dichotomous scoring is helpful when the HONC is used to predict continued smoking (i.e., is a person with any symptom more likely to smoke than a person with no symptoms?).

Continuous scoring – The HONC as a measure of the degree of diminished autonomy.

The number of symptoms a person endorses serves as a measure of the extent to which autonomy has been diminished.

Some researchers prefer to provide multiple response options for questionnaire items, e.g., *never, sometimes, most of the time, always*. In certain situations, this can improve the statistical properties of a survey. When this has been done with the HONC, its performance was not improved.[20] Having more response options complicates the scoring because the total score does not coincide with the number of individual symptoms. Therefore we recommend the Yes/No response format.

Researchers who wish to measure frequency or severity of symptoms may do so by adding to the yes/no format additional questions about any item endorsed by a smoker. Here is an example: *Have you ever felt like you were addicted to tobacco?* A smoker who checked "yes" would then respond to: How often have you felt addicted? (*Rarely, Occasionally, Often, Very Often*) On a scale from 1 (*hardly at all*) to 10 (*extremely*), how addicted have you felt?

WHERE CAN I GET THE HONC?

The HONC may be used without permission and free of charge. It is available in English, Dutch, Finnish, French, German, Greek, Italian, Polish, Portuguese and Spanish on our website (http://fmchapps.umassmed.edu/honc). It has also been translated into Arabic and Korean.

A NOTE ABOUT THE SUBJECTIVE SYMPTOMS MEASURED BY THE HONC

Research methodologists might lament that the symptoms on the HONC are all subjective. Even the item concerning a failed quit attempt might be considered by some to be subjective, since who is to say if the effort was sincere? We believe that at its core addiction is an internal emotional and physiological process that can best be measured subjectively. This may explain why the HONC has better psychometric properties than some measures that focus on observable behaviors.

This emphasis on how the smoker feels is diametrical to the behavior-oriented approach taken by the DSM and ICD, which deemphasize the smoker's internal experience. In our minds this is analogous to defining love by describing dating behaviors while ignoring what it feels like to be in love.

WHAT ARE THE PSYCHOMETRIC PROPERTIES OF THE HONC?

Even with its reliance on subjective symptoms, the HONC has excellent psychometric properties. It performs equally well when used with smokers of any age, gender, racial or ethnic background, and level of experience with smoking. Because the HONC evaluates addiction independent of cigarette intake, it is particularly useful for the purpose of comparing levels of autonomy between populations of smokers who differ in their daily cigarette consumption. Examples include adolescent versus adult smokers, or smokers in affluent countries versus developing countries where economic constraints limit cigarette consumption.

FACTOR STRUCTURE

Factor analyses with both adolescent and adult smokers consistently reveal that the items on the HONC measure a single dimension. Inter-item correlations are generally low to moderate, indicating that each item makes a unique contribution to the total score.

INTERNAL CONSISTENCY

In four samples totaling over 700 adolescent smokers between 12 and 18 years old, Cronbach's alpha ranged from 0.90 to 0.94.[16, 18, 20, 21] When the HONC is used with adolescent smokers, inter-item correlations are generally moderate, typically falling between 0.5 and 0.7. In a survey of 300 college student current smokers (median age = 20 - 21 years old), Cronbach's alpha was 0.89, and inter-item correlations were generally moderate (mean *phi* = 0.44, range = 0.18 – 0.70).[22] The students in that sample were largely light smokers; only 40% smoked daily and 48% smoked fewer than five cigarettes per day. In one survey of 1102 adult smokers (mean age = 39 years; mean daily cigarette consumption = 17.5), Cronbach's alpha was 0.83.[23] In a follow-up survey of 1130 smokers (mean age = 41 years;

mean daily cigarette consumption = 18.5), it was 0.82.[24] Inter-item correlations in both surveys were low to moderate, with an average *phi* coefficient of 0.32 (range = 0.11 – 0.59).

TEST-RETEST RELIABILITY

In a study of 74 students, ages 14 to 16 years, the intraclass correlation was 0.88 over a two-week period. Individual HONC items generally showed good to excellent reliability over time: Median Yules' Y = 0.71, range = 0.41 – 0.82.[21] Among 66 adolescent past-month smokers in Montreal, the mean test-retest reliability (Kappa) over a two week span was 0.79, ranging from 0.61 for 'nervous, anxious, restless' to 0.93 for 'felt addicted to tobacco'.[20]

The HONC is also stable over long periods of time. In a study of adolescent smokers ages 14-20, the intraclass correlation over six months was 0.93 ($n = 98$); over one year it was 0.91 ($n = 83$).[16] The test-retest reliability has not been assessed in an adult population.

CONCURRENT VALIDITY

A consequence of diminished autonomy is an increased likelihood of continued smoking and the development of tolerance. HONC scores for youths at different smoking stages can be compared to evaluate the concurrent validity of the HONC. HONC scores correlate well with smoking status. In ninth grade students, HONC scores greater than zero were reported by 16% of youths who had only experimented briefly with smoking, by 50% of occasional smokers, and 100% of regular smokers, both current and former.[21]

A similar relationship between HONC scores and smoking status was found among 241 Canadian adolescents (ages 12-13 at the beginning of the prospective study) who had smoked in the preceding three months. At least one HONC symptom was reported by 52% of experimenters, 78% of sporadic smokers, 94% of monthly smokers, and 100% of weekly and daily smokers.[12] The HONC is a much more sensitive measure than the ICD-10 criteria: in this study the criteria for an ICD-10 diagnosis was met by none of the experimenters, 3% of sporadic smokers, 5% of monthly smokers, 19% of weekly smokers, and 66% of daily smokers. The early appearance of diminished autonomy provides an explanation for why such a high proportion of novice smokers continue to use tobacco, causing them to progress to the point where they meet the diagnostic criteria.

Among college students, most of whom were not daily smokers, those who smoked fewer days per month or fewer cigarettes per day had lower HONC scores than those who smoked more frequently.[22] Similarly, students who smoked their first cigarette more than an hour after they awoke had lower HONC scores than those who smoked sooner after awakening. Finally, students who had ever smoked daily had higher HONC scores than did those who had never been daily smokers.

Daily cigarette consumption is not a gold standard for the measurement of addiction. We have found that daily cigarette consumption represents a fairly good proxy for diminished autonomy among novice smokers, but not among long-term smokers. Among novice smokers, those who suffer from diminished autonomy begin to escalate their consumption while those smokers who are free of such symptoms maintain low levels of consumption.[25]

At this stage consumption rates do reflect diminished autonomy, and the HONC correlates above 0.65 with the number of cigarettes consumed on smoking days and the number of days smoked in the preceding month.[16]

The picture is completely different in adult smokers. Over years of smoking, variability between individuals in the rate of daily consumption appears to be driven more by factors other than addiction, for example, the nicotine content of the preferred brand, whether smoking is allowed in the home and workplace, and the genetically determined rate of nicotine metabolism. We have found that cigarette consumption represents a very poor proxy for diminished autonomy in adult smokers. In a study of 1130 adult smokers, the HONC correlated just above 0.2 with the number of cigarettes consumed per day and the number of days smoked in the preceding month.[24]

Many studies have shown that individuals who initiate smoking at a younger age have more difficulty quitting. Consistent with this, adults who started to smoke at a younger age had higher HONC scores. Among adults, those who availed themselves of pharmacological aids when attempting to achieve abstinence had higher HONC scores (and scores on the Fagerström Test of Nicotine Dependence) than those who did not use such aids.[24] College students who began smoking before 15 years of age reported more HONC symptoms than did those who began smoking later.[22]

PREDICTIVE VALIDITY

In a 30-month prospective study of the natural history of tobacco use in a cohort of 679 7th grade students, endorsement of a single item on the HONC was associated with a failed attempt at cessation, continued smoking until the end of follow up, and daily smoking. HONC scores correlated 0.65 with the maximum amount smoked and at almost 0.8 with the maximum frequency of smoking.[9] Progression beyond smoking one cigarette per day was seen almost exclusively in youths who had diminished autonomy as indicated by the HONC.[25]

In a prospective study of 215 adolescent smokers (ages 14 to 20), predictive validity of the HONC was high. Each additional HONC symptom increased the likelihood of smoking at the six-month follow-up by 29% after controlling for age and days smoked at baseline. Similarly, each additional HONC symptom increased the likelihood of smoking at the one-year follow-up by 21% after controlling for the number of cigarettes consumed per smoking day at baseline.[16]

The HONC can be used as a dichotomous indicator of diminished autonomy (a zero score versus a score of 1-10). Smokers who score zero on the HONC are asymptomatic; they enjoy full autonomy over their use of tobacco. Smokers who report one or more symptom are symptomatic; they have diminished autonomy. Far more adolescent smokers with HONC symptoms at baseline reported smoking six months later (86%) than did those who reported no HONC symptoms (41%). Similarly, far more youths who were symptomatic at baseline reported smoking one year later (80%) than did their initially asymptomatic counterparts (52%).[16]

CAN I SHORTEN THE HONC TO MAKE ITS USE MORE PRACTICAL?

Due to space or time constraints, researchers often ask about shorter versions of the HONC. If you wish to shorten the HONC, keep in mind that each item has been reported as the first symptom of diminished autonomy in some smokers. Thus, leaving out any item will reduce the sensitivity of the measure a little. Our analyses indicate that the internal consistency (Cronbach's alpha) of the scale is affected very little by dropping any single item. However, care must be taken, as alpha is typically dependent on the number of items in a scale, so omitting too many items from the HONC may reduce its reliability. Table 2 presents Cronbach's alpha for the HONC with each item removed.

Table 2. Cronbach's alpha if each item is removed from the HONC

| | Adolescents | | Adults | |
| | Study | | Study | |
	1 [a]	2 [b]	1 [c]	2 [d]
Have you ever tried to quit, but couldn't?	0.91	0.91	0.82	0.82
Do you smoke *now* because it is really hard to quit?	---	0.90	0.82	0.80
Have you ever felt like you were addicted to tobacco?	0.90	0.90	0.82	0.80
Do you ever have strong cravings to smoke?	0.90	0.90	0.82	0.80
Have you ever felt like you really needed a cigarette?	0.91	0.90	0.83	0.81
Is it hard to keep from smoking in places where you are not supposed to?	0.91	0.91	0.84	0.82
When you haven't used tobacco for a while ... OR When you tried to stop smoking ...				
did you find it hard to concentrate because you couldn't smoke?	0.91	0.90	0.82	0.81
did you feel more irritable because you couldn't smoke?	0.90	0.90	0.81	0.79
did you feel a strong need or urge to smoke?	0.90	0.89	0.81	0.79
did you feel nervous, restless or anxious because you couldn't smoke?	0.91	0.89	0.80	0.79
Overall Cronbach's alpha	0.92	0.91	0.83	0.82

Adolescents: [a] Study 1 (*n* = 215 current smokers: Reference 16); [b] Study 2 (*n* = 153 monthly smokers: Reference 18).

Adults: [c] Study 1 (*n* = 1102 current smokers: Reference 23); [d] Study 2 (*n* = 1130 current smokers: Reference 24).

HOW DOES THE HONC COMPARE TO OTHER MEASURES OF NICOTINE DEPENDENCE?

The HONC vs. the Modified Fagerström Tolerance Questionnaire (MFTQ)[26-28]

We compared a 9-item version of the HONC (inadvertently omitting item 2, "Do you smoke now because it is really hard to quit?") with the MFTQ in a sample of 215 adolescent current smokers in a prospective evaluation of an anti-smoking intervention.[16] Baseline HONC scores ranged from 0 to 9 (out of a potential maximum score of 9) and the mean HONC score was 4.2; 23% of subjects reported no symptoms. Baseline MFTQ scores ranged from 0 to 17 (out of a potential maximum score of 19) and the mean MFTQ score was 8.0.

The modal score on the MFTQ was 5, which represented almost 9% of subjects, and only 3% of subjects received a score of 0.

The HONC demonstrated greater internal consistency and greater stability between baseline and six- and twelve-month follow-up than did the MFTQ. The individual HONC items also demonstrated fair to good stability, while the individual MFTQ items demonstrated poor stability. After controlling for age and the number of smoking days per month at baseline, the HONC predicted the likelihood that adolescents would be smoking at the six- and twelve-month follow-up, with each additional HONC symptom increasing the likelihood of smoking by 29% at six months post treatment and by 21% at one year. In contrast, after controlling for the number of cigarettes consumed per smoking day at baseline, a one quartile increase in MFTQ score increased the risk of smoking at the six-month follow-up by 64%, but the MFTQ did not enter the equation predicting smoking at one year post treatment.[16]

The HONC vs. the Fagerström Test of Nicotine Dependence (FTND)[29]

We compared the HONC with the FTND in a sample of 1130 experienced adult smokers.[24] Both the HONC and the FTND measured single dimensions, but the internal consistency of the HONC (Cronbach's alpha = 0.82) was significantly higher than that of the FTND (Cronbach's alpha = 0.61). Although men and women had comparable scores on the HONC, men had higher FTND scores. The two measures did not differ in their correlation with the number of smoking days per month. Even with the cigarette consumption item removed, the FTND was more strongly associated with the number of cigarettes smoked per day than the HONC. Both measures were similarly negatively correlated with age at smoking initiation. Smokers who used nicotine replacement therapy or bupropion during a cessation attempt had higher scores on both measures than did those who did not use such aids. Smokers who maintained abstinence for at least three days had lower scores on both measures than those who were unsuccessful in maintaining abstinence for that long. This demonstrates that the HONC is at least as good as the FTND in determining which smokers are more addicted.

Which HONC Symptoms Are Most Common?

Table 3 presents the proportion of adolescent smokers who endorsed each HONC symptom, based on five studies of youths between 14 and 20 years of age whose smoking experience ranged from simply inhaling on a cigarette once to daily smoking.[12, 16, 18, 21, 30] Table 4 presents the proportion of adult smokers who endorsed each HONC symptom, based on three studies of adults between 18 and 88 years of age, all of whom were current smokers and whose consumption ranged from a few cigarettes per month to heavy daily smoking.[22-24]

Table 3. Proportion of adolescent smokers endorsing each HONC symptom

	%
Have you ever tried to quit, but couldn't?	40
Do you smoke *now* because it is really hard to quit?	29
Have you ever felt like you were addicted to tobacco?	41
Do you ever have strong cravings to smoke?	62
Have you ever felt like you really needed a cigarette?	67
Is it hard to keep from smoking in places where you are not supposed to?	19
When you haven't used tobacco for a while … OR When you tried to stop smoking …	
did you find it hard to concentrate because you couldn't smoke?	31
did you feel more irritable because you couldn't smoke?	34
did you feel a strong need or urge to smoke?	45
did you feel nervous, restless or anxious because you couldn't smoke?	35

[a] References 12, 16, 18, 21, 30.

Table 4. Proportion of adult smokers endorsing each HONC symptom

	Study		
	1 [a]	2 [b]	3 [c]
Have you ever tried to quit, but couldn't?	74	72	42
Do you smoke *now* because it is really hard to quit?	69	63	26
Have you ever felt like you were addicted to tobacco?	83	83	55
Do you ever have strong cravings to smoke?	85	85	62
Have you ever felt like you really needed a cigarette?	93	91	80
Is it hard to keep from smoking in places where you are not supposed to?	42	45	11
When you haven't used tobacco for a while … OR When you tried to stop smoking …			
did you find it hard to concentrate because you couldn't smoke?	44	42	22
did you feel more irritable because you couldn't smoke?	72	71	37
did you feel a strong need or urge to smoke?	78	80	50
did you feel nervous, restless or anxious because you couldn't smoke?	69	66	39

[a] Study 1: n = 1102; Reference 23
[b] Study 2: n = 1130; Reference 24
[c] Study 3: n = 300; Reference 22.

WHAT ARE THE CONTROVERSIES AROUND THE TRADITIONAL DEFINITIONS OF DEPENDENCE AND ADDICTION?

The generic criteria for diagnosing dependence on any substance are listed below (from DSM-IV-TR)[3]

A maladaptive pattern of substance use, leading to clinically significant impairment or distress, as manifested by three (or more) of the following, occurring at any time in the same 12-month period:

1. *tolerance*, as defined by either of the following:

(a) a need for markedly increased amounts of the substance to achieve intoxication or desired effect

(b) markedly diminished effect with continued use of the same amount of the substance

(Tolerance to nicotine is described as "a more intense effect of nicotine the first time it is used during the day and the absence of nausea and dizziness with repeated intake, despite regular use of substantial amounts of nicotine.")

2. *withdrawal*, as manifested by either of the following:

(a) the characteristic withdrawal syndrome for the substance (Nicotine withdrawal includes a cluster of symptoms immediately preceded by drastic curtailment or cessation of use "*after using daily for at least several weeks*" [italics added].)

(b) the same (or a closely related) substance is taken to relieve or avoid withdrawal symptoms

3. the substance is often taken in larger amounts or over a longer period than was intended
4. there is a persistent desire or unsuccessful efforts to cut down or control substance use
5. a great deal of time is spent in activities necessary to obtain the substance (e.g., visiting multiple doctors or driving long distances), use the substance (e.g., chain-smoking), or recover from its effects
6. important social, occupational, or recreational activities are given up or reduced because of substance use
7. the substance use is continued despite knowledge of having a persistent or recurrent physical or psychological problem that is likely to have been caused or exacerbated by the substance (e.g., current cocaine use despite recognition of cocaine-induced depression, or continued drinking despite recognition that an ulcer was made worse by alcohol consumption).

There are several problems inherent in the use of DSM or ICD criteria [2, 3] to determine whether a smoker is addicted. These criteria were derived from clinical observations of alcoholics [31, 32] and were not based on any explicit theory of addiction. The criterion for tolerance lacks face validity as an index of addiction. Why would a person be considered an addict because he or she could tolerate a larger dose of nicotine without experiencing nausea, or because the first cigarette of the day was more pleasurable? The idea that withdrawal cannot be experienced except after prolonged daily smoking is contradicted by a substantial body of literature.[6-16] The use of a substance in larger amounts or over longer periods than intended (criterion 3) concerns binge use of substances like alcohol or cocaine and does not reflect smokers' behavior; smokers do not go on benders. Of the criteria, only withdrawal (criterion 2) and unsuccessful efforts to control use (criterion 4) have face validity as indicators of diminished autonomy. Several others would indicate diminished autnomy only under certain conditions. Spending time obtaining and using tobacco (criterion 5) would not indicate diminished autonomy if the person did so out of enjoyment, but would if the frequent use was required to keep withdrawal symptoms in check. Giving up social activities in order to smoke (criterion 6) would not indicate diminished autonomy if the person simply preferred smoking to socializing, but would if prior attempts to socialize were thwarted by withdrawal symptoms. Smoking despite harm (criterion 7) would not indicate diminished autonomy if the person felt the pleasure derived from smoking was worth the price, but would if attempts at cessation had been unsuccessful. This discussion is intended to highlight some of the difficulties of measuring the construct of dependence in the absence of a clear consensus as to what it entails. The concept of diminished autonomy over tobacco was developed in part to avoid the pitfalls of the long-standing controversy about the nature of tobacco dependence.

HOW DOES THE CONCEPT OF AUTONOMY PROVIDE UNIQUE INSIGHTS INTO THE NATURE OF ADDICTION?

It can be easily argued that all concepts of addiction and dependence are artificial man-made constructs.

Neuroscientists study the neurophysiological changes that occur in the brain as a result of nicotine use. The goal of this research is to identify the mechanisms that cause addiction so that these might be countered or reversed. It is important that the measures used to identify addiction in human tobacco users correspond to real events in the brain. If a measure of addiction is "artificial," it is unlikely to correspond to the observed patterns of brain alterations. It is likely that the neurological processes that underlie addiction begin before the smoker is aware of the first symptom, and the onset of these processes will be missed if the beginning of dependence is identified as the point in time when the third symptom appears. To the degree that measures of addiction rely on self-harm or cultural responsibilities they are also less likely to align with neurophysiological processes. For example, two different smokers might differ in whether they develop lung cancer or heart disease (use despite harm) but the brain processes causing their smoking might be identical. Direct measures of smokers' thoughts and feelings are more likely to parallel the underlying neurophysiological processes. The HONC relies entirely on subjective evaluation.

WHAT HAVE WE LEARNED ABOUT SMOKING THROUGH THE LENS OF DIMINISHED AUTONOMY?

We have learned that...

- Youths frequently experience diminished autonomy over tobacco use within days to weeks of initiating intermittent smoking.[8] While most smokers develop symptoms rapidly, some are more resilient.
- The average rate of consumption at the onset of symptoms is two cigarettes, one day per week.[9]
- Two-thirds of youths have symptoms prior to the onset of daily smoking.[9]
- Autonomy is diminished one symptom at a time; addiction is incremental, not dichotomous.

- Individuals develop the various symptoms in different sequences.
- Most "chippers" have diminished autonomy over their use of tobacco.[33]
- The appearance of a single symptom of diminished autonomy is a strong predictor of continued smoking.[8, 16]
- Even prior to the onset of daily smoking, many smokers are unsuccessful in their quit attempts.[25]
- Adult "social smokers" who smoke only a few days each week experience withdrawal symptoms.[33, 34]
- A single cigarette can relieve withdrawal symptoms in intermittent smokers for days.[34]
- Withdrawal symptoms appear before substantial tolerance to nicotine develops, indicating that the form of tolerance that requires smokers to smoke a half pack per day or more is not the cause of withdrawal symptoms.[9, 17]
- Having withdrawal symptoms does not necessarily mandate maintaining minimum serum levels of nicotine in the blood throughout the day.[34]
- The stage theory that states that dependence follows a prolonged period of steady use is wrong.
- Girls develop symptoms at a quicker rate than boys.[9, 12, 17]
- Youths have many more symptoms of diminished autonomy than would be expected based upon how much they smoke in comparison to adults.[21, 23]
- Daily cigarette consumption correlates well with the severity of diminished autonomy in novice smokers, but quite poorly in long-term smokers.[16, 24]
- Very few smokers have only one HONC symptom; for those who do, the situation is only temporary as additional symptoms develop quickly.
- The ten symptoms on the HONC appear in different orders and combinations in different individuals, indicating individual variability in trajectories.[8]
- Craving is the most commonly reported presenting symptom (the first to appear), but withdrawal symptoms are also commonly reported as presenting symptoms.[8]
- Smokers populate every point on the HONC scale from 0 to 10, in a skewed unimodal bell-shaped distribution with a mean of 7 for adult smokers.[22-24] Diminished autonomy is distributed over a continuous spectrum of severity.

WHAT ARE THE ADVANTAGES OF THE HONC?

The HONC has many advantages over other putative measures of nicotine addiction. First, each HONC item has face validity as a symptom of diminished autonomy. Second, it is a very sensitive measure of the first symptoms of addiction. Third, the HONC is valid with adolescents and adults of all ages, and because it does not confound addiction with the amount smoked, it can be used with infrequent and heavy smokers alike. Fourth, it has excellent psychometric properties. Fifth, it can be used as either a dichotomous or a continuous measure. Sixth, because the HONC score equals the total number of symptoms, it is easily interpretable. Seventh, it can be administered in an interview or as a self-completed survey. Most importantly, the HONC is part of a unique triad that provides a unified view of tobacco addiction from neurobiology to behavior. The triad includes a construct with face validity – autonomy over tobacco, a thoroughly validated tool for measuring autonomy, and a detailed theory that integrates clinical observations and neurophysiological processes.

REFERENCES

[1] *Jacobellis v. Ohio*. U.S. 378: 184, 1964.

[2] World Health Organization. *International statistical classification of diseases and related health problems (10th revision)*; World Health Organization: Geneva, 1992.

[3] American Psychiatric Association. *Diagnostic and statistical manual of mental disorders (4th ed., text revision)*; American Psychiatric Association: Washington, D.C., 2004.

[4] Russell, M.A.H. Nicotine intake and its regulation. *Journal of Psychosomatic Research.* 1980, *24*, 253-264.

[5] Leventhal, H.; Cleary, P.D. The smoking problem: A review of the research and theory in behavioral risk modification. *Psychological Bulletin.* 1980, *88*, 370-405.

[6] An, L.; Lein, E.; Bliss, R.; Pallonen, U.; Hennrikus, D.; Farley, D.; Hertel, A.; Perry, C.; Lando, H. Loss of autonomy over nicotine use among college social smokers [POS2-035 Abstract]. In *Proceedings of the 10th Annual Meeting of the Society for Research on Nicotine and Tobacco*: Scottsdale, Arizona, 2004.

[7] Barker, D. Reasons for tobacco use and symptoms of nicotine withdrawal among adolescent and young adult tobacco users-United States, 1993. *MMWR Morbidity and Mortality Weekly Report.* 1994, *43*, 745-750.

[8] DiFranza, J.R.; Rigotti, N.A.; McNeill, A.D.; Ockene, J.K.; Savageau, J.A.; St Cyr, D.; Coleman, M. Initial symptoms of nicotine dependence in adolescents. *Tobacco Control.* 2000, *9* (3), 313-319.

[9] DiFranza, J.R.; Savageau, J.A.; Rigotti, N.A.; Fletcher, K.; Ockene, J.K.; McNeill, A.D.; Coleman, M.; Wood, C. Development of symptoms of tobacco dependence in youths: 30 month follow up data from the DANDY study. *Tobacco Control.* 2002, *11* (3), 228-235.

[10] Goddard, E. *Why children start smoking*; Office of Population Censuses and Surveys HMSO: London, UK, 1990;

[11] McNeill, A.D.; West, R.J.; Jarvis, M.; Jackson, P.; Bryant, A. Cigarette withdrawal symptoms in adolescent smokers. *Psychopharmacology.* 1986, *90*, 533-536.

[12] O'Loughlin, J.; DiFranza, J.; Tyndale, R.F.; Meshefedjian, G.; McMillan-Davey, E.; Clarke, P.B.; Hanley, J.; Paradis, G. Nicotine-dependence symptoms are associated with smoking frequency in adolescents. *American Journal of Preventive Medicine.* 2003, *25* (3), 219-225.

[13] O'Loughlin, J.; Kishchuk, N.; DiFranza, J.; Tremblay, M.; Paradis, G. The hardest thing is the habit: a qualitative investigation of adolescent smokers' experience of nicotine dependence. *Nicotine and Tobacco Research.* 2002, *4* (2), 201-209.

[14] Riedel, B.W.; Robinson, L.A.; Klesges, R.C.; McLain-Allen, B. Ethnic differences in smoking withdrawal effects among adolescents. *Addictive Behaviors.* 2003, *28*, 129-140.

[15] Strong, D.R.; Kahler, C.W.; Ramsey, S.E.; Abrantes, A.; Brown, R.A. Nicotine withdrawal among adolescents with acute psychopathology: an item response analysis. *Nicotine and Tobacco Research.* 2004, *6*, 547-557.

[16] Wellman, R.J.; DiFranza, J.R.; Pbert, L.; Fletcher, K.E.; Flint, A.; Young, M.H.; Druker, S. A comparison of the psychometric properties of the hooked on nicotine checklist and the modified Fagerström tolerance questionnaire. *Addictive Behaviors.* 2006, *31* (3), 486-495.

[17] O'Loughlin, J.; Bancej, C.; Gervais, A.; Meshefedjian, G.; Tremblay, M. Milestones in the natural course of cigarette use onset in adolescents [PA 12-2]. In *Proceedings of the 12th Annual Meeting of the Society for Research on Nicotine and Tobacco*: Orlando, Florida, 2006.

[18] DiFranza, J.R.; Savageau, J.A.; Fletcher, K.; Ockene, J.K.; Rigotti, N.A.; McNeill, A.D.; Coleman, M.; Wood, C. Measuring the loss of autonomy over nicotine use in adolescents: the DANDY (Development and Assessment of Nicotine Dependence in Youths) study. *Archives of Pediatrics and Adolescent Medicine.* 2002, *156* (4), 397-403.

[19] DiFranza, J.R.; Wellman, R.J. A sensitization-homeostasis model of nicotine craving, withdrawal, and tolerance: Integrating the clinical and basic science literature. *Nicotine and Tobacco Research.* 2005, *7* (1), 9-26.

[20] O'Loughlin, J.; Tarasuk, J.; Difranza, J.; Paradis, G. Reliability of selected measures of nicotine dependence among adolescents. *Annals of Epidemiology.* 2002, *12* (5), 353-362.

[21] Wheeler, K.C.; Fletcher, K.E.; Wellman, R.J.; Difranza, J.R. Screening adolescents for nicotine dependence: the Hooked On Nicotine Checklist. *Journal of Adolescent Health.* 2004, *35* (3), 225-230.

[22] Wellman, R.J.; McMillen, R.C.; DiFranza, J.R. Assessing college students' autonomy over smoking with the Hooked on Nicotine Checklist. *Journal of American College Health, In press.*

[23] Wellman, R.J.; DiFranza, J.R.; Savageau, J.A.; Godiwala, S.; Friedman, K.; Hazelton, J. Measuring adults' loss of autonomy over nicotine use: The Hooked on Nicotine Checklist. *Nicotine and Tobacco Research.* 2005, *7* (1), 157-161.

[24] Wellman, R.J.; Savageau, J.A.; Godiwala, S.; Savageau, N.; Friedman, K.; Hazelton, J.; DiFranza, J. A comparison of the Hooked on Nicotine Checklist and the Fagerström Test of Nicotine Dependence in adult smokers. *Nicotine and Tobacco Research.* 2006, *8* (4), 575-580.

[25] Wellman, R.J.; DiFranza, J.R.; Savageau, J.A.; Dussault, G.F. Short-term patterns of early smoking acquisition. *Tobacco Control.* 2004, *13* (3), 251-257.

[26] Prokhorov, A.V.; De Moor, C.; Pallonen, U.E.; Hudmon, K.S.; Koehly, L.; Hu, S. Validation of the modified Fagerström tolerance questionnaire with salivary cotinine among adolescents. *Addictive Behaviors.* 2000, *25* (3), 429-433.

[27] Prokhorov, A.V.; Pallonen, U.E.; Fava, J.L.; Ding, L.; Niaura, R. Measuring nicotine dependence among high-risk adolescent smokers. *Addictive Behaviors.* 1996, *21* (1), 117-127.

[28] Prokhorov, A.V.; Koehly, L.M.; Pallonen, U.E.; Hudmon, K.S. Adolescent nicotine dependence measured by the Modified Fagerström Tolerance Questionnaire at two time points. *Journal of Child and Adolescent Substance Abuse.* 1998, *7*, 35-47.

[29] Heatherton, T.F.; Kozlowski, L.T.; Frecker, R.C.; Fagerstrom, K.O. The Fagerström Test for Nicotine Dependence: a revision of the Fagerström Tolerance Questionnaire. *British Journal of Addiction.* 1991, *86* (9), 1119-1127.

[30] O'Loughlin, J.; DiFranza, J.; Tarasuk, J.; Meshefedjian, G.; McMillan-Davey, E.; Paradis, G.; Tyndale, R.F.; Clarke, P.; Hanley, J. Assessment of nicotine dependence symptoms in adolescents: a comparison of five indicators. *Tobacco Control.* 2002, *11* (4), 354-360.

[31] Edwards, G. The alcohol dependence syndrome: a concept as a stimulus to enquiry. *British Journal of Addiction.* 1986, *81*, 171-183.

[32] Edwards, G.; Gross, M.M. Alcohol dependence: provisional description of a clinical syndrome. *British Medical Journal.* 1976, *1*, 1058-1061.

[33] Wellman, R.J.; DiFranza, J.R.; Wood, C. Tobacco chippers report diminished autonomy over smoking. *Addictive Behaviors.* 2006, *31* (4), 717-721.

[34] Fernando, W.W.S.A.; Wellman, R.J.; DiFranza, J.R. The relationship between level of cigarette consumption and latency to the onset of retrospectively reported withdrawal symptoms. *Psychopharmacology.* 2006, *188* (3), 335-342 .

In: Psychological Tests and Testing Research Trends   ISBN: 978-1-60021-569-8
Editor: Paul M. Goldfarb, pp. 211-230   © 2007 Nova Science Publishers, Inc.

Chapter 10

SHORT-FORM SPORT ORIENTATION QUESTIONNAIRE (SF-SOQ): TESTING THE FACTOR STRUCTURE AND INVARIANCE ACROSS ATHLETES WITH AND WITHOUT DISABILITIES

*N. A. Stavrou[1] and E. K. Skordilis[2]**

[1] Laboratory of Motor Behavior and Sport Psychology
[2] Laboratory of Adapted Physical Activity/Developmental and Physical Disabilities
Department of Physical Education and Sport Sciences
National and Kapodistrian University of Athens, Greece

ABSTRACT

The study examined: a) the factor structure of the Short-Form Sport Orientation Questionnaire (SF-SOQ) (Skordilis and Stavrou, 2005) in two separate groups of athletes, with and without disabilities, through confirmatory factor analysis (CFA) and b) the equivalence of the SF-SOQ factor structure, across the two groups, through multisample analyses. The SF-SOQ incorporates 15 items, under the following three factors: "Competitiveness" (7 items), "Win Orientation" (5 items) and "Goal Orientation" (3 items).The participants were five hundred and thirty (530) athletes, classified in two groups of 273 athletes with disabilities and 257 athletes without disabilities. Three alternative nested models were examined for the first purpose [a: a three first-order correlated factor model (FM_{3C}), b: a three first-order uncorrelated factor model (FM_{3U}), and c: a single first-order factor model (FM_1)]. The results were in accordance to the sport achievement orientation theory (Gill and Deeter, 1988), since: a) the three first-order correlated factor SF-SOQ model-FM_{3C} provided an acceptable fit to the data, whereas the models of: b) three uncorrelated-FM_{3U} and c) single first-order-FM_1 factors, provided poor fit. Accordingly, the multisample analyses revealed that the three sport orientation factors were not equivalent across the two groups. The SF-SOQ items varied, in their relationship to the underlying measurement construct, meaning that these items were perceived and interpreted differently between athletes with and without disabilities.

* Address correspondence: Dr. Emmanouil K. Skordilis, 7 Miltiadou street, Glyfada 16675, Athens, Greece.

Overall, the SF-SOQ may be used with confidence to examine separate groups of athletes, either with or without disabilities. However, meaningful differences between athletes who differ according to disability status may not be undertaken in the future.

Keywords: sport orientation, confirmatory factor analysis, multisample analysis.

INTRODUCTION

The sport-specific achievement motivation theory of Gill and Deeter (1988) guided the present study. According to Gill and Deeter (1988), the above theory was based on the general achievement motivation concept, 'widely recognized as a capacity to experience pride in accomplishment or a disposition to strive for success across various achievement situations and standards' (p. 191). Further, Page, O'Connor, and Wayda (2000) stated that the above theory was based on the work of Atkinson and McClelland (McClelland, 1961), suggesting that achievement behavior is based on personality and situational factors. These factors have a direct influence on individual motives to avoid failure and/ or perceive success in sports (Page et al., 2000; Zoerink and Wilson, 1995).

Gill and Deeter (1988) developed the Sport Orientation Questionnaire (SOQ), as a multidimensional and sport specific measure, in an attempt to describe individual differences in sport achievement settings. The SOQ incorporates 25 items, classified under the three factors of 'Competitiveness' (13 items), 'Win Orientation' (6 items) and 'Goal Orientation' (6 items). Gill and Deeter (1988) used separate samples of university and high school students and stated that 'we believe that we have sufficient evidence for reliability and validity so that our sport achievement orientation measure may be used to address various questions about sport and exercise behavior' (p. 200). However, several fit indexes presented (e.g. GFI = .779, .743, AGFI = .738, .696, RMSR = .122, .174) departed from the appropriate range, leading to the general conclusion that the SOQ incorporates psychometric weaknesses and must be reevaluated in the future.

The work of Gill and Deeter (1988) has offered to researchers the opportunity to use the SOQ, in order to describe the sport orientations, in a variety of settings (e.g. sport participants vs non participants), populations (e.g. individuals with vs individuals without disabilities) etc. In the able-body literature, for example, individuals who participate in: a) sport and non sport activities (Gill, Dzewaltowski, and Deeter, 1988), b) different sports (Acevedo, Dzewaltowski, Gill, and Noble, 1992; Gill and Dzewaltowski, 1988;), c) local high school teams (Martin and Gill, 1991), d) university level teams (Finkenberg, Moode, and DiNucci, 1998; Kleppinger, 1995; Lerner and Locke, 1995; Swain and Jones, 1992), etc, have been examined. Further, the SOQ has been tested repeatedly, in different countries, such as Filipinas (Martin and Gill, 1995), Australia (Marsh, 1994b), Taiwan (Kang, Gill, Acevedo, and Deeter, 1990), Japan (Wakayama, Watanabe, Murai, and Inomata, 2004), Greece (Karteroliotis, 1995), etc., providing, therefore, understanding of sport orientations across a variety of cultures.

The SOQ has been used with several groups of athletes with disabilities in the past too (Martin, Adams-Mushett, and Smith, 1995; Page et al., 2000; Skordilis, 1998; Skordilis, Gavriilidis, Charitou and Asonitou, 2003; Zoerink and Wilson, 1995). Martin et al. (1995) examined the athletic identity and sport orientation of adolescent, international swimmers with disabilities. The researchers found that the participants exhibited high competitiveness and goal orientations, while their win orientation was only moderate. Zoerink and Wilson (1995) examined the sport orientations in a group of athletes with and without intellectual disabilities. The disability group of athletes participated at the International Special Olympics, while the non disable group competed in national, collegiate level, athletics. The researchers concluded that the group of athletes with disabilities were similar to their counterparts without disabilities. Page et al. (2000) examined the different sport orientations exhibited in a group of athletes with physical disabilities, competing at the Paralympic track and field trials. The participants varied according to onset (congenital and acquired) gender, age (adolescents and adults) and classification. The researchers found no mean differences across gender, onset, age and classification, suggesting the examination of wider samples, with measuring instruments specifically constructed for athletes with disabilities.

Skordilis (1998) examined individuals with physical disabilities who differed according to gender, sport involved (basketball and marathon racing) and onset of experienced disability. The researchers found that males scored higher on competitiveness, females scored higher on goal orientation, while no differences were evident for win orientation. Further, basketball players scored higher than marathoners on win and lower on goal orientation, while no differences were evident on competitiveness. Finally, no significant differences were evident among groups who differed according to onset.

Skordilis et al. (2003) compared the sport achievement orientations in separate groups of basketball athletes. The above groups were comprised from: a) professional able-body athletes, b) amateur able-body athletes and c) amateur athletes with physical disabilities. The researchers found that win orientation was the factor that significantly separated the three groups. Specifically, professional athletes were more oriented towards winning than their amateur counterparts, either with or without disabilities.

Experts in disability research (Sherrill and O'Connor, 1999; Yun and Ulrich, 2002) indicated the importance of providing validity and reliability information for the samples examined. According to Sherrill and O'Connor (1999), for example, only if a specific sample has been tested repeatedly then validity and reliability evidence may be generalized. Yun and Ulrich (2002) stated that 'subsequent uses of an instrument in new situations and/ or with different attributes of population should be preceded by validity estimation procedures to ensure appropriateness of its use' (p. 34). Further, Sawilowsky (2000) stated that 'it remains a question for the editors and the editorial boards of academic journals as to why the importance of citing a test's reliability estimate for the sample in the study has not been emphasized' (p. 198). Based on the above sample specific validity and reliability evidence theory, the construct validity of the SOQ was recently examined for marathon athletes and basketball players with disabilities, using exploratory (Skordilis, Koutsouki, Asonitou, Evans, Jensen, and Wall, 2001) and confirmatory factor analytic procedures (Skordilis, Sherrill, Yilla, Koutsouki, and Stavrou, 2002). The initial exploratory factor analysis (Skordilis et al., 2001) indicated a poor fit of several items with the Competitiveness and Goal Orientation factors. The factor structure of the SOQ therefore was found to differ between athletes with and without disabilities. Specifically, the major factor of Competitiveness was divided into the Self-referenced Competitiveness and Other-referenced Competitiveness. The separate confirmatory factor analysis (Skordilis et al., 2002), confirmed the above findings and, overall, the psychometric weaknesses of the SOQ model. Skordilis et al. (2002) concluded that a new measuring instrument is essential to describe the sport orientations of wheelchair athletes.

Recently, Skordilis and Stavrou (2005) found that a short-form SOQ (SF-SOQ) overcomes the psychometric weaknesses of the SOQ (Gill and Deeter, 1988) and is valid for wheelchair basketball athletes. The SF-SOQ provided acceptable fit indices and Cronbach's alpha reliability coefficients. The error variances, the factor loadings and the intercorrelations among the SF-SOQ factors were at the appropriate range. Further, Skordilis and Stavrou (2005) examined the SF-SOQ structure across gender. Specifically, they examined whether the conceptualization of sport achievement orientation was similar between men and women wheelchair basketball athletes with disabilities. The researchers found similar measuring properties across gender, indicating that the conceptualization of sport achievement orientation was similar between men and women athletes with physical disabilities who participate in wheelchair basketball.

Based on the above, it appears that the SF-SOQ adequately explains the sport orientations of athletes with physical disabilities. Further, the application of the SF-SOQ, to athletes without disabilities, has not been examined yet. According to Skordilis and Stavrou (2005), the SF-SOQ may be re-examined in the future to strengthen the previous findings. Therefore, the present study was designed to examine, through confirmatory factor analysis, the factorial structure of the SF-SOQ, across separate samples of athletes with and without disabilities. Further, our second research objective was to examine, through multisample confirmatory factor analysis, the invariance of the SF-SOQ model across the two groups. With regard to the first research objective, we anticipated that the SF-SOQ would be valid and reliable for the two samples examined. Concerning the second objective, however, we had no previous evidence to lead into a specific research hypothesis and our findings were mainly exploratory.

METHOD

Participants

Five hundred and thirty (530) athletes volunteered to participate in the present study. The total sample was divided in two groups: a) two hundred and fifty seven (257) athletes without disabilities and b) two hundred and seventy three (273) athletes with physical disabilities. The disability sample was comprised from 231 males and 42 females, participating in individual (48 athletes) and team (225 athletes) sports, with a mean age of 35 years (SD = 8.45). The mean competitive experience was approximately 10 years (M = 9.78, SD = 7.44). The group of athletes without disabilities (185 males and 72 females), participating in individual (81 athletes) and team (176 athletes) sports, was comprised from 223 amateur and 34 professional athletes. Their ages ranged from 16 to 31 years (M = 22.61, SD = 2.60), while their competitive experience ranged from 1 to 18 years (M = 5.51, SD = 3.88).

Measuring Instrument

The SF-SOQ of Skordilis and Stavrou (2005) was used for the purposes of the present study. The SF-SOQ was based on the work of Gill and Deeter (1988), who developed the Sport Orientation Questionnaire (SOQ) as a multidimensional, sport specific construct, to assess sport achievement orientations.

Sport Orientation Questionnaire (SOQ)

The Sport Orientation Questionnaire (SOQ; Gill and Deeter, 1988) is a self-reported instrument which is used to examine athletes' sport orientations. The original questionnaire consists of 25 items comprising three factors named "competitiveness" (13 items), "win orientation" (6 items), and "goal orientation" (6 items). Participants responded on a 5-point Likert-type scale, anchoring from 5 "Strongly agree" to 1 "Strongly disagree".

Gill and Deeter (1988) used exploratory and confirmatory factor analyses in separate samples of university and high school students. The results indicated low fit indices for the three factor solution of the SOQ. Specifically, exploratory factor analysis (EFA), using varimax and oblique rotations, provided a medium percentage of explained variance (49.6%). The primary factor-loadings of the items to their associated factors indicated values above .40 (Tabachnick and Fidell, 2006). However, several items had double high factor loadings, indicating that they did not measure an exact, pre hypothesized factor.

Confirmatory factor analysis indices of the SOQ model did not reach the cutoff criteria of adequate fit, providing psychometric weaknesses for the three factor SOQ model (Goodness of Fit Index <.900, Adjusted Goodness of Fit Index <.900, Root Mean Square Residuals > .080). However, the intraclass reliability (IR) ranged from .84 to .94, and the test-retest (r) reliability coefficients from .73 to .89. Gill and Deeter (1988) concluded that the above reliability coefficients were adequate and the instrument could be used in the future for measuring sport achievement orientation.

The construct validity of the SOQ was recently examined for marathon athletes and basketball players with disabilities using exploratory (Skordilis et al., 2001) and confirmatory factor analytic procedures (Skordilis et al., 2002). The initial exploratory factor analysis (Skordilis et al., 2001) indicated a poor fit for several items. Specifically, the major factor of competitiveness was divided into the "self-referenced competitiveness" and "other-referenced competitiveness". The separate confirmatory factor analysis (Skordilis et al., 2002), confirmed the above findings and, overall, the psychometric weaknesses of the model. Skordilis et al. (2002) concluded that a new measuring instrument is essential to describe the sport orientations of wheelchair athletes.

Short-Form Sport Orientation Questionnaire (SF-SOQ)

The SF-SOQ (Skordilis and Stavrou, 2005) was used for the purposes of the present study. Based, on previous research findings and the theory of sample-specific validity and reliability (Pedhazur and Pedhazur-Schmelkin, 1991; Sherrill and O'Connor, 1999; Thomas and Nelson, 1996; Yun and Ulrich, 2002), Skordilis and Stavrou (2005) evaluated the SOQ factors of Gill and Deeter (1988), underlying sport orientations. Skordilis and Stavrou (2005) found that a short-form instrument (SF-SOQ) was valid for athletes with disabilities. Specifically, Skordilis and Stavrou (2005) based on a series of criteria (Bentler, 1995; Bradley, 1982; Tabachnick and Fidell, 1996; West, Finch, and Curran, 1995), excluded ten

(10) items, and reached the proposed SF-SOQ model. The SF-SOQ is consisting of fifteen (15) items, classified under the followings factors: (a) competitiveness: 3, 9, 11, 13, 15, 17, and 21, (b) win orientation: 2, 6, 10, 14, and 22, and (c) goal orientation factor: 8, 12, and 20. Confirmatory factor analysis of the SF-SOQ provided acceptable fit to the data since fit indices reached the cutoff criteria (SF-SOQ indices: χ^2/df ratio = 2.21, Non-Normed Fit Index = .892, Comparative Fit Index = .911, Robust Comparative Fit Index = .935, Standardized Root Mean Squared Residual = .058, Root Mean Squared Error of Approximation = .071, 90% CI of RMSEA = .057 - .84). The error variances, the factor loadings and the intercorrelations among the SF-SOQ factors were in the appropriate range. Cronbach's alpha reliability coefficients (Cronbach, 1951) were: .84 for competitiveness, .74 for goal orientation, and .81 for win orientation, indicating that the SF-SOQ factors were internally consistent. Further, the factor structure of the short-form SOQ was tested for its consistency across gender. Specifically, it was examined whether the conceptualization of sport achievement orientation was equivalent between male and female wheelchair basketball athletes with disabilities. The fit indices of multisample analysis indicated invariance of the measuring properties across gender (χ^2/df ratio = 1.65, CFI = .90, NNFI = .89). In other words, the conceptualization of sport achievement orientation was similar, between men and women athletes with physical disabilities who participate in wheelchair basketball.

Procedure

The athletes were recruited by either contacting their coaches or the athletes themselves. Initially, the athletes were informed about the purpose of the study and the methodology of the measurement. The confidential nature of the data was made clear, and the athletes were asked whether they were willing to complete the questionnaires. Then, they were asked to complete a consent form, the demographic information data sheet, and the SF-SOQ. The athletes completed the questionnaire during their free time in non-competitive situations, based on their previous experience as sport participants. Both groups of athletes were encouraged to select the responses closely reflective of their perceptions as athletes.

Statistical Analysis

The factor structure of the SF-SOQ was examined through confirmatory factor analysis, using the EQS software (Bentler, 1995). The SF-SOQ items were uniquely allowed to load on the appropriate factors, according to the original scale proposed by Gill and Deeter (1988). The item loadings on the remaining factors were fixed to 0.00. The factors for the model identification were fixed to 1.00. Covariances among the factors were free estimated (Bentler, 1995). As Hoyle and Panter (1995) recommended, absolute and incremental fit indices were used to estimate the sufficiency of the measurement models. The following indices were used to examine the fit of the measurement models: (a) Chi-square (χ^2) (Bentler and Bonett, 1980; Long, 1983), (b) χ^2/df ratio (Byrne, 1989; Kelloway, 1998), (c) AIC and CAIC indices (Akaike, 1987; Bozdogan, 1987), (d) Non-Normed Fit Index (NNFI) (Bentler and Bonett, 1980; McDonald and Marsh, 1990), (e) Comparative Fit Index (CFI) (Byrne, 1989; Marsh, 1994a), (f) Robust Comparative Fit Index (RCFI) (Byrne, 1989), (g) Standardized Root Mean

Squared Residual (SRMR) (Bollen, 1989; Tabachnick and Fidell, 2006), and (h) Root Mean Squared Error of Approximation (RMSEA) (Steinger, 1990). Also, the Parsimonious Normed Fit Index (PNFI) [PNFI = (df_{model}/df_{indep}) x NFI] was used to estimate the degree of parsimony in the models (James, Mulaik, and Brett, 1982; Kelloway, 1998). The usefulness of PNFI is to compare measurement models, showing that the model with the higher parsimonious fit is better. The Akaike's Information Criterion (Akaike, 1987) (AIC) and the Bozdogan's (1987) consistent version of Akaike's Information Criterion (CAIC) were also used, as two important indices for estimating the comparative adequacy among competing models (Bentler, 1995). The AIC and CAIC are not normed on a zero-to-one scale, and they do not have a specified range of acceptable values. The AIC and CAIC indices with the lowest values, among competing models, demonstrated an improved and more parsimonious fit of the model.

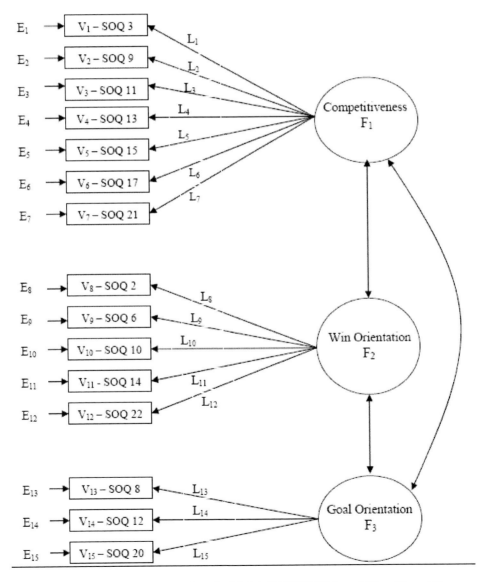

Figure 1. Short-Form Sport Orientation Questionnaire Model (SF-SOQ) (15 items) (Skordilis and Stavrou, 2005).

The χ^2 provides information regarding the differences of covariances between the model-reproduced and the actual, and it is positively affected by the sample size (Hu and Bentler, 1995; Kline, 1998). The χ^2/df ratio can be used for judging model fit (Jörsekog, 1969). In order to indicate acceptable fit of a model, the χ^2/df ratio should be close to 2 and less than 3 (Bollen, 1989). However, the df refer to the number of model fixed parameters which are not affected by the sample size (Marsh, Balla, and McDonald, 1988). Thus, there is a positive relationship between χ^2/df ratio and sample size (Kahn, 2006). Given the dependency of the chi-square statistics on sample size (Bentler and Bonnett, 1980; Byrne, 1994), and the fact that the chi-square values are not accurate for evaluating the exact fit of a model (Quintana and Maxwell, 1999), additional indices were examined. The NNFI, CFI and the RCFI indices range from 0 to 1, with values above .90 representing acceptable fit of the model (Jöreskog and Sörbom, 1993). The Standardized Root Mean Squared Residual (SRMR) and Root Mean Squared Error of Approximation (RMSEA) were used to examine the residuals. The lower than .05 SRMR values indicate a very good application of the model, while values between .05 and .10 represent a rather acceptable fit (Bollen, 1989; Tabachnick and Fidell, 2006). According to Hu and Bentler (1999), the cutoff criteria for SRMR and RMSEA are lower than .08 and .06 respectively, while Steinger (1990) suggests that values close to or lower than .05 demonstrate an acceptable fit. The 90% CI (confidence interval) around the RMSEA point should contain .05 to indicate close-model fit to the data (Browne and Cudeck, 1993). Finally, the ratio of sample size to the model free parameters in the present study was greater than 7:1, exceeding the minimum ratio of 5:1, recommended by Bentler and Wu (2002).

To test the internal consistency, the following indices were estimated for each SF-SOQ subscale: (a) the means and the range of item means, inter-item correlations, and item-total correlations, and (b) Cronbach's a coefficient. Tabachnick and Fidell (2006) suggested that, for an acceptable internal consistency, Cronbach's a coefficient should exceed .70.

Initially, the factor structure of the SF-SOQ model was examined separately for the two groups of athletes (with and without disabilities). For this reason, three alternative SF-SOQ models were tested independently (Byrne, 1994). In order to provide further validity evidence and to test the SF-SOQ factor structure across the two groups (athletes with and without disability), multisample (MSA) (multiple-groups) analyses were conducted. The simultaneous examination of the factor structure of the SF-SOQ across disability provides information regarding the similarity or equivalence of the baseline model. Similarity is important since it is meaningless to discuss differences between groups, if the SF-SOQ does not measure the same constructs between them (Bentler, 1995; Marsh, 1993). The similarity was tested in the SF-SOQ through three separate MSA. The first MSA examined the invariance of variance/covariance matrices. Then, the equivalence of factor loadings, which refers to the equality of coefficients linking observed and latent variable, and the equivalence of item's uniquenesses, which represents the equality of item's random and specific-error variance, were tested through two additional MSA (Byrne and Watkins, 2003; Jöreskog and Sörbom, 1993).

RESULTS

Confirmatory Factor Analysis of SF-SOQ

Descriptive Statistics

The means (M), standard deviations (SD) of the 15 items of the SF-SOQ, for the two groups of athletes (with and without disabilities), are resented in table 1. Regarding the distributional properties in the disability group, the items mean univariate skewness was –.973 and the mean univariate kurtosis items was .920. Mardia's (1970) coefficient of multivariate kurtosis (normalized estimate) was 25.881, indicating acceptable multivariate kurtosis among the items. For the group of athletes without disability, the mean univariate skewness was –1.453, whereas the mean univariate kurtosis was 1.956. Further, the Mardia's (1970) normalized multivariate kurtosis statistic was 32.155. It should be noted that Mardia's coefficient (normalized estimate) is reported for descriptive reasons (Tabachnick and Fidell, 2006), since it is positively related to the sample size (Bollen, 1989; Mardia, 1970). Therefore, the maximum likelihood was considered the appropriate method in the subsequent confirmatory factor analysis (CFA), because it provided accurate absolute and relative fit indices with observed categorical data of varying degrees of skewness or kurtosis (Hutchinson and Olmos, 1998; Olson, Foss, Troye, and Howell, 2000).

Table 1. Means (M), Standard Deviations (SD), Items Loadings (L), and Uniqueness (U) of the SF-SOQ, for Athletes With and Without Disabilities

	Athletes Without Disabilities		Athletes With Disabilities		Athletes Without Disabilities		Athletes With Disabilities	
	M	SD	M	SD	L	U	L	U
Item 2 (W)	4.47	.90	4.07	.92	.648	.761	.705	.709
Item 3 (C)	4.30	.83	4.49	.71	.448	.894	.652	.758
Item 6 (W)	4.34	1.02	3.59	1.11	.653	.757	.756	.654
Item 8 (G)	4.16	1.12	4.04	1.01	.416	.909	.639	.769
Item 9 (C)	3.81	1.24	4.42	.69	.316	.949	.683	.730
Item 10 (W)	3.51	1.51	3.62	1.19	.647	.762	.613	.790
Item 11 (C)	4.56	.73	3.90	1.03	.457	.890	.703	.711
Item 12 (G)	4.62	.78	4.14	.93	.623	.782	.743	.670
Item 13(C)	4.75	.61	4.07	1.07	.677	.736	.643	.766
Item 14 (W)	3.36	1.37	2.47	1.10	.594	.804	.623	.783
Item 15 (C)	4.66	.67	4.35	.64	.689	.724	.667	.745
Item 17 (C)	4.46	.86	4.27	.74	.732	.681	.599	.801
Item 20 (G)	4.25	.92	4.12	.90	.445	.896	.761	.649
Item 21 (C)	4.25	.97	4.36	.70	.495	.869	.713	.701
Item 22 (W)	4.58	.77	3.69	1.09	.529	.849	.616	.788

Note: C = competitiveness, W = win orientation, G = goal orientation.

Examining Baseline Models

A single-group CFA was employed in order to establish the baseline model, as a prerequisite for testing the factor invariance of the SF-SOQ across the two separate samples (athletes with and without disabilities). The baseline model represents the one that best fits the data in a parsimonious and substantive way. For this reason, in addition to the "a priori" specification of the three first-order factor SF-SOQ model, with the three factors of competitiveness, win orientation, goal orientation derived from the theory (Gill and Deeter, 1988), additional specifications of alternative models, as potential explanations of the observed data structure, were applied (Breckler, 1990; MacCallum, Wegener, Uchino, and Fabrigar, 1993; Mulaik, James, Van Alstine, Bennett, Lind, and Stillwell, 1989). Thus, three alternative models were examined: (a) a three first-order correlated factor model (FM_{3C}), according to the theory, (b) a three first-order uncorrelated factor model (FM_{3U}), and (c) a single first-order factor model (FM_1). The FM_{3U} model examined the level of independence of the SF-SOQ factors, whereas FM_1 model was specified in order to determine the unidimensionality of the SF-SOQ.

The item loadings of the FM_{3U} for athletes with disabilities ranged from .599 to .761 (mean factor loadings = .674), whereas the mean item loadings for the single first-order factor model (FM_1) was .579, with a range of .404 to .725 (table 1). The average off-diagonal standardized residual for the M_{3U} was 0.044, showing that the model fits the items. With regard to the group of athletes without disability, the item loadings for the hypothesized three first-order factor model (FM_{3U}), ranged from .316 to .732 (mean factor loadings = .558). The average off-diagonal standardized residual was 0.052, showing an acceptable fit of the model. In addition, the mean item loading was .408 for the single first-order factor model (FM_1), with the items loading values ranging from .333 to .657.

The intercorrelations among the SF-SOQ factors indicated differences between the two groups of athletes. The intercorrelations between: a) competitiveness and goal orientation, b) competitiveness and win orientation, and c) goal and win orientation were .711, .642, and .433 for the disability group, and .551, .681, and .566 for the able-body group of athletes respectively.

Table 2 provides the fit indices of the examined baseline models for the two groups of athletes. The testing procedure of the competing models, for both samples, indicated that the hypothesized three first-order correlated factor model provided adequate fit to the data, since absolute and incremental fit indices reached the cut-off criteria. On the other hand, the single first-order factor model (FM_1) and the uncorrelated three first-order factor model (FM_{3U}) indicated poor fit to the data, since none of the indices reached the criteria of acceptable fitting. In other words, the fit indices did not support either the unidimensionality of sport orientation, or the independence of the SF-SOQ factors. In addition, the χ^2 difference among the hypothesized three first-order factor model (FM_{3C}) and the competing models (FM_{3U}, FM_1), as well as the AIC, CAIC and PNFI values, indicated that the FM_{3C} is the best fitting and superior among the three alternative baseline models (table 2).

Table 2. Fit Indices of Three Alternative Models of the SF-SOQ, for Athletes With and Without Disabilities

	Absolute Fit Indices						Incremental Fit Indices			Parsimonious Fit Indices		
	Scaled χ^2	Unadjusted χ^2	df	χ^2/df	RMSEA (90% CI)	SRMR	NNFI	CFI	RCFI	AIC	CAIC	PNFI
Athletes Without Disabilities												
FM_{3C}	129.744	165.933	87	1.907	.060 (.046 - .074)	.065	.884	.905	.921	-6.067	-397.287	.727
FM_{3U}	213.589	274.069	90	3.045	.089 (.077 - .101)	.161	.744	.781	.777	94.069	-315.348	.609
FM_1	235.586	316.522	90	3.517	.099 (.087 - .111)	.085	.686	.730	.737	136.522	-182.133	.631
Athletes With Disabilities												
FM_{3C}	151.498	191.068	87	2.196	.066 (.053 - .079)	.054	.914	.929	.930	17.068	-383.956	.683
FM_{3U}	307.436	388.439	90	4.316	.110 (.099 - .122)	.229	.761	.795	.763	208.439	-206.414	.645
FM_1	322.310	412.719	90	4.586	.115 (.103 - .126)	.086	.742	.779	.746	232.719	-182.133	.570

Model Comparisons	$\Delta\chi^2$	Δ_{df}	p
Athletes Without Disabilities			
Model FM_{3C} vs Model FM_{3U}	83.845	3	<.001
Model FM_{3C} vs Model FM_1	105.842	3	<.001
Athletes With Disabilities			
Model FM_{3C} vs Model FM_{3U}	197.371	3	<.001
Model FM_{3C} vs Model FM_1	221.651	3	<.001

Note. Scaled χ^2 = Satorra-Bentler scaled test statistic; Unadjusted χ^2 = chi-square statistic for the model, df = degrees of freedom for the model, $\Delta\chi^2$ = χ^2 difference, Δ_{df} = df difference

FM_{3C} = three first-order factor model with correlated factors, FM_{3U} = three first-order factor model with uncorrelated factors, FM_1 = single first-order factor model.

Internal Consistency

The internal consistency of the SF-SOQ factors, using Cronbach's a coefficient alphas, were estimated (Cronbach, 1951). In the disability group, Cronbach alpha internal consistency indices were acceptable: .84 for competitiveness, .80 for win orientation, .76 for goal orientation, and .88 for the total SF-SOQ. The Cornbach's a for the group of athletes without disabilities were .71, .70, and .69, for the three factors of competitiveness, win orientation, and goal orientation respectively, and .80 for the total SF-SOQ. The inter-item correlations as well as the item-factor correlations indicated that the factors were internally consistent, for both groups of athletes.

MULTISAMPLE CFA ON THE SOQ: TESTS FOR MEASUREMENT INVARIANCE ACROSS THE TWO GROUPS

Adequate factor structure was provided for the "a priori" hypothesized SF-SOQ, for both groups of athletes. However, the well-fitting models do not mean that same parameters describe adequately responses of both groups. For the above reason, the acceptable factor structure (i.e., "loose" cross-validity; MacCallum, Roznowski, Mar, and Reith, 1994), was the first step. The following step was to test whether the variance-convariance matrices across the two groups, underlying the SF-SOQ items, were invariant. Based on the above, a series of multi-sample CFAs were conducted to test the invariance of the factor structure of the SF-SOQ baseline models, across the two groups of athletes. However, the invariant variance-covariance matrices ($M_{Var/Cov}$) does not indicate that measurement parameters are invariant since it provides contradictory results (Byrne, 1998; Li, Harmer, and Acick, 1996; Motl and Controy, 2001). Subsequently, the invariance of factor loadings (M_{Load}) and the equality of item uniquenesses (M_{Uniq}) were tested across groups. The results of nested tests of the measurement invariant SF-SOQ models, are presented in table 3.

In the first multisample analysis, the invariant variance-covariance matrices ($M_{Var/Cov}$) were tested across the two groups of athletes. The χ^2/df ratio, NNFI, CFI, SRMR, RMSEA, as well as 90% CI of the RMSEA supported the invariance of observed variance/covariance matrices for both groups. However, the invariant of variance/covariance does not indicate that the measurement parameters, across the two groups, are identical (Byrne, 1989; Li et al., 1996; Rock, Werts, and Flaugher, 1978). The equivalence of measured parameters across the two groups was examined, therefore, in order to support that group responses were similar or identical. For this reason, the invariance of item loadings and uniqueness was tested, in order to determine if the factor patterns were invariant. The item loadings (M_{Load}) and uniquenessess (M_{Uniq}) were equally constrained across the two groups. The fit indices of the two multisample analyses impaired the model fit, indicating that sport orientation factors are not equivalent between able and disable athletes. In other words, the results showed that the three correlated first-order factor SF-SOQ model was not identical between athletes with and without disabilities.

Table 3. Fit Indices of the SF-SOQ – Multi-sample Confirmatory Factor Analysis

	Unadjusted χ2	df	χ^2/df	NNFI	CFI	SRMR	RMSEA (90% CI)
$M_{Var/Cov}$	378.381	177	2.138	.896	.912	.066	.046 (.040 – .053)
M_{Load}	463.340	189	2.452	.867	.881	.103	.053 (.046 – .058)
M_{Uniq}	701.928	189	3.714	.752	.777	.107	.072 (.066 – .077)

Note. Unadjusted χ^2 = chi-square statistic for the hypothesized model, df = degrees of freedom for the hypothesized model

$MM_{Var/Cov}$ = factor variance – covariance constrained to be equal across athletes with and without disabilities, MM_{Load} = factor loadings constrained to be equal across athletes with and without disabilities, MM_{Uniq} = uniquenesses constrained to be equal across athletes with and without disabilities.

CONCLUSION

The purpose of the present study was twofold. The first was to provide the best fitting baseline factor structure of the SF-SOQ, for the two separate groups of athletes, with and without disabilities. The second purpose was to examine the invariant factor structure of the SF-SOQ, across the two samples, through multisample analyses. The results of confirmatory factor analysis (CFA) provided acceptable fit to the data, supporting the hypothesized, according to theory (Gill and Deeter, 1988), three first-order correlated factor model (FM_{3C}). The fit indices of the FM_{3C} reached the cutoff criteria, whereas the indices of the alternative models (FM_{3U} and FM_1) did not attain the acceptable values. In addition, Cronbach's a indices indicated that the SF-SOQ factors, as well as the SF-SOQ total score, were internally reliable and consistent.

Subsequent analyses revealed that the sport orientation structure was noninvariant across the two groups of athletes. The multisample CFA revealed that the hypothesized three-factor structure of the SF-SOQ is nonequivalent between athletes with and without disabilities. Conclusively, the two groups do not have an identical conceptualization of the examined sport orientation factors (competitiveness, goal orientation and win orientation). The above finding suggests that the SF-SOQ does not measure the same underlying construct across the two groups. In other words, certain items of the SF-SOQ varied, in their relationship to the sport orientation construct, meaning that these items were perceived and interpreted differently across the two groups.

The sample specific validity and reliability evidence theory (Sherrill and O'Connor, 1999; Yun and Ulrich, 2002), offered the solid theoretical background to examine the construct validity of the instrument for athletes with disabilities. Further, previous research findings supported the testing of the construct validity of the instruments used to describe the sport orientations of individuals with disabilities (Page et al., 2000; Zoerink and Wilson, 1995). Zoerink and Wilson (1995) examined the sport orientations of individuals with intellectual disabilities and stated that their findings 'may be limited by the ability of the subjects to understand the constructs tested' (p. 40). Page et al. (2000) examined athletes competing at the Paralympic trials and stated that it is essential to examine sport orientations with measures specifically designed to be administered to athletes with disabilities. Based on the above, Skordilis et al. (2001) used exploratory factor analysis and found that the competitiveness and goal orientation factors differed in a sample of athletes with physical disabilities (basketball players and marathoners), compared to the university and high school samples reported by Gill and Deeter (1988). Later, Skordilis et al. (2002) used confirmatory factor analysis to examine a hypothetical, five factor SOQ model. The CFA did not adequately explain the five factor structure, leaving the area open for future research. Finally, Skordilis and Stavrou (2005) used confirmatory factor analysis and found that a short-form of the instrument (SF-SOQ) was valid for basketball athletes with physical disabilities. The SF-SOQ provided also acceptable Cronbach's alpha reliability coefficients, suggesting that it may be perceived as a valid and reliable measuring instrument describing the sport orientations of athletes with disabilities.

Skordilis and Stavrou (2005) further tested the factorial structure of the SF-SOQ across gender. Specifically, it was examined whether the conceptualization of sport achievement orientation was similar between men and women basketball athletes with physical disabilities. The researchers found that the sport achievement orientation construct was similar between the two groups of men and women, suggesting that meaningful comparisons across gender may be undertaken in the future. Skordilis and Stavrou (2005) concluded that future research is important to examine additional sample characteristics such as age, competitive level, and experience of athletes' participation. Further, it may be of interest to examine the factor structure of the SF-SOQ among athletes who differ in a variety of settings, such as professional *vs* non-professional, experienced *vs* non experienced, adults *vs* non adults, etc.

Overall, the present findings, concerning the disability sample, are in agreement with the literature. The construct validity of the SF-SOQ was tested and was proved to be a valid and reliable measuring instrument for the examination of sport orientations in athletes with physical disabilities. Researchers may feel confident in the future to use the SF-SOQ as a valid and reliable multidimensional construct, with the three correlated factors of competitiveness, win orientation and goal orientation.

Concerning the first research objective, the present findings are both in agreement and disagreement with the able-body literature. Gill and Deeter (1988) developed the sport orientation measure and stated that there was sufficient evidence of validity and reliability. Later, Gill et al. (1988) reported divergent and convergent validity evidence, while Kang et al. (1990) reported adequate findings of discriminant validity. However, the confirmatory factor analytic results of Kang et al. (1990) revealed Goodness of Fit Index-GFI below the acceptable range (GFI = .735), suggesting that further construct validity evidence was required.

Lerner and Locke (1995) examined, among others, the sport orientations in a group of undergraduate students. The researchers found that the sport orientation measure was: a) related to performance, and b) valid for the sample examined. Marsh (1994b) however, examined the similarity of several measuring instruments, and stated that future researchers need to be aware of jingle and jangle fallacy when using several measuring instruments. The researcher concluded that 'there is a need in sport psychology, as well as other areas of psychological and educational research, to evaluate more critically the interpretations of psychological measures using a construct validity approach' (p. 377).

Wakayama et al, (2004) used exploratory factor analysis to develop the sport achievement orientation questionnaire, in a sample of Japanese athletes. The researchers found that the Japanese version of the measure incorporated three separate but interrelated factors, with sufficient validity and reliability evidence. Finally, Karteroliotis (1995) examined the construct validity of the sport orientation measure in a sample of university students from Greece. The researcher found, through confirmatory factor analysis, that the fit indices departed from the appropriate range. Karteroliotis (1995) concluded that further item analysis is required 'to determine whether specific items are contributing only to the scales they were intended to measure' (p. 5).

Overall, the development of the sport orientation measure (Gill and Deeter, 1988) allowed researchers, in the able-body literature, to present validity evidence in different populations and settings. According to the previous findings, only evidence of discriminant, divergent, and convergent validity were reported. Adequate construct validity findings, however, based on factor analytic methods, were only evident in the study of Wakayama et al. (2004). The present findings supported our research objective, since sufficient construct validity and internal consistency evidence for the SF-SOQ was found, in our group of athletes without disabilities. Therefore, the SF-SOQ may be used, if reconfirmed in the future, in the able-body literature too, as a valid instrument to describe the sport orientations of athletes without disabilities.

The noninvariace findings of the SF-SOQ model revealed that certain items had different meaning across the two groups of athletes (with and without disabilities). This finding is in agreement with Skordilis et al. (2002) who conducted a confirmatory factor analysis in the responses of adult athletes with physical disabilities. The researchers stated that only eight competitive and four goal orientation items were grouped under their respective factors. More specifically, the major factor of competitiveness appeared 'to be a more complex entity for wheelchair athletes than for able-bodied athletes and was divided into two separate elements' (p. 205). The first element was named self-referenced competitiveness, in which the participants compared themselves through internal aspects of excellence. The second element was named other-referenced competitiveness, were participants exhibited excellence through external aspects in sports competition. Skordilis et al. (2002) concluded that the division of the major factor of competitiveness 'is logical when the diversity of wheelchair and able-bodied groups of athletes is considered' (p. 205).

In a later study, Skordilis and Stavrou (2005) conducted multisample CFA in male and female athletes with physical disabilities. The similar SF-SOQ factorial structure was perceived important since it was meaningless to discuss differences between groups (e.g., males and females), if the SF-SOQ did not measure the same exact construct for each. Skordilis and Stavrou (2005) supported the invariance of the SF-SOQ, suggesting that meaningful gender comparisons may be undertaken in the future for athletes with disabilities.

Further, Page, O'Connor, and Peterson (2001) examined the factors underlying achievement motivation in a group of elite athletes with physical disabilities. The researchers used interview questions based on the sport achievement orientation model of Gill and Deeter (1988). The qualitative thematic analysis revealed that the major factors for participating in competitive sports were the: a) social outlet, b) promoting fitness, c) delaying the effects of disability and d) affirming competence and being a serious competitor. The above factors may be perceived as unique in the disability literature and certainly differ from those reported by Gill and Deeter (1988). Overall, the findings of Page et al. (2001) may explain, to an extend, the present differences concerning the SF-SOQ structure of athletes with and without disabilities.

According to our literature review, no published research studies were found using multisample analysis, to examine the sport orientations across separate samples of able-bodied individuals. Therefore, we only related our findings to previous reports in the able-bodied literature, using a similar construct, named the Task and Ego Orientation in Sport Questionnaire-TEOSQ (Duda, 1989). Li, Harmer, Duncan, Duncan, Acock, and Yamamoto (1998) for example, examined two samples of college students for cross validation purposes. The researchers found that, for both samples (calibration and validation), the psychometric properties of the TEOSQ items were consistent with theory. The items were grouped around two orthogonal factors, named task orientation and ego orientation, suggesting that the TEOSQ may be applied with confidence in the college student population. Li et al. (1996) examined the measurement invariance and latent mean structure of the TEOSQ, in male and female college students. The researchers found that the two factors of task and ego orientation were similarly conceptualized according to gender. Li et al. (1996) concluded that meaningful comparisons across gender may be obtained in the future. Finally, Chi and Duda (1995) examined the TEOSQ invariance across four separate samples of: a) intercollegiate athletes, b) college students, c) high school athletes and d) junior high school sport participants. The researchers found that the factorial structure of the TEOSQ was not invariant across the four groups, meaning that they possessed a different conceptualization of task and ego orientation. Chi and Duda (1995) recommended that 'both single-group and multi-sample CFAs must be employed to examine the psychometric properties of other established or recently developed sport psychology assessments' (p. 97).

Overall, the SF-SOQ is a valid and reliable measuring instrument for the examination of sport orientations, separate for athletes with and without disabilities. The SF-SOQ model, however, is not similarly perceived from the above groups. Meaningful comparisons, therefore, across disability status, may not be undertaken in the future. Possibly, the new way to address the above issue is the development of a new sport orientation construct, taking under consideration the specific attributes of both groups. Through the four separate steps of Yun and Ulrich (2002) for collecting construct related validity evidence (a: define the construct, b: formulate hypothesis, c: run the statistics and d: gather empirical evidence to support hypothesis), we may lead to the sport orientation measure that will allow future researchers to examine the differences across disability status.

REFERENCES

Akaike, H. (1987). Factor analysis and AIC. *Psychometrika, 52*, 317-332.

Acevedo, E. O., Dzewaltowski, D. A., Gill, D. L., and Noble, J. M. (1992). Cognitive orientations of ultramarathoners. *The Sport Psychologist, 6*, 242-252.

Bentler, P.M., and Wu, E.J.C. (2002). *EQS 6 for Windows: User's guide*. Encino, CA: Multivariate Software.

Bentler, P. M. (1995). *EQS Structural Equations Program manual*. Los Angeles, CA: BMDP Statistical Software.

Bentler, P. M., and Bonett, D. G. (1980). Significance tests and goodness of fit in the analysis of covariance structures. *Psychological Bulletin, 88*, 588-606.

Bollen, K. A. (1989). *Structural equations with latent variables*. New York: Wiley.

Bordogan, H. (1987). Model selection and Akaike's information criteria: The general theory and its analytical extensions. *Psychometrika, 52*, 345-370.

Bradley, J. V. (1982). The insidious L-shaped distribution. *Journal of the Psychonomic Society, 20*, 85-88.

Breckler, S. J. (1990). Applications of covariance structure modeling in psychology: Cause for concern? *Psychological Bulletin, 107*, 260-273.

Browne, M. W., and Cudeck, R. (1993). Alternative ways of assessing model fit. In K. A. Bollen and J. S. Long (Eds.), *Structural equation models* (pp. 136-162). Newbury Park, CA: Sage.

Byrne, B. M. (1989) *A primer of LISREL: basic applications and programming for confirmatory factor analytic models*. New York: Springer-Verlag.

Byrne, B. M. (1994). *Structural equation modeling with EQS and EQS/Windows: Basic concepts, applications, and programming*. Thousand Oaks, CA: Sage.

Byrne, B. M. (1998). *Structural equation modeling with LISREL, PRELIS, and SIMPLIS: Basic concepts, applications, and programming*. New York: Lawrence Erlbaum.

Byrne, B. M., and Watkins, D. (2003). The issue of measurement invariance revisited. *Journal of Cross-Cultural Psychology, 34*, 15-175.

Chi, L., and Duda, J. L. (1995). Multi-sample confirmatory factor analysis of the Task and Ego Orientation in Sport Questionnaire. *Research Quarterly for Exercise and Sport, 66*, 91-98.

Cronbach, L. J. (1951). Coefficient alpha and the internal structure of tests. *Psychometrika, 16*, 297-334.

Duda, J. L. (1989). Relationship between task and ego orientation and the perceived purpose of sport among high school athletes. *Journal of Sport and Exercise Psychology, 11*, 318-335.

Finkenberg, M. E., Moode, F. M., and DiNucci, J. M. (1998). Analysis of sport orientation of female collegiate athletes. *Perceptual and Motor Skills, 86*, 647-650.

Gill, D. L., and Deeter, T. E. (1988). Development of the Sport Orientation Questionnaire. *Research Quarterly, 59*, 191-202.

Gill, D. L., and Dzewaltowski, D. (1988). Competitive orientations among intercollegiate athletes: Is winning the only thing? *The Sport Psychologist, 2*, 212-221.

Gill, D. L., Dzewaltowski, D., and Deeter, T. E. (1988). The relationship of competitiveness and achievement orientation to participation in sport and non-sport activities. *Journal of Sport and Exercise Psychology, 10*, 139-150.

Hoyle, R. H., and Panter, A. T. (1995). Writing about structural equation models. In R. H. Hoyle (Ed.), *Structural equation modeling: Concepts, issues and applications* (pp. 158 – 176). Thousand Oaks, CA: Sage.

Hu, L., and Bentler, P. M. (1999). Cutoff criteria for the fit indexes in covariance structure analysis: Conventional criteria versus new alternatives. *Structural Equation Modeling, 6*, 1-55.

Hutchinson, S. R., and Olmos, A. (1998). Behavior of descriptive fit indices in confirmatory factor analysis using ordered categorical data. *Structural Equation Modeling, 5*, 344-364.

James, L. R., Mulaik, S. A., and Brett, J. M. (1982). *Causal analysis: Assumptions, models, and data*. Beverly Hills, CA: Sage.

Jöreskog, K. G. (1969). A general approach to confirmatory maximum likelihood factor analysis. *Psychometrika, 34*, 183-202.

Jöreskog, K. G., and Sörbom, D. (1993). *LISREL 8: Structural modeling with the SIMPLES command language*. Hillsdale, NJ: Erlbaum.

Kahn, J. H. (2006). Factor analysis in counselling psychology research, training, and practice: Principles, advances, and applications. *The Counseling Psychologist, 34*, 684-718.

Kang, L., Gill, D. L., Acevedo, E. O., and Deeter, T. E. (1990) Competitive orientations among athletes and nonathletes in Taiwan. *International Journal of Sport Psychology, 21*, 146-157.

Karteroliotis, C. E. (1995). *The Greek version of Sport Orientation Questionnaire*. Paper presented at the IV European Congress of Psychology, Athens, Greece.

Kelloway, E. K. (1998). *Using LISREL for structural equation modeling: A researcher's guide*. Thousand Oaks, CA: Sage.

Kleppinger, A. (1995). *Gender differences in goal orientation and sport orientation*. Unpublished master's thesis, Springfield College, Springfield, MA.

Kline, R. B. (1998). *Principles and practice of structural equation modeling*. New York: Guilford Press.

Lerner, B. S., and Locke, E. A. (1995). The effects of goal setting, self-efficacy, competition, and personal traits on the performance of an endurance task. *Journal of Sport and Exercise Psychology, 17*, 138-152.

Li, F., Harmer, P., and Acock, A. (1996). The Task and Ego Orientation in Sport Questionnaire: Construct equivalence and mean differences across gender. *Research Quarterly for Exercise and Sport, 68*, 228-238.

Li, F., Harmer, P., Duncan, T. E., Duncan, S. C., Acock, A., and Yamamoto, T. (1998). Confirmatory factor analysis of the Task and Ego Orientation in Sport Questionnaire with cross-validation. *Research Quarterly for Exercise and Sport, 69*, 276-283.

Long, J. S. (1983). *Confirmatory factor analysis*. Newbury Park, CA: Sage.

MacCallum, R., Roznowski, M., Mar, C. M., and Reith, J. V. (1994). Alternative strategies for cross-validation of covariance structure models. *Multivariate Behavioral Research, 29*, 1-32.

MacCallum, R. C., Wegener, D. T., Uchino, B. N., and Fabrigar, L. R. (1993). The problem of equivalent models in applications of covariance structure analysis. *Psychological Bulletin, 114*, 185-199.

Mardia, K. V. (1970). Measures of multivariate skewness and kurtosis with application. *Biometrika, 57*, 519-530.

Marsh, H. W. (1993). The multidimensional structure of physical fitness: Invariance over gender and age. *Research Quarterly for Exercise and Sport, 64*, 256-273.

Marsh, H. W. (1994a). Confirmatory factor analysis models of factorial invariance: a multifaceted approach. *Structural Equation Modeling, 1*, 5-34.

Marsh, H.W. (1994b). Sport motivation orientations: Beware of jingle-jangle fallacies. *Journal of Sport and Exercise Psychology, 16*, 365-380.

Marsh, H. W., Balla, J. R., and McDonald, R. P. (1988). Goodness-of-fit indices in confirmatory factor analysis: The effect of sample size. *Psychological Bulletin, 103*, 391-410.

Martin, J. J., Adams-Mushett, C., and Smith, K. L. (1995). Athletic identity and sport orientation of adolescent swimmers with disabilities. *Adapted Physical Activity Quarterly, 12*, 113-123.

Martin, J. J., and Gill, D. L. (1991). The relationships among competitive orientation, sport-confidence, self-efficacy, anxiety, and performance. *Journal of Sport and Exercise Psychology, 13*, 149-159.

Martin, J. J., and Gill, D. L. (1995). Competitive orientation, self-efficacy and goal importance in Filipino marathoners. *International Journal of Sport Psychology, 26*, 348-358.

McClelland, D. C. (1961). *The achieving society*. New York, NY: Free Press.

McDonald, R. P., and Marsh, H. W. (1990). Choosing a multivariate model: Noncentrality and goodness-of-fit. *Psychological Bulletin, 107*, 247-255.

Motl, R. W., and Conroy, D. E. (2001). The Social Physique Anxiety Scale: Cross validation, factorial invariance, and latent mean structure. *Measurement in Physical Education and Exercise Science, 5*, 81-95.

Mulaik, S. A., James, L. R., Alstine, J. V., Bennett, N., Lind, S., and Stillwell, C. D. (1989). Evaluation of goodness-of-fit indices for structural equation models. *Psychological Bulletin, 105*, 430-445.

Olson, U. H., Foss, T., Troye, S. V., and Howell, R. D. (2000). The performance of ML, GLS, and WLS estimation in structural equation modelling under conditions of misspecification and nonnormality. *Structural Equation Modeling, 7*, 557-595.

Page, S., O'Connor, E., and Peterson, K. (2001). Leaving the disability ghetto. A qualitative study of factors underlying achievement motivation among athletes with disabilities. *Journal of Sport and Social Issues, 25*, 40-55.

Page, S. J., O'Connor, E. A. and Wayda, V. K. (2000). Exploring competitive orientation in a group of athletes participating in the 1996 Paralympic trials. *Perceptual and Motor Skills, 91*, 491-502.

Pedhazur, E., and Pedhazur-Schmelkin, L. (1991). *Measurement, design, and analysis: An integrated approach*. Hillsdale, NJ: Erlbaum.

Quintana, S. M., and Maxwell, S. E. (1999). Implications of recent developments in structural equation modeling for counseling psychology. *The Counseling Psychologist, 27*, 485-527.

Rock, D. A. Werts, C. E., and Flaugher, R. L. (1978). The use of analysis of covariance structures for comparing the psychometric properties of multiple variables across populations. *Multivariate Behavioral Research, 13*, 403-418.

Sawilowsky, S. (2000). Reliability: Rejoinder to Thompson and Vacha-Haase. *Educational and Psychological Measurement, 60*, 196-200.

Sherrill, C., and O'Connor, J. (1999). Guidelines for improving adapted physical activity research. *Adapted Physical Activity Quarterly, 16*, 1-8.

Skordilis, E. K. (1998). *Competitive, goal, and sport orientations of wheelchair athletes*. Unpublished doctoral dissertation, Springfield College, Springfield, MA.

Skordilis, E. K., Gavriilidis, A., Charitou, S., and Asonitou, K. (2003). Comparison of sport achievement orientation of male professional, amateur, and wheelchair basketball athletes. *Perceptual and Motor Skills, 97*, 483-490.

Skordilis, E. K., Koutsouki, D., Asonitou, K., Evans, E., Jensen, B., and Wall, K. (2001). Sport orientations and goal perspectives of wheelchair athletes. *Adapted Physical Activity Quarterly, 18*, 304-315.

Skordilis, E. K., Sherrill, C., Yilla, A., Koutsouki, D., and Stavrou, N. A. (2002). Use of the Sport Orientation Questionnaire with wheelchair athletes: examination of evidence for validity. *Perceptual and Motor Skills, 95*, 197-207.

Skordilis, E. K., and Stavrou, N. A. (2005). Sport orientation model for wheelchair basketball athletes. *Perceptual and Motor Skills, 100*, 1081-1096.

Steinger, J. H. (1990). Structural model evaluation and modification: an interval estimation approach. *Multivariate Behavioral Research, 25*, 173-180.

Swain, A. B., and Jones, J. G. (1992). Relationships between sport achievement orientation and competitive state anxiety. *The Sport Psychologist, 6*, 42-54.

Tabachnick, B. G., and Fidell, L. S. (2006). *Using multivariate statistics* (5th ed.). New York: Pearson Education.

Thomas, J., and Nelson, J. (1996) *Research methods in physical activity* (3rd ed.). Champaign, IL: Human Kinetics.

Wakayama, H., Watanabe, E., Murai, G., and Inomata, K. (2004). Development of the sport achievement orientation questionnaire for Japanese athletes by exploratory factor analysis. *Perceptual and Motor Skills, 98*, 533-541.

West, S. G., Finch, J. F., and Curran, P. J. (1995). Structural equation models with non-normal variables: Problems and remedies. In R. H. Hoyle (Ed.), *Structural equation modeling: Concepts, issues, and applications* (pp. 56-75). Thousand Oaks, CA: Sage.

Yun, J., and Ulrich, D. (2002). Estimating measurement validity: A tutorial. *Adapted Physical Activity Quarterly, 19*, 32-47.

Zoerink, D. A., and Wilson, J. (1995). The competitive disposition: Views of athletes with mental retardation. *Adapted Physical Activity Quarterly, 12*, 34-42.

In: Psychological Tests and Testing Research Trends   ISBN: 978-1-60021-569-8
Editor: Paul M. Goldfarb, pp. 231-249   © 2007 Nova Science Publishers, Inc.

Chapter 11

ASSESSMENT OF PROSPECTIVE MEMORY: A REVIEW OF DATA FROM LABORATORY-BASED PARADIGMS AND ECOLOGICALLY VALID TASKS

Raymond C. K. Chan[1] , Tianxiao Yang[2], Ya Wang[2,3] and Yonghong Qi[2]

[1] Neuropsychology and Applied Cognitive Neuroscience Laboratory, Institute of Psychology, Chinese Academy of Sciences, Beijing, China
[2] Neuropsychology and Applied Cognitive Neuroscience Laboratory, Department of Psychology, Sun Yat-Sen University, Guangzhou, China
[3] Life Science Faculty, Sun Yat-Sen University, Guangzhou, China

ABSTRACT

The present chapter aims to review the assessment of prospective memory (PM) in healthy subjects and clinical populations. In particular, the purposes of this chapter are three-fold: (1) To evaluate the pros and cons of different types of PM tasks: event-based, time-based and activity-based, (2) To discuss the issue of ecological validity in clinical practice, (3) To evaluate the effect sizes of PM deficits in patients with neurological disorders. Moreover, we also illustrate the potential aging effect on PM using both experimental-based and ecologically valid paradigms. The present findings provide us a comprehensive view about aging effect by comparing three age groups: young, young old and older old. Three different types of laboratory-based PM showed different aging patterns, event-based PM tasks show a general decline pattern while aging effect of time-based PM only obvious when comparing the young and the young old. Activity-based PM did not show any aging effect, which implies different aging process of three types of PM. However, both executive function and retrospective memory failed to show the relationship with PM with one exception—one high cognitive demanding ecological valid time-based PM (open-and-close door in hotel test), was found consistent significant correlations with executive function, suggesting that executive function is not needed in PM unless PM performance is difficult or competing with other tasks for cognitive resources.

Keywords: prospective memory, cognitive process, executive function, healthy aging, neurological disorders.

INTRODUCTION

Prospective memory (PM) is a brand new concept that points to the future instead of remembering from the past, which is different from conventional retrospective memory. Millions of questions emerge when we consider it as a research topic. We may want to know the nature of PM and how it functions? In what aspect does PM differ from other types of memory, for example, retrospective memory? Is it just a component of Executive function? Is there any aging effect on PM performances? More important, what role does it play in clinical cases like Alzheimer's disease (AD) and traumatic brain injury (TBI)? In this chapter, we attempt to address the core issues of PM step by step, particularly focusing on the psychological testing of PM in healthy and clinical populations.

DEFINITIONS OF PROSPECTIVE MEMORY

Prospective memory (PM) is defined as remembering to perform an intended action at a particular point in the future (Craik, 1986; Kliegel, Martin, McDaniel and Einstein, 2002). Some (e.g., Kvavilashvili and Ellis, 1996; Meacham and Leiman, 1975) further refer PM to be a memory to represent the realization of intentions that must be delayed over a fixed period of time, maybe minutes, hours, or days. Therefore, it differs from retrospective memory (e.g., recognition of past information) that there are no external cues or prompts to trigger a controlled search of memory (Einstein and McDaniel, 1990, 1996). Figure 1 demonstrates the essence of a PM task, as suggested by Ellis and Kvavilashvili (2000). First, there must be a delay between encoding and retrieval of the prospective task. Second, there should be no explicit prompt provided when the event to act arises. Third, participants should engage in an ongoing task with an interruption in between the whole process of performing the prospective task.

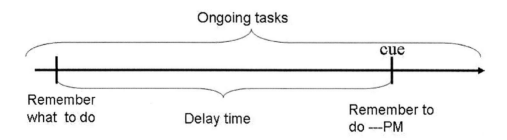

Figure 1. Operational definition of Prospective Memory.

According to these criteria, PM is considered to be overlapping with retrospective memory (recall and recognition) but is more complex. It may also involve cognitive components similar to those of executive function, e.g., intention organization, monitoring of intention. Although there has been a steady increase in the number of studies devoted to understanding the cognitive processes and neural mechanisms supporting PM, mainly in the aging populations, relatively few studies have been specifically conducted to examine the reliability and validity of these so-called PM tasks.

THREE TYPES OF PM: EVENT-BASED, TIME-BASED AND ACTIVITY-BASED

Basically, PM task can further be classified to three types according to different particular points of future. These are the event-based, time-based and activity-based PM tasks. Event-based PM involves the subject's ability to perform an intended action when meeting certain person or the objects (acting as cues), e.g., remembering to return a book when meeting someone. Time-based PM captures the subject's ability to remember an intended action and to perform the corresponding action at an appropriate time in the future, e.g., have an appointment with someone at eight o'clock. Finally, activity-based PM is specifically designed to assess whether the subject carries out certain action that coincides with the end of an ongoing activity, e.g., turning off the gas after cooking. Different paradigms, ranging from experimental tasks to everyday life subjective complaints, could be used to examine these different types of PM function in both healthy and clinical populations. We will illustrate the pros and cons of these paradigms separately.

LABORATORY-BASED PARADIGMS OF PM TASKS

The laboratory-based paradigms used for studying PM performance were mainly derived from the dual-task paradigm designed by Einstein and McDaniel (1990). In their experiment, the participants were told the main aim was the ongoing task—short-term memory. They emphasized the ongoing tasks in order to lessen the importance of PM function throughout the experiment. After the short-term memory instructions, participants were told that the experiment had a secondary interest in their ability to remember to do something in the future. They had to press a response key on the computer keyboard whenever a particular target event occurred. Here, we can see the basic rationale of the laboratory-based PM task: PM tasks embedded in the ongoing task.

However, experiment design requires exquisite control over any confounding variables, either by controlling them or setting them as independent variables. Several factors warrant discussion here. First, performance of PM task itself can be influenced by its complexity (the amount of PM tasks) (Einstein, Holland, McDaniel and Guynn, 1992) and unfamiliarity of PM (Einstein and McDaniel, 1990). Second, cues of PM can be of great importance, like cues detection (McDaniel, Guynn, Einstein and Breneiser, 2004), cue accessibility and cue sensitivity (West, Bowry and Krompinger, 2006), different difficulty levels of initial retrieval (Einstein, McDaniel, Manzi, Cochran, and Baker, 2000). Third, the environment of PM, that is, non-PM factors may also influence the PM performance. For example, ongoing task demands may affect the performance of PM tasks, concerning people's limited processing ability in certain time (Einstein, Smith, McDaniel and Shaw, 1997; Einstein, McDaniel,

Thomas, Mayfield, and Shank, 2005). Moreover, subjective factors like motivation or PM importance to the task can be one of the influencing factors (Kliegel, Martin, McDaniel and Einstein, 2004).

As mentioned above, controlling the factors is important but may not be perfect. One accusation of dual-tasks paradigm (by Einstein and McDaniel) is using short-term memory as ongoing task. When retrospective memory serves as ongoing tasks of PM, the aging effects of retrospective memory became larger, due to the interference of PM (Henry et al, 2004). Alternatively, PM may also be affected by retrospective memory ongoing tasks. In this situation, exploring of the relationship between retrospective memory and PM can be inaccurate. Moreover, experimental paradigms are different from naturalistic PM task, particularly the ongoing task. In addressing this limitation, some studies used word task – a task more akin to everyday life task – to compensate the insufficiency of ecological validity of laboratory-based paradigm.

Most recently, the advance of neuroimaging techniques make the locations of neural substrates of PM feasible. Okuda et al. (1998) and Burgess et al. (2001, 2003a, 2003b) demonstrated that the BA10 in the prefrontal cortex, including medial and lateral rostral regions and right lateral prefrontal and inferior parietal regions, may be the locations contributing most to a proper PM function. Most tests in these studies are either simple numeration tasks or perception judgment tasks to rule out language interference. Our team adapted this paradigm in a subsequent study among the healthy elder people (Yang, Chan, Lin, and Zheng, submitted). In so doing, we deleted the prejudge process by asking the participants judged the different directions of arrow in the middle without the pre-judge of the two bars (the process demonstrated in figure 2). The appearance of PM task was reduced from 20% to 5% percent, preventing repetition effect. The findings showed that both laboratory event-based PM performance (p<0.001) and ecological valid event-based PM performance (p<0.05) indicated a significant aging effect. None of other PM tests revealed aging effect. However, it is worth noticing that more executive function and retrospective memory related to a complex ecologically valid PM test (Item of open-close door Hotel, cognitive demanding) than related to other PM tests, suggesting executive function only involves when the task is highly demanding for cognitive control.

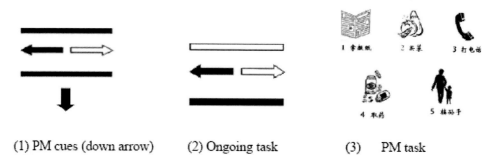

(1) PM cues (down arrow)   (2) Ongoing task   (3)   PM task

Figure 2. Laboratory event-based PM adopted from a recent study (Adapted from Yang et al., 2006).

ECOLOGICAL VALID PM TASKS

We have argued that the findings generated from laboratory-based PM may not be directly translated to everyday life scenarios. Actually, there may be cases that participants score well or within the normal range of PM tasks may still complain a lot of their everyday life PM functions. This may be due to the fact that the realization of delayed intentions or the creation of an intention to do something at a future time is largely self-initiated in real life scenarios, whereas most of these "markers" are triggered by experimental cues in the laboratory-based tasks. In short, the ecological validity and the predictive validity of these laboratory-based PM tasks should be interpreted cautiously. Therefore, another approach to studying PM function in clinical groups is to adopt a more ecologically valid paradigm or using a simulated environment to elicit any PM deficits.

In early years, PM was studied in a naturalistic environment (West, 1988; Poon and Schaffer, 1982; Dobbs and Rule,1987).Typical procedure was to ask young and old participants to call the experimenter on the telephone at a particular time one evening , to send in a postcard on a specified date, or to return a questionnaire at certain time. Most of studies focused on time-based PM tasks, in which the time interval is an important variable, termed delay, the intention formation and the execution of the action. However, in one study (Nigro and Cicogna, 2000), results seemed contradictory against our intuitive notion that longer the delay, worse the remembering to act. The delay affected neither the occurrence of remembering nor its accuracy. However, this approach has been criticized of having no control over the interval time (Poon and Schaffer, 1982; Dobbs and Rule, 1987; West, 1988; Einstein and McDaniel.1990). For example, when the delay time intervals last for several days, the elders may write a note or ask the family to remind them for completing the delayed task. All these external factors may facilitate a better "remembering" performance of the PM task

Another form of ecological valid PM test was devised from the concept of multiple-task test. For example, in the sub-task of door opening and closing of the Hotel Test (Manly et al., 2002), participant is required to remember to press buttons in order to open and close the garage at a pre-set time frame. The Rivermead Behavioral Memory Test (RBMT; Wilson, Cockburn, and Baddeley, 1985) also comprises two subtests of PM. One is specifically designed to capture activity-based PM performance (remembering taking back a belonging in the end of the whole test).The other is used to assess the time-based and event-based PM performance (remembering to ask certain questions when the alarm rings twenty minutes later). The clinical sensitivity and psychometric properties of this RMBT has been demonstrated rendering its wide applications (e.g., Cockburn and Smith, 1988, 1991, 1994; Evans andWilson, 1992; Huppert and Beardsall, 1993; Wisemann, Ratcliff, Chase, Laporte, Robertson, and Colantonio, 2000). However, we should be very careful when using these simulated daily-working tasks as PM evaluation in clinical settings because results may be totally different from simple PM task that embeds in other tests.

Therefore, some types of self-report questionnaires have been developed to evaluate everyday life subjective complaints of PM function, e.g., Prospective Memory Questionnaire (PMQ) (Hannon et al.,1990). PMQ is a 74-item questionnaire capturing for 5 dimensions of PM: long-term episodic tasks, short-term episodic tasks, long-term habitual tasks, short-term habitual tasks, and techniques to assist recall. These types of questionnaires have been commonly used in clinical settings for examining the efficacy of intervention programme (e,g., Sohlberg, White, Evans and Mateer, 1992a, 1992b; Raskin and Sohlberg, 1996; Smith, Della, Logie and Maylor, 2000; Heffernan Ling and Scholey, 2001). However, whether self-rating of prospective memory can best reflect the actual performance warrants further discussion (Roche, Fleming and Shum, 2002; Zeintl, Kliegel, Rast and Zimprich D, 2006).

RELATIONSHIPS TO EXECUTIVE FUNCTIONS

When exploring the relationship between PM and other cognitive aspect, like retrospective memory or executive function, the whole experimenting process will include various tests. The arrangement of the sequence is important. One most important part of PM is its delay. The choice of tests during PM intention and action should be well considered especially when other types of PM test are also included. If the tests during delay of event-based PM and time-based PM were different in cognitive demanding, different level of rehearsal in delay may be suspected. We should be very careful about the order of tests implementation. For example, when assessing a time-based PM, the time cue may coincide with other neuropsychological tests involving time perception, and thus confound the ultimate outcome.

AGING EFFECT ON THE SUBTYPES OF PM TASKS

The aging effect on the PM performances is still not clear. According to the literature, performance of event-based PM will be intact when comparing the young with the young-old. However, a recent meta-analysis also found that event-based PM did decline with advancing age ($r = -0.34$) (Henry et al., 2004). The contradictory results made the predication more difficult. In order to illustrate the aging effect on the three subtypes of PM tasks, we have compared the PM performances between young adults, young-old and older-old people using the experimental paradigms and ecological tests we discussed above (Yang et al., submitted). We found that there was a main aging effect on both the experimental event- and time-based PM tasks showed significant declining pattern across all age groups [$F(84) = 37.69$, $p < 0.001$], particularly between young adult and young-old ($p < 0.05$). No significant aging effect was found in the experimental activity-based PM task. Similar significant findings were found in the ecological test (Hotel Test) between the young adults and young old ($p < 0.001$) but not between young-old and older-old.

On the contrary, there was a different pattern observed in the retrospective memory performances in these age sub-groups. There was aging effect on the logical memory (semantic memory) ($p < 0.001$) and visual reproduction (visual memory) ($p < 0.05$) between young adults and young-old participants, but not between young-old and older-old participants. However, both performances of visual memory showed significant decline across all age sub-groups. We would then notice that there is a different declining pattern between PM and retrospective memory, suggesting some basic differences between these two types of memory. Nevertheless, the aging pattern of logical memory is quite similar to that of

ecologically valid test of PM (i.e., a time-based PM sub-test in the Hotel Test), which is highly cognitive demanding.

REHABILITATION ASSESSMENT OF PM

Up to the present moment, very few studies have focused on PM rehabilitation and most of these studies were concerned with the PM performances in patients with traumatic brain injury whose PM performance seemed to be impaired. It is also not currently possible to perform a comprehensive assessment of PM ability in a rehabilitation setting because no standardized test is yet available. The probable reason for the paucity of PM assessment material is that it is difficult to devise a comprehensive assessment that does not require testing in real-life situations with all the logistical problems that entails. As mentioned above briefly, the most relevant test is the Rivermead Behavioural Memory Test (RBMT) (Wilson et al., 1985), which was developed as a method of identifying everyday memory problems. However, only two, or possibly three, items in the RBMT relate to prospective memory, an insufficient number on which to base a realistic assessment of prospective memory ability.

At present, PM questionnaires are commonly used in clinical PM assessments, such as Prospective Memory and Retrospective Memory Questionnaire (PRMQ) (Smith et al.2000), Prospective Memory Questionnaire (PMQ) (Fleming, 2005), Comprehensive assessment of Prospective Memory (CAPM) (Waugh, 1999). The PRMQ is a 16-item questionnaire which was developed to allow participants to rate the frequency with which they make particular types of memory errors. Participants rated how often each type of memory failure occurred on a 5-point scale: Very Often, Quite Often, Sometimes, Rarely, Never. The questions came from eight categories reflecting different aspects of memory, with two questions for each category. The eight categories were: prospective short-term self-cued, prospective short-term environmentally-cued, prospective long-term self-cued, prospective long-term environmentally-cued, retrospective short-term self-cued, retrospective short-term environmentally-cued, retrospective long-term self-cued, retrospective long-term environmentally-cued. This questionnaire includes retrospective memory and prospective memory in everyday life. From this self-rating questionnaire, we can gain some insights into any distinction between prospective and retrospective memory performance in everyday life (Crawford et al., 2003). However, few items as it is, even this questionnaire does not capture all aspects of everyday prospective remembering problems often reported by adults. So it may be not sensitive to be used in rehabilitation assessments.

Another assessment specifically designed to measure prospective memory function is the Comprehensive Assessment of Prospective Memory (CAPM) (Waugh, 1999), which was developed to overcome some shortcomings associated with the PMQ. It's a questionnaire that does not just measure the frequency of prospective memory failure (as in the PMQ), but also evaluates the perceived amount of concern about these memory lapses and the reasons why people are successfully or unsuccessfully performing prospective memory tasks. There are three main sections of this questionnaire designed to assess the frequency, severity and process of PM failure. The Section A (Frequency scale) was used in a rehabilitation study in brain injury (Fleming, 2005). These two components in the section A which were found applicable in four separate samples of normal adults in differing age categories, as well as an analysis in which all participants were pooled. Two items that were not included in the components were 'leaving the stove on' and 'walking into a room and forgetting why you went there'. These two components could be categorized as `common' and `uncommon' prospective memory lapses. The uncommon PM lapses related to basic activities of daily living (BADL), that is, daily self-care tasks (e.g. dressing, eating, personal grooming and hygiene). The common PM failures related to instrumental activities of daily living (IADL), that is, household management activities (e.g. managing finances, shopping, and meal preparation).The reliability of the CAPM is supported by the Cronbach's α for the BADL and IADL components (viz., .79 and .92). The validity of the CAPM is supported by the theory of consistent group differences (between individuals in three different age groups and between participants with brain injury and matched controls).

Although some of the questionnaires have preferable validity, they still have some limitations. Subjects often could not remember their prospective memory as clearly as they could do in retrospective memory tasks. They usually remembered the PM tasks they had remembered to do but were not conscious of those they had ignored. An optional method is using a version of the questionnaire which is produced for the carer to rate the patients and some basic data about the carer himself/herself could be taken as you need. Keeping diary be used as PM rehabilitation assessment can give us more details of the participants, but can not be suitable for every prospective situation, such as the participants who received no education.

Some researchers employed naturalistic methods to assess the effects of the PM intervention. These methods that require participants to operate recording devices at predetermined times or places, such as returning a card, press the designed button, making a telephone call or telling the researcher something in response to a pre-assigned cue. These kinds of studies are conducted outside the laboratory, where subjects have the opportunity to use compensatory strategies which were taught in the rehabilitation program. But these tests involve a minimal amount of experimental control, which could leads to interpretive problems. For example, telephone task (Schmidt et al., 2001) asked the participants to call an answering machine during working hours once a day on Monday, Tuesday, Thursday, Friday at a specified time during two weeks (max. 8 times). Calling times were not allowed to coincide with fixed daily routines. Although the reliability of this task was moderate ($r = 0.53$), telephone call may not make on time for a variety of reasons, including inadequate planning or lack of motivation and so on. So the results may be hard to interpretive.

Some experimental paradigms described above, such as some designed computer procedure, are also used in the rehabilitation assessments. But the clinical utility of these paradigms is often limited. There are several reasons for this. First, reliability of the variety of tasks used have been disappointing low (e.g. Schmidt et al., 2001) or even have not been reported. Second, as we have already discussed in the previous session, there are few test item and simple responses in most assessments, which making it difficult to quantify individual differences and to identify the components of the tasks that a person is failing. Third, some of the computer procedures can not give the participants enough time or chance to use the strategies taught in the rehabilitation program.

In an exploratory study (Brooks et al., 2004), the author devised an assessment using virtual reality (VR). VR is an interactive computer technology that can create the illusion of being in an artificial world that can be manipulated, and within which one can be move around. A form of VR may be presented on a computer monitor and can be explored and manipulated using a joystick or other control device. Virtual environments using this technology can be designed to represent many real-life situations and are programmed to record accurate measurements of performance within them. They can combine aspects of the realism of 'naturalistic' scenarios with the control of laboratory-based studies. It may be more suitable to be used in rehabilitation of PM.

PM DEFICITS IN PATIENTS WITH NEUROLOGICAL AND PSYCHIATRIC DISORDERS

Since the construct of PM is relatively new, its corresponding performance in different clinical groups is still not fully known yet. In this section, we attempt to present a preliminary review on the PM performance in patients with neurological and psychiatric disorders. A systematic literature search was conducted in EBSCOhost (including Academic Source Premier, PsycINFO, PsycARTICLES, ERIC, MEDLINE, Psychology and Behavioral Sciences Collection) and ScienceDirect between the periods of January 1980 to September, 2006. In particular, we only limited our search to three clinical groups: patients with traumatic brain injury and stroke, patients with neurological degeneration (mainly Dementia), and patients with schizophrenia.

For the traumatic brain injury and stroke group, we used keywords such as prospective memory and brain injury (69 articles were found); prospective memory and stroke (2 articles were found). Papers were excluded if there were no full papers available, papers with repeated samples, and papers without sufficient information to calculate the effect size of PM deficits between patients and healthy controls. As a result, 12 studies were reviewed and the details are summarized in table 1. The effect size ranges from 0 to 2.58, with most studies showing a modest to large effect size of PM deficits in patients with traumatic brain injury. There are two points that warrant further discussion. First, most of these studies were limited to experimental paradigms of using different types of paradigms, mainly event-based paradigms, to examine the corresponding PM performances of the patients. Very few studies on time- and activity-based PM have been conducted and the actual effect size of these two PM subtypes is not yet fully clear. Second, similar to our arguments above, most of the studies were limited to experimental or laboratory-based paradigms. There are only two studies (Brooks et al., 2004, Knight et al., 2006) attempting to address these issues. The ecological validity and discriminative predictability have not been fully addressed in these studies. The development of a more ecological valid test such as the Hotel Test and the use of appropriate facilities such as virtual reality (Brooks et al., 2004) and videotaping on real life scenario (Knight et al., 2006) may be useful in addressing this issue.

Table 1. Prospective memory in traumatic brain injury and stroke compared to controls

Studies	Patients type	PM tasks	Patient		Control		statistics	Effect size
			Mean	SD	Mean	SD		
*Brooks et al., 2004	42 stroke cases and 29 healthy controls	time	0.39	0.35	0.58	0.32	t(48)=2.02 p = 0.05	0.58
		activity	0.27	0.31	0.61	0.33	t(48)=3.83 p < 0.001	1.11
		event	0.31	0.4	0.66	0.4	t(48)=3.05 p = 0.004	0.88
**Carlesimo et al., 2004	16 patients with severe TBI and 16 healthy controls	time and event					Z=4.59 (U test) p < 0.001	1.56
*Daum and Mayes, 2000	10 patients with frontal lesion and 10 healthy controls	event	1.5	1.3	2.8	0.6	p = 0.035	1.28
	10 patients with posterior lesion and 10 healthy controls	event	1.5	1.3	2.8	0.6	p = 0.035	1.28
#Fortin et al., 2003	10 patients with traumatic brain injury and 12 healthy controls	Time (end point timing error)	0.4		1.0		p = 0.003	0.6
*Groot et al., 2002	26 patients with brain injury and 28 healthy controls	time and event (CBPMT)	4.5	2.29	7.29	1.12	t(53)=6.39 p < 0.001	1.55
*Kliegel et al., 2004	7 patients with traumatic brain injury and 19 healthy controls	complex (intention re-instantiation)	0.14	0.38	0.95	0.23	p < 0.001	2.58
*Knight et al., 2005	25 patients with traumatic brain injury and 20 healthy controls	event	11.48	3.59	14.95	2.76	p < 0.001	1.08
*Knight et al., 2006	20 patients with traumatic brain injury and 20 healthy controls	Event, low distraction	0.29	0.26	0.59	0.31		1.05
		Event, high distraction	0.15	0.20	0.43	0.35		0.98
**Maujean et al., 2003	17 patients with severe brain injury and 14 healthy controls	event					F(1,27)=7.10 p < 0.05	1.03

Table 1. (Continued).

Studies	Patients type	PM tasks	Patient		Control		statistics	Effect size
*Schmitter-Edgecombe and Wright, 2004	24 severe traumatic brain injury cases and 24 healthy controls	Event, focal cue	0.78	0.26	0.91	0.16		0.60
		Event, peripheral cue	0.78	0.29	0.90	0.22		0.47
*Shum et al., 1999	12 patients with severe traumatic brain injury and 12 healthy controls	event, time	0.66	0.31	0.89	0.18	$F(1,22)=9.41$ $p < 0.01$	0.91
		activity	0.81	0.20	0.94	0.11	$t(22)=2.21$ $p < 0.05$	0.81
**Mathias et al.,2005	25 patients with moderate and severe brain injury and 25 healthy controls	event, belonging	3.4	0.8	3.6	0.6	$p = 0.151$[##]	0.28
		event, appointment	1.6	0.6	1.9	0.3	$p = 0.014$[##]	0.63
		event, delayed message	3	0.2	3	0.2	$p = 0.5$[##]	0
		time, timer test	1	0.9	1.6	0.6	$p = 0.013$[##]	0.79
		time, envelope test	1	0.9	1.7	0.7	$p = 0.004$[##]	0.86

* Calculation of effect size (Cohen's *d* calculated by mean and SD)

** Cohen's *d* presented in the paper

Effect size calculated by subtracting the two proportions

The p value in this study used one tail t-test.

Table 2. Prospective memory in neurological degenerated patients

Studies	Patient type	PM type	Patient		Control		statistics	Effect size
			Mean	SD	Mean	SD		
[#]Bravin et al., 2000	40 patients with multiple sclerosis and 36 healthy controls	time based, Pulse task	0.31		0.61		$X^2(1)=6.95$ $p < 0.025$	0.30
		time based, Clerical task	0.42		0.62		$X^2(1)=2.62$ $p > 0.05$	0.20
[§]Brunfaut et al., 2000	Experiment 2: 27 untrained patients with Korsakoff syndrome and 24 alcoholic controls	event	0.53		0.88		$F(1,33)=17.28$ $p < 0.0002$	1.45
[#]Huppert et al.,2000	388 patients with early dementia and 11956 healthy cohorts	activity	0.54		0.08			0.46
[*]Katai et al., 2005	20 patients with Parkinson disease and 20 healthy controls	event	1.5	1.6	3.2	1	$p < 0.01$	1.27
		time	13.6	12.4	17.1	16.3		0.24
[*]Kazui et al., 2005	48 Alzheimer's cases and 48 healthy controls	RBMT, belonging	0.7	1	3.1	1.1	$p < 0.001$	2.28
		RBMT, appointment	0.2	0.4	1.4	0.7	$p < 0.001$	2.1
		RBMT, message immediate	1.8	0.9	2.8	0.4	$p < 0.001$	1.44
		RBMT, message delayed	0.7	0.8	2.8	0.4	$p < 0.001$	3.32
[#]Jones et al., 2006	46 preclinical Alzheimer's cases and 188 healthy controls	activity	0.19		0.41		$X^2=4.54$ $p = 0.02$	0.22
[§]Maylor et al., 2002	30 Alzheimer's cases and 24 healthy controls	Exp1: event, time					$F(1,50)=18.72$ $p < 0.001$	1.22
		Exp2: event					$F(1,34)=7.22$ $p < 0.02$	0.92

[*] Calculation of effect size (Cohen's *d* calculated by mean and SD)

[#] Effect size calculated by subtracting the two proportions

[§] Effect size calculated by F and degree of freedom.

For the neurological degeneration group, we used the keywords such as prospective memory and Alzheimer (28 papers were found); prospective memory and dementia (36 studies were found); prospective memory and multiple sclerosis (4 studies were found); prospective memory and Korsakoff syndrome (1 study was found). However, after eliminating those studies according to the exclusion criteria, there were only 7 studies remained for analysis (table 2). The effect size ranges from 0.2 to 3.32, with most studies showing a small to modest effect size of PM deficits in these clinical groups except Kazui et al. (2005) showing large effect sizes. However, because these clinical groups consist of a wide range of patients with different neuropathology such as Alzheimer's disease and Parkinson's disease, the present findings only serve as preliminary indices of PM deficits. In addition to the points discussed in the brain injury group, most of the studies on dementia used the questionnaires and naturalistic paradigms to explore the corresponding PM deficits in this clinical group. However, most of them did not include sufficient data for effect size calculation and therefore were not included in the present table. For example, Smith et al. (2000) found that Alzheimer disease patients reported highest PM failures in the population-based study, and PM failure frustrated their carers more than retrospective memory failures. Maylor et al. (2000) made a naturalistic study on normal aging and dementia, and found the intention superiority effect that was thought to be important in prospective memory was impaired in old and dementia participants.

Table 3. Prospective memory in schizophrenic patients

Studies	Patient type	PM type	Statistics	effect size
[§]Elevevag et al., 2003	20 patients with chronic schizophrenia (most were incomplete response to conventional treatments) and 20 healthy controls	habitual PM	$F(1,38)=15.67$ $p < 0.001$	1.28
[§]Kumar et al., 2005	42 patients with schizophrenia (drug free for at least 3 months or drug naive) and 42 healthy controls	event	$F(1,82)=22.16$ $p < 0.0001$	1.04
[§]Shum et al., 2004	60 chronic schizophrenic patients and 60 healthy controls	event, time, activity	$F(1,118)=65.61$ $p < 0.05$	1.49

[§] Effect size calculated by F and degree of freedom.

For the schizophrenic group, we used the keywords such as prospective memory and schizophrenia (8 studies were found).However, there were 5 studies without detailed information for effect size calculation and leaving 3 papers for the present table 3. Moreover, there were no mean and SD given in these papers. We calculated the effect size with the use of degree of freedom and related statistics (e.g., F- or t-values). The effect size of PM deficits in schizophrenic patients is generally large (d ranges from 1.04 to 1.49). However, the results should be interpreted with cautious. First, the number of studies available for analysis is so few that the generalizability of the present findings is limited. Second, schizophrenia is a complex disease with phase-specific features, e.g. first-onset episode may be different from chronic cases. Third, treatment effect of atypical and typical antipsychotic medication may differ from each other. These all confounding factors should therefore be addressed in order to have a more global picture of PM performances in patients with specific phase of schizophrenia.

SELF-AWARENESS AND OTHER CONFOUNDING FACTORS OF SUBJECTIVE SELF-REPORT OF PM

In addressing the issue of self-report of PM performance in neurological and psychiatric disorders, we should be cautious to the impairment of self-awareness observed in these clinical groups. Brooke et al. (2004) found that despite there were significant differences of PM performances between stroke patients and healthy controls, the patients did not subjectively rate their PM as being worse than controls Furthermore, patients with traumatic brain injury may sometime demonstrate the so-called "memory introspection paradox", that is the patients may rate themselves according to their pre-morbid PM capacity but not the present situation Roche et al. (2002). All these findings suggest both the performance and self-awareness in PM may be impaired in neurological patients especially brain injury patients. Other factors that may affect PM performances include emotion (anxiety, and stress) (Nater et al., 2006), individual difference (Obsessive compulsive disorder tendency) (Cuttler and Graf, 2006), and drug addiction (alcohol, ecstasy) (Heffernan and Bartholomew, 2006; Heffernan, Jarvis, Rodgers, Scholey, and Ling, 2001; Heffernan, Ling and Scholey, 2001; Zakzanis, Young, and Campbell, 2003). Therefore, these factors should all be taken into consideration when assessing the PM performances in neurological and psychiatric patients.

CONCLUSION

The present chapter has reviewed the pros and cons of different types of PM tasks in healthy and clinical populations. In particular, we have emphasized on the comparison of the three subtypes of PM tasks, namely event-based, time-based and activity-based. In view of the recent development of the PM construct and its paucity of examining the effect of PM deficits in different clinical populations, we have conducted a mini meta-analysis PM deficits in patients with traumatic brain injury, neurological degeneration diseases and schizophrenia. Despite the moderate to large effect sizes of PM deficits in these clinical groups, there are relatively few clinical trials or programmes specifically designed to intervene these deficits. Therefore, future direction of PM study should focus more onto the development of an effective intervention programme of PM deficits as well as the development of a more systematic approach to evaluating the efficacy of any new medication on PM performances in clinical populations.

REFERENCES

Bravin, J.H., Kinsella, G.J., Ong, B., and Vowels, L. (2000). A Study of Performance of Delayed Intentions in Multiple Sclerosis. *Journal of Clinical and Experimental Neuropsychology*,22(3),418-429.

Brooks, B.M., Rose, F.D., Potter, J., Jayawardena, S., and Morling, A. (2004). Assessing stroke patients' prospective memory using virtual reality. *Brain Injury*, 18(4), 391-401.

Brunfaut, E., Vanoverberghe, V., and d'Ydewalle, G. (2000). Prospective remembering of Korsakoffs and alcoholics as a function of the prospective-memory and on-going tasks. *Neuropsychologia*, 38, 975-984.

Burgess, P. W., Quayle, A.L.C., and Frith, C.D. (2001). Brain regions involved in prospective memory as determined by positron emission tomography. *Neuropsychologia, V39, 545-555*

Burgess, P. W., Scott, S. K. and Frith, C.D. (2003). The role of the rostral frontal cortex (area 10) in prospective memory: a lateral versus medial dissociation. *Neuropsychologia, V 41, 906-918*

Burgess, P. W., Veitch, E., Quayle, A.L.C., and Frith, C.D. (2003). The cognitive and neuroanatomical correlates of multitasking .*Neuropsychologia, V 38, 848-863*

Carlesimo, G.A., Casadio, P., and Caltagirone, C. (2004). Prospective and retrospective components in the memory for actions to be performed in patients with severe closed-head injury. *Journal of the International Neuropsychological Society*,10,679-688.

Cockburn, J., and Smith, P.T.(1988) Effects of age and intelligence on everyday memory tasks. *In M.M.Gruneberg, P.E.Morris, and R.N.Sykes (Eds.), Practical aspects of memory: Current research and issues, 2; Clinical and educational implications, 132-136. Chichester, UK: Wiley*

Cockburn, J., and Smith, P. T. (1991). The relative influence of intelligence and age on everyday memory. *Journals of Gerontology, Series B: Psychological Sciences and Social Sciences, 46, P31-P36.*

Cockburn, J., and Smith, P. T. (1994). Anxiety and errors of prospective memory among elderly people. *British Journal of Psychology, 85,273-282*

Craik, F. I. M. (1986). A functional account of age differences in memory. In F. Klix and H. Hagendorf (Eds.), *Human memory and cognitive capabilities: Mechanisms and performances, 409-422*

Crawford, J.R., Smith, G., Maylor, E. A., Della Sala, S., and Logie. R. H. (2003). The Prospective and Retrospective Memory Questionnaire (PRMQ): Normative data and latent structure in a large non-clinical sample. *Memory*, 11(3), 261-275.

Cuttler, C., and Graf, P. (2006). Sub-clinical compulsive checkers' prospective memory is impaired. *Journal of Anxiety Disorders.*

Daum, I., and Mayes, A.R. (2000). Memory and executive function impairments after frontal or posterior cortex lesions. *Behavioral Neurology*,12,161-173.

Dobbs, A. R., and Rule, B. G. (1987). Prospective Memory and Self reports of Memory Abilities in Older Adults. *Canadian Journal of Psychology, 41, 209-222.*

Einstein,G.O., Holland, L.J., Mark A. McDaniel and Guynn, M.J.(1992). Age-Related Deficits in Prospective Memory: The Influence of Task Complexity. *Psychology and Aging, 7, 471-478*

Einstein,G.O., and McDaniel, M.A., (1990). Normal Aging and Prospective Memory. *Journal of Experimental Psychology: Learning, Memory, and Cognition, 16, 717-726*

Einstein, G. G., and McDaniel, M.A. (1996). Retrieval processes in prospective memory: Theoretical approaches and some new empirical findings. In M. Brandimonte, G. O. Einstein, and M.A. McDaniel (Eds.). *Prospective memory: Theory and applications,* pp. 115-141. Mahwah, NJ: Erlbaum.

Einstein,G.O., McDaniel, M.A., Manzi, M., Cochran, B., and Baker, M. (2000) Prospective Memory and Aging: Forgetting Intentions Over Short Delays. *Psychology and Aging, 15, 671-683*

Einstein,G.O., McDaniel, M.A.; Thomas, R., Mayfield, S., Shank, H., Morrisette, N., Breneiser, J. (2005). Multiple Processes in Prospective Memory Retrieval: Factors Determining Monitoring Versus Spontaneous Retrieval. *Journal of Experimental Psychology: General, 134, 327-342.*

Einstein,G.O., Smith, R.E, McDaniel, M.A., and Shaw, P.(1997). Aging and Prospective Memory: The Influence of Increased Task Demands at Encoding and Retrieval. *Psychology and Aging, 12, 479-488*

Ellis, J.A., and Kvavilashvili, L. (2000). Prospective memory in 2000: Past, present, and future directions. *Applied Cognitive Psychology, 14, S1-S9.*

Elvevag, B., Maylor, E.A., and Gilbert, A.L. (2003). Habitual prospective memory in schizophrenia. *BMC Psychiatry, 3(9).*

Evans ,J., and Wilson, B.A.(1992) A memory group for individuals with brain injury. *Clinical Rehabitation, 6, 75-81*

Fleming, J. M., Shum, D., JStrong, J., and Lightbody, S. (2005). Prospective memory rehabilitation for adults with traumatic brain injury: A compensatory training programme. *Brain Injury*, 19(1): 1-10

Fortin, S., Godbout, L., Braun, CMJ. (2003).Cognitive structure of executive deficits in frontally lesioned head trauma patients performing activities of daily living. *Cortex,*39,273-291.

Groot, Y.C., Wilson, B.A., Evans, J., and Watson, P. (2002). Prospective memory functioning in people with and without brain injury. *Journal of the International Neuropsychological Society,*8,645-654.

Hannon, R., Adams, P., Harrington, S., Fries-Dias, C. and Gibson, M. T. (1995) Effects of brain injury and age on prospective memory self-rating and performance. *Rehabilitation Psychology 40, 289–297.*

Heffernan, T.M., and Bartholomew, J. (2006). Does Excessive Alcohol Use in Teenagers Affect Their Everyday Prospective Memory? *Journal of Adolescent Health,*39,138-140.

Heffernan, T.M., Jarvis, H., Rodgers, J., Scholey, A.B., and Ling, J. (2001). Prospective memory, everyday cognitive failure and central executive function in recreational users of Ecstasy. *Human Psychopharmacology*, 16,607-612.

Heffernan, T.M., Ling, J., and Scholey, A.B. (2001). Subjective ratings of prospective memory deficits in MDMA ('ecstasy') users. *Human Psychopharmacology*, 16, 339-344.

Henry,J.D., MacLeod, M.S., Phillips,L.H., and Crawford, J.R.(2004).A Meta-Analytic Review of Prospective Memory and Aging. *Psychology and Aging, 19, 27-39*

Huppert, F.A. and Beardsall, L.(1993). Prospective memory impairment as an early indicator of dementia. *Journal of Clinical and Experimental Neuropsychogy, 15,805-821.*

Huppert, F.A., Johnson, T., and Nickson, J. (2000). High prevalence of prospective memory impairment in the elderly and in early-stage dementia: Findings from a population-based study. *Applied Cognitive Psychology*,14,S63-S81.

Jones, S., Livner, A., and Backman, L. (2006). Patterns of Prospective and Retrospective Memory Impairment in Preclinical Alzheimer's Disease. *Neuropsychology*, 20(2),144-152.

Katai, S., Maruyama, T., and Ikeda, S. (2005). Event based and time based prospective memory in Parkinson's disease. *Journal of Neurology, Neurosurgery and Psychiatry*,74,704-709.

Kazui, H., Matsuda, A., Hirono, N., Mori, E., Miyoshi, N., Ogino, A., Tokunaga, H., Ikejiri, Y., Takeda, M. (2005). Everyday Memory impairment of Patients with Mild Cognitive Impairment. *Dementia and Geriatric Cognitive Disorders,*19,331-337.

Kliegel, Eschen, Thone-Otto. (2004). Planning and realization of complex intentions in traumatic brain injury and normal aging. *Brain and Cognition*,56,43-54.

Kliegel,M., Martin,M., McDaniel,M.A., and Einstein, G.O.(2002). Complex Prospective Memory and Executive Control of Working memory: *A Process Model. Psychologische Beitrage, 44, 303-318.*

Kliegel,M., Martin,M., McDaniel, M.A, Einstein,G.O.(2004) Importance effects on performance in event-based prospective memory tasks, Psychology Press, 12, 553 – 561

Knight, R., Harnett, M., and Titov, N. (2005). The effects of traumatic brain injury on the predicted and actual performance of a test of prospective remembering. *Brain injury*,19(1),27-38.

Knight, RG., Titov, N., Crawford. (2006). The effects of distraction on prospective remembering following traumatic brain injury assessed in a simulated naturalistic environment. *Journal of the International Neuropsychological Society*, 12(1),8-16.

Kumar, D., Nizamie, S.H., and Jahan, M. (2005). Event-based Prospective Memory in Schizophrenia. *Journal of Clinical and Experimental Neuropsychology*,27,867-872.

Kvavilashvili, L., and Ellis, J. (1996). Varieties of intention: Some distinctions and classifications. In M. Brandimonte, G. O. Einstein, and M.A. McDaniel (Eds). *Prospective memory: Theory and application,* pp. 23-51. Mahwah, NJ: Erlbaum.

Manly,T., Hawkins,K., Evans. J., Woldt,K., and Robertson, I.H. (2000). Rehabilitation of executive function: facilitation of effective goal management on complex tasks using periodic auditory alerts, *Neuropsychologia,* 40,271-281

Mathias, JL., Mansfield, KM. (2005). Prospective and declarative memory problems following moderate and severe traumatic brain injury. *Brain Injury*, 19(4),271-282.

Maujcan, A., Shum, D., and McQueen, R. (2003). Effect of cognitive demands on prospective memory in individuals with traumatic brain injury. *Brain Impairment*,4(2),135-145.

Maylor, EA., Darby, RJ., Sala, SD. (2000). Retrieval of performed versus to-be-performed tasks: A naturalistic study of the intention-superiority effect in normal aging and dementia. *Applied Cognitive Psychology*, 14,S83-S98.

Maylor, EA., Smith, G., Sala, SD., Logie, RH. (2002). Prospective and retrospective memory in normal aging and dementia: An experimental study. *Memory and Cognition*,30(6),871-884.

McDaniel,M.A., Guynn,M.J., Einstein,G.O., and Breneiser,J. (2004). Cue-Focused and Reflexive-Associative Processes in Prospective Memory Retrieval. *Journal of Experimental Psychology: Learning, Memory, and Cognition, 30,605-614.*

Meacham, JA., and Leimen, B. (1975)., Remembering to perform future actions. In U. Neisser (Ed.), Memory observed, pp. 327-336. San Francisco: Freeman.

Nater, U.M., Okere, U., Stallkamp, R., Moor, C., Ehlert, U., and Kliegel, M. (2006). Psychosocial stress enhances time-based prospective memory in healthy young men. *Neurobiology of Learning and Memory.*

Nigro, G., Cicogna,P.C. (2000) Does Delay Affect Prospective Memory Performance? *European Psychologist, 5, 3, 228-233.*

Okuda,J., Fuji,T., Yamadori,A., Kawashima,R., Tsukiura,T., Fukatsu,R., Suzuki,K., Ito,M., and Fukuda, H (1998): Participation of the prefrontal cortices in prospective memory: evidence from a PET study in humans. *Neuroscience Letters, 253, 127-130*

Poon,L.W., and Schaffer,G. (1982). Prospective Memory in Young and Elderly Adults. *Paper presented at the annual meeting of the American Psychological Association, Washington, DC.*

Raskin, S. and Sohlberg, M. (1996). An investigation of prospective memory training in two individuals with traumatic brain injury. *Journal of Head Trauma Rehabilitation, 11, 32-51.*

Roche, N., Fleming, J.M., and Shum, D. (2002). Self-awareness of prospective memory failure in adults with traumatic brain injury. *Brain Injury,*16(11),931-945.

Schmidt, I. W., Berg, I. J., and Deelman, B. G. (2001). Prospective memory training in older adults. *Educational Gerontology*, 27: 455-478

Schmitter-Edgecombe, M., and Wright, M.J. (2004). Event-Based Prospective Memory Following Severe Closed-Head Injury. *Neuropsychology,*18(2),353-361.

Shum, D., Ungvari, G.S., Tang, W., and Leung, J.P. (2004). Performance of Schizophrenia Patients on Time-,Event-, and Activity-Based Prospective Memory Tasks. *Schizophrenia Bulletin*, 30(4),693-701.

Shum, D., Valentine, M., and Cutmore, T. (1999). Performance of Individuals with Severe Long-Term Traumatic BrainInjury on Time-, Event-, and Activity-Based Prospective Memory Tasks. *Journal of Clinical and Experimental Neuropsychology,*21(1),49-58.

Smith, G., Della Sala, S., Logie, R. H., and Maylor, E. A. (2000). Prospective and retrospective memory in normal aging and dementia: A questionnaire study. *Memory.* 8(5), 311-321

Sohlberg, M., White, O., Evans, E, and Mateer, C. (1992a). Background and initial case studies into the effects of prospective memory training. *Brain Injury, 6, 129-138.*

Sohlberg, M. White, O., Evans, E., and Mateer, C. (1992b) An investigation into the effects of prospective memory training. *Brain Injury, 6, 139-154.*

Waugh, N. (1999). Self-report of the young, middle-aged, young-old and old-old individuals on prospective memory functioning. Unpublished Honours Thesis, School of Applied Psychology, Griffith University, Brisbane.

West,R.L. (1988). Prospective memory and aging: In M. M. Gruneberg, P. E. Morris, and R. N. Sykes (Eds.). *Practical aspects of memory, Vol. 2, pp. 119-125*

West,R., Bowry.,R and Krompinger,J., (2006). The effects of working memory demands on the neural correlates of prospective memory. *Neuropsychologia, 44, 197-207*

Wilson,B.A., Cockburn, J., and Baddeley, A.D. (1985). The Rivermead Behaviroal Memory Test. *Titchfield, UK: Thames Valley Test Co.*

Wiseman,K.A., Ratcliff,G.., Chase,S., Laporte,D.J., Robertson,D.U., and Colantonio, A.(2000). Does a test of functional memory during the post-acute period predict long-term outcome of traumatic brain injury? *Brain and Cognition, 44, 14-18.*

Yang, T., Chan, R. C. K., Lin, H., and Zheng, L. (submitted). Aging effect on prospective memory in healthy Chinese elder people.

Zakzanis, K.K., Young, D.A., and Campbell, Z. (2003). Prospective memory impairment in abstinent MDMA (Ecstasy) users. *Cognitive Neuropsychiatry,*8(2),141-153.

Zeintl, M., Kliegel, M., Rast, P., Zimprich, D. (2006). Prospective memory complaints can be predicted by prospective memory performance in older adults, *Dementia and geriatric cognitive disorders, Vol, 22(3):209-15.*

In: Psychological Tests and Testing Research Trends
Editor: Paul M. Goldfarb, pp. 251-263

ISBN: 978-1-60021-569-8
© 2007 Nova Science Publishers, Inc.

Chapter 12

MEASURING DISABILITY AND FUNCTION IN INDIVIDUALS WITH MULTIPLE SCLEROSIS: PSYCHOMETRIC PROPERTIES OF THE ABBREVIATED LATE-LIFE FUNCTION AND DISABILITY INSTRUMENT

Robert W. Motl, Erin M. Snook,
Jessica L. Gosney and Edward McAuley
Department of Kinesiology and Community Health
University of Illinois at Urbana-Champaign, IL USA

ABSTRACT

The measurement of functional limitations and disability in individuals with multiple sclerosis (MS) has been plagued by definitional ambiguity and measurement limitations. The abbreviated Late Life-Function and Disability Inventory (LL-FDI) was recently developed based on accepted definitions of functional limitations and disability, and has been supported as having strong measurement properties in samples of older adults. This study examined the structural and external aspects of score validity for the LL-FDI in individuals with MS. Individuals with MS completed the LL-FDI and three measures of physical activity. Structural aspects of score validity for the LL-FDI were established using confirmatory factor analysis (CFA). The CFA supported the existence of two factors of personal and social aspects of disability for the disability frequency and limitations subscales of the LL-FDI, and three factors of upper extremity function, basic lower extremity function, and advanced lower extremity function for the functional limitations subscale of the LL-FDI. External aspects of score validity for the LL-FDI were established based on expected differences in mean scores between individuals with relapsing-remitting MS and primary and secondary progressive MS and examination of the pattern of correlations between mean scores with the measures of physical activity. Our results support the structural and external aspects of score validity for the LL-FDI in individuals with MS, and we recommend that future researchers use this scale when measuring functional limitations and disability in this population.

INTRODUCTION

Multiple sclerosis (MS) is a chronic and progressive disease of the central nervous system (National Multiple Sclerosis Society [NMSS], 2005) and functional limitations and disability are inevitable consequences of the disease. MS involves a presumed attack by the immune system of the myelin sheath that surrounds the axons of neurons in the brain, brain stem, spinal cord, and optic nerves. This results in demyelination and axonal transection and interferes with the salutatory conduction of action potentials along axons of the neurons. The interference with conduction of action potentials results in multiple symptoms including loss of function and feeling in limbs, fatigue, loss of balance and coordination, pain, cognitive dysfunction, and depression (NMSS, 2005; Lublin, 2005). Ultimately, the symptoms lead to functional limitations and disability. That is, 50% of individuals will require the use of an aid for walking (i.e., reach an Expanded Disability Status Scale score of 6.0) and 10% will require a wheelchair within 15 years after the onset of MS (Weinshenker et al., 1989; Runmarker and Anderson, 1993). Nearly 90% of individuals will have functional limitations and disability within 25 years after the onset of MS (Frohman, Racke, and van den Noort, 2000).

Although it is well accepted that functional limitations and disability are the result of MS, current measures of those constructs are inadequate and lack sensitivity for detecting the types of change experienced by people with MS (Coulthard-Morris, 2000). This is, in part, attributable to the very nature of the disease (Rudick et. al., 1996) were the clinical course of MS is unpredictable and varies among individuals and across time (Coulthard-Morris, 2000). Another contributing factor is that existing measures have not been developed within an established model of physical disablement that provides sound operational definitions of functional limitations and disability.

The measurement of functional limitations and disability in MS might benefit by consideration of the disablement process. Based on Nagi's (1976) model of the disablement process and Verbrugge and Jette's (1994) operational definitions, Guralnik and Ferrucci (2003) differentiated functional limitations and disability as two important components of the disablement process. Functional limitations can be described as an individual's reduced capacity to carry out activities that are relevant for effective community living such as walking, lifting, climbing, reaching, and handling everyday objects. Disability can be described as an individual's performance of socially defined roles and tasks within a sociocultural and physical environment (Nagi, 1976). Hence, functional limitations involve the performance of discrete tasks whereas disability focuses on behavioral repertoires, and restrictions in one's ability to walk (i.e., functional limitations) result in problems with activities that are required for one's employment, personal care, and recreation (i.e., disability).

The original (Jette et al., 2002) and abbreviated (McAuley, Konopack, Motl, Rosengren, and Morris, 2005) versions of the Late-Life Function and Disability Instrument (LL-FDI) represent methodological advancements in the measurement of functional limitations and disability. The original LL-FDI was developed based on the disablement process and consists of three components, namely Functional Limitations, Disability Frequency, and Disability Limitations. The original LL-FDI was developed using a sample of 150 adults aged 60 years and older, and contained a comprehensive battery of items that avoided problems such as ceiling and floor effects by spreading items across a broad range of activities (Jette et al., 2002). We recently revised and abbreviated the LL-FDI based on an examination of its psychometric properties and construct validity in a sample of older women (McAuley et al., 2005). This abbreviated version of the LL-FDI had an acceptable 15-item solution for the Functional Limitations component and an acceptable 8-item solution for both the Disability Frequency and Disability Limitation components. The Functional Limitations component consisted of three subscales of advanced lower extremity function, basic lower extremity function, and upper extremity function. The Disability Frequency and Disability Limitations components each consisted of two subscales of performing social and personal role activities. This abbreviated instrument demonstrated high correlations with the original LL-FDI scales. Construct validity for the abbreviated LL-FDI was supported based on correlations with measures of physical function, body composition, and physical activity. The abbreviated LL-FDI appears to be an effective instrument for assessing function and disability in older women, although continued determination of its structural and construct aspects of validity is recommended in similar and different populations.

Although the LL-FDI was developed primarily for use with older adults, its content and conceptual underpinnings make it amenable for use with diseased populations. Indeed, the content of this scale has relevance for individuals with MS. Hence, this study examined the structural and external aspects of score validity for the abbreviated LL-FDI in individuals with MS. We initially tested the structural validity of the Disability and Functional Limitations components of the abbreviated LL-FDI using standard covariance modeling procedures and confirmatory factor analysis. After testing the structural validity, we examined the reliability of the scales using estimates of internal consistency derived using Cronbach's coefficient alpha. Finally, we tested the external aspects of score validity for the abbreviated LL-FDI based on known-groups comparisons of scores between individuals with relapsing-remitting and progressive forms of MS and correlations with measures of physical activity.

METHODS

Participants

The sample consisted of individuals with MS who were recruited through contact with the Greater Illinois, Indiana, and Gateway chapters of the NMSS. Recruitment was conducted by contacting facilitators of local self-help groups and placing advertisements in the *MS Connection* quarterly publication of the Great Illinois chapter of the NMSS. The sample included 288 individuals (244 females, 44 males) with MS. Of the 288 participants, 239 self-reported being diagnosed with relapsing-remitting MS (RRMS) and 49 self-reported being diagnosed with either primary progressive MS (PPMS) or secondary progressive MS (SPMS). The mean duration of MS (i.e., time since diagnosis) was 9.6 years (SD = 7.6). The sample was primarily Caucasian (93%), married (64%), currently employed (58%), and well educated (25% had some college education and 41% were college graduates) with a median annual household income of greater than $40,000 (63%). The mean age of the sample was 47.4 years (SD = 10.3).

Measures

LL-FDI

The abbreviated LL-FDI (McAuley et al., 2005) is a multidimensional measure of function and disability with good psychometric properties (Jette et al., 2002). The function component of the abbreviated LL-FDI contains a 15-item self-report measure of functional limitations (limitations in a person's ability to do discrete actions or activities) that correspond with advance lower extremity function, basic lower extremity function, and upper extremity function. An example item for the advance lower extremity function was "How much difficulty do you have with going up and down a flight of stairs outside, without using a handrail?". An example item for the basic lower extremity function was "How much difficulty do you have using a step stool to reach into a high cabinet?". An example item for the upper extremity function was "How much difficulty do you have unscrewing the lid off a previously unopened jar without using any devices?". The 15-items were rated on a 5-point scale of 1 (none) and 5 (cannot do) and were reverse-scored and then averaged to form composite measures of advance lower extremity function, basic lower extremity function, and upper extremity function with higher scores representing better functioning; scores for each subscale range between 5 and 25.

The disability component of the abbreviated LL-FDI contains an 8-item measure of disability frequency (i.e., frequency of performing socially-defined tasks) and an 8-item measure of disability limitations (i.e., limitations with performing socially-defined tasks) that both correspond with social and personal components of disability. An example item for the social component of disability limitations was "To what extent do you feel limited in visiting friends and family in their homes?". An example item for the personal component of disability limitations was "To what extent do you feel limited in taking care of your own personal care needs?". The 8-items for the disability frequency component were rated on a 5-point scale of 1 (never) and 5 (very often). The 8-items for the disability limitation component were rated on a 5-point scale of 1 (not at all) and 5 (completely). The items on both scales were reverse-scored and then averaged to form composite measures of social and personal components of disability frequency and limitations with higher scores representing less disability; scores for each subscale range between 4 and 20.

Physical Activity

We measured physical activity using the Godin Leisure-Time Exercise Questionnaire (GLTEQ; Shephard and Bouchard, 1985), short-form of the International Physical Activity Questionnaire (IPAQ; Craig et al., 2003), and an ActiGraph accelerometer. We have previously provided validity evidence for the measures of physical activity in individuals with MS (Gosney, Scott, Snook, and Motl, in press; Motl, Snook, McAuley, and Scott, 2006). The GLTEQ is a self-administered 2-item measure of usual physical activity that has been widely used in epidemiologic, clinical, and behavioral change studies. The first question has three open-ended items that measure the frequency of strenuous (e.g., jogging), moderate (e.g., fast walking), and mild (e.g., easy walking) exercise for periods of more than 15 minutes during one's free time in a typical week. The weekly frequencies of strenuous, moderate, and mild activities are multiplied by 9, 5, and 3 metabolic equivalents, respectively, and summed to form a measure of total leisure activity. The second question is ordinal with three options and measures the frequency of engaging in any regular activity long enough to work up a sweat during a typical week. This study did not include the sweat index in the data analyses because of autonomic nervous system disturbances that commonly result in sweating disturbances among those with MS.

The short-form of the IPAQ was designed as an instrument for population surveillance of physical activity among adults and contains 6 items that measure the frequency and duration of vigorous-intensity activities, moderate-intensity activities, and walking during a seven-day period. The respective frequency and duration values for vigorous, moderate, and walking activities are initially multiplied, and the resulting volumes of vigorous, moderate, and walking activities are multiplied by 8, 4, and 3.3 metabolic equivalents (METs), respectively, and then summed to form a continuous measure of physical activity in MET-minutes/week. The short-form of the IPAQ includes an additional question that measures time spent sitting as an indicator of sedentary activity and that is not included as part of the summary physical activity score. This study did not include the sitting item in the data analyses because we were not interested in sedentary behavior.

The ActiGraph single-axis accelerometer (model 7164 version, Health One Technology, Fort Walton Beach, FL) was used as an objective measure of physical activity. This accelerometer contains a single, vertical axis piezoelectric bender element that generates an electrical signal proportional to the force acting on it. Acceleration detection ranges in magnitude from 0.05 - 3.2 Gs and the frequency response ranges from 0.25 - 2.5 Hz. Motion outside normal human movements is rejected by a band-pass filter. The acceleration/deceleration signal is digitized by an analog-to-digital converter and numerically integrated over a pre-programmed epoch interval yielding activity counts. Hence, activity counts are a summation of accelerations measured during a cycle period that is established along with start time during an initialization phase. The counts represent a quantitative measure of activity over time, and are linearly related to the intensity of a participant's physical activity during a cycle period. The cycle period, or epoch, can range from 1 second to 10 minutes, and in this study was set to be 1 minute. Each accelerometer was checked for accuracy using manufacturer-recommended hardware and software and calibrated, if necessary. We further checked each accelerometer for accuracy using a walking test (15 minutes of walking at 80 m·min^{-1} on a treadmill). All accelerometers were accurate based on manufacturer recommended criteria and our walking test. Participants recorded the exact time the units were worn in a log on a daily basis.

Procedure

The procedure for this study was approved by an Institutional Review Board, and all participants provided written informed consent. The participants completed a battery of questionnaires that included the abbreviated LL-FDI, GLTEQ, and IPAQ, and wore the accelerometer during the waking hours (i.e., the moment upon getting out of bed in the morning through the moment of getting into bed in the evening), except while showering, bathing, and swimming, for a seven-day period. The participants recorded the time that the accelerometer was worn on a log, and this was verified by inspection of the minute-by-minute accelerometer data. Participants received $20 and a pedometer as remuneration after completing the measures and wearing the accelerometer.

Data Analysis

Factorial Validity

The fit of measurement models for the components of the abbreviated LL-FDI was examined using confirmatory factor analysis with maximum likelihood estimation in LISREL 8.50. Briefly, researchers using confirmatory factor analysis postulate an "a priori" measurement model linking observed variables with latent factors, and then test that model for its ability to fit the data. The "a priori" measurement model specifies the pattern of fixed and freed parameters in matrices containing factor loadings, factor variances and covariances, and item uniquenesses. Maximum likelihood was selected to estimate the freed parameters in matrices because it is the standard estimation technique (Hoyle and Panter, 1995) and has resulted in accurate absolute and relative fit indices with ordered categorical data of varying degrees of kurtosis (Hutchinson and Olmos, 1998).

The fit of the measurement models was evaluated based on the chi-square statistic, standardized root mean square residual (SRMR), comparative fit index (CFI), and inspection of standardized residuals and modification indices. The chi-square statistic assesses perfect fit of the model to the data (Bollen, 1989). The SRMR is the average of the standardized residuals between the specified and obtained variance-covariance matrices. The SRMR should be less than .08 to indicate good model fit (Hu and Bentler, 1999). The CFI is an incremental fit index, and tests the proportionate improvement in fit by comparing the target model to a baseline model with no correlations among observed variables (Bentler, 1990). CFI values approximating 0.90 and 0.95 were indicative of acceptable and good model-data fit, respectively (Bentler, 1990; Hu and Bentler, 1999). Large standardized residuals and modification indices are an indication of specific sources of model misfit for the data (Bollen, 1989).

Internal Consistency

After testing the factorial validity, we next examined the internal consistency of subscale and overall composite scores from the disability and functional components of the abbreviated LL-FDI. The analysis of internal consistency was undertaken using Cronbach's coefficient alpha and SPSS for Windows 14.0.

Construct Validity

The first method of establishing the construct validity of scores on the abbreviated LL-FDI involved comparisons of disability and function subscale scores between individuals with RRMS and those with PPMS/SPMS. This was accomplished using a one-way (Groups: RRMS vs. PPMS/SPMS) multivariate analysis of variance (MANOVA) on scores from function and disability frequency and limitation components of the abbreviated LL-FDI. The multivariate main effect was decomposed using univariate F-ratios and the magnitude of the group differences were expressed using Cohen's d. The second method of examining the construct validity of scores on the abbreviated LL-FDI involved examining correlations with measures of physical activity. This was accomplished using Pearson product-moment correlations computed between scores from the function and disability component of the abbreviated version of the LL-FDI with scores from the three measures of physical activity. Both the MANOVA and correlation analysis were undertaken using SPSS for Windows 14.0.

RESULTS

Factorial Validity

Disability Component – Frequency Items

We initially tested the fit of two, correlated factors consisting of personal and social roles for the 8-item Disability, Frequency component of the abbreviated LL-FDI. The model represented a good fit for the data (χ^2 = 34.65, df = 19, p = .02, SRMR = .05, CFI = 0.96). Inspection of the standardized residuals and modification indices did not indicate any specific source of misfit. All factor loadings were statistically significant, and the items and factor loadings for the model are presented in table 1. The standardized correlation between the personal and social role factors was statistically significant (φ = 0.50).

Table 1. Standardized factor loadings for the items on the Disability-Frequency and Disability-Limitation scales of the LL-FDI

Items	Disability, Frequency		Disability, Limitations	
	Personal	Social	Personal	Social
Take care of local errands	.766		.764	
Prepare meals	.490		.722	
Take care of personal care needs	.461		.701	
Take care of household business	.534		.631	
Go out to public places		.730		.797
Visit friends		.652		.666
Travel out of town		.615		.771
Invite family and friends into home		.640		.714

Disability Component – Limitation Items

We then tested the fit of two, correlated factors consisting of personal and social roles for the 8-item Disability, Limitation component of the abbreviated LL-FDI. This model represented an excellent fit for the data (χ^2 = 36.14, df = 19, p = .01, SRMR = .03, CFI = 0.98), and an inspection of the standardized residuals and modification indices did not indicate any specific source of misfit. All factor loadings were statistically significant, and the items and factor loadings for the final model are presented in table 1. The standardized correlation between the personal and social role factors was statistically significant (φ = 0.80).

Function Component

We finally tested the fit of three, correlated factors consisting of advanced lower body extremity function, basic lower body extremity function, and upper extremity function for the 15-item Function component of the abbreviated LL-FDI. The model represented an adequate, but not good fit for the data (χ^2 = 276.88, df = 87, p = .0001, SRMR = .05, CFI = 0.92). Inspection of the standardized residuals and modification indices combined with examination of item content resulted in the addition of correlated uniqueness between items 14 and 15 and items 3 and 4 on the basic lower body extremity and upper extremity function factors, respectively. This model provided an improved and good fit for the data (χ^2 = 219.51, df = 85,

p = .0001, SRMR = .05, CFI = 0.95). Inspection of the standardized residuals and modification indices did not indicate any additional specific source of misfit. All factor loadings were statistically significant, and the items and factor loadings for the final model are presented in table 2. There were statistically significant standardized correlations between advanced lower body extremity function and basic lower body extremity function (φ = .86), advanced lower body extremity function and upper extremity function (φ = .60), and basic lower body extremity function and upper extremity function (φ = .65).

**Table 2. Standardized factor loadings for the items
on the Functional Limitations scales of the LL-FDI**

Items	ALEF	BLEF	UEF
Go up and down 1 flight, no rails	.828		
Carry while climb stairs	.882		
Walk 1 mile with rests	.772		
Go up and down 3 flights inside	.768		
Run one-half mile	.675		
Get into and out of car		.748	
Bend over from a standing position		.729	
Pick up a kitchen chair		.784	
On and off a step stool		.828	
Walk around one floor of home		.713	
Pour from a large pitcher			.841
Remove wrapping with hands only			.788
Hold full glass of water in 1 hand			.588
Use common utensils			.669
Unscrew lid without assistive device			.659

Note. ALEF = advanced lower extremity function. BLEF = basic lower extremity function. UEF = upper extremity function.

Internal Consistency

The estimates of internal consistency were acceptable for the personal (α = .63) and social (α = .75) roles subscale scores and composite score (α = .74) for the 8-item Disability, Frequency component of the abbreviated LL-FDI. The estimates of internal consistency were good for the personal (α = .79) and social (α = .82) roles subscale scores and composite score (α = .87) for the 8-item Disability, Limitations component of the abbreviated LL-FDI. The estimates of internal consistency were good for the advanced lower body extremity function (α = .89), basic lower body extremity function (α = .88), and upper extremity function (α = .84) subscales and composite score (α = .92) for the 15-item Function component of the abbreviated LL-FDI.

Differences between Types of MS on the Components of the Abbreviated LL-FDI

The MANOVA identified a significant main effect of type of MS on subscales of the abbreviated LL-FDI [F (7,271) = 7.01, p < .001]. Examination of univariate follow-up analyses indicated that the overall multivariate effect could be best explained by differences in the basic and advanced lower extremity subscales of the Function component of the LL-FDI, personal and social roles subscales of the Disability, Limitations component of the abbreviated LL-FDI, and personal roles subscale of the Disability, Frequency component of the abbreviated LL-FDI (values of p < .05). Individuals with RRMS reported fewer limitations with personal and social tasks and less difficulty with advanced and basic lower extremity tasks than did individuals with PPMS and SPMS, and the differences were generally moderate-to-large in magnitude. The mean scores, standard deviations, and effect sizes are provided in table 3.

Table 3. Mean scores on abbreviated LL-FDI subscales by type of multiple sclerosis

	RRMS	PPMS/SPMS	
	M (SD)	M (SD)	d
Disability, Frequency Social	13.0 (2.9)	12.9 (3.2)	0.03
Disability, Frequency Personal	17.4 (2.5)	16.6 (3.4)	0.30
Disability, Limitation Social	16.2 (3.3)	14.1 (3.4)	0.62
Disability, Limitation Personal	17.0 (3.0)	15.0 (3.4)	0.64
Function, Advanced Lower Extremity	11.2 (4.6)	7.6 (3.7)	0.77
Function, Basic Lower Extremity	16.8 (3.2)	13.4 (4.3)	0.94
Function, Upper Extremity	15.8 (3.3)	14.9 (3.2)	0.27

Note. RRMS = relapsing-remitting multiple sclerosis. PPMS = primary-progressive multiple sclerosis. SPMS = secondary-progressive multiple sclerosis. M = mean score. SD = standard deviation. d = effect size expressed as Cohen's d.

Correlations between Abbreviated Components of the LL-FDI and Measures of Physical Activity

All correlations between scores from the abbreviated version of the LL-FDI with scores from the measures of physical activity were statistically significant and small-to-moderate in magnitude. The correlations indicated that more physically active individuals with MS reported less difficulty in function, more frequent participation in personal and social role activities, and fewer limitations in performance of social and personal role activities. The correlations are provided in table 4.

Table 4. Pearson product-moment correlations between scores from the abbreviated version of the LL-FDI and measure of physical activity

LL-FDI component	Physical Activity Measures		
	ACCEL Counts·wk^{-1}	GLTEQ	IPAQ MET min·wk^{-1}
Disability, Frequency			
1. Personal Roles	.22	.20	.21
2. Social Roles	.11	.20	.17
Disability, Limitations			
3. Personal Roles	.33	.24	.20
4. Social Roles	.25	.21	.16
Function			
5. Upper Extremity Function	.32	.23	.15
6. Basic Lower Extremity Function	.42	.29	.24
7. Advanced Lower Extremity Function	.56	.41	.30

Note. All correlations are statistically significant ($p < .05$) based on a one-tailed test. ACCEL = accelerometer. GLTEQ = Godin Leisure-Time Exercise Questionnaire. IPAQ = International Physical Activity Questionnaire.

DISCUSSION

This study examined the psychometric properties of the abbreviated LL-FDI in a sample of individuals with MS. We were initially interested in confirming the factor structure of the three components (i.e., Function, Frequency, and Limitation) of the LL-FDI and then examining the reliability and the construct validity of the measure based on differences between individuals with RRMS and PPMS/SPMS and correlations with objective and self-report measures of physical activity.

Our analyses provided preliminary support for the structural validity, reliability, and construct validity of scores from the Frequency and Limitation scales of the Disability component of the LL-FDI in individuals with MS. The measurement model with two, correlated factors of social and personal roles provided an excellent fit for the 8-items on both the Frequency and Limitation components of the Disability component of the LL-FDI. Subsequent analyses provided evidence of acceptable internal consistency for the subscales and the overall composite score for both the Frequency and Limitation scales of the Disability component of the LL-FDI. Support for the construct validity was based on examination of the difference between individuals with RRMS and PPMS/SPMS in mean scores on the Frequency and Limitation components of the Disability component of the LL-FDI and inspection of relationships with measures of physical activity. Those with RRMS reported fewer limitations with personal and social tasks than those with PPMS and SPMS, and physical activity was associated with more frequent and less limited participation in personal and social activities. Overall, our findings provide preliminary support for the interpretation of scores on the Frequency and Limitation Disability components of the LL-FDI as measures of personal and social aspects of disability in those with MS.

Beyond the disability component, our analyses provided preliminary support for the structural validity, reliability, and construct validity of scores from the Functional Limitations component of the LL-FDI. Although our initial test of the structural validity did not provide evidence of an excellent fit for the measurement model, the addition of two interpretable correlated uniquenesses resulted in a good fit of the measurement model with three, correlated factors consisting of advanced lower body extremity function, basic lower body extremity function, and upper extremity function for the 15-item Function component of the abbreviated LL-FDI. The estimates of internal consistency were good for the three subscales and overall composite scores for the 15-item Function component of the abbreviated LL-FDI. Support for the construct validity was based on examination of the difference between individuals with RRMS and PPMS/SPMS in mean scores on the Functional Limitations components of the LL-FDI and inspection of relationships with the three measures of physical activity. Those with RRMS reported fewer functional limitations with advanced and basic lower extremity function than those with PPMS and SPMS, and physical activity was associated with fewer functional limitations and the strongest correlations were observed with advanced lower extremity function. Overall, our findings provide preliminary support for the interpretation of scores on the Functional Limitations components of the LL-FDI as measures of advanced and basic lower extremity function and upper extremity function in those with MS.

The abbreviated LL-FDI might represent a major methodological advancement in the study of function and disability in MS. This is based on satisfaction of important considerations when selecting a measure of function and disability in MS, namely sound evidence of psychometric properties and clinical usefulness (Coulthard-Morris, 2000). Our study provided preliminary evidence for psychometric soundness based on the structural validity, reliability, and construct validity of scores from the abbreviated LL-FDI in this sample of individuals with MS. Based on the perspective of clinical usefulness, the abbreviated LL-FDI has low time of administration (5-10 minutes) and degree of respondent burden and high degrees of relative ease of use and user-friendliness combined with the provision of a user manual and training guidelines for the original LL-FDI that are equally applicable for the abbreviated LL-FDI. Other strong features of the abbreviated LL-FDI include the conceptual reasoning behind its development and its basis in Nagi's (1976) disablement framework.

Despite our positive preliminary support, there are several directions for future research in evaluating the psychometric properties of the abbreviated LL-FDI in individuals with MS. One direction for future research involves an examination of correlations between scores from the abbreviated LL-FDI with other self-report measures with relevance for function and disability such as the Expanded Disability Status Scale, Performance Scales, Multiple Sclerosis Impact Scale, and Multiple Sclerosis Walking Scale. Another direction includes an examination of the relationship between scores from the Functional Limitations component of the abbreviated LL-FDI with measures of physical function such as the six-minute walk and climbing and descending stairs. One final direction for future research involved an examination of the sensitivity of the abbreviated LL-FDI based on serial administrations over time in the presence and absence of a treatment for MS, comparisons of the instrument with other criteria of change such as patient or clinician perception, and comparison of the relative responsiveness of the instrument with other instruments of the same entity. Such inquires will provide a clearer picture of the validity of the abbreviated LL-FDI as a measure of function and disability in those with MS.

The continued study of function and disability in MS is important because this is one of the most common neurological diseases among adults 20-50 years of age, affecting approximately 400,000 Americans during the prime years of productivity (NMSS, 2005). Indeed, an estimated 50–80% of individuals with MS are unemployed and disabled within 10 years of disease onset (Rao et al., 1991). The rates of MS and associated unemployment and disability have underscored the importance of examining strategies for reducing functional limitations and disability in this population. Accordingly, future research might consider examining the influence of physical activity on functional limitations and disability in individuals with MS and this could be best accomplished based on Nagi's disablement process model (1976) and the abbreviated LL-FDI. The disablement model and its operational definitions (Verbrugge and Jette, 1994) describe the transitions from pathology (i.e., disease, for example, MS) into impairment (i.e., dysfunction and structural abnormalities in specific body systems, for example, demyelenation of axons in central nervous system), impairment into functional limitations (i.e., restrictions in basic physical and mental actions, for example, walking one mile), and functional limitations into disability (i.e., difficulty doing activities of daily living, for example, activities that are required for one's employment, personal care, and recreation). The disablement model has recently been extended (Stewart, 2003) such that symptoms serve as a step between impairment and functional limitations. Using the abbreviated LL-FDI and a measure of MS-related symptoms, the disablement process model would afford a test of the influence of physical activity on disability, including the possibilities that symptoms and functional limitations serve as entry points for explaining any effect of physical activity on disability in persons with MS.

REFERENCES

Bentler, P.M. (1990). Comparative fit indexes in structural models. *Psychological Bulletin, 107*, 238–246.

Bollen, K.A. (1989). *Structural Equations with Latent Variables*. New York: Wiley-Interscience.

Coulthard-Morris, L. (2000). Clinical and rehabilitation outcome measures. In J.S. Burks and K.P. Johnson (Eds.), *Multiple sclerosis: Diagnosis, medical management, and rehabilitation* (pp. 221-290). New York, NY: Demos.

Craig, C.L., Marshall, A.L., Sjostrom, M., Bauman, A.E., Booth, M.L., Ainsworth, B. E., et al. (2003). International physical activity questionnaire: 12-country reliability and validity. *Medicine and Science in Sports and Exercise*, 35, 1381-1395.

Frohman, E.M., Racke, M., and van den Noort, S. (2000). To treat, or not to treat: The therapeutic dilemma of idiopathic monosymptomatic demyelinating syndromes. *Archives of Neurology, 57*, 930-932.

Godin, G., and Shephard, R.J. (1985). A simple method to assess exercise behavior in the community. *Canadian Journal of Applied Sport Science, 10,* 141-146.

Gosney, J.L., Scott, J.A., Snook, E.M., and Motl, R.W. (in press). Physical activity and multiple sclerosis: Validity of self-report and objective measures. *Family and Community Health*.

Guralnik, J.M., and Ferrucci, L. (2003). Assessing the building blocks of function: Utilizing measures of functional limitation. *American Journal of Preventive Medicine, 25*, (Suppl.), 112-121.

Hoyle, R.H., and Panter, A.T. (1995). Writing about structural equation models. In R.H. Hoyle (Ed.), *Structural equation modeling: Concepts, issues, and applications* (pp. 158-176). Newbury Park, CA: SAGE.

Hu, L., and Bentler, P.M. (1999). Cutoff criteria for fit indices in covariance structure analysis: Conventional versus new alternatives. *Structural Equation Modeling, 6*, 1-55.

Hutchinson, S.R., and Olmos, A. (1998). Behavior of descriptive fit indices in confirmatory factor analysis using ordered categorical data. *Structural Equation Modeling, 5*, 344–364.

Jette, A.M., Haley, S.M., Coster, W.J., Kooyoomjian, J.T., Levenson, S., Heeren, T., et al. (2002). Late life function and disability instrument: I. Development and evaluation of the disability component. *Journals of Gerontology A: Biological Sciences and Medical Sciences, 57*, M209-M216.

Lublin, F.D. (2005). Clinical features and diagnosis of multiple sclerosis. *Neurology Clinics, 23*, 1-15.

McAuley, E., Konopack, J.F., Motl, R.W., Rosengren, K., and Morris K.S. (2005). Measuring disability and function in older women: Psychometric properties of the late-life function and disability instrument. *Journals of Gerontology A: Biological Sciences and Medical Sciences. 60*, 901-909.

Motl, R.W., McAuley, E., Snook, E. M., and Scott, J. A. (2005). Validity of physical activity measures in ambulatory individuals with multiple sclerosis. *Disability and Rehabilitation, 28*, 1151-1156.

Nagi, S.Z. (1976). An epidemiology of disability among adults in the United States. *Milbank Quarterly, 54*, 439-467.

National Multiple Sclerosis Society (2005). *Multiple sclerosis information sourcebook.* New York: Information Resource Center and Library of the National Multiple Sclerosis Society.

Rao, S. M., Leo, G. J., Ellington, L., Nauretz, T., Bernardin, L., and Unverzagt, F. (1991). Cognitive dysfunction in multiple sclerosis: II. Impact on employment and social functioning. *Neurology, 41*, 692-696.

Rudick, R., Antel, J., Confavreux, C., Cutter, G., Ellison, G., Fischer, J., et al. (1996). Clinical outcomes and assessment in multiple sclerosis. *Annals of Neurology, 49*, 469-479.

Runmarker, B., and Andersen, O. (1993). Prognostic factors in multiple sclerosis incident cohort with twenty-five years of follow-up. *Brain, 116*, 117-134.

Stewart, A.L. (2003). Conceptual challenges in linking physical activity and disability research. *American Journal of Preventive Medicine, 25*, (Suppl.), 137-140.

Verbrugge, L.M., and Jette, A.M. (1994). The disablement process. *Social Science in Medicine, 38*, 1-14.

Weinshenker, B.G., Bass, B., Rice, G.P., Noseworthy, J., Carriere W., Baskerville, J., et al. (1989). The natural history of multiple sclerosis: A geographically based study. Clinical course and disability. *Brain, 112*, 133-146.

In: Psychological Tests and Testing Research Trends   ISBN: 978-1-60021-569-8
Editor: Paul M. Goldfarb, pp. 265-281   © 2007 Nova Science Publishers, Inc.

Chapter 13

METHODOLOGICAL TOPICS TO DEVELOP A NEW OUTCOME MEASURE

Masami Akai and Tokuhide Doi*

Department of Rehabilitation for Movement Functions,
Research Institute, National Rehabilitation Center
Tokorozawa, Saitama, Japan
Fukuoka Clinic, Adachi, Tokyo, Japan

ABSTRACT

The concept of "outcomes" has become widely accepted in clinical medicine as a means to evaluate the results of a medical intervention. In the past there was a reluctance to place a high value on patients' perceptions, but it is now generally agreed that patient-based outcomes are a valuable method of determining function and quality of life. In order for any outcome-based instrument to be useful, it must be user-friendly for both the clinician and patient, but it must be also statistically reliable and valid. These goals can be achieved through careful preparation by experts, sufficient feedback from patient groups, and by comparing objective clinical data with the results of the outcome instrument itself.

In this chapter, we would like to focus on the following 4 methodological issues and other related topics;

1. Selection of appropriate content for question items

For most outcome instruments, an ordinal scale is used with 3 to 5 choices ranging from a negative extreme to a positive extreme. However, grading schemes sometime use unclear phrasing which results in a misunderstanding by the patient. It is important, therefore, to ensure that the choice of content is comprehensive, yet unambiguous.

2. Relationships among items

Multivariate analyses are often used to statistically evaluate the strength of a relationship between a dependent variable and multiple independent variables. However, the assumption that the relationships are linear may not always be true in the case of

---

* Corresponding Address: Masami Akai, MD, PhD; Department of Rehabilitation for Movement Functions, Research Institute, National Rehabilitation Center Japan, 4-1 Namiki, Tokorozawa, Saitama 359-8555, Japan; TEL: +81-42-995-3100 (ext 3001), FAX: +81-42-995-3132, e-mail: akai@rehab.go.jp

outcome measures. It is necessary to use information criteria or data-specific multiple comparisons to check relationships among instrument items.

3. Construct validity

Categorical principal component analysis (CPCA) is a powerful statistical tool to reveal the patterns of shared variation or interrelationships within a score matrix. Through CPCA, items are clustered into related groups and dimensionally rotated. The number of dimensions – in effect, grouping clusters – is determined through scree plot or testing.

4. Evaluation of non-parametric tests

Non-parametric tests are commonly used in psychometric assessment, which involve the analysis of the difference between the median and its 95% confidence interval within a set of data. No standard method for estimation of the result of non-parametric calculations has been determined for evaluating outcomes instruments, but some promising methodologies deserve special attention.

INTRODUCTION

In clinical studies, where effective therapy must take into account the diversity of patients and disease symptoms, it is difficult to find a direct "intervention-outcome" or "cause-result" relationship from a treatment intervention. In order to investigate the effectiveness of a certain therapy from a collection of clinical cases, it is necessary to eliminate the unique conditions found in individual cases and to extract the essential characteristics common to all cases.

Recently, the concept of "outcomes" to evaluate medical interventions by comparing pre- and post-treatment effects has been widely accepted in clinical medicine. Assessment of interventional results based on health-related quality of life or patient-based outcomes brings us a greater understanding about patients' value judgments, and in turn, increases our ability to develop accurate psychometric instruments. In the past there was reluctance to put a high value on patients' perceptions, but it is now generally agreed that patient-based outcomes are important, and should be assessed directly with proper instruments [1].

Outcomes research should appropriately evaluate what patients think of the results of the medical intervention they were given. Psychometric assessments that fail to accurately correlate question responses to actual patient perceptions may obfuscate meaningful trends and/or cause healthcare professionals to waste resources on treatments with little benefit. It is absolutely important, therefore, to obtain information in terms of functional status, health-related quality of life and other related data, through valid and reliable psychological assessment of patients' values and perceptions [2]. In this chapter we would like to explain, based on our research experiences, the process of developing a new outcomes instrument (i.e. a patient-focused ordinal scale questionnaire) based on the process proposed by Suk et al [3]. (table 1)

1. BUILDING A COLLABORATIVE TEAM

1.1. Collaborative Team

To develop a new outcomes instrument, it is important to first organize a collaborative team including clinicians in the targeted field, a methodologist (clinical epidemiologist and/or biostatistician), and if possible, patients. Once the team is in place, the members need to develop a process with clear and attainable goals:

1. Develop a set of question items, and if necessary, cut down the number to a manageable size
2. Conduct a pretest to formulate a measuring scale for the question items
3. Check for criterion-related and other validities, and reliability
4. Define the measuring concept and check for construct validity
5. Evaluate the question items based on steps 3 and 4 and modify or delete items as necessary
6. Group the edited question items and confirm the integrity of the new outcomes instrument.

There are several necessary steps to be statistically tested using multivariate or other analyses, requiring a comprehensive understanding of statistical methodologies [4-6]. Unfortunately, there are few clinical epidemiologists or biostatisticians who also have a deep knowledge of clinical practice in our country.

1.2. Generic Instruments and Disease-Specific Instruments

There are two kinds of questions that can be formulated to measure patient perceptions of health-related quality of life: generic or disease-specific. Generic instruments are used across different diseases and different cultural backgrounds. The majority of instruments are designed to be multi-dimensional and to give comprehensive overviews. There are several well-known generic measures of health-related quality of life, including the Sickness impact profile, Nottingham health profile, and Short Form-36 [7-11]. Disease-specific instruments, as the name implies, are more focused on precise aspects of patient health. They are developed to provide relevant content related to a particular disease or site of the body. This kind of specification makes these instruments more suitable to detect smaller and/or key changes within a particular disease or condition.

2. SELECTION OF QUESTION ITEMS; CONTENT VALIDITY

2.1. Translation and Evaluation of Foreign Language Outcomes Instruments

It is not so difficult to translate the overall content of an outcomes instrument into vernacular language, but it is much more difficult to accurately verify psychometric validity.

The existence of cross-cultural differences is one of the basic problems in trying to develop a universal standard of medical outcome assessment. Dissimilar interpretations of question items based on linguistic or cultural differences are common, thereby compromising content validity.

We experienced this problem first-hand when we used the Roland-Morris Disability Questionnaire (RDQ) for low back pain on Japanese patients.[12, 13] In the RDQ there were some questions which Japanese found difficult to answer in the "either/or" format presented, e.g., "stay at home" in the question 1, or "jobs around the house" in the question 21. In question 19 of the RDQ, patients were asked about their capability to do self-care with or without someone's help, yet Japanese patients tended to interpret the question with regard to relationships with their surroundings.

2.2. Selection of Appropriate Content for Question Items

To select the most appropriate content of a new instrument, the initial set of questions should be developed collaboratively and with sufficient review and revision. Clinicians with extensive first-hand experience with the targeted disease/condition are usually very skilled at identifying key question items. Through repeated discussions among the team, the content of each question should be determined based on its pertinence to the aims of the questionnaire. Each question should also reflect the contemporary lifestyles of the targeted patient group.

Some older outcomes instruments combined patient symptoms and clinical physiological findings into a single performance score. These types of instruments make it difficult to develop a grading scale that accurately weights empirical data and subjective judgments, and they may cause confusion because a lumped score fails to provide information regarding different aspects of a disease or condition.

For most outcome instruments consisting of question items, an ordinal scale is used ranging from a negative extreme to a positive extreme. However, grading schemes sometimes comprise unclear phrasing which results in a misunderstanding by the patient. It is important, therefore, to ensure that the choice of content is comprehensive, yet unambiguous. Most outcomes instruments use a scale with 3 to 5 grades for each item. However, poorly constructed scales may not encompass the whole targeted sphere of a particular question. For example, a 5-point scale with the positive and negative extremes "unable to do" and "able to do" may, at first glance appear straightforward. Yet in our development of a chronic low back pain instrument, subjects were sometimes physically able to perform a task, but chose to avoid it when possible. Therefore, we found that a more appropriate grading scale consisted of "hard to do" and "not hard to do". Effective grading scales should also be able to discriminate between the frequency and severity of a disease, as these are separate phenomena. In order to check the validity or reliability of a scale, a statistical analysis is essential. However, the team must decide whether the data from the instrument will be parametric or non-parametric. In other words, data that are not normally distributed must be evaluated differently; an issue that is often overlooked by researchers not sufficiently knowledgeable about statistics [14].

2.3. Pilot Study

Once the first version of the questionnaire has been drafted, a pilot test should be conducted on a small group of patients. Face validity is basically assured by a panel of experts who evaluate the relevance of the content, and the pilot study is used to confirm this. The difference between face validity and content validity is explained by Guyatt et al. [15] as follows: "Face validity examines whether an instrument appears to be measuring what it is intended to measure, and content validity examines the extent to which the domain of interest is comprehensively sampled by the items, or questions, in the instrument."

Revision of the questions is continued as necessary. During this process, the aim of the outcomes instrument may also be refined. Practical issues such as the length of time to complete the questionnaire, and the presence of confusing or personally-uncomfortable questions should be carefully examined. A poorly designed questionnaire will result in poor compliance and unreliable results.

3. Relationships among Items

3.1. Cluster Structure of Outcomes Instrument

We developed the Japanese knee osteoarthritis measure (JKOM), a self-administered, disease-specific instrument, which includes questions about patient pain in level walking, standing or climbing stairs, physical functions related to the activities of daily living, and social participation [16]. Based on the ICF concept, we assumed that the disabilities associated with knee osteoarthritis patients were as follows:

- Health condition: osteoarthritis
- Impairment: knee pain
- Activity limitation: difficulty in mobility-related daily activities
- Participation restriction: difficulty in participating in social activities

However it is necessary to confirm whether the aims of questionnaire developer are well reflected in the answers of patients. To understand the essential characteristics of this multi-faceted disease, statistical tools are available to define the cluster structure of the questions within the instrument. Factor analysis and principal component analysis, and the recently introduced Akaike information criterion are useful, powerful tools to that we have used to analyze latent structures within newly created outcomes instruments.

3.2. Akaike Information Criterion (AIC)

The Akaike information criterion (AIC), developed by Akaike in 1971, is a measure of the goodness of fit of an estimated statistical model. The AIC is an operational way of trading off the complexity of an estimated model against how well the model fits the data [17]. It is a popular method for comparing the adequacy of multiple, possibly non-nested models and able to assess the relationship between two items.

Because it is a very general method, the AIC has been applied to a wide range of situations relevant to cognitive psychology [18]. For instance, the AIC is often used as a measure of model adequacy in both structural equation modeling and time series analysis. The AIC is also applied in factor analysis, regression, and latent class analysis. A sample of other recent contexts in which the AIC has been employed includes competitive testing of models of categorization, modeling of mixture distributions, modeling of luminance detection, and modeling of perception with the use of stochastic catastrophe models.

We used the AIC to investigate the construct structure and domain of items within a newly developed questionnaire for low back pain in Japan. The JLEQ is a self-administered, disease-specific measure, and consists of 30- items, including 7 questions regarding low back pain during the last few days, 17 questions regarding the problems in daily activity due to low back pain during the last few days, and 6 questions regarding the conditions during the last one month [19].

Two to four dimension multiple cross tabulation was performed with JLEQ, resulting in $31929 (= {}_{30}C_2 + {}_{30}C_3 + {}_{30}C_4)$ combinations. AIC values were calculated for all the combinations and sorted in ascending order using Categorical Data Analytic Procedure 2 (CATDAP2). The AIC analysis revealed that there were some two item groupings but no groups with 3 or 4 items. No confounding factors were found.

The AIC calculation produced $435(= {}_{30}C_2)$ "minimal distance" assortments of 2 items groupings. The spatial relationship of the calculated groupings is shown in figure 1 (animated TIFF). The plot was created using Graph-Layout, an applet written in the JAVA programming language [Sun Microsystems I. Graph.java 1.9. 1999].

In figure 1, the items related to lying down and rising from a horizontal position were located in the right lower region of the plot, while those related to coordinated lower limb and lumbar spine movement were grouped in the left lower region. The items associated with posture and movements of lumbar spine without locomotion were clustered in the right middle region, while locomotion and work or house-hold task items were clustered in the left middle region. Finally, social and psycho-emotional items were located in the upper region of the plot.

In the past when modeling with non-parametric data, we often faced a so-called "horse-shoe effect", in which a distortion occurred in the ordination diagrams. Because data from ordinal or Guttman scales often cause plotted graphs to assume a horseshoe like U-shape or bell-curve, the effect is often observed for very long gradients in principal components analysis. To avoid this horse-shoe problem, we have found that the above described AIC analysis is an effective way to investigate the construct structure and domain of items.

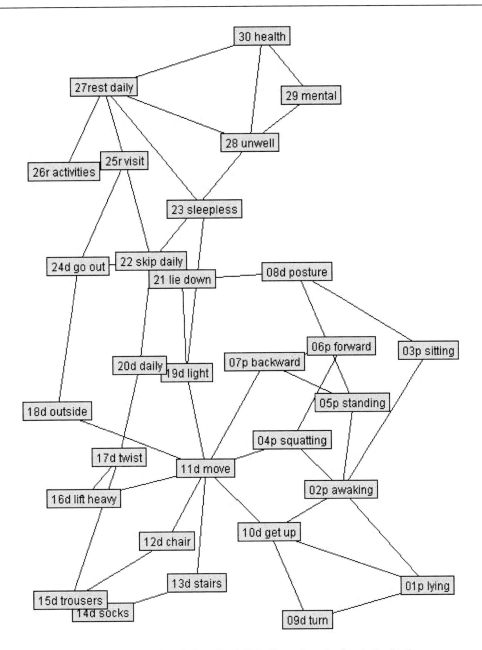

Figure 1. From our Questionnaire for Chronic Low Back Pain (Japan Low back pain Evaluation Questionnaire; JLEQ); The numbers indicate the content of each item in JLEQ; d=abbreviation for difficulty, p=abbreviation for pain. Related question items and their spatial representations are as follows:
Lying down and rising from a horizontal position--right lower region
Coordinated lower limb and lumbar spine movement--left lower region
Posture and movements of lumbar spine without locomotion--right middle region
Locomotion and work or house-hold task items--left middle region
Social and psycho-emotional items--upper region
Supplemental data including an animation of Figure 1 (Gr.aph Layout in animated GIF) are available online at: http://breezeway.fc2web.com/JLEQ/jleq_aic_layout.ppt.

3.3. Reliability of Tests

Reliability is directly related to the quality of an instrument and is a measure of its consistency. If not so, observed changes found in patient group could not be attributed to the treatment effect, but to the methodological problems in measurement [20].

Reproducibility is the main concept of reliability and consists of inter-observer and intra-observer reliabilities. Inter-observer (inter-rater) reliability describes how closely different observers rate the same subject. A well designed instrument should produce consistent scores on different occasions by different raters. Intra-observer (intra-rater) reliability is related to the consistency of the results of one patient on separate occasions using the same rater. This is also called "test-retest" reproducibility and is usually assessed by an interclass correlation coefficient (ICC) in the case of parametric data, and by a Kappa coefficient in the case of non-parametric data. Internal consistency is a measure of the reliability of related questions to produce similar scores, and can be determined by calculating Cronbach's alpha for each subscale or items [21]. The answers obtained through the questionnaire should be consistent and reflect the psychological condition of the patient.

4. Meaning of Measurement: Construct Validity

4.1. Latent Structure of Construct Validity

Construct validity is a more quantitative assessment than content validity. As construct validity is pluralistic in its intrinsic nature, its conceptual structure has some domains or subgroups [20]. Therefore in order to check construct validity, it is necessary to investigate the latent structure of a new outcomes instrument and to compare it with other similar instruments. Just like a diagnostic test, construct validity has two aspects similar to sensitivity and specificity. Convergent validity is a measure of the degree of relatedness between two instruments that observe the same target or concept (e.g. low back pain or knee osteoarthritis in our past experience). It is reasonable – in fact desirable – that the scores on different instruments are similar for questions that are related to the same aspect of a disease or condition. If there is low correlation, and one of the instruments in the comparison is a gold standard, then it can be said that the new instrument is not validly measuring the disease and needs to be revised. Divergent validity, on the other hand, is a measure of the correlation between two instruments that observe different aspects within a similar framework. With divergent validity, high correlations indicate that the two instruments are too similar and, therefore, the new instrument will be unable to provide new or different aspects of the disease. Convergent and divergent validity are interlocking components of construct validity, yet determining acceptable values for each is a qualitative assessment and should be considered very carefully.

4.2. Multivariate Analyses

Multivariate analyses are often used to statistically evaluate the strength of a relationship between multiple independent (explanatory) variables and a dependent (objective) variable. However, the assumption that the relationships are linear may not always be true in the case of outcomes instruments. It is necessary to use information criteria or data-specific multiple comparisons to check relationships among instrument items.

Objective variable = simple equation of multiple explanatory variables

Factor analysis is a useful tool to evaluate latent factors or structures which are unable to be measured directly through simple linear regression. The two types of factor analysis are Exploratory Factor Analysis and Confirmatory Factor Analysis. The former is used to determine the factors that explain objective variable drift without a hypothesis or theoretical basis, while the later is used to check the factors and their affected variables or inter-factorial relationships on the basis of previously observed findings. In exploratory factor analysis, a latent factor is defined as an objective variable that is under the influence of several explanatory variables. The strength of the contributions of each variable is expressed by a loading pattern of factors. Factor extraction is the process of finding "common factors" that affect the objective variable and assigning a loading influence value to them.

4.3. Dimensional Structure

The dimensions of the measurement instrument have to be consistent with the various groups investigated [22]. It should be tested among the items correlating with the same kind of subscale scores in all patients. It is especially important because pooled analyses usually evaluate outcomes in diagnostically mixed patient groups. Traditional methods to investigate the dimensional structure of measurement are factor analysis or principal component analysis and Rasch analysis. The Rasch measurement model, based on items response theory, is able to explore whether all items of the scale measure a single dimension of a scale or not [23]. It is also able to convert an ordinal scale into an interval scale. If the items examined did not fit the model, it will show that those items measure a different construct.

In exploratory factor analysis the most important step is determining the number of factors. The scoring distribution of each factor indicates the correlation matrix in order of the largest value in each dimension. The researchers must determine the cut-off point for accepting a factor or not.

Scree Test and Mathematical Rotation

A scree test can be used to identify the point (factor load criterion) where the decreasing percentage of variance explained by the factors levels off [24]. From our knee osteoarthritis data, the appropriate cut off point for the number of factor dimensions was found to be 2 or 3, which in effect, means that the number of grouping clusters was 2 or 3. (figure 2a)

To interpret most factor analysis applications, the factors should be adjusted, i.e. rotated, mathematically to more clearly define their clusters [25]. After mathematical rotation of the three-dimensional graph and the divided subgroups, the data are then converted into a two-dimensional graph to show the question item interrelationships.

4.4. Categorical Principal Component Analysis

In cases where there is no objective variable (external criterion) identified, principal component analysis is used to condense the number of explanatory variables and to examine their characteristics. It is also possible to transform an ordinal scale into an interval scale with this technique.

Categorical principal component analysis (CATPCA) simultaneously quantifies categorical variables while reducing the dimensionality of the data. This procedure is another powerful statistical tool to reveal the patterns of shared variation or inter-relationships within a score matrix, and to investigate factor loading patterns or background architecture, even from ordinal scale data. Through CATPCA and its proper rotation, question items are clustered into related groups. We developed a CATPCA program to analyze our data written in the SYNTAX language for use with statistic software such as SPSS (SPSS Inc. Chicago, Illinois 60606). During processing of the JOKM results, factor analysis was performed on the assumption that the questionnaires provided quantitative data, followed by a categorical principal component analysis to confirm the dimensional structure. The results of the JKOM original version are shown in figure 2b. The construct structure consisted of three item clusters.

4.5. The Mathematical Dealing of Factor Analysis and Principal Component Analysis

Multivariate analysis, in which a dependent (objective) variable is explained by multiple independent (explanatory) variables, is realized in the assumption of linear regression. Generally speaking, the scoring values derived from an outcomes instrument should not be regarded as quantitative data due to the fact that they are derived from ordinal scales. Factor analyses and principal components analysis (PCA) that combine dichotomous scores and continuous values in their algebraic computations should only, in the strictest sense, be interpreted qualitatively. However, it is still possible to test the assumption of the linearity of factor and question item relationships by using information criteria or multiple comparisons based on the nature of the data where necessary.

Factor analysis is similar to principal components analysis, except that the former tries to find common factors accounting for as much of the total variance as possible, while the latter seeks to reduce the number of putative underlying factors.

Retest with Factor Analysis

We performed several repeated mathematical rotations of the JKOM data to converge the factors, and then the varimax rotated item patterns were extracted to display the results of the factor-loading pattern. After reselection of the items and modulation of their expression we performed the test again to improve the questionnaire. We found three clearly separated domains of the loading pattern, i.e., (figure 2c)

(1) pain,

(2) limited mobility related to daily activities,

(3) restricted participation in social life and health perception.

Our factor analysis of the JKOM data illustrated that there were underlying item clusters that were a reflection of the multidimensional and interrelated structure of the new instrument, thereby providing a new insight to patient perspectives and self-image according to developer's intention.

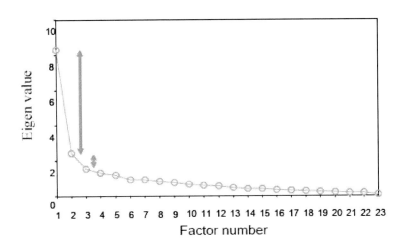

a.

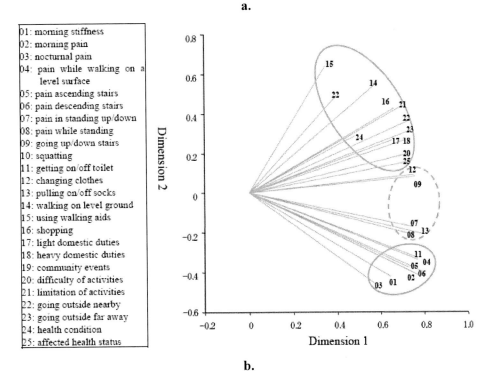

b.

Figure 2. Continued.

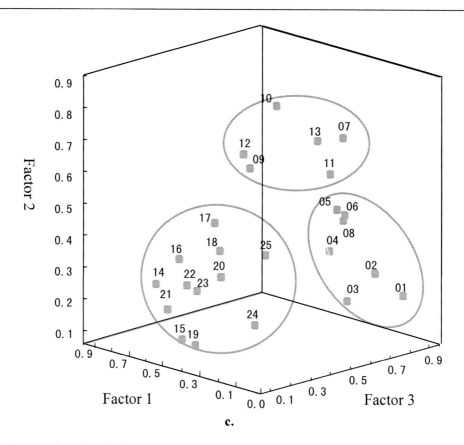

c.

Figure 2. From our Questionnaire for Knee Osteoarthritis (Japanese Knee Osteoarthritis Measure; JKOM).
2a: In factor analysis the most important step is determining the number of factors. The scoring distribution
of each factor indicates the correlation matrix in order of the largest value in each dimension. A scree test can
be used to identify the point (factor load criterion) where the decreasing percentage of variance explained by
the factors levels off. From the knee osteoarthritis data, the appropriate cut off point for the number of factor
dimensions was found to be 2 or 3.
2b: Categorical principal component analysis (CATPCA) simultaneously quantifies categorical variables
while reducing the dimensionality of the data. Through CATPCA and its proper mathematical rotation,
question items are clustered into related groups. The numbers indicate the content of each item in the JKOM.
2c: Exploratory factor analysis is a powerful statistical tool to reveal the patterns of shared variation or interrelationships within a score matrix, and to investigate factor loading patterns or background architecture,
even from ordinal scale data. The result shows that three domains are clearly separated; (1) pain, (2)
limitation in mobility related to daily activity, and (3) restriction of social participation and health perception.

5. COMPARISON WITH OTHER TESTS: CRITERION-RELATED VALIDITY

5.1. Criterion-Related Validity

New outcomes instruments should be evaluated relative to previously existing ones with
direct comparisons performed in the same patient population. The checkpoint used for direct
comparisons is known as criterion-related validity. Criterion-related validity evaluates
whether an instrument correlates highly with an existing "gold standard" test of the same
disease or condition. When a gold standard does not exist, it is possible to use a less-

established, but related test for comparison. In the vast majority of emerging research areas, however, gold standards or related instruments do not exist, making it difficult to test external criterion validity.

5.2. Comparison with other Tests

Conventionally, as a check of concurrent validity, Pearson's Correlation coefficient is widely used for two variables from parametric continuous data, while Kendall's rank correlation coefficient (tau), or Spearman's Correlation coefficient may be used for categorical data or non parametric variables.

We have examined concurrent validity within similar subscales that are supposed to be equivalent and highly correlated. For example, to test the concurrent validity of a low back pain questionnaire, the authors compared disease-specific items related to "depression" with generic "mental health" items from the SF-36 [13].

Correlation coefficients, however, are calculated from the comparison of different continuous data, for example, height and weight. When measuring similar parameters, even with two different scales, it is natural to expect a high correlation to some extent. Therefore it is not appropriate to put too much significance onto the value of correlation coefficient.

6. EVALUATION OF NON-PARAMETRIC TESTS

6.1. Meaning of P-Value

When comparing two or more groups, there is often a statistical significance result reported as a p-value. However, a p-value does not indicate the amount of difference or ratio found between samples. A small p-value does not mean a greater difference between groups, therefore it is important to distinguish the difference between p-value for statistical hypothesis testing and estimation with confidence intervals. The p-value is not an indicator of measurement error or uncertainty but the probability that the observation result happens by chance with a value from 0 to 1. If the degree of difference between two groups is deemed to be most important, then confidence intervals should be used.

6.2. Normalization of Original Data

The next important problem at the stage of data processing is the nature of data from a statistical point of view. The concepts of "mean" and "standard deviation" can only be correctly applied to normal distributions. Normality is evaluated by histograms or distribution plots for the variable. If the data are normally distributed and of the sample size is sufficient large, a parametric statistical test can be used.

We would like to describe a typical example from our daily laboratory data. Histograms of such data showed that total protein had a typical bell-shaped normal distribution, but hemoglobin and the hepatic enzyme GOT were skewed. In order to normalize these skewed distributions, it was possible to transform them with an exponential square calculation for hemoglobin and a logarithm value calculation for GOT. Following these mathematical manipulations, the skewed parameters assumed a normal distribution. However, in cases where normalization cannot be achieved through mathematical operations, such as in the case of bimodally distributed (i.e. two-peaks) data, non-parametric statistical methods must be used. In parametric tests it is not so difficult to calculate parameter means and 95% confidence intervals. However, for non-parametric tests that are commonly used in psychometric assessment, box and whisker plots that display the median and percentiles (e.g. 25% and 75%) are more appropriate.

6.3. Median and Its 95% Confidence Interval

From a practical point of view, when we compare two treatments, we have to know not only which one is the more efficient therapy but also by how much it is better. Statistical significance of a certain finding depends not only upon the degree of deviation from the null hypothesis but also upon the sample size of the deviation observed.

In non-parametric data, a commonly used statistical value is the median. It is somewhat difficult work, however, to compare medians from two sets of non-parametric data because the values cannot be directly compared in the same manner as continuous parametric data. The subjective perceptions of two parameters may be meaningfully related, but a quantitative evaluation of medians with an estimation range, such as 95% confidence intervals, cannot be performed [26]. No standard method for estimation of the results of non-parametric calculations has been yet determined for evaluating outcomes instruments, but some promising methodologies deserve special attention. For example, Campbell and Gardner described their method to give the median and its 95% confidence interval. [27]

7. CLINICAL UTILITY

7.1. Data Form

The data collection form is important to collect all the information of participants. The design of the data form should start early in the protocol development process.

Farell and Spark proposed the following simple tips for the design of data forms [28]

- Always collect raw data, if necessary it can be categorized later.
- Build in cross checks for important times and dates.
- Ask questions in an order that will make sense to the person completing the form.
- Line up boxes, to reduce the risk of any being missed.
- Make the forms look attractive, don't clutter them up or use too small of a font.
- Get professional advice, for example from your local medical illustration department.

7.2. Clinical Testing of a Newly Developed Instrument

Once a new instrument or questionnaire has been written, a pilot study with a small sample of representative patients should be conducted. The questionnaire should be easy to understand, able to be completed in a relatively brief time, and concise in terms of utility. Patients to be interviewed are not always familiar with these kinds of questionnaires, so it is important to check face validity at this stage, i.e., are the meanings of the questions interpreted by the patients in the intended manner? Dichotomous questions such as "yes-no" are often poorly answered because they do not provide a suitable description of patients' thinking. In terms of clinical use of the instrument, it is also important to think about the effort that researchers will have to exert in order to conduct the questionnaire and collect the completed data. A well designed outcomes instrument will also be responsive to changes in a patient's condition. Questions should be able to target different aspects of the disease or condition, and the grading scale should have enough choices so that even a relatively minor, but meaningful, improvement or deterioration can be detected. Following the pilot study, reselection of questions is the next important step. Based on the various psychometric analyses of each question item (e.g. validity, reliability, responsiveness), some of the questions may need to be modified, new questions added, and others deleted. Finally, once the new questionnaire has been developed, it should be sent to other researchers for appraisal. In fact, as no instrument is perfect when first reported, it will likely need continual refinement as feedback is received. (table 2)

7.3. Necessary Steps in Ethics

Approval by the Institutional Review Board (IRB) or ethics committee is required before patient recruitment can start. Such committees must include both clinical and non-medical members and follow the guidelines set in the Declaration of Helsinki [29]. The main role of the committee is to ensure that both scientific and ethical aspects of the trial are conducted appropriately. The operational protocol of the trial including consent form, data collection forms, information leaflet for patients, and letters to attending doctors, co-medical staff, and participants must be prepared. A scientific justification of the study aims and the validity of the methods to be used, as well as an ethical estimation of risks, informed consent measures, and the steps taken to ensure protection of personal information must be clearly delineated. These documents should be completed according to the guidelines of the IRB, and in the case of patients, be written in a clear and easily understood manner.

Finally, agreement by patients to participate in the trial should be confirmed in writing.

CONCLUSION

The concept of "outcomes" has become widely accepted in clinical medicine as a means to evaluate the results of a medical intervention. In the past there was a reluctance to place a high value on patients' perceptions, but it is now generally agreed that patient-based outcomes are a valuable method of determining function and quality of life. In order for any outcome-based instrument to be useful, it must be user-friendly for both the clinician and patient, but it must be also statistically reliable and valid. These goals can be achieved through careful preparation by experts, sufficient feedback from patient groups, and by comparing objective clinical data with the results of the outcome instrument itself.

REFERENCES

[1] Ware JE. Measuring patients' views; the optimum outcome measure. *BMJ.* 306: 1429-1430, 1993

[2] Guyatt GH, Kirshner B, Jaeschke R. Measuring health status; What are the necessary measurement properties? *J. Clin. Epidemiol.* 12: 1341-1345,1992

[3] Suk M, Hanson BP, Norvell DC, et al. *AO Handbook; Musculoskeletal outcomes measures and instruments; 155 instruments evaluated and assessed.* AO publishers, Davos, 2005

[4] McDowell I, Newell C. *The theoretical and technical foundations of health measurement. Measuring health; A guide to rating scales and questionnaires.* (2nd ed.), Oxford University Press, New York, 1996

[5] Bowling A. *Measuring disease; A review of disease-specific quality of life measurement scales.* (2nd ed.), Open University Press, Buckingham, 2001

[6] Streiner DL, Norman GR. *Health measurement scales; a practical guide to their development and use.*(3rd ed), Oxford University Press, Oxford, 2003

[7] Bergner M, Bobbitt RA, Kressel S, et al. The sickness impact profile; Conceptual formation and methodology for the development of a health status measure. *Int. J. Health Serv.* 6:393-415, 1976

[8] Bergner M, Bobbitt RA, Carter W, et al. The sickness impact profile; Development and final revision of a health status measure. *Med. Care.* 19:787-805,1981

[9] Hunt SM, Mckenna SP, McEwen J, et al. The Nottingham health profile. Subjective health status and medical consultations. *Soc. Sci. Med.* 15A:221-229, 1981

[10] Ware JA, Sherbourne CD. The MOS 36-item short-form health survey (SF-36); I .Conceptual framework and item selection. *Med. Care.* 30:473-483,1992

[11] McHorney CA, Ware JA, Raczek AE. The MOS 36-item short-form health survey;.Psychometric and clinical tests of validity in measuring physical and mental health constructs. *Med. Care.* 31:247-263,1993

[12] Roland M, Morris R. A study of the natural history of back pain. Part I: development of a reliable and sensitive measure of disability in low-back pain. *Spine.* 8:141-144, 1983

[13] Suzukamo Y, Fukuhara S, Kikuchi S, et al. Validation of the Japanese version of the Roland-Morris Disability Questionnaire. *J. Orthop. Sci.* 8:543-548, 2003

[14] Svensson E. guidelines to statistical evaluation of data from rating scales and questionnaires. *J. Rehab. Med.* 33:47-48,2001

[15] Guyatt GH, Feeny DH, Patrick DL. Measuring health-related quality of life. *Ann. Intern. Med.* 118:622-629,1993

[16] Akai M, Doi T, Fujino K, Iwaya T, Kurosawa H, Nasu T. An outcome measure for Japanese people with knee osteoarthritis. *J. Rheumatol.* 32:1524-1532, 2005

[17] Akaike H. Information theory and an extension of the maximum likelihood principle. In: *Proceedings of the Second International Symposium on Information Theory.* (Petrov BN, Caski F. edts), Akademiai Kiado, Budapest, 1973, pp.267-281

[18] Wagenmakers EJ, Farrell S. AIC model selection using Akaike weights. *Psychon. Bull. Rev.* 11:192-196, 2004

[19] Shirado O, Doi T, Akai M, Fujino K, Hoshino Y, Iwaya T. An outcome measure for Japanese people with chronic low back pain; An introduction and validation study of Japan Low back pain Evaluation Questionnaire (JLEQ). Spine (in submission)

[20] Riegelman RK. *Studying a study and testing a test; How to read the medical evidence.* (5th ed.), Lippincott Williams and Wilkins, Philadelphia, 2005

[21] Cronbach LJ. Coefficient alpha and the internal structure of tests. *Psychometrica,* 16:297-334, 1951

[22] Dekker J, Dallmeijer AJ, Lankhorst GJ: Clinimetrics in rehabilitation medicine; current issues in developing and applying measurement instruments. *J. Rehabil. Med.* 37:193-201, 2005

[23] Tesio L. Measuring behaviours and perceptions; Rasch analysis as a tool for rehabilitation research. *J. Rehabil. Med.* 35:105-115, 2003

[24] Cattell RB. The scree test for the number of factors. *Multivariate Behav. Res.* 1:245-276, 1966

[25] Kaiser HF. The varimax criterion for analytic rotation in factor analysis. *Psychometrica.* 23:187-200, 1958

[26] Hodges JR, Lehmann EL. Estimates of location based on rank tests. *Ann. Math. Statist.* 34: 598-611, 1963

[27] Campbell MJ, Gardner MJ. Medians and their differences. In: *Statistics with Confidence.* (2nd ed.), (Altman DG, Machin D, Bryant TN, Gardner MJ. eds), *BMJ. Books,* Bristol, 2000, pp.36-44

[28] Farrell B, Spark P. Building resources for randomized trials. In: *Clinical Trials.* (Duley L, Farrell B. eds), *BMJ Books,* London, 2002, pp.80

[29] World Medical Association. Recommendation guiding physicians in biomedical research involving human subjects. As adopted by the 18th World Medical Assembly, Helsinki, June 1964

In: Psychological Tests and Testing Research Trends
Editor: Paul M. Goldfarb, pp. 283-293

ISBN: 978-1-60021-569-8

Chapter 14

A SIMPLE BEDSIDE TEST TO DETECT AND EVALUATE INTENTIONAL NEGLECT

J.C. Bier[1]*, F. Degreef[1], S. Camut[2] and M. Vokaer[1]

[1] Department of Neurology and [2] Department of Occupational Therapy
Erasme Hospital, Université Libre de Bruxelles, Brussels, BELGIUM.

ABSTRACT

The detection of intentional neglect requires time and equipment. In order to simplify its detection, we developed new software running on Microsoft Windows®, inverting right-left horizontal movements of the mouse cursor while leaving its vertical movements unchanged. We observed on eight successive subjects, that the software increased the expression of attentional neglect and detected intentional neglect. To conclude, we developed a simple, fast and objectively analyzable bedside test to detect and evaluate intentional neglect.

Keywords: neglect, intentional, test, software

INTRODUCTION

Stroke represents one of the leading causes of morbidity in many countries. Indeed, in 1992, at least 70% of the patients who survive one year after stroke remain disabled (Bonita R. 1992). Among impairments following stroke, hemispatial visual neglect is recognized as an important factor associated with a poor functional outcome (Jehkonen M, *et al.* 2000)(Denes G, *et al.* 1982)(Stone SP, *et al.* 1992). Hemispatial visual neglect is defined as a defect of perception, attention, representation, and/or of performing actions in the contralateral area to a cerebral lesion despite normal motor and perception functions (Rode G,

---

* Address Correspondence and reprint requests to Dr. Jean-Christophe Bier, Hôpital Erasme; Service de Neurologie (3ème étage); Route de Lennik, 808, B-1070 Bruxelles; Belgique. e-mail : Jean-Christophe.Bier@ulb.ac.be Tel: 00322 555 34 29 Fax: 00322 555 39 42.

et al. 2003). Visual neglect induces many functional disabilities in everyday life. It is found in at least 40% of patients with acute stroke (Kalra L, *et al.* 1997). When present, hemispatial visual neglect worsens prognosis, especially when the right hemisphere is damaged (Kalra L, *et al.* 1997). Many authors consider neglect as lateralized attention impairment (Driver J, Mattingley JB. 1995). However, hemispatial visual neglect is a complex phenomenon that can be divided into different nosological entities, which may be isolated or associated. This neurological deficit may be predominantly object-centred or scene-based, externalised or internalised, motor (intentional) or perceptual (attentional) (Tegnér R, Levander M. 1991)(Harvey M, Kramer-McCaffery T, *et al.* 2003).

To date, no therapy has formally proven long term effectiveness in neglect (Cappa SF, *et al.* 2005). On a pragmatic model, therapeutics could be non specific, bottom-up targeted stimulation, top-down targeted stimulation, manipulation of inhibitory processes and manipulation of arousal mechanism (Robertson and Murre. 1999). Even if some studies showed statistical benefits of various technics, the great deal of these trials attests theirs lack of reproducible, durable, efficiencies. This is the case for various combined training therapies (Antonucci A, *et al.* 1995)(Pizzamiglio L, *et al.* 1992)(Vallar G, *et al.* 1997), including at a functional level (Stanton KM, *et al.* 1983), for alertness training programs (Hommel M, *et al.* 1990)(Ladavas E, *et al.* 1994)(Robertson IH, *et al.* 1995)(Kerkhoff G. 1998)(Heilman KM *et al.* 1987), for visual scanning training alone (Young GC, *et al.* 1983)(Weinberg J, *et al.* 1977), for some kind of visual spatial motor cueing (Kalra L, *et al.* 1997)(Lin KC, *et al.* 1996)(Frassinetti F, *et al.* 2001), with kinetic stimuli (Butter CM, *et al.* 1990)(Pizzamiglio L, *et al.* 1990)(Butter CM and Kirsch N. 1995), for the use of video feedback (Tham K and Tegnér R. 1997), or the use of visuomotor feedback (Harvey M, Hood B, *et al.* 2003). This is also the case for vestibular stimulations (Rode G and Perenin MT. 1994)(Rode G, *et al.* 1998)(Rorsman I, *et al.* 1999), for neck transcutaneous electrical stimulation (Vallar G, *et al.* 1995)(Guariglia C, *et al.* 1998)(Perennou DA, *et al.* 2001), vibration (Schindler I, *et al.* 2002), or changes in orientation (Wiart L, *et al.* 1997). This is yet the case for the use of computer training (Webster JS, *et al.* 2001). Finally, this is the case for forced left visual deviation (Beis JM, *et al.* 1999)(Butter CM and Kirsch N. 1992)(Walker R, *et al.* 1996), with the use of prism goggle treatment (Rossetti Y, *et al.* 1998)(Angeli V, *et al.* 2004)(Frassinetti F, *et al.* 2002)(Farne A, *et al.* 2002). The discrepancy between much more outcomes could be due, at least in part, to the clinical difficulty to differentiate diverse neglects syndromes which could have various responses to treatment. (Malhotra PA, *et al.* 2006) The same way, it is difficult to distinguish between attentional and intentional visual neglect in clinical practice, still it could help understanding and secondarily treating this symptom (Rode G, *et al.* 2003)(Harvey M, Kramer-McCaffery T, *et al.* 2003).

The aim of this study was to evaluate the efficacy and clinical feasibility of our new software on personal computer developed to differentiate intentional from attentional visual neglect.

METHODS

Personal Computer

We developed the Mouse Cursor movement Inversion Software running on Microsoft Windows®, inverting right-left horizontal movements of the mouse cursor while leaving vertical movements unchanged. Albert test (Albert ML. 1973) alone or together with Bell cancellation test (Gauthier L, et al. 1989), were performed with the mouse cursor movement inversion software before and after the movements inversion. At the test beginning, the cursor was automatically positioned at the screen's center. Patients: Prior to inclusion in the study, the "ethics committee-approved informed consent form" was signed by the patients. All patients were right handed, older than 18 years old and presented hemispatial visual neglect following a right ischemic stroke. All patients had more than 20/30 on Mini Mental State Examination. For each patient Motor Index (Demeurisse G, et al. 1980) was performed together with evaluation. Statistical analysis: Statistical Package for Social Sciences 10 software was used for the analysis. In view of the limited sample, we used non-parametric tests such as "Spearman's rho" for the correlations and "Wilcoxon's signed rank test" for sample comparison. For these analyses we defined:

1. Reflect of neglect on Albert test (N) and Bell cancellation test (N') as the ratio of the difference between the number of omissions in the left hemi space of the screen (A) and the number of omissions in the right hemi space (B) by the total number to be cancelled (17 for Albert test and 20 for Bell cancellation test): $N = (A - B)/20$ and $N' = (A - B)/17$. N and N' where set at 1 when all pictures in the left hemi space were omitted.

2. Reflect of neglect in case of inversion (I and I') were defined in the same way as N and N'.

3. Reflect of left movements as a percentage of movements in left hemi screen directly measured by the software with and without inversion on Albert test (M_a, M_a') and Bell cancellation test (M_b, M_b').

4. Variation of omissions on Albert test (Δn) and Bell cancellation test ($\Delta n'$) as the ratio of the difference between Reflect of neglect in case of inversion (I or I') and Reflect of neglect in normal conditions (N or N') by Reflect of neglect in normal conditions (N or N'): $\Delta n = [(I - N)/N] \times 100$ and $\Delta n' = [(I' - N')/N'] \times 100$. Δn and $\Delta n'$ were set at 0% when I = N and I' = N'. Δn or $\Delta n'$ were set at 100% when N or N' = 0 and different from I or I'.

5. Variation of movements on Albert test (Δm_a) and Bell cancellation test (Δm_b) as the ratio of the difference between Reflect of left movements in case of inversion (M') and Reflect of left movements in normal conditions (M) by Reflect of left movements in normal conditions (M): $\Delta m = [(M' - M)/M] \times 100$. Δm was set at 0% when M = M' and set at 100% when M = 0 and was different from M'.

Controls: We evaluate the ability of our test to detect neglect in an unselected population. Thus, in our department of rehabilitation, we tested it on five consecutive patients who performed blindly a more complete neuropsychological testing which included an evaluation of time and space orientation, digit span (forwards and backward), block tapping test, Buschke selective reminding task and informal investigation of verbal expression and comprehension, the Bachy-Langedock test which is a confrontation naming task using line-drawings (Bachy-Langedock M.N. 1989), executive evaluations by the Winconsin Card Sorting Test, Stroop test and verbal fluency ("p", "r", animals and fruits), visual spatial abilities assessments with the Rey complex figure or La Ruche which is a visual-spatial learning task, in which patients were presented with a 5 learning trials kind of symmetric matrix comprising 45 squares. Ten of those squares were filled with black colour. On each trial, the matrix is presented to patient for 45 seconds and he had to learn the location of the ten black squares. He is then given an empty matrix and has to cross the squares corresponding to the black ones on the model (Violon A., and Wijns Ch. 1984). In neglected suspected cases, line bisection task (during which the patient is asked to bisect the middle of various lines randomly disposed on a paper) and drawing copy task of five objects horizontally disposed was performed. If deficits on attention were suspected, ten different visual and auditory tests were performed with the computerized standardized attentional tasks: Test for Attentional Performance (Zimmerman P, Fimm B. 1995) (Drepper J, et al. 1999) (Gouzoulis-Mayfrank E, et al. 2000) Subjects were seated in an isolated and quiet room in front of a 14'' computer screen at a viewing distance of 40-50 cm. Tests included Alertness (20 trials preceded by an acoustic warning, 20 not preceded by an acoustic warning), Crossmodal Integration (20 trials), Divided attention (20 squares, 20 sounds, and 30 squares + sounds) with the visual task "squares" consisting of crosses appearing randomly in a 4 x 4 matrix. Subject having to press a key as soon as the crosses form the corners of a square. A regular sequence of high and low tones being presented during the acoustical task "sounds" with subject having to detect an irregularity in the sequence. During the test "squares and sounds" first and second test are simultaneously combined, Flexibility (60 stimuli), Go/NoGo (25 trials), Vigilance (32 trials), and Working memory (60 trials). For each test, reaction times and error rates were recorded. An error is defined as an omission, anticipation, or latency over 2000 milliseconds.

RESULTS

These five controls (table 3) included in order from case 1 to case 5:

1. 57 years old, right hemianopsic woman, with no visual neglect observed, but executive and attentional dysfunctions confirmed on tests and due to a left posterior cerebral artery stroke. Note that she forgot 2 left and one right Bell cancellation test on cancellation task with the mouse cursor movement inversion software after inversion.

2. 50 years old diplopic woman presenting multiple sclerosis, with no neglect observed, but mild defects of tonic alertness and of divided attention. She performed perfectly on the mouse cursor movement inversion software.

3. 30 years old man presenting left neglect due to a right median cerebral artery stroke. Hemispatial visual neglect was confirmed to be attentional on test with our mouse cursor movement inversion software test.

4. 51 years old woman presenting left visual neglect due to large right anterior and median cerebral artery stroke (carotid thrombosis). neglect was confirmed to be attentional on test with our mouse cursor movement inversion software test.

5. 46 years old man with mild working memory deficits subordinate to a right deep focal ischemic stroke. He performed well on tasks with the mouse cursor movement inversion software.

Table 1. Epidemiologic data
Hemispatial Visual Neglect Patients

NUMBER	1	2	3	4	5	6	7	8
AGE	69	60	71	55	56	44	74	71
GENDER	M	W	W	M	M	W	M	W
STROKE LOCALISATION	R MCA	R MCA	R MCA	R MCA	R MCA	R MCA	R MCA	R MCA
DATE OF STROKE	06 May	22 May	30 may	04 February	18 December	01 March	25 February	22 March
DATE OF EVALUATION	31 May	5 June	12 June	12 July	12 July	12 July	12 July	15 April

Epidemiologic data: M : man ; W : woman ; R MCA : right medial cerebral artery.

Table 2. Results of the tests patient by patient

Test	Value	1	2	3	4	5	6	7	8
Albert test	M_a	60,88	41,76	47,67	45,85	55,73	48,72	50,87	51,65
	M_a'	43,19	27,76	16,03	60,15	51,75	42,87	59	41,87
	Δm_a	29,06	33,52	66,37	31,19	7,14	12,01	15,98	18,94
	N	0	5/20	1/20	1/20	0	0	0	0
	I	0	20/20	13/20	0	0	3/20	0	0
	Δn	0	300	1200	100	0	100	0	0
Bell cancellation	M_b	55,4	3,21	39,13	50,5	47,31	59,82	53,21	
	M_b'	38,48	9,82	15,88	65,1	59,11	25,21	48,57	
	Δm_b	30,54	205,92	59,42	28,91	24,94	57,86	8,72	
	N'	6/17	17/17	4/17	1/17	4/17	-2/17	1/17	
	I'	6/17	17/17	17/17	-3/17	5/17	10/17	1/17	
	$\Delta n'$	0	0	325	400	25	600	0	
Motor index		47%	85%	22%	36%	33%	24%	60%	54%
MMSE		30/30	27/30	29/30	27/30	25/30	26/30	30/30	29/30

Results of the tests patient by patient: $M_{a\ and\ b}$: reflect of movement as the percentage of movement in left hemi screen directly measured by the software without inversion on Albert and bell cancellation tests. ; $M_{a\ and\ b}'$: reflect of movement as the percentage of movement in left hemi screen directly measured by the software with inversion on Albert and cancellation tests. ; $\Delta m_{a\ and\ b}$: variation of movement on Albert and cancellation tasks as $\Delta m = [(M' - M)/M] \times 100$ with Δm set as 0% when $M = M'$ and set as 100% when $M = 0$ and was different of M'. ; N: reflect of omissions on Albert test with $N = (A - B)/20$ when $X < 20$. With A = number of omissions in the left hemi space of the screen, B = number of omissions in the right hemi space, and X = total consecutive left omissions on the full screen. N was set as 1 in case of $X \geq 20$. ; I: reflect of neglect in case of inversion, defined as N but with inversion. ; N': reflect of omissions on Bell cancellation test with $N' = (A - B)/17$ when $X < 17$. With A = number of omissions in the left hemi space of the screen, B = number of omissions in the right hemi space, and X = total consecutive left omissions on the full screen. N was set as 1 in case of $X \geq 17$. ; I': reflect of neglect in case of inversion, defined as N'. ; Δn: variation of omissions as $\Delta n = [(I - N)/N] \times 100$ with Δn set as 0% when $I = N$ and set as 100% when $N = 0$ and was different of I. ; $\Delta n'$: variation of omissions as $\Delta n' = [(I' - N')/N'] \times 100$ with $\Delta n'$ set as 0% when $I' = N'$ and set as 100% when $N' = 0$ and was different of I'. ; MMSE: Mini Mental State Examination.

Table 3. Results of the tests control by control

Test	Value	1	2	3	4	5
Albert test	M_a		53,56			52,65
	M_a'		55,86			48,31
	N		0			0
	I		0			0
Bell cancellation	M_b	50,45	45,42	42,23	75,53	
	M_b'	40,34		45,7	52,44	
	N'	0	0	5/17	5/17	
	I'	1/17		12/17	5/17	

Results of the tests control by control: $M_{a\ and\ b}$: reflect of movement as the percentage of movement in left hemi screen directly measured by the software without inversion on Albert and bell cancellation tests. ; $M_{a\ and\ b}'$: reflect of movement as the percentage of movement in left hemi screen directly measured by the software with inversion on Albert and cancellation tests. ; N: reflect of omissions on Albert test with N = (A - B)/20 when X < 20. With A = number of omissions in the left hemi space of the screen, B = number of omissions in the right hemi space, and X = total consecutive left omissions on the full screen. N was set as 1 in case of X ≥ 20. ; I: reflect of neglect in case of inversion, defined as N but with inversion. ; N': reflect of omissions on Bell cancellation test with N' = (A - B)/17 when X < 17. With A = number of omissions in the left hemi space of the screen, B = number of omissions in the right hemi space, and X = total consecutive left omissions on the full screen. N was set as 1 in case of X ≥ 17. ; I': reflect of neglect in case of inversion, defined as N'.

Thereafter, 8 subjects were included. Four patients were tested during the month following their stroke, the others, more than four months after (table 1). When considering N, N', I, I', M_{a-b}, M_{a-b}', Δn, Δn', and $Δm_{a-b}$ for each tests (table 2), we observed that the median p25 and p75 N and N' (Reflect neglect by number of omissions) were 0 and 0,05 for the Albert test and 0,0588 and 0,3529 for the Bell cancellation test. This difference however was non significant (p=0,063). In all cases but patient 4, the cursor movement inversion resulted even in an increase or stabilization of the omission number (I ≥ N; I' ≥ N'). For patient 4, the cursor movement's inversion resulted in an inversion of his omissions (especially for Bell cancellation test) (figure 1). Movement's analysis confirmed an increase of the left movement's predominance in this isolated case. There was no correlation on Spearman's test between Δn (Variation of omissions on Albert test) and $Δm_a$ (Variation of left movements on Albert test) (ρ = 0,949; non significant) and between Δn' (Variation of omissions on Bell cancellation test) and $Δm_b$ (Variation of left movements on Bell cancellation test) (ρ = 0,111; non significant).

Normal conditions   Inversion of cursor movement conditions

A   B

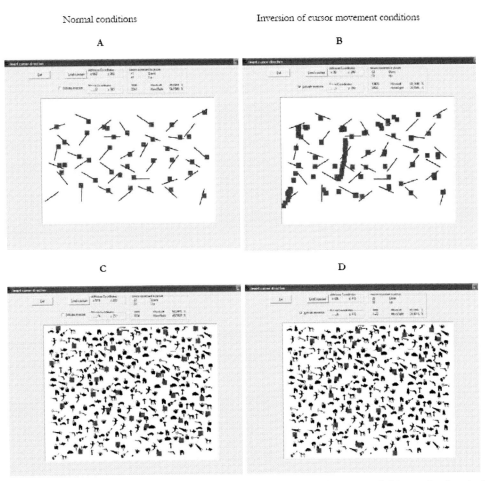

C   D

Patient n°4 : predominant intentional neglect : Patient 4 is the only case of this study that had predominantly intentional neglect. He clearly neglected bells on the inferior left part of the field in normal condition (C), and symmetrically on the right in case of inversion (D). However, there are three left bells forgotten yet for six on the right in inversion. Movement analysis confirmed an increase of the left movement predominance in this isolated case but showed also, especially on Albert test, that he presented perseverations added to his neglect (B).

Figure 1. Patient n°4 : predominant intentional neglect.

DISCUSSION

We developed a simple, fast and objectively analyzable test to detect and evaluate intentional neglect. Considering omissions, we have shown that on our mouse cursor movement inversion software, as already described on paper-pencil tests (Wilson B, *et al.* 1987)(Werth R. 1993), distracters increase the expression of visual neglect. Indeed, for all seven (but two particular cases: n°4 and n°6) patients who performed both test, N' was greater than N. Patient 4 made only one omission in both tests. Patient 6 made no omissions on Albert test and substantially more omissions on Bell cancellation test, but with more right omissions in this single case. Median N' has been necessarily decreased by this way as N' was negative in this isolated case. The non significant difference (p=0,063) between median N (0,00) and median N' (0,2353) is likely due to these two cases and to the insufficient patients number included in this preliminary study. Moreover, we observed that inversions of cursor movements increased, in the same way as distracters do, the expression of attentional neglect. Indeed, except for patient 4, I and I' were systematically similar to, or greater than, N and N'. This is probably due to the charge of attention used to cross movements and sight. Capacity of attention is decreased and performance fall similarly. Results of our controls cases are in perfect line with these hypotheses. Indeed, controls 3 and 4 presented attentional spatial visual hemineglect which was well detected by our mouse cursor movement inversion software evaluation. As expected, in control 3, inversions of cursor movements increased the expression of his attentional neglect. Control 1 forgot two left, but one right, bells on cancellation task with the mouse cursor movement inversion software after inversion. She did not presented neglect but hemianopia with executive and attentional dysfunctions confirmed on Test for Attentional Performance. Thus, confirming the hypothesis of attentional dependence of our task's results in case of crossing movements and sight.

Patient 4 is the only case of this study that had predominantly intentional neglect (figure 1). He clearly neglected bells on the inferior left part of the field in normal condition, and symmetrically on the right in case of inversion. Noteworthy, patient 4 forgot three left bells but six right bells in inversion. This could be due to the partial attentional component of his predominantly intentional hemispatial visual neglect. Movement analysis confirmed all of these observations but showed also that patient 4 presented perseverations added to his hemispatial neglect.

If we consider the absence of correlation on the Spearman's test between Δn (variation of omissions on Albert test) and Δm_a (variation of left movements on Albert test) ($\rho = 0,949$; non significant) and between $\Delta n'$ (variation of omissions on Bell cancellation test) and Δm_b (variation of left movements on Bell cancellation test) ($\rho = 0,111$; non significant), we conclude that these analysis (omissions and movements) did not give one isolated information twice. Movement's analysis has certainly more value than an anecdotic case by case survey.

Noteworthy, if this preliminary study has no clear implications for theories regarding neglect, for neuroanatomical substrates of neglect or for rehabilitation of neglect, it confirmed that our test is a simple, fast and robust way to detect intentional visual neglect, and that it helps evaluating hemispatial neglect being it attentional or intentional. This open the way for further systematic large samples studies to understand these benefits.

REFERENCES

Albert ML. (1973) A simple test of visual neglect. *Neurology*; 23: 658-664.

Angeli V, Benassi MG, Ladavas E. (2004) Recovery of oculomotor bias in neglect patients after prism adaptation. *Neuropsychologia*; 42: 1223-1234.

Antonucci A, Guariglia C, Judica A, Magnotti L, Paolucci S, Pizzamiglio L, Zoccolotti P. (1995) Effectiveness of neglect rehabilitation in a randomized group study. *J. Clin. Exp. Neuropsychol*; 17: 383-389.

Bachy-Langedock, M.N. (1989) Batterie d'examen des troubles en dénomination. Bruxelles : *Editest*.

Beis JM, André JM, Baumgarten A, Challier B. (1999) Eye patching in unilateral spatial neglect: efficacy of two methods. *Arch. Phys. Med. Rehabil*; 80: 71-76.

Butter CM, Kirsch NL, Reeves G. (1990) The effect of lateralized kinetic visual cues on visual search in patients with unilateral spatial neglect following right hemisphere lesions. *Restor. Neurol. Neurosci*; 2: 39-46.

Butter CM and Kirsch N. (1992) Combined and separate effects of eye patching and visual stimulation on unilateral neglect following stroke. *Arch. Phys. Med. Rehabil*; 73: 1133-1139.

Butter CM and Kirsch N. (1995) Effect of lateralized kinetic visual cues on visual search in patients with unilateral spatial neglect. *J. Clin. Exp. Neuropsychol*; 17: 856-867.

Cappa SF, Benke T, Clarke S, Rossi B, Stemmer B and Van Heugten CM. (2005) EFNS guidelines on cognitive rehabilitation: report of an EFNS task force. *Eur. J. Neurol*; 12: 665-680.

Demeurisse G, Demol O, Robaye E. (1980) Motor Evaluation in Vascular Hemiplegia. *Eur. Neurol*; 19: 382-389.

Denes G, Semenza C, Stoppa E, Lis A. (1982) Unilateral spatial neglect and recovery from hemiplegia: a follow up study. *Brain*; 105: 543-552.

Drepper J, Timmann D, Kolb FP, Diener HC. (1999) Non-motor associative learning in patients with isolated degenerative cerebellar disease. *Brain*; 122 (Pt 1): 87-97.

Driver J, Mattingley JB. (1995) Selective attention in humans: normality and pathology. *Curr. Opin. Neurobiol*; 2: 191-197.

Farne A, Rosetti Y, Tonolio S, Ladavas E. (2002) Ameliorerating neglect with prism adaptation: visuo-manual and visuo-verbal measures. *Neuropsychologia*; 40: 718-792.

Frassinetti F, Rossi M, Ladavas E. (2001) Passive limb movements improve visual neglect. *Neuropsychologia*; 39: 725-733.

Frassinetti F, Angeli V, Meneghello F, Avanzi S, Ladavas E. (2002) Long-lasting amelioration of visuospatial neglect by prism adaptation. *Brain*; 125: 608-623.

Gauthier L, Dehaut F, Joanett J. (1989) The Bell test: A quantitative and qualitative test for visual neglect. *Int. J. Clin. Neuropsychol*; 11: 49-54.

Gouzoulis-Mayfrank E, Thimm B, Rezk M, Hensen G, Daumann J. (2000) Impaired cognitive performance in drug free users of recreational ecstasy (MDMA) *J. Neurol. Neurosurg. Psychiatry*; 68: 719-725.

Guariglia C, Lippolis G, Pizzamiglio L. (1998) Somatosensory stimulation improves imagery disorders in neglect. *Cortex*; 34: 233-241.

Harvey M, Hood B, North A, Robertson IH. (2003) The effects of visuomotor feedback training on the recovery of hemispatial neglects symptoms: assessment of a 2-weeks and follow-up intervention. *Neuropsychologia*; 41: 886-893.

Harvey M, Kramer-McCaffery T, Dow L, Murphy PJ, Gilchrist ID. (2003) Categorisation of "perceptual" and "premotor" neglect patients across different tasks: is there strong evidence for a dichotomy? *Neuropsychologia*; 40: 1387-1395.

Heilman KM, Watson RT, Valenstein E, Goldberg ME. (1987) Attention: behavior and neural mechanism. In: Plum, F. (Ed.), *Handbook of physiology, Section I: The Nervous System, vol. 5*. American Physiology Society, Bethesda, MD, pp. 461-481.

Hommel M, Peres B, Pollack P, Memin B, Besson G, Gaio JM, Perret J. (1990) Effects of passive tactile and auditory stimuli on left visual neglect. *Arch. Neurol*; 47: 573-576.

Kalra L, Perez I, Gupta S, Wittink M. (1997) The influence of visual neglect on stroke rehabilitation. *Stroke*; 28: 1386-1391.

Kerkhoff G. (1998) Rehabilitation of visuospatial cognition and visual exploration in neglect : a cross-over study. *Restor. Neurol. Neurosci*; 12: 27-40.

Ladavas E, Menghini G, Umilta C. (1994) A rehabilitation study of hemispatial neglect. *Cogn. Neuropsychol*; 11: 75-95.

Lin KC, Cermack SA, Kinsbourne M, Trombly CA. (1996) Effects of left-sided movements on line bisection in unilateral neglect. *J. Int. Neuropsychol. Soc*; 2: 404-411.

Malhotra PA, Parton AD, Greenwood R, Husain M. (2006) Noradrenergic modulation of space exploration in visual neglect. *Ann. Neurol*; 59: 186-190)

Perennou DA, Leblond C, Amblard B, Micallef JP, Herisson C, Pelissier JY. (2001) Transcutaneous electric nerve stimulation reduces neglect-related postural instability after stroke. *Arch. Phys. Med. Rehabil*; 82: 440-448.

Pizzamiglio L, Frasca R, Guariglia C, Incoccia C, Antonucci G. (1990) Effect of optokinetic stimulation in patients with visual neglect. *Cortex*; 26: 535-540.

Pizzamiglio L, Antonucci G, Judica A, Montenero P, Razzano C, Zoccolotti P. (1992) Cognitive rehabilitation of the hemineglect disorder in chronic patients with unilateral right brain damage. *J. Clin. Exp. Neuropsychol*; 14: 901-923.

Robertson IH, Tegnér R, Tham K, Lo A, Nimmo-Smith I. (1995) Sustained attention training for unilateral neglect: theoretical and rehabilitation implications. *J. Clin. Exp. Neuropsychol*; 17: 416-430.

Robertson and Murre. (1999) Rehabilitation of brain damage: brain plasticity and principles of guided recovery. *Psychological Bulletin*; 125: 544-575.

Rode G and Perenin MT. (1994) Temporary remission of representational hemineglect through vestibular stimulation. *Neuroreport*; 5: 869-872.

Rode G, Tiliket C, Charopain P, Boisson D. (1998) Postural asymmetry reduction by vestibular caloric stimulation in left hemiparetic patients. *Scand. J. Rehabil. Med*; 30: 9-14.

Rode G, Pisella L, Rosetti Y, Farne A, Boisson D. (2003) Bottom-up transfer of sensory-motor plasticity to recovery of spatial cognition: visuomotor adaptation and spatial neglect. *Prog. Brain Res*; 142: 273-287.

Rorsman I, Magnusson M, Johansson BB. (1999) Reduction of visuo-spatial neglect with vestibular galvanic stimulation. *Scand. J. Rehabil. Med*; 31: 117-124.

Rossetti Y, Rode G, Pisella L, Farne A, Li L, Boisson D, Perenin MT. (1998) Prism adaptation to rightward optical deviation rehabilitates left hemispatial neglect. *Nature*; 395: 166-169.

Schindler I, Kerkhoff G, Karnath HO, Keller I, Goldenberg G. (2002) Neck muscle vibration induces lasting recovery in spatial neglect. *J. Neurol. Neurosurg. Psychiatry*; 73: 412-419.

Stanton KM, Pepping M, Brockway JA, Bliss L, Franckel D, Waggener S. (1983) Wheelchair transfer training for right cerebral dysfunctions: an interdisciplinary approach. *Arch. Phys. Med. Rehabil*; 64: 276-280.

Stone SP, Patel P, Greenwood RJ, Halligan PW. (1992) Measuring visual neglect in acute stroke and predicting its recovery: the visual neglect recovery index. *J. Neurol. Neurosurg. Psychiatry*. 55: 431 -436.

Tegnér R, Levander M. (1991) Through a looking glass. A new technique to demonstrate directional hypokinesia in unilateral neglect. *Brain*; 114: 1943-1991.

Tham K and Tegnér R. (1997) Video feedback in the rehabilitation of patients with unilateral neglect. *Arch. Phys. Med. Rehabil*; 78: 410-413.

Vallar G, Rusconi ML, Barozzi S, Bernardini B, Ovadia D, Papagno C, Cesarani, A. (1995) Improvement of left visuo-spatial hemineglect by left-sided transcutaneous electrical stimulation. *Neuropsychologia*; 33: 73-82.

Vallar G, Guariglia C, Magnotti L, Pizzamiglio L. (1997) Dissociation between position sense and visual-spatial components of hemineglect through a specific rehabilitation treatment. *J. Clin. Exp. Neuropsychol*; 19: 763-771.

Violon, A., and Wijns, Ch. (1984) La Ruche: Test de perception et d'apprentissage progressif en mémoire visuelle. *Belgique : Edition de l'Application des Techniques Modernes.*

Walker R, Young AW, Lincoln NB. (1996) Eye patching and the rehabilitation of visual neglect. *Neuropsychol. Rehabil*; 6: 219-231.

Webster JS, Mc Farland PT, Rapport LJ, Morrill B, Roades LA, Abadee PS. (2001) Computer-assisted training for improving wheelchair mobility in unilateral neglect patients. *Arch. Phys. Med. Rehabil*; 82: 769-775.

Weinberg J, Diller L, Gordon WA, Gerstman LJ, Lieberman A, Lakin P, Hodges G, Ezrachi O. (1977) Visual scanning training effect on reading-related tasks in acquired right brain damage. *Arch. Phys. Med. Rehabil*; 58: 479-486.

Werth R. (1993) Shifts and omissions in spatial reference in unilateral neglect. In Robertson IJ, Marshall J, eds. *Unilateral neglect: clinical and experimental studies*: L Erlbaum Associates, 222-226.

Wiart L, Bon Saint Côme A, Debelleix X, Petit H, Joseph PA, Mazaux JM, Barat M. (1997) Unilateral neglect syndrome rehabilitation by trunk rotation and scanning training. *Arch. Phys. Med. Rehabil*; 78: 424-429.

Wilson B, Cockburn J, Halligan PW. (1987) Development of a behavioral test of visuospatial neglect. *Arch. Phys. Med. Rehabil;* 68: 98-102.

Young GC, Collins D, Hren M. (1983) Effect of pairing scanning training with block design training in the remediation of perceptual problems in left hemiplegics. *J. Clin. Neurpsychol*; 5: 201-212.

Zimmerman P, Fimm B. (1995) Test for Attentional Performance (TAP). Herzogenrath; *Psytest.*; website: http://www.psytest-fimm.com/

In: Psychological Tests and Testing Research Trends   ISBN 978-1-60021-569-8
Editor: Paul M. Goldfarb, pp. 295-310   © 2007 Nova Science Publishers, Inc.

Chapter 15

USING THE RASCH MODEL FOR PREDICTION

Karl Bang Christensen[*]
National Institute of Occupational Health,
Lersø Parkallé 105, 2100 KBH Ø, Denmark

Abstract

Rasch measurement is widely used for measurement of latent variables in psychological testing, education, health status measurement, and other fields. The Rasch model expresses ideal measurement requirements and much research has dealt with testing whether these assumptions are met in real data. Latent variables are often of interest in terms of their relation to other variables, some examples being self rated health as predictor of mortality or psychosocial work environment factors as predictors of job turnover. This chapter deals with prediction of a binary outcome variable using latent variables measured using the Rasch model. Three approaches are compared: (i) prediction using the sufficient score, (ii) prediction using the estimated values for each person, and (iii) prediction based on a joint model. Extensions of the Rasch model including uniform differential item functioning and uniform local dependence between items are also discussed. The approaches are illustrated and motivated using an example from occupational epidemiology.

Introduction

Different frameworks for modeling of latent variables exist, most notably structural equation models (Bollen, 1989) and item response theory models (van der Linden & Hambleton, 1997).

Structural equation models are used to model the relation between theoretical variables in the presence of measurement error. Item response theory models are used in situations where several questions (or items) are used for ordering of a group of subjects with respect to a unidimensional latent variable. This means that focus is on relative comparisons in terms of higher/lower, better/worse, agree/disagree.

Applications of structural equation models have been motivated by a desire to describe correlation structures, combining a factor analytic approach (the measurement model) with

---

[*]E-mail address: KBC@AMI.DK

regression models for the latent variables (the structural model). Structural equation models have been formulated for latent response variables measured using ordinal categorical variables (Muthén, 1979, 1984) yielding a flexible, but complex class of models. Item response theory models on the other hand are formulated directly for observed ordinal categorical responses. Applications of item response theory models have focussed on modeling the response process taking place and assuring the quality of measurement by testing the assumptions of the model, with less emphasis on modeling of structural relations between observed and latent variables.

Item response theory models express ideal requirements of scales and are thus natural tools when validating scales. The work presented here deals with measurement and statistical modeling of latent variables using the simplest type of item response theory models; the class of Rasch measurement models, (Rasch, 1960; Fischer & Molenaar, 1995). Measurement within item response theory can be viewed as comparisons (between persons or between a person and a reference population). The Rasch model is based on a requirement of (specific) objective comparison: a comparison of two persons using a single item is required to be invariant of the choice of item. The term specific is used to emphasize that the claim for objectivity is made within a given frame of reference defined by a specific population and a specific set of permissible items.

The Rasch model has traditionally been a framework for measurement alone, but the requirements can be applied in an extended framework for item responses, latent variables, and observed covariates: Graphical Rasch models (Kreiner & Christensen, 2002). The traditional Rasch modeling framework has been extended in two ways: (i) to include relations between items and covariates (Kelderman, 1984, 1992; Kelderman & Rijkes, 1994) yielding loglinear Rasch models and (ii) to include relations between the latent variable and covariates (Andersen & Madsen, 1977; Zwinderman, 1991; Adams, Wilson, & Wu, 1997) yielding latent regression models. A framework including both of these extensions has also been discussed (Christensen, Bjorner, Kreiner, & Petersen, 2004).

The example, taken from occupational epidemiology, shows how measurement precision can be increased and also illustrates the use of loglinear Rasch models as measurement models.

Measurement Models

The traditional framework for the Rasch model consists of a unidimensional latent variable θ responsible for the correlation between the observed items $x_1, \ldots, x_I$. The conditional probability given the person parameter θ is

$$p(x_i|\theta) = \frac{\exp(x_i\theta + \eta_{ix_i})}{\sum_l \exp(l\theta + \eta_{il})} \qquad (i = 1, \ldots, I, x = 0, 1, \ldots, H) \qquad (1)$$

yielding a monotonous relation between the latent variable θ and the item response x_i. The item parameters can be interpreted through the locations $-(\eta_{ix} - \eta_{i,x-1})$, $x = 1, \ldots, H$ of the H threshold between adjacent response categories.

The item parameters are the same for every person in the sample expressing absence of differential item functioning: the response depends only on the value of the latent variable and not on other variables like age and gender. Absence of differential item functioning is a prerequisite of simple meaningful comparisons. The assumption

$$p(x_1, \ldots, x_I | \theta) = p(x_1 | \theta) \cdots p(x_I | \theta) \qquad (2)$$

of local independence expresses that the latent variable θ accounts for all correlation between the items $x_1, \ldots, x_I$. The joint distribution of the item responses $x_1, \ldots, x_I$ is given by the probabilities

$$p(x_1, \ldots, x_I | \theta) = \frac{\exp(t\theta + \sum_i \eta_{ix_i})}{K(\eta, \theta)}, \qquad (3)$$

where $K(\eta, \theta) = \prod_i \sum_l \exp(l\theta + \eta_{il})$ is a normalizing constant. The total sum score $t = \sum_i x_i$ is seen to be a sufficient statistic for θ. The item parameters can be estimated using a conditional approach without distributional assumptions about the latent variable yielding item parameter estimates that are conditionally consistent.

The assumption of absence of differential item functioning can be relaxed by including an interaction between an item, say x_a, and a covariate, say X, yielding

$$p(x_1, \ldots, x_I | \theta, X) = \frac{\exp(t\theta + \sum_i \eta_{ix_i} + \kappa(x_a, X))}{K(\eta, \theta, X)}. \qquad (4)$$

The assumption of local dependence can be relaxed by including an interaction between items, say x_a and x_b, yielding

$$p(x_1, \ldots, x_I | \theta) = \frac{\exp(t\theta + \sum_i \eta_{ix_i}) + \nu(x_a, x_b))}{K(\eta, \theta, X)} \qquad (5)$$

Including extensions like (4) and (5) yields a loglinear Rasch model (Kelderman, 1984). This makes it possible to study the relation of the latent variable in a setting where uniform local dependence and uniform differential item functioning is modeled. The term uniform indicates that for all values of θ the same relation between item parameters or between item parameters and covariates is included.

Importantly the score is sufficient in this model. The item parameters can be estimated using a conditional approach without distributional assumptions about the latent variable (Kelderman, 1984, 1992). This yields item parameter estimates that are conditionally consistent.

For the models (3), (4), and (5) the sufficiency of the total score t is the prerequisite of the most important feature of the Rasch models: separation of the item parameters from the person parameters. This feature also applies to the regression models discussed in what follows.

Latent Regression Models

Modeling of ordinal data with random effects has a very long tradition in item response theory (Andersen & Madsen, 1977; Mislevy, 1984, 1985, 1987; Zwinderman, 1991; Andersen, 1994; Hoijtink, 1995; Adams, Wilson, & Wu, 1997; Adams, Wilson, & Wang,

1997; Zwinderman, 1997; Janssen, Tuerlinckx, Meulders, & De Boeck, 2000; Fox & Glas, 2001; Kamata, 2001; Maier, 2001). Many specialized computer programs have also been developed within psychometrics. Procedures like PROC NLMIXED in SAS, the NLME library in Splus, and gllamm (Rabe-Hesketh, Pickles, & Skrondal, 2001) in Stata has made nonlinear random effects models a standard tool. Latent regression models are linear regression models where the outcome variable is a latent variable, that is, a combination of (3) and a linear structure

$$\theta = X\delta + \epsilon, \qquad X\delta = X_1\delta_1 + \ldots + X_k\delta_k, \qquad \epsilon \sim N(0, \xi^2). \qquad (6)$$

Using a two-stage estimation approach, where consistent estimates of item parameters are inserted, the latent regression model (6) is a generalized linear model (Christensen et al., 2004). Many articles describe Taylor-series methods for Generalized linear mixed models (Harville & Mee, 1984; Stiratelli, Laird, & Ware, 1984; Gilmour, Anderson, & Rae, 1985; Schall, 1991; Breslow & Clayton, 1993; Wolfinger & O'Connel, 1993; McGilchrist, 1994), however such methods can produce biased results (Rodriguez & Goldman, 1995; Lin & Breslow, 1996). The two-stage estimation procedure yields unbiased estimates of regression parameters (Christensen et al., 2004), but asymptotic standard errors of estimated regression parameters are too small, and must be interpreted with caution.

The separation properties of the Rasch models (3), (4), and (5) stemming from the sufficiency of the total score t also applies to these regression models: the measurement part can be separated from the regression (or structural) part of the model. This has been outlined in the context of graphical Rasch models (Kreiner & Christensen, 2002). If the data fits the Rasch model, inference about the latent variable can be based on the graphical Rasch model shown in Figure .

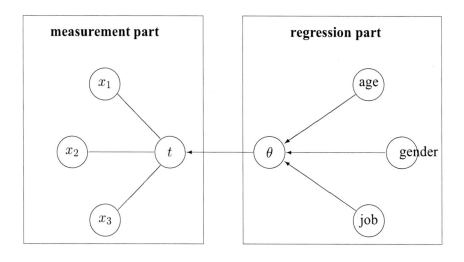

Figure 1. Example of the structure of a graphical Rasch model.

If data fits a loglinear Rasch model, inference can be based on a graphical loglinear Rasch model (Kreiner & Christensen, 2004) shown in Figure .

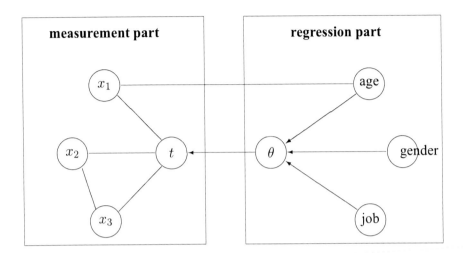

Figure 2. Example of the structure of a graphical loglinear Rasch model. Incorporating differential item functioning, cf. (4), and local dependence, cf. (5).

Another consequence of the separation property is that goodness of fit tests can be performed in two steps: First the fit of the Rasch model to the data can be evaluated, and in a second step the goodness of fit of the postulated latent structure (6) can be evaluated. Several fit statistics comparing observed and expected score distributions have been proposed (Christensen & Kreiner, 2004).

Logistic Regression with a Latent Predictor

Consider a logistic regression model for a dichotomous variable Y with distribution given by

$$P(Y = 1|\eta) = \frac{\exp(\eta)}{1 + \exp(\eta)} \qquad P(Y = 0|\eta) = \frac{1}{1 + \exp(\eta)} \qquad (7)$$

and the linear structure

$$\eta = X\beta, \qquad X\beta = X_1\beta_1 + \ldots + X_k\beta_k. \qquad (8)$$

This yields a simple structure of the odds

$$O(\eta) = \frac{P(Y = 1|\eta)}{P(Y = 0|\eta)} = \exp(\eta) \qquad (9)$$

and the effect on the dichotomous outcome variable Y of a one unit increase of a covariate, say X_1, can be interpreted in terms of the Odds Ratio

$$OR = \frac{\exp((X_1 + 1)\beta_1)}{\exp(X_1\beta_1)} = \exp(\beta_1). \tag{10}$$

In what follows, focus is on a two-dimensional model combining the logistic regression model with the latent regression model (6):

$$\begin{bmatrix} \eta \\ \theta \end{bmatrix} = \begin{bmatrix} X\beta + \gamma\theta \\ X\delta + \epsilon \end{bmatrix} \qquad \epsilon \sim N(0, \xi^2). \tag{11}$$

A more general version of the logistic regression model including random effects

$$\eta = X\beta + \omega, \qquad X\beta = X_1\beta_1 + \ldots + X_k\beta_k, \qquad \omega \sim N(0, \sigma^2), \tag{12}$$

is sometimes preferred. The interpretation of parameters in the presence of random effects is more complicated: The effect of the covariates can be interpreted as median odds ratios taking variation into account, and heterogeneity can be quantified using the median odds ratio (Larsen, Petersen, Budtz-Jørgensen, & Endahl, 2000). This number can be interpreted as the odds ratio between the person at highest risk and the person at lowest risk for two randomly chosen persons. The model combining the random effects logistic regression model with the latent regression model (6) has the same structure as (11):

$$\begin{bmatrix} \eta \\ \theta \end{bmatrix} = \begin{bmatrix} X\beta + \gamma\theta + \omega \\ X\delta + \epsilon \end{bmatrix} \qquad \begin{bmatrix} \omega \\ \epsilon \end{bmatrix} \sim N\left(\begin{bmatrix} 0 \\ 0 \end{bmatrix}, \begin{bmatrix} \sigma^2 & 0 \\ 0 & \omega^2 \end{bmatrix} \right). \tag{13}$$

The probabilities in the logistic regression model thus depend on the η parameters taking the form

$$\begin{aligned} \eta &= X\beta + \gamma\theta + \omega \\ &= X\beta + \gamma(X\delta + \epsilon) + \omega \\ &= X(\beta + \gamma\delta) + (\gamma\epsilon + \omega). \end{aligned}$$

The effect of a one unit increase of the covariate X on the outcome variable Y is thus divided into the direct effect of β and the effect $\gamma\delta$ mediated through the latent covariate. The variance $V(\gamma\epsilon + \omega) = V(\gamma\epsilon) + V(\omega)$ is also divided into two parts $V(\gamma\epsilon) = \gamma^2\xi^2$ and $V(\omega) = \sigma^2$. The model (13) can be written

$$\begin{bmatrix} \eta \\ \theta \end{bmatrix} = \begin{bmatrix} 1 & \gamma \\ 0 & 1 \end{bmatrix} \begin{bmatrix} X\beta \\ X\delta \end{bmatrix} + \begin{bmatrix} 1 & \gamma \\ 0 & 1 \end{bmatrix} \begin{bmatrix} \omega \\ \epsilon \end{bmatrix} \qquad \begin{bmatrix} \omega \\ \epsilon \end{bmatrix} \sim N(0, \begin{bmatrix} \sigma^2 & 0 \\ 0 & \xi^2 \end{bmatrix}).$$

and the framework can be extended to include more than one latent covariate as a predictor. Let $\theta = \begin{bmatrix} \theta_1 & \cdots & \theta_D \end{bmatrix}'$ denote a D-dimensional vector of latent variables, and write $\gamma = \begin{bmatrix} \gamma_1 & \cdots & \gamma_D \end{bmatrix}, \epsilon = \begin{bmatrix} \epsilon_1 & \cdots & \epsilon_D \end{bmatrix}'$. The structure

$$\begin{bmatrix} \eta \\ \theta \end{bmatrix} = \begin{bmatrix} 1 & \gamma \\ 0 & I \end{bmatrix} \begin{bmatrix} X\beta \\ X\delta \\ \vdots \\ X\delta \end{bmatrix} + \begin{bmatrix} 1 & \gamma \\ 0 & I \end{bmatrix} \begin{bmatrix} \omega \\ \epsilon \end{bmatrix} \tag{14}$$

is of the same kind as (13). More than one latent predictor can thus be included.

Implementation in Conquest

The computer program ConQuest (Wu, Adams, & Wilson, 1998) can be used to fit multi-dimensional latent regression models where the same fixed effects influence all latent variables and where no restrictions on the variance-covariance matrix can be introduced. The logistic regression model with a random effect is equivalent to a Rasch model for one item and the logistic regression model with latent predictors can thus be fitted in ConQuest.

When $\Omega = V(\epsilon)$ is denotes the variance-covariance of the D-dimensional latent predictor the variance-covariance matrix of the error term in (14) is

$$V \begin{bmatrix} \omega \\ \epsilon \end{bmatrix} = \begin{bmatrix} \sigma^2 & 0 \\ 0 & \Omega \end{bmatrix}$$

and there are no restrictions on the variance-covariance matrix

$$V \begin{bmatrix} \eta \\ \theta \end{bmatrix} = \begin{bmatrix} \sigma^2 + \gamma \Omega \gamma' & \gamma \Omega \\ \Omega \gamma' & \Omega \end{bmatrix}.$$

The parameters of interest can thus be computed from an estimate of the variance-covariance matrix as

$$\gamma = \Omega^{-1} \begin{bmatrix} V(\eta, \theta_1) \\ \vdots \\ V(\eta, \theta_l) \end{bmatrix} \quad \text{and} \quad \sigma^2 = V(\eta, \eta) - \gamma \Omega \gamma'.$$

Implementation in SAS

The possibility of fitting the dichotomous Rasch model in standard software has existed for a long time (Tjur, 1982; Kelderman, 1984; TenVergert, Gillespie, & Kingma, 1993), and similar approaches to polytomous Rasch models have also been discussed (Agresti, 1993). Many other tests of fit of the Rasch model can easily be implemented in standard software: the Tjur test (Tjur, 1982; Kreiner & Christensen, 2002), Mantel-Haenszel procedures (Holland & Thayer, 1988; Kreiner & Christensen, 2002), and logistic regression techniques, (Swaminathan & Rogers, 1990; Zumbo, 1999) are examples of this.

Item parameter estimation using conditional maximum likelihood estimation, latent regression models, and logistic regression models with a latent predictors have been implemented in SAS macros (Christensen & Bjorner, 2003).

Example

The data considered in this section come from a large study on burnout and job satisfaction in Danish health care workers: the PUMA study (Borritz et al., 2006). The sub sample studied here consists of employees in home care for the elderly in two areas: a large city and small town. Answers from 576 persons were included, and 187 (32.5%) of these stated that given the possibility to choose job again they would not choose the same type of job. This differed between the two areas: 21% in the small town and 44% in the urban area.

This variable is of interest as a proxy for job satisfaction and as predictor of job turnover - something which is very expensive for the health care sector.

Three psychosocial work environment factors are used as predictors: skill discretion, relevant information (predictability), and role conflicts. Together with this three-dimensional latent predictor the observed variables age, gender and area (small town or city) are also included in the analysis.

Three logistic regression models are compared. They introduce the latent predictor in the model by: (i) including the raw scores $\eta = X\beta + \gamma_{(i)}t + \omega$, (ii) including estimated values for each person $\eta = X\beta + \gamma_{(ii)}\hat{\theta} + \omega$, or (iii) by the joint model

$$\eta = X\beta + \gamma_{(iii)}\theta + \omega \qquad \theta = X\delta + \epsilon. \qquad (15)$$

The parameter $\gamma_{(i)}$ quantifies the effect of a one point increase on the sum score scale, and the parameters $\gamma_{(ii)}$ and $\gamma_{(iii)}$ quantify the effect of a one point increase on the latent scale.

The effect estimates based on estimated values $\hat{\theta}$ and on sum scores t are not directly comparable, but dividing estimated values and scores by their standard deviation yields comparable effect estimates: the effect on the risk of job turnover of a an increase of one standard deviation.

The odds ratios based on the parameters $\gamma_{(ii)}$ and $\gamma_{(iii)}$ are immediately comparable because these parameters are on the same scale.

The Effect of Role Conflicts

Four items were used to measure role conflicts (Table 1).

Table 1. Wording of the four items used to measure role conflicts.

some	Do you do things at work, that are accepted by some persons, but not by others?
contr.	Are you met with contrasting demands in your work?
diff.	Do you sometimes do things that should have been done differently?
unness.	Do you sometimes do things that seem unnecessary?
	Responses - To a large extent, To some extent, Somewhat, Not very much, To a very small extent/ No

The response categories are scored $0, 1, 2, 3, 4$, and based on these responses total scores t taking values $0, 1, \ldots, 16$ are computed. The Rasch model was found to fit the data adequately and based on this model estimates $\hat{\theta}$ of the latent predictor are computed for each person. The estimated effects of role conflicts on the risk of job turnover computed using (i) the sum score t, and (ii) the estimated values $\hat{\theta}$ are shown in Table 2. these analyzes yield virtually identical effect estimates: People who experience more role conflicts are less likely to choose the same job again. The estimated effects of role conflicts on the risk of job turnover computed using (ii) the estimated values $\hat{\theta}$, and (iii) the joint model (15) are shown in Table 3.

Table 2. Estimated effect of role conflicts on risk of job turnover computed using (i) sum score t, and (ii) estimated values $\hat{\theta}$. Odds ratios show effect of a one standard deviation increase and are adjusted for gender and age.

(i) sum score t	OR=1.70	(95% CI: 1.40-2.06)
(ii) estimate $\hat{\theta}$	OR=1.65	(95% CI: 1.37-2.01)

Table 3. The effect of role conflicts on the risk of job turnover. Odds ratios show the effect of one unit increase and are adjusted for the effect of gender and age.

(ii) estimate $\hat{\theta}$	OR=1.48	(95% CI: 1.27-1.72)
(iii) joint model	OR=1.85	(95% CI: 1.46-2.34)

The predicted effect based on estimates $\hat{\theta}$ is considerably smaller than the one based on the joint model (15), presumably because the measurement error inherent in the estimates is not taken into account. Introducing the effect of area in the model the structural parameter is $\gamma = 0.59$. The area effect in the model (15) is

$$\beta + \gamma\delta = 0.97 + 0.32 = 1.29,$$

and this means that $\frac{0.32}{1.29} = 25\%$ of the area difference is explained by the differences in role conflicts.

The Effect of Predictability

Two items were used to measure predictability (Table 4)

Table 4. Wording of the two items used to measure predictability.

all	Do you get all the information you need to do your job well?
in time	Do you get information about important decisions and changes in time?
	Responses - To a large extent, To some extent, Somewhat, Not very much, To a very small extent/ No

A latent regression model based on the Rasch model did not show good fit to the data: a Pearson type goodness of fit test was rejected, but observed skewness and the observed kurtosis not outside the confidence intervals (Christensen & Kreiner, 2004). Response categories are scored $0, 1, 2, 3, 4$, and total scores t taking values $0, 1, \ldots, 8$ are computed. Again different ways of introducing the latent predictor in the model are compared. The estimated effects of predictability on the risk of job turnover computed using (i) the sum score t, and (ii) the estimated values $\hat{\theta}$ are shown in Table 5.

Table 5. Estimated effect of role conflicts on risk of job turnover computed using (i) sum score t, and (ii) estimated values $\hat{\theta}$. Odds ratios show effect of an increase of one standard deviation and are adjusted for the effect of gender and age.

(i) sum score t	OR=0.50	(95% CI: 0.41-0.61)
(ii) estimate $\hat{\theta}$	OR=0.54	(95% CI: 0.44-0.66)

Again the conclusion is the same - people who do not receive relevant information are less likely to choose the same job again. The estimated effects of predictability on the risk of job turnover computed using (ii) the estimated values $\hat{\theta}$, and (iii) the joint model (15) are shown in Table 6.

Table 6. The effect of predictability on the risk of job turnover. Odds ratios show the effect of one unit increase and are adjusted for the effect of gender and age.

(ii) estimate $\hat{\theta}$	OR=$\exp(\gamma_{(ii)})$	=	0.81	(95% CI: 0.76-0.87)
(iii) joint model	OR=$\exp(\gamma_{(iii)})$	=	0.76	(95% CI: 0.70-0.82)

again the effect estimates based on $\hat{\theta}$ is smaller than the one based on the joint model (15). Introducing the effect of area in the model the structural parameter is $\gamma = -0.37$. The area effect in the model (15) is

$$\beta + \gamma\delta = 1.13 + 0.22 = 1.35,$$

so only $\frac{0.22}{1.35} = 16\%$ of the area difference is explained by the differences in predictability.

The Effect of Skill Discretion

Four items were used to measure skill discretion (Table 7).

Table 7. Wording of the four items used to measure skill discretion.

init.	Does your job require you to take the initiative?
learn	Do you have the possibility of learning new things through your work?
skills	Can you use your skills or expertise in your work?
vary	Is your work varied?
	Responses - To a large extent, To some extent, Somewhat, Not very much, To a very small extent

Response categories are scored $0, 1, 2, 3, 4$, and total scores t taking values $0, 1, \ldots, 16$ are computed. The estimated effects of predictability on the risk of job turnover computed using (i) the sum score t, and (ii) the estimated values $\hat{\theta}$ are shown in Table 8.

Table 8. Estimated effect of skill discretion on risk of job turnover computed using (i) sum score t, and (ii) estimated values $\hat{\theta}$. Odds ratios show effect of an increase of one standard deviation and are adjusted for the effect of gender and age.

(i) sum score t	OR=0.49	(95% CI: 0.40-0.60)
(ii) estimate $\hat{\theta}$	OR=0.47	(95% CI: 0.38-0.58)

Again the two methods yield the same conclusion: people with low skill discretion are less likely to choose the same job again. The estimated effects of predictability on the risk of job turnover computed using (ii) the estimated values $\hat{\theta}$, and (iii) the joint model (15) are shown in Table 9.

Table 9. The effect of predictability on the risk of job turnover. Odds ratios show the effect of one unit increase and are adjusted for the effect of gender and age.

(ii) estimate $\hat{\theta}$	OR=0.56	(95% CI: 0.48-0.66)
(iii) joint model	OR=0.49	(95% CI: 0.39-0.61)

Conclusions are similar: skill discretion decreases the risk of job turnover. Effect estimates based on $\hat{\theta}$ are smaller than those based on the joint model (15). Introducing the effect of area in the model the structural parameter is $\gamma = -0.67$. The area effect in the model is

$$\beta + \gamma\delta = 0.75 + 0.40 = 1.15,$$

so $\frac{0.40}{1.15} = 35\%$ of the area difference is explained by the differences in skill discretion.

Analysis of differential item functioning disclosed specific group differences. Health care workers in the urban area report that their job requires them to take the initiative much more often than health care workers in the small town who, based on responses to the other items, would be expected to have the same skill discretion. Health care workers over 50 systematically score lower on the item 'Do you have the possibility of learning new things through your work?'. Using loglinear Rasch model these specific differences can be included in the model. The effect of including these specific differences is evident in terms of the goodness of fit of latent regression models (Christensen & Kreiner, 2004): A latent regression model based on the Rasch model yielded highly significant Pearson test statistics and observed skewness and the observed kurtosis were outside the confidence intervals. A latent regression model based on the loglinear Rasch model showed much better fit.

In a model based on a loglinear Rasch model the estimated area effect is larger: $\gamma = -0.87$. The area effect is

$$\beta + \gamma\delta = 0.81 + 0.54 = 1.35,$$

so a larger proportion ($\frac{0.54}{1.35} = 40\%$) of the area difference is explained by the differences in skill discretion, when a better measurement model is used.

Multivariate Latent Predictor

Next the model

$$\eta = X\beta + \gamma_1\theta_1 + \gamma_2\theta_2 + \gamma_3\theta_3 + \omega \qquad (16)$$

with three latent predictors is considered. The effect of the observed covariates age, gender, and area (the row vector X) and of the latent covariates skill discretion (θ_1), predictability (θ_2), and role conflicts (θ_3) on the outcome variable (y) is studied. An overview of the relation between observed and latent variables is given in Figure .

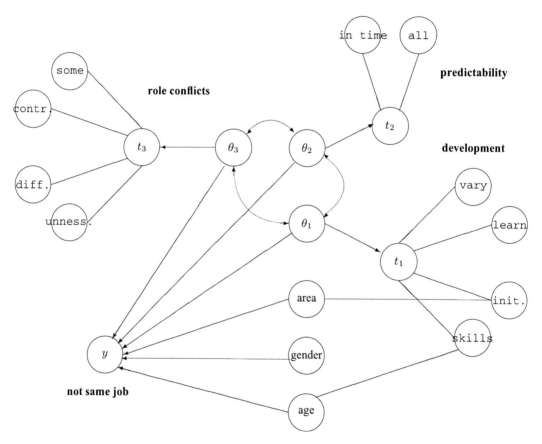

Figure 3. The structure of the regression model with three latent covariates. Structural relations from observed covariates to latent variables can be included yielding direct and mediated effect estimates (not shown).

The structural parameters are $\gamma_1 = -0.79$, $\gamma_2 = -0.30$ and $\gamma_3 = 0.21$ and the area effect is

$$\beta + \gamma_1\delta_1 + \gamma_2\delta_2 + \gamma_3\delta_3 = 0.48 + 0.48 + 0.37 + 0.12 = 1.45,$$

so $\frac{0.48+0.37+0.12}{1.45} = 67\%$ of the area difference is explained by the differences in the latent covariate.

Conclusion

Latent variables are often of interest in terms of their relation to other variables, e.g. self rated health as predictor of death or psychosocial factors as predictor of absence from work or job turnover. The use of unreliable explanatory variables yields biased estimates of regression parameters and can lead to misleading statistical inference (Carroll, Ruppert, & Stefanski, 1995; Fuller, 1987). Measurement error models have been applied in different research areas to model errors-in-variables problems, incorporating error in the response as well as in the covariates. Most of the attention has focused on linear measurement error models.

Rasch measurement models have been widely used and studied in great detail in the last forty years because its mathematical simplicity and the sufficiency of the raw score are desirable properties of a measurement model. Sufficiency is important for validation of measurement instruments, where raw scores will often be used when reporting results, but this feature can also be used to construct regression models based on increased measurement precision.

Analysis based on standardized estimated values $\hat{\theta}$ and on standardized sum scores t yielded virtually identical effect estimates. This is not surprising given that there is a one to one correspondence between t and $\hat{\theta}$ the sufficiency of the score t. Effect estimates based on $\hat{\theta}$ are smaller than those based on the joint model (15), this is probably because the uncertainty of the estimates $\hat{\theta}$ is ignored. This difference in estimated effect size was most outspoken in the situation with four items fitting the Rasch model, and less so in the two other situations. When misfit of the Rasch model can be identified as local dependence or as differential item functioning the modeling framework can be extended to loglinear Rasch models.

The example illustrated how the effect of psychosocial exposures can explain differences in risk of job turnover. The analysis of single latent predictors showed that people with low skill discretion, people who do not receive relevant information, and people who experience many role conflicts are less likely to choose the same job again. These differences explained between 16 and 40% of the area effect. The two most important factors were found to be predictability and skill discretion. With respect to job turnover the psychosocial factors accounted for 67% of the difference between the two areas.

References

Adams, R. J., Wilson, M., & Wang, W. C. (1997). The multidimensional random coefficients multinomial logit model. *Applied Psychological Measurement*, 21, 1–23.

Adams, R. J., Wilson, M., & Wu, M. (1997). Multilevel item response models: An approach to errors in variables regression. *Journal of Educational and Behavioral Statistics*, 22(1), 47–76.

Agresti, A. (1993). Computing conditional maximum likelihood estimates for generalized Rasch models using simple loglinear models with diagonals parameters. *Scandinavian Journal of Statistics*, 20(1), 63–71.

Andersen, E. B. (1994). *Latent regression analysis* (Research Report No. 106). Department of Statistics, University of Copenhagen.

Andersen, E. B., & Madsen, M. (1977). Estimating the parameters of the latent population distribution. *Psychometrika*, *42*, 357–374.

Bollen, K. A. (1989). *Structural equations with latent variables*. New York: J Wiley & Sons.

Borritz, M., Rugulies, R., Bjorner, J. B., Villadsen, E., Mikkelsen, O. A., & Kristensen, T. S. (2006). Burnout among employees in human service work: design and baseline findings of the puma study. *Scandinavian Journal of Public Health*, *34*, 49–58.

Breslow, N. E., & Clayton, D. G. (1993). Approximate inference in generalized linear mixed models. *Journal of the American Statistical Association*, *88*(1), 9–25.

Carroll, R. J., Ruppert, D., & Stefanski, L. A. (1995). *Measurement error in nonlinear models*. London: Chapman & Hall.

Christensen, K. B., & Bjorner, J. B. (2003). *SAS macros for Rasch based latent variable modelling* (Tech. Rep. No. 03/13). Department of Biostatistics, University of Copenhagen. (available from http://pubhealth.ku.dk/bs/publikationer)

Christensen, K. B., Bjorner, J. B., Kreiner, S., & Petersen, J. H. (2004). Latent regression in loglinear Rasch models. *Communications in Statistics. Theory and Methods*, *33*(6), 1295–1313.

Christensen, K. B., & Kreiner, S. (2004). Testing the fit of latent regression models. *Communications in Statistics. Theory and Methods*, *33*(6), 1341–1356.

Fischer, G. H., & Molenaar, I. W. (1995). *Rasch models - foundations, recent developments, and applications* (G. H. Fischer & I. W. Molenaar, Eds.). Springer-Verlag.

Fox, J. P., & Glas, C. A. W. (2001). Bayesian estimation of a multilevel IRT model using Gibbs sampling. *Psychometrika*, *66*, 271–288.

Fuller, W. A. (1987). *Measurement error models*. New York: J Wiley & Sons.

Gilmour, A. R., Anderson, R. D., & Rae, A. L. (1985). The analysis of binomial data by generalized linear mixed model. *Biometrika*, *72*, 593–599.

Harville, D. A., & Mee, R. W. (1984). A mixed-model procedure for analyzing ordered categorical data. *Biometrics*, *40*, 393–408.

Hoijtink, H. (1995). Linear and repeated measures models for the person parameters. In G. H. Fischer & I. W. Molenaar (Eds.), *Rasch models - foundations, recent developments, and applications* (pp. 203–214). Springer-Verlag.

Holland, P. W., & Thayer, D. T. (1988). Differential item performance and the mantel-haenszel procedure. In H. Wainer & H. I. Braun (Eds.), *Test validity* (pp. 129–145). Lawrence Erlbaum Associates.

Janssen, R., Tuerlinckx, F., Meulders, M., & De Boeck, P. (2000). A hierarchial IRT model for criterion-referenced measurement. *Journal of Educational and Behavioral Statistics*, *25*(3), 285–306.

Kamata, A. (2001). Item analysis by the hierarchial generalized linear model. *Journal of Educational Measurement*, *38*(1), 79–93.

Kelderman, H. (1984). Loglinear Rasch model tests. *Psychometrika*, *49*, 223–245.

Kelderman, H. (1992). Computing maximum likelihood estimates of loglinear models from marginal sums with special attention to loglinear item response theory. *Psychometrika*, *57*, 437–450.

Kelderman, H., & Rijkes, C. P. M. (1994). Loglinear multidimensional IRT models for polytomously scored items. *Psychometrika*, *59*(2), 149–176.

Kreiner, S., & Christensen, K. B. (2002). Graphical Rasch models. In M. Mesbah, M.-L. T. Lee, & B. F. Cole (Eds.), *Statistical methods for quality of life studies: Design, measurements and analysis* (pp. 187–203). Kluwer Academic Publishers.

Kreiner, S., & Christensen, K. B. (2004). Analysis of local dependence and multidimensionality in graphical loglinear Rasch models. *Communications in Statistics. Theory and Methods, 33*(6), 1239–1276.

Larsen, K., Petersen, J. H., Budtz-Jørgensen, E., & Endahl, L. (2000). Interpreting parameters in the logistic regression model with random effects. *Biometrics, 56,* 909–914.

Lin, X., & Breslow, N. E. (1996). Bias correction in generalized linear mixed models. *Journal of the American Statistical Association , 91,* 73–89.

Maier, K. S. (2001). A Rasch hierarchial measurement model. *Journal of Educational and Behavioral Statistics, 26*(3), 307–330.

McGilchrist, C. E. (1994). Estimation in generalized mixed models. *Journal of the Royal Statistical Society B, 56*(1), 61–69.

Mislevy, R. J. (1984). Estimating latent distributions. *Psychometrika, 49,* 359–381.

Mislevy, R. J. (1985). Estimation of latent group effects. *Journal of the American Statistical Association, 80,* 993–997.

Mislevy, R. J. (1987). Exploiting auxiliary information about examinees in the estimation of item parameters. *Applied Psychological Measurement , 11,* 81–91.

Muthén, B. (1979). A structural probit model with latent variables. *Journal of the American Statistical Association , 74,* 807–811.

Muthén, B. (1984). A general structural equation model with dichotomous, ordered categorical, and continous latent variable indicators. *Psychometrika, 49,* 115–132.

Rabe-Hesketh, S., Pickles, A., & Skrondal, A. (2001). *Gllamm manual* (Tech. Rep. No. 2001/01). Department of Biostatistics and Computing, Institute of Psychiatry, King's College, London. (available from http://www.iop.kcl.ac.uk/IoP/Departments/BioComp/programs/gllamm.html)

Rasch, G. (1960). *Probabilistic Models for some Intelligence and Attainment Tests .* Copenhagen: Danish National Institute for Educational Research (Expanded edition, Chicago: University of Chicago Press; 1980).

Rodriguez, G., & Goldman, N. (1995). An assessment of estimation procedures for multilevel models with binary response. *Journal of the Royal Statistical Society, Series A , 158,* 73–89.

Schall, R. (1991). Estimation in generalized linear models with random effects. *Biometrika, 78,* 719–727.

Stiratelli, R., Laird, N. M., & Ware, J. H. (1984). Random effects models for serial observations with binary response. *Biometrics, 40,* 961–971.

Swaminathan, H., & Rogers, H. J. (1990). Detecting differential item functioning using logistic regression procedures. *Journal of Educational Measurement , 27,* 361–370.

TenVergert, E., Gillespie, M., & Kingma, J. (1993). Testing the assumptions and interpreting the results of the Rasch model using log-linear procedures in SPSS. *Behaviour Research Methods, Instruments, & Computers , 25*(3), 350–359.

Tjur, T. (1982). A connection between Rasch's item analysis model and a multiplicative Poisson model. *Scandinavian Journal of Statistics , 9,* 23–30.

van der Linden, W. J., & Hambleton, R. K. (Eds.). (1997). *Handbook of modern Item Response Theory*. Springer-Verlag.

Wolfinger, R., & O'Connel, M. (1993). Generalized linear mixed models: A pseudo-likelihood approach. *J Statist. Comput. Simul.*, *48*, 233–243.

Wu, M., Adams, R. J., & Wilson, M. R. (1998). *ACER Conquest: Generalized item response modelling software*. Australian Council for Educational Research.

Zumbo, B. D. (1999). *A handbook on the theory and methods of differential item functioning (DIF): Logistic regression as a unitary framework for binary and likert-type (ordinal) item scores*. Ottowa, ON: Directorate of Human Resources Reasearch and Evaluation, Department of National Defense.

Zwinderman, A. H. (1991). A generalized Rasch model for manifest predictors. *Psychometrika*, *56*, 589–600.

Zwinderman, A. H. (1997). Response models with manifest predictors. In W. J. van der Linden & R. K. Hambleton (Eds.), *Handbook of modern Item Response Theory* (pp. 245–258). Springer-Verlag.

In: Psychological Tests and Testing Research Trends   ISBN: 978-1-60021-569-8
Editor: Paul M. Goldfarb, pp. 311-320   © 2007 Nova Science Publishers, Inc.

Chapter 16

ASSESSING THE PSYCHOMETRIC AND LANGUAGE EQUIVALENCY OF THE CHINESE VERSIONS OF THE INDEX OF NAUSEA, VOMITING, AND RETCHING AND THE PRENATAL SELF-EVALUATION QUESTIONNAIRE

Fan-Hao Chou[1], Kay C. Avant[2], Shih-Hsien Kuo[3] and Han-Fu Cheng[4]

[1] School of Nursing, Kaohsiung Medical University, Kaohsiung;
[2] School of Nursing, The University of Texas at Austin, Austin, Texas, USA
[3] Basic Medical Science Education Center, Fooyin University, Taliao Hsiang, Kaohsiung County, Taiwan
[4] Department of Midwifery, Fooyin University, Taliao Hsiang, Kaohsiung County, Taiwan

ABSTRACT

This study was an initial psychometric test of the Chinese versions of the Index of Nausea, Vomiting, and Retching (INVR) and the Prenatal Self-Evaluation Questionnaire (PSEQ) in pregnant Taiwanese women. Although there already is evidence that the English-language versions of the scales are reliable and valid, it is important to verify the proper psychometric characteristics of the Chinese versions. Forward and backward translation, and a multiphase instrumentation study describing internal consistency, test-retest reliability, and content validity of the translated versions were conducted. A convenience sample was recruited from prenatal clinics in the south of Taiwan. Three measurement instruments were used in this study: the demographic inventory (DI), the INVR, and the PSEQ. Thirty pregnant women participated in the study. Both the internal consistency and stability coefficients of the INVR and PSEQ were satisfactory. The indices of content validity (CVI) for the Chinese versions of these two instruments were both 1.0, indicating that they are acceptable for use among Taiwanese pregnant women. This was the first instrumentation study of the INVR and PSEQ applied to Taiwanese pregnant women. Researchers could use this study as a model for future translation and application of psychometric instrumentation.

Keywords: psychometric equivalence, nausea, vomiting, maternal psychosocial adaptation.

Pregnancy can be stressful and often causes uncomfortable physical symptoms. Chief among these are nausea and vomiting, which affect not only the physical and mental condition of pregnant women [1], but also the subsequent relationship between a mother and her newborn. The mother's adaptation to pregnancy provides a foundation for the mother-newborn relationship to come, and forms one step in achieving the maternal tasks of "seeking and ensuring safe passage through pregnancy and childbirth", "binding-in to the child", "acceptance by others", and "giving of oneself" [2,3].

Nausea and vomiting can increase stress [4,5], which can adversely affect maternal adaptation [6]. Therefore, pregnancy-induced nausea and vomiting may be a significant factor in maternal psychosocial adaptation during pregnancy. Research on this particular issue has been lacking, particularly in Taiwan. Knowledge of the possible effects of nausea and vomiting during pregnancy may help parent-child nurses better understand how to provide appropriate prenatal care, and provide data for comparative research or practical application for other countries. Nurses can then design and implement suitable comprehensive interventions for these women in Taiwan and elsewhere.

Two instruments, the Index of Nausea, Vomiting, and Retching (INVR) and the Prenatal Self-Evaluation Questionnaire (PSEQ), are currently available to study pregnancy-induced nausea and vomiting and maternal psychosocial adaptation. There are, however, no Chinese language versions of these measurement scales for Taiwanese women, despite the strong empirical evidence for the reliability and validity of the English-language versions. Researchers should consider the issues of cultural and linguistic translation when selecting instruments to be applied in a different country, for example, as with adapting English-language based instruments for use in a Taiwanese population. In adapting an instrument, its reliability and validity are achieved by establishing the equivalence of the original and the translated instrument's psychometric characteristics, in addition to properly translating the concepts and language [7]. In general, forward and backward translations and expert review satisfy the conceptual issues, while field tests can best establish the proper equivalence of psychometric characteristics [7,8].

Forward and backward translations can be accomplished through direct translation by the researcher, after which another bilingual translator can do the back translation.

The two versions of the translation can then be checked by an expert or experts for adequacy [7–9]. In addition to these translation steps to verify and validate the translation of an instrument, decentering, in which "successive iterations of translations are done until both forms are appropriate for their respective cultures" [10], can further enhance the cultural and linguistic translation of an instrument [10,11].

To establish the reliability and validity of the Chinese versions, therefore, is a critical task prior to any study conducted with the INVR and PSEQ in Taiwan. The first aim of this study was to translate the INVR and PSEQ scales into Chinese. The second aim was to conduct initial psychometric testing of the INVR and PSEQ (including evaluating the readability, item clarity and initial psychometric characteristics) in pregnant Taiwanese women before using the scales in an exploratory study with a larger sample [12].

RELIABILITY AND VALIDITY OF THE ENGLISH VERSIONS

The INVR was designed to measure the severity of nausea and vomiting and includes subjective and objective measurements. It is an 8-item instrument that uses a 5-point Likert scale and consists of three subscales: nausea (range, 0–12), vomiting (range, 0–12), and retching (range, 0–8), giving a total range of 0–32. The INVR was developed from the INV-1 and INV-2 [13], both of which had good evidence for reliability and validity [14–18]. For example, the Cronbach's α of the INV-1 were 0.89–0.97 (n = 25–30) for 12 administrations of a version in oncology patients; the split-half correlations were 0.83–0.99 (n = 25–32) for 11 of the 12 administrations. The concurrent validity of the INV-1 was determined using Spearman's correlation coefficient, r_s = 0.87 (n = 18), by comparing the ratings of unhospitalized chemotherapy patients with those of a family member or significant other. The reliability of the INV-2 was 0.98 (Cronbach's α) (n = 309) for oncology patients [17] and 0.83 (n = 102) to 0.88 (n = 60) in pregnant women [14,18].

In a parallel-form study, Rhodes and McDaniel determined the reliability of the INVR as a replacement for INV-2 [19]. The INVR uses the same symptom components and item-order as the INV-2, but has different descriptions. The INVR is designed with eight introductory statements and for each statement there are five response choices. The INVR is more concise and easier to read than the INV-2. Rhodes and McDaniel compared the responses of subjects to the INV-2 and the INVR. The percentage agreements and Spearman correlations between each of the eight items on the two scales were 79–98% and 0.71–0.95 (n = 159), respectively. The Spearman's coefficient was 0.87 (n = 159) for the total INVR and the INV-2. The data revealed that the INVR and INV-2 were equivalent in measuring nausea, vomiting, and retching in obstetric (n = 40), oncologic (n = 60), and medical/surgical (n = 59) populations. Rhodes and McDaniel, therefore, recommended use of the INVR in future studies [19].

The PSEQ is used to measure maternal psychosocial adaptation during pregnancy and was developed from the Lederman framework of maternal psychosocial adaptation.

It is a 79-item instrument using a four-point Likert scale (1 = not at all, to 4 = very much so) and measures conflict in the maternal developmental tasks of pregnancy. The scale is composed of seven domains: acceptance of pregnancy, identification of a motherhood role, relationship with her mother, relationship with her husband, preparation for labor, fear of helplessness and loss of control in labor, and concern for the well-being of self and baby [2,20–22]. The possible range of summed scores for the PSEQ scale is 79–316. Higher scores indicate greater perception of conflict or lack of adaptation.

This instrument has been used and demonstrated as valid and reliable through various studies with different populations [21,23,24]. The samples in these studies included primigravidas and multigravidas in different trimesters of pregnancy and in different ethnic groups. For instance, in one study, the Cronbach's α of the PSEQ in each of the three trimesters of pregnancy among the seven dimensions was, in order, 0.74–0.91 (n = 196–203), 0.71–0.93 (n = 297–302), and 0.73–0.92 (n = 367–377). Previous studies have provided evidence for the predictive and construct validity of the PSEQ. To examine the effects of prenatal maternal adaptation on maternal anxiety in labor, Lederman, for example, performed a longitudinal study (from the third trimester to active-phase labor) in 53 normal multigravidas using the PSEQ and the Labor Anxiety Scale [21]. The results showed that the PSEQ could predict anxiety in labor, supporting the predictive validity of the PSEQ.

In Taiwan, there was a Chinese version of the INV-2, but no reliability and validity data for the INVR or the INV-2 in maternal research have been reported. The researcher, therefore, had to determine the reliability and validity of the INVR Chinese version. There was no Chinese version of the PSEQ. The researcher, therefore, needed to translate the PSEQ and determine the reliability and validity of the Chinese version.

METHODS

Research Design and Study Population

This was a translation and multiphase instrumentation study to determine internal consistency, test-retest reliability, and face and content validity in the translated versions of the INVR and the PSEQ.

The population of concern was Taiwanese pregnant women. Thirty pregnant women were recruited into the study. The criteria for selection were: no previous history or currently diagnosed medical disease and no pregnancy complications; aged from 18 to 44 years old; and speaks, reads, and writes Chinese. The researcher used a convenience sampling technique, collecting data from prenatal clinics in two teaching hospitals in Kaohsiung, Taiwan.

Translation

The researcher obtained permission to use the INVR and PSEQ from the original authors. The two instruments were then translated from English to Chinese by two bilingual academics, the researcher, and a Taiwanese associate professor with a PhD in a health- care field. A doctoral candidate majoring in foreign language education with a concentration in English as a second language back translated the Chinese versions of the INVR and PSEQ into English. This bilingual doctoral candidate had never seen the English versions of the INVR and PSEQ. The equivalence of the original and back- translated scales was evaluated by a nursing professor who is an expert in parent-child nursing. The instruments were modified as necessary, based on the decentering procedure. Only minor revisions were required.

Data Collection

The researcher used a self-report method to collect data. Data collection began after obtaining approval from the Human Subjects Committee of the institution. Participants were informed that all the information gathered from the study would be kept confidential. The researcher first screened potential participants who came to prenatal care clinics, and informed them of the aim of the study and the time needed for self-administration of the instruments. After obtaining informed consent, the researcher gave willing participants the demographic inventory (DI), INVR and PSEQ scales to fill out. When the participants completed the questionnaires at the clinics, the researcher also gave them a second set of the INVR and PSEQ scales in an envelope to take home and fill out. All participants were notified that they had the right to withdraw from the study at any time. They could also refuse to respond to any question that might make them feel uncomfortable. Participants' names and other identifying information were not on the questionnaires, and a code number was assigned to ensure confidentiality. All the data remained accessible only to the researcher. All participants were asked to provide suggestions about the wording of the instruments, in order to determine face validity.

These steps were continued until 30 participants were obtained. One week later, the researcher received the second set of questionnaires from these participants by return mail. Each participant received a small gift from the researcher after she had completed the study. In addition, participants could obtain free nursing consultation from the researcher.

Data Analysis

Data were analyzed using SPSS, version 9.0 for Windows (SPSS Inc, Chicago, IL, USA). The internal consistency and test–retest reliability coefficients were examined for the INVR and the PSEQ scales. The content validity and face validity were also assessed for the Chinese versions of both scales. Data are given as mean ± standard deviation.

RESULTS

The 30 pregnant women in this study ranged in age from 18 to 41 years with a mean age of 27.23 ± 5.14 years. The gestational stage of these women ranged from 7 to 38 weeks with a mean of 25.83 ± 9.90 weeks. Most participants in this sample had a college education (40.0%, $n = 12$), followed by a senior high school education (36.7%, $n = 11$). More than half of the participants in this sample were employed (53.3%, $n = 16$) and more than half (56.7%, $n = 17$) were primigravida. Most women had nausea and vomiting (73.3%, $n = 22$).

Content and Face Validity

According to Streiner and Norman, 3–10 experts are appropriate for a panel of experts [8]. For this study, three experts were chosen from related research and practical fields to estimate the content validity of the Chinese language versions of the INVR and PSEQ. The first panel member was a School of Nursing professor with a PhD in nursing and more than 20 years of experience researching and working with perinatal women in Taiwan. The second was an obstetric physician with more than 10 years of experience working with pregnant patients with nausea and vomiting. The last was a School of Nursing faculty member who also worked part-time in the obstetric clinics of a hospital. She had several years of research experience with Taiwanese pregnant women.

These three experts were asked to independently rate the Chinese versions of the INVR and PSEQ in terms of the two instruments' applicability to pregnant women in Taiwan, including their content and cultural relevance and language equivalence to the original instruments. A three point scale was used to rate each item as not applicable, applicable with some revision, or applicable. Based on the opinions of the three experts, the sixth item of the INVR, which uses "a cup" to describe the amount of vomiting, might need to be further interpreted using concrete numbers, since there are several different sizes of cups in Taiwanese daily life. This item was therefore clarified with a number ("a cup is equal to 250 ml") after the statement. After the revision in light of the experts' opinions, the index of content validity (CVI) of both these translated instruments was 1.0 [25]. The CVIs indicated that the INVR and PSEQ Chinese versions were acceptable for use among pregnant women in Taiwan, based on the experts' evaluation.

According to the responses from the expert panel and the participants in the study, the instrument was modified as necessary to build face validity. Face validity "refers only to the appearance of the instrument to the layman" and "does not provide evidence for validity" [25]. If an instrument has face validity, however, response rates may increase [25]. Therefore, the face validity of the INVR and PSEQ Chinese-language versions was estimated by a bilingual pregnant woman who had earned a bachelor's degree in Taiwan, had lived in the USA for more than 2 years and, at the time of the study, was 33 weeks pregnant. She could respond easily to all items on both scales. She proposed that only one item of the PSEQ needed to be slightly reworded in Chinese. In the item, "It will be hard for me to balance child care with my other commitments and activities," the "my" in the Chinese- language version seemed redundant. The word "my" was therefore omitted.

Reliability

The INVR total scores ranged from 0 to 29 (mean, 8.0 ± 8.8) for the 30 participants. For the three subscales of the INVR, the means for nausea, vomiting, and retching were 3.7 ± 3.8, 2.1 ± 3.2, and 2.2 ± 2.6, respectively.

In this study, the reliability coefficient for the INVR scale using Cronbach's α was 0.94. The 1-week test-retest reliability coefficient determined by intraclass correlation coefficient (ICC) was 0.97. Both the internal consistency and stability coefficients of the INVR scale were high and satisfactory.

The PSEQ total scores ranged from 84 to 204 (mean, 144.0 ± 27.9). The scores on the seven subscales were: acceptance of pregnancy, 25.9 ± 6.8; identification of a motherhood role, 25.2 ± 6.6; relationship with her mother, 16.0 ± 4.8; relationship with her husband, 15.3 ± 4.1; preparation for labor, 19.5 ± 5.5; fear of helplessness and loss of control in labor, 19.1 ± 5.6; and concern for the well-being of self and baby, 23.1 ± 6.0.

The reliability coefficient for the entire PSEQ scale using Cronbach's α was 0.93. The ICC test-retest reliability coefficient at 1 week was 0.95. The Cronbach's α coefficients of the seven subscales were: acceptance of pregnancy, 0.82; identification of a motherhood role, 0.81; relationship with her mother, 0.77; relationship with her husband, 0.68; preparation for labor, 0.80; fear of helplessness and loss of control in labor, 0.79; and concern for the well-being of self and baby, 0.81. The 1-week test-retest reliability coefficients of these subscales were 0.91, 0.85, 0.89, 0.93, 0.96, 0.94, and 0.83, respectively. Both the internal consistency and stability coefficients of the PSEQ scale were satisfactory.

DISCUSSION

These results show that the Chinese-language versions of the INVR and PSEQ scales had satisfactory internal consistency and stability coefficients. The CVI for both Chinese versions was 1.0, indicating that they are acceptable for use among Taiwanese pregnant women.

There are no related studies using the INVR. However, as US studies reveal that the INVR and INV-2 are equivalent in measuring nausea, vomiting, and retching in obstetric populations, the INVR scores in this study were compared with INV-2 scores from previous studies. In this study, the reliability of the INVR scale was 0.94. This was a little lower than Rhodes et al reported when using the INV-2 in oncology patients [17], but higher than Belluomini et al. and Zhou et al. reported with the INV-2 in pregnant women [14,18]. The reliability of the PSEQ scale was 0.93, which was consistent with previous Western studies [21,23,24].

The INVR total score in this study (mean, 8.0 ± 8.8) was lower than that reported by Belluomini et al., using the INV-2 in American women within the first 10 weeks of pregnancy who received pretreatment (mean, 12.6 ± 5.7; $n = 30$) or no pretreatment (mean, 11.5 ± 4.9; $n = 30$) [14]. Table 1 compares the three subscales of the INVR in this study with the two subscales of the INV-2 in two other studies [14,18]. The findings in this study are roughly equivalent to those of previous studies except that the score on the nausea subscale was lower than Belluomini et al. reported for pretreated pregnant women (mean, 8.4 ± 2.2) and the control group (mean, 8.0 ± 2.5) [14]. One explanation for the difference may be the different sampling criteria used: Belluomini et al. included women with symptoms of nausea and vomiting during pregnancy, while this study included women with or without nausea and vomiting during pregnancy. Another possible reason for the higher scores for nausea reported by Belluomini et al. may be due to the absence of a retching subscale and inclusion of retching in the nausea subscale.

Table 2 compares the seven subscales of the PSEQ in this study with those from three other studies [21,23,24]. The results of this study are similar to those of previous studies, where, for example, the mean score of the "relationship with her mother" subscale was similar to those Halman et al. reported for third-trimester fertile and infertile pregnant women [23]. However, it was lower than the means reported by Stark and Lederman for third-trimester pregnant women [24,21]. The mean score of the "relationship with her husband" subscale was also higher than the scores reported by Halman et al. for third-trimester fertile and infertile pregnant women [23], but lower than the scores reported by Stark [24] and Lederman [21] for third-trimester pregnant women. The mean scores of "acceptance of pregnancy," "identification of a motherhood role," and "concern for the well-being of self and baby," however, were higher than the mean scores in the three previous studies. One possible reason is that this study included all three trimesters and the three other studies focused only on the third trimester.

Because the third trimester is closer to labor and delivery, the women may have been more accepting of their pregnancy, had more identification with a motherhood role, and had more concern for the well-being of themselves and their babies.

Table 1. Mean and standard deviation of the three subscales of the Index of Nausea, Vomiting, and Retching compared with two different studies using the Index of Nausea and Vomiting–2

Subscale	Present study (*n* = 30)	Zhou et al. (*n* = 103)[18]	Belluomini et al. (*n* = 60)[14]	
			Pre-treatment	Control group
Nausea	3.7 ± 3.8	3.4 ± 0.7	8.4 ± 2.2	8.0 ± 2.5
Vomiting	2.1 ± 3.2	1.5 ± 0.6	2.1 ± 2.5	1.8 ± 2.7
Retching	2.2 ± 2.6	1.9 ± 0.8	–	–

Table 2. A comparison of the mean ± standard deviation of the seven subscales of the Prenatal Self-Evaluation Questionnaire in four different studies

Subscale	Present study (*n* = 30)	Stark (*n* = 43-63)[24]		Lederman (*n* = 115-119)[21]	Halman et al. (*n* = 97-261)[23]	
		Older Gravidas	Younger Gravidas		Fertile	Infertile
Acceptance of pregnancy	25.9±6.8	22.2±6.2	22.2±7.0	22.3±7.0	19.7±5.7	18.8±4.3
Identification of a motherhood role	25.2±6.6	21.2±4.1	20.9±5.3	20.2±4.6	21.0±4.7	20.2±4.3
Relationship with her mother	16.0±4.8	18.6±6.6	16.7±6.6	17.3±6.9	16.1±6.3	15.9±6.7
Relationship with her husband	15.3±4.1	16.7±5.2	16.0±5.4	16.2±5.1	13.8±3.8	14.1±3.8
Preparation for labor	19.5±5.5	17.5±5.2	18.8±4.8	15.9±4.5	17.0±4.8	16.6±4.6
Fear of helplessness and loss of control in labor	19.1±5.6	16.8±4.4	19.1±4.1	18.2±4.2	17.2±4.1	16.4±3.8
Concern for the well-being of self and baby	23.1±6.0	17.2±4.6	18.2±4.8	16.5±4.8	17.0±4.4	16.9±4.1

Methodological Issues

Two instruments, the INVR and PSEQ, that did not have Chinese-language versions were subjected to direct and back translations. The psychometric properties of the INVR and PSEQ Chinese versions indicated satisfactory validity and reliability with indices of content validity of 1.0 and of reliability above 0.93. To increase the external validity and the theoretical basis for these two scales in Taiwan, further research should evaluate these Chinese versions in different Taiwanese populations, such as a larger sample in similar populations or other pregnant populations and settings in Taiwan.

During the process of this study, many pregnant women proposed that the PSEQ scale had too many items (79 items). Therefore, a short form may be worth developing for both cost-effectiveness and the benefit of subjects.

REFERENCES

[1]   Deuchar N. Nausea and vomiting in pregnancy: A review of the problem with particular regard to psychological and social aspects. *Br. J. Obstet. Gynaecol.* 1995;102:6–8.

[2]   Beck CT. Available instruments for research on prenatal attachment and adaptation to pregnancy. *Am. J. Matern. Child Nurs.* 1999;24:25–32.

[3]   Rubin R. *Maternal Identity and the Maternal Experience.* New York: Springer, 1984.

[4]   Jarnfelt-Samsioe A, Eriksson B, Waldenstrom J, et al. Some new aspects on emesis gravidarum: Relations to clinical data, serum electrolytes, total protein and creatinine. *Gynecol. Obstet. Invest.* 1985;19:174–86.

[5]   O'Brien B, Naber S. Nausea and vomiting during pregnancy: Effects on the quality of women's lives. *Birth.* 1992;19:138–43.

[6]   Reece MS. Stress and maternal adaptation in first-time mothers more than 35 years old. *Appl. Nurs. Res.* 1995;8:61–6.

[7]   Scientific Advisory Committee. Instrument review criteria. *Medical Outcomes Trust Bulletin*, September, I–IV, 1995.

[8]   Streiner D, Norman G. *Health Measurement Scales: A Practical Guide to their Development and Use,* 2nd edition. Oxford: Oxford University Press, 2001.

[9]   Sechrest L, Fay TL, Hafeez Zaidi SM. Problems of translation in cross-cultural research. *J. Cross Cult. Psychol.* 1972;3:41–56.

[10]   Ferketich S, Phillips L, Verran J. Development and administration of a survey instrument for cross-cultural research. *Res. Nurs. Health.* 1993;16:227–30.

[11]   Chapman DW, Carter JF. Translation procedures for the cross cultural use of measurement instruments. *Educ. Eval. Policy Anal.* 1979;1:71–6.

[12]   Fox R, Ventura M. Small scale administration of instruments and procedures. *Nurs. Res.* 1983;32:122–5.

[13]   Rhodes VA, McDaniel RW. Measuring nausea, vomiting, and retching. In: Frank-Stromborg M, Olsen SJ, eds. *Instruments for Clinical Health-care Research.* Sudbury, MA: Jones and Bartlett, 1997:509–17.

[14]   Belluomini J, Litt RC, Lee KA, et al. Acupressure for nausea and vomiting of pregnancy: A randomized, blinded study. *Obstet Gynecol.* 1994;84:245–8.

[15]   O'Brien B. *Nausea and Vomiting During Pregnancy: A Descriptive Correlational Study.* Unpublished doctoral dissertation, Chicago: Rush University, 1990.

[16]   Rhodes VA, Watson PM, Johnson MH. A self-report tool for assessing nausea and vomiting in chemotherapy. *Oncol. Nurs. Forum.* 1983;10:11.

[17]   Rhodes VA, Watson PM, Johnson MH, et al. Patterns of nausea, vomiting, and distress in patients receiving antineoplastic drug protocols. *Oncol. Nurs. Forum.* 1987;14:35–43.

[18]   Zhou Q, O'Brien B, Relyea J. Severity of nausea and vomiting during pregnancy: What does it predict? *Birth.* 1999;26:108–14.

[19]   Rhodes VA, McDaniel RW. The index of nausea, vomiting, and retching: A new format of the index of nausea and vomiting. *Oncol. Nurs. Forum.* 1999;26:889–93.

[20]   Lederman RP. *Psychosocial Adaptation in Pregnancy.* Englewood Cliffs, New Jersey: Prentice-Hall, 1984.

[21] Lederman RP. *Psychosocial Adaptation in Pregnancy,* 2nd edition. New York: Springer, 1996.

[22] Lederman RP, Lederman E, Work BA, et al. Relationship of psychological factors in pregnancy to progress in labor. *Nurs. Res.* 1979;28:94–7.

[23] Halman LJ, Oakley D, Lederman R. Adaptation to pregnancy and motherhood among subfecund and fecund primiparous women. *Matern. Child Nurs. J.* 1995;23:90–100.

[24] Stark MA. Psychosocial adjustment during pregnancy: The experience of mature gravidas. *J. Obstet. Gynecol. Neonatal. Nurs.* 1997;26:206–11.

[25] Waltz CF, Strickland OL, Lenz ER. *Measurement in Nursing Research,* 2nd edition. Philadelphia: F. A. Davis, 1991.

INDEX

B

C

E

N

O

P

Q